Cultural Topographies of the New Berlin

Cultural Topographies of the New Berlin

Karin Bauer and Jennifer Ruth Hosek

berghahn
NEW YORK · OXFORD
www.berghahnbooks.com

First published in 2018 by

Berghahn Books

www.berghahnbooks.com

© 2018, 2019 Karin Bauer and Jennifer Ruth Hosek
First paperback edition published in 2019

Library of Congress Cataloging-in-Publication Data

A CIP data record is available from the Library of Congress

British Library Cataloguing in Publication Data

A catalogue record for this book is available from the British Library

ISBN 978-1-78533-720-8 hardback
ISBN 978-1-78920-522-0 paperback
ISBN 978-1-78533-721-5 ebook

Contents

Part III: Reimagining Integration

Part IV: Berlin Memoryscapes of the Present

Illustrations

Figures

Table

Introduction

Karin Bauer and Jennifer Ruth Hosek

Since the fall of the Wall in 1989, Berlin has seen intense social, political, and cultural transformation. Berlin (West) lost its postwar insularity and Berlin (East) its status as capital of the German Democratic Republic as they fused into a center of influence in the middle of Europe. The New Berlin's reputation as a global city has risen consistently since the end of the Cold War and the concomitant shift of relations of power. Now one of the pillars of the European Union, the German capital faces its challenges with a diverse—and some argue inconsistent—set of policies and approaches. In the current political context, Berlin stands as a symbol for the perception of Germany as Europe's status-quo power that in the wake of Brexit will increasingly attract financial and human capital and expand its presence on the global stage.

From the postwar years onward, narratives, images, and metaphors forefronting opportunity and novelty have painted Berlin as an economic and avant-garde playground. Provocative monikers such as "urban frontier" imply adventure, danger, advantage to be gained in the overcoming of adversity, and a paucity of inhabitants relative to abundant resources. Deploying postcolonial critique more frequently brought to bear on earlier histories and Southern geographies, Christine Hentschel illuminates this phenomenon today. She quotes an "activist for creative newcomers" to highlight his way of seeing a working-class neighborhood of Berlin: "Neukölln's charm is that it is raw and rough. Like a raw diamond. One can still jump around, can realize one's dreams. . . . There is the space and you can still occupy it."[1] Such wide putatively open spaces beg for exploitation and promise blooming landscapes of opportunity for the enterprising. Of course, as contributors to the invaluable anthology *The Berlin Reader* show in their analyses, this frontier is not void of inhabitants, but full of resistance. Importantly, the urban frontier concept, which expanded in the 1960s into a core element of city planning, is market-based and privileges economic growth. In Berlin's case, it comes with a particular twist, because the integration of East and West Berlin uniquely maps a phenomenon that Saskia Sassen has noted in relation to U.S. cities: "[N]eglect and accelerated obsolescence produce vast spaces for rebuilding the center according to the requirements of whatever regime of urban accumulation or pattern of spatial organization of the urban economy prevails at a given time."[2]

The "poor but sexy" New Berlin has undergone a rapid process of urban renewal that has significantly altered its central neighborhoods and its entire social and cultural fabric. While the effects are felt throughout, the impact of this gentrification is to date most visible in the central areas. Simultaneously, perceptions of what constitutes the "center" have and are continuously shifting toward quartiers that were once considered peripheral—the former margins of Neukölln, Friedrichshain, and Wedding are now the new hot spots. Gentrification is also expressed and furthered by the city's branding and "Imagineering" campaigns that spin Berlin as the city of clubbers, advertising and management consultants, designers, architects, restaurateurs, and contributors to the ever-expanding art, music, film, and literary scenes. Seen critically, these groups are associated with the plague and opportunity of urban accumulation and touristification and belong, in more general terms, to what Richard Florida has infamously termed the "creative class," behind whose glitzy lifestyle images and practices often lurk economically dubious realities. The de facto economic precarity of many freelancers and startup workers reminds by extension that being truly poor may not truly be sexy. For those endowed with the wealth of their parents' generation, their appropriation of a typically marginal label garners them cultural capital that compensates for the tangible commodities that they do not produce.

Contemporary Berlin is perceived to be a liberated place inhabited by free spirits, a central German outpost where raw urbanity still shines through. It is the meeting place of former dissidents from East and West, underground punks and political activists, conscientious objectors, alternative lifestyle advocates, and bohemians. Its gritty underbelly remains part of its lure and lore. Like the old West Berlin and the Berlin of the 1990s, the New Berlin still holds the reputation of a place that has not cleaned itself up completely and that remains a fertile ground for radical and edgy subcultures and for countless associations and communities that mobilize on glocal levels against the myriad effects brought about by rampant speculation, globalization, and gentrification. The New Berlin harbors enclaves of political, social, and technological disenchantment and a preference for physical over virtual realities. Increasingly, artists who flocked to Berlin in search of inspiration, community, and a germane working environment have come to take on activist roles defending community projects and access to affordable work and living spaces against urban development driven by investors, politicians, and "imagineers." Johannes Novy and Claire Colomb have found an "increasing mobilization of cultural producers in oppositional movements in an era of wholesale instrumentalization of culture and 'creativity' in contemporary processes of capitalist urbanization."[3]

This volume probes recent developments and their inherent contradictions, including the tensions between Berlin's creative city identification and its urban challenges, multiculturalism and Germanness, historical memories and institutionalized memorialization, slick surfaces of redevelopment and rough underground economies, forward-looking attitudes and nostalgia, and the uncompromising honing of radical edges amid concomitant institutionalization and domestication of squatters, subcultures, and other alternatively capitalized communities and geographies. In examining both the governmental and institutional strategies of shaping the New Berlin and the practices on the ground, this volume offers multifaceted perspectives that seek to intervene in and complicate official narratives and broaden the horizon of scholarly inquiry of cultural, memory, and urban studies. It brings together the expertise of scholars from an array of disciplines who engage their topics from interdisciplinary perspectives.

The contributions assembled here offer historicized perspectives on the ways in which participation in urban life and contestation of urban developments since the 1990s are negotiated by those who occupy, experience, and study the city. As Berlin scholars we are keenly aware of our own roles in the material production of the New Berlin, as well as in the production of signifying practices codifying the city as sign, metaphor, text, and symptom. In studying Berlin, many of us have been occupying physically and intellectually the "free" spaces, the "voids" available in the 1990s and the early 2000s and the gentrified spaces of today, thus participating in the very production of the space that we research and critique.

As a site of memory and memorialization, Berlin is, as Karen E. Till points out, "haunted with landscapes that simultaneously embody presences and absences, voids and ruins, intentional forgetting and painful remembering."[4] The continuing relevance of these landscapes of memory lies in the questions they raise in the present. In the past twenty years, the "voids" of Berlin have disappeared at an unanticipated rate and speed and with them the "spaces of hope" for alternative urban restructuring with which these "voids" were invested.[5] As Andreas Huyssen remarked, "Since much of central Berlin in the mid-1990s is a gigantic construction site, a hole in the ground, a void, there are indeed ample reasons to emphasize the void rather than to celebrate Berlin's current state of becoming."[6] Huyssen is here referring to spaces vacated or destroyed in order to build the economic and governmental heart of the New Berlin. Uncritically describing as "voids" sites such as the terrain of the former Wall—the strip of land between the inner and outer walls—or the formerly dilapidated Gründerzeit apartment buildings in East Berlin's Mitte and Prenzlauerberg risks forgetting their historical and contemporary meanings and the practices that shaped and were shaped in them.

The putative emptiness of the "death strip"—in which, moreover, protesters of gentrification and globalization settled post-1990—and the dilapidated buildings of central city Eastern Berlin—which many citizens, particularly dissenters, called home—testify to the economic and ideological schisms between and within East and West that still have not been overcome. Furthermore, mislabeling economically underleveraged areas as voids can legitimate re-focus on profit maximization. Consider why in the 2000s, a *Tacheles* at the site of the former Kaufhaus Wertheim with its bomb-damaged roof half-open to the sky is seen so differently from the *Gedächtniskirche* with its bomb-damaged "hollow tooth" standing open to the sky, although their conditions were both results of aerial assaults. Over the last decades, each of these less-than-fully-intact buildings was an integral part of Berlin's and the national landscape. Today, the former alternative art and meeting space *Tacheles* sits barricaded, awaiting redevelopment,[7] yet the *Gedächtniskirche* remains a prominent memorial. The diverging status of these two locations indicates a very different perception of voids, ruins, or "authentic sites"—one that stems primarily from the ideological point of view of the stakeholder.

As Huyssen reminds us, human-made voids are created with particular intent and purpose: excavating what had been there in order to create space for the timely, planned, managed, and branded arrival of the New. Topographies understood to be caught in the past become "there and then" frontiers awaiting "here and now" plentitude.[8] Already in 1997, Huyssen found much of the hope invested in Berlin's urban development misplaced. He speculated that "Berlin may be *the* place to study how this new emphasis on the city as cultural sign, combined with its role as capital and the pressures of large-scale developments, prevents creative alternatives and represents a false start into the twenty-first century. Berlin may be well on the way to squandering a unique chance."[9] This volume reassesses "the city as cultural sign" by probing the impact of urban development (Ward, Erek and Gantner), marketing and branding strategies (Sark, Kutch), image politics (Ingram, Janzen), imaginary cityscapes (Steckenbiller, Gölz, Schütze), debates of ethnicity and integration (Ülker, Schuster-Craig, Amit), and ideological battles for primacy of historical meaning and interpretation (Eisenhuth and Krause, Pogoda and Traxler, Kranz and Cohen). The contributions examine a wide array of debates, art works, texts, films, comics, and practices that reflect on the forces that have shaped the New Berlin since the 1990s. Framing their investigation in historical terms, the contributions examine how these developments are impacting perceptions of the city, as well as the experiences and lived practices of its inhabitants today.

Along with Henri Lefebvre we assume that all space is social space, a product of complex interpersonal, political, and economic processes. This volume brings together investigations that highlight the interrelation of the modes of production of what Lefebvre refers to as the triad of "perceived—conceived—lived" realms.[10] Lefebvre distinguishes between "spatial practice" (the way in which perceived space and daily urban reality intersect), "representations of space" (space as conceived by urban planners, social engineers, and strategists asserting scientific knowledge, governmental and professional authority), and "representational space" (the lived spaces of inhabitants and of artists, writers, and philosophers who describe, imagine, and represent it).[11] The differentiation between perceptions, conceptualizations, and representations of the lived city usefully reminds us of the "centrality of embodied experience to the production, reproduction and contestation of urban space."[12] "Space considered in isolation is an empty abstraction," because space is produced through physical, mental, and social fields that interact in a dialectical fashion.[13] In examining the functions of various urban spaces and experiences, including subcultures (Ingram, Sark); alternative spaces and cultures (Amit, Ward); monuments, historic sites, and cultural memory (Eisenhuth and Krause, Pogoda and Traxler, Erek and Gantner, Kranz and Cohen); festivals (Janzen); and artistic expressions (Schuster-Craig, Kutch, Janzen, Steckenbiller, Gölz, Schütze), the contributions to this volume reflect on a wide array of material, mental, and everyday practices that constitute and construct the social space of Berlin.

Resonant, too, for thinking through the constructions of Berlin, is Michel de Certeau's differentiation between the notions of strategy and tactics. Linked to institutions, governments, corporations, and organizations, strategies aim at creating and maintaining regulations that support hegemonic power structures. Perhaps more loosely applied, strategies, in the context of our volume, refer to policies that attempt to construct and regulate the "city as sign," and several contributions examine aspects of how these strategies are forged and deployed (Ward, Eisenhuth and Krause, Pogoda and Traxler, Erek and Gantner, Ülker, Janzen). In contrast, tactics are created and deployed by users and consumers—literally and figuratively by those walking the streets. Tactics evade strict boundaries and may poach, oppose, undermine, and interfere with the order and structures established by the strategic exercise of power. Several contributions here examine tactics used to disrupt strategies and to contest dominant concepts, planning activities, perceptions, representations, and images (Sark, Ingram, Kutch, Schuster-Craig, Steckenbiller, Amit, Janzen, Kranz and Cohen).

In reflecting on recent transformation in historical perspective, the contributions highlight that as the "voids" disappear, the material traces of Berlin's history turn into contested territory. Berlin as "palimpsest of different times and histories"[14] implies forgetting, filling, rewriting, and reshaping of memory and remembrance. As history is appropriated, revised, managed, and showcased, certain historical sites become monuments and certain historical events are memorialized, while others are abandoned. In contesting "forgetting," appropriation, and economically and politically motivated erasures of historical and cultural memory, this volume presents a complex, multifaceted view of Berlin, a montage—to speak in Huyssen's terms—and an affirmation of the "necessarily palimpsestic texture of urban space."[15]

In choosing "cultural topographies" as a title to this volume, we want to buttress our emphasis on the connection between spatial production and historical memory. In using the plural rather than the singular, we indicate our commitment not only to plurality and the illumination of the heterogeneous character of the present but also to the continuing scrutiny of Berlin's storied history as it manifests physically. The chapters of this book delineate an uneven and contested territory that is always also a work in progress. Topographies are not mere descriptions of places but refer to the spatial mapping and delineation of features and surface configurations.[16] Drawing on J. Hillis Miller's concept of topography, this volume is conceived as a multilayered montage "like the transparencies superimposed in palimpsest on a map, each transparency charting some different feature of the landscape beneath … the landscape 'as such' is never given, only one or another of the ways to map it."[17] Resonating with Certeau's "Walking in the City," this volume maps a layered, fragmentary topography via un- and underexplored pathways, writing the urban text much like the pedestrian in the city whose "intersecting writings compose a manifold story."[18]

What is Berlin today? In asking this question, the contributions to this volume seek to understand the multifaceted cultural shifts taking place in contemporary Berlin within the context of its storied history. Berlin today still bears the open wounds and hidden scars of some of the most significant historical transformations of the twentieth and twenty-first centuries. From Imperial Germany, the Weimar Republic, the Third Reich, the Cold War, and the fall of the Wall, contemporary Berlin is a metropolis of "ghosts." A multicultural city with an as-yet comparatively low cost of living, a highly educated workforce, decent economic prospects, and engaged residents, Berlin has considerable potential and the opportunity to create a unique and inclusive urban environment that will foster strong local communities, equity, and civic participation.

While the New Berlin promotes itself as a creative center populated by a young, dynamic, cosmopolitan class of globalized citizens from all over the world, its economy is fragile; its debt load and unemployment rates are high. The city's promotional and branding strategies are driven by urban managers and marketing experts who recognize and value creativity as it relates to the bottom line. In other words, creative endeavors are not thought of as alternatives to "extant market-, consumption- and property-led development strategies, but as low-cost, feel-good *complements*. Creativity plans do not disrupt these established approaches to urban entrepreneurialism and consumption-oriented place promotion, they *extend* them."[19] Such reinvention of urban space has entailed the forgetting and deletion of certain marginalized cultural identities in favor of "sexier" urban pleasures: "Current conflicts over the right to the city in Berlin, especially those led by new social movements challenging neoliberal urban policies, often mask the endurance of old forms of exclusion as well as the formation of new kinds of dispossession. ... [T]here seems to be little reflection on the way in which [these movements] have also activated mechanisms of revalorization that have destabilized existing use and led to the continued economic marginalization and displacement of other groups, most notably East Berliners, migrants, and the poor."[20]

Cautionary accounts of urban development are all the more relevant and urgent with the New Berlin having become a new home for nearly 80,000 refugees and asylum seekers in 2015 and with more migrants expected to settle or stay temporarily in the city in the next years. Like other urban centers and other parts of Germany and Europe, Berlin's most urgent challenge is not just to provide shelter but to find effective ways to integrate the newcomers and sojourners into the economic, political, social, and cultural fabric of the city. Institutions and many private Berliners have mobilized, trying to meet the challenge of welcoming refugees into the fold of urban life by offering language courses and vocational training, and organizing benefits and neighborhood events. Artists, musicians, and writers are founding initiatives to facilitate cultural integration of the new residents, inviting participation in and offering free tickets to cultural events. These initiatives take place amid fervent debates among Germans who doubt or oppose Germany's official immigration and refugee policies. Angela Merkel's famous "We can do it!" is often met with skepticism. Some Germans unconvinced by their chancellor's optimistic message ask how it can be done, while others angrily demand her ouster and the closing of the borders; violence simmers, and right-wing political parties and groups have seen considerable gains in state and local elections. Implicit to questions of "how" to facilitate the settlement of refugees are not only economic concerns but also anxieties about what is perceived to be an unprecedented challenge to German national and cultural identity. The arrival of 140,000 new residents within a two-year period of time puts Berlin's "culture of welcome" (*Willkommenskultur*) to the test while setting in motion yet another transformation of a city perpetually in flux. Marike Janzen's examination, in this volume, of the *internationale literaturfestival* and Jenny Erpenbeck's novel *Gehen, ging, gegangen* (*Going, Went, Gone*) offers a critical reflection on efforts to engage new arrivals to the city and interact with the refugees. Johanna Schuster-Craig's contribution provides a salient critique of the broader implications of integration debates, arguing for a shift from models of integration to models of participation.

This collection addresses some of the most salient issues facing Berlin, offering an impetus for reflection, further research, and debate about its present, past, and future in the hope that the newish capital will continue to be built on its resistance potential. Our contributors ask an array of questions, including: What are the social and institutional barriers hindering civic engagement? How do non-German residents navigate Berlin? How does the New Berlin engage the social and political imagination? How is Berlin represented and with which effects? What is distinct about its urban aesthetic and imagery? What role has Berlin to play in the articulation of a contemporary German national and supranational identity? All of them illuminate how particular cultural narratives about the city are deployed for concrete ends.

In the November 2016 special issue of *Seminar* on Berlin, we wrote:

> Cities have long challenged, captivated, and inspired the cultural imag-
> ination of their inhabitants and non-inhabitants alike. In contemporary
> society, urban areas seem to gain importance in every imaginable way
> and are recognized as privileged sites. ... However, these urban narra-
> tives of ambition and creation are often undercut by material realities
> and ethnic, religious, and social tensions and are shot through with a
> myriad of thwarted aspirations.[21]

Since our work in that project, Berlin and other German and European
cities have been challenged to rethink their positions and aspirations as
the doors are being pried open to what some term Fortress Europe. European cities have been experiencing what seem to be unprecedented
shifts due to global upheaval and concomitant movement of people.
Northern cities in particular function as beacons for better futures.
While the magnitude of the current refugee situation in Europe is unprecedented, the changes affecting European cities through economic
factors and migration participate in a much larger global pattern that
scholars such as Mike Davis have recently historicized. While in the first
half of the twentieth century city centers were occupied by well-off
urban dwellers, Davis shows the shift that took place as impoverished
workers and peasants gradually took up their "right to the city,"[22] which
included work, even under poor conditions mightily shaped by global
market forces. Often governments did not strengthen infrastructure and
opportunities in response to needs of the new arrivals.[23] The resultant
urban slums in the developing world are part of what today's migrants
reaching the Global North are fleeing; although Northern gatekeepers
mostly turn these "economic migrants" away.

Meanwhile, a culture of "new urbanism" has been attracting middle-
and upper-class nationals and internationals back to reconstructed city
centers across the globe. Urban renewal promises cities with less crime
and grime and more productivity and pleasure through enterprises and
tax bases, yet such gentrification also reconfigures the city back to a
situation akin that of the early twentieth-century demographics Davis
describes. The deep privilege of revitalized city centers is so ubiquitous
as to be invisible or expected, so commonplace as to be normative.
Yet, few city governments have developed successful policies even for
securing affordable housing, and it is more often than not due to the
determination of principled protestors and housing activists that cities are stalled in succumbing to the demands of real-estate developers
and venture capitalists. Berlin in the 1990s seemed different from these

old-growth bastions of self-legitimating inequality. Its new arrivals experienced openness and affordability that engendered what seemed to be the creation of new solutions for many a malaise. In this new central European capital with space to grow, many believed themselves to be creating new narratives rather than different expressions of old problems. The chapters in this volume variously touch upon, illuminate, and analyze what is turning out to be in many instances a limited-time offer, a space of utopian *Zwischennutzung*—take the famous case of *Tacheles*—that is increasingly becoming or being made unsustainable in the face of global, national, and local pressures.

Under the heading "Contesting Gentrification: Subculture to Mainstream," we bring together three contributions that examine various ways in which gentrification is negotiated and contested in contemporary Berlin. In "Cultural History of Post-Wall Berlin: From Utopian Longing to Nostalgia for Babylon," Katrina Sark articulates shifts in the *Zeitgeist* of the city from the early 1990s to the present. The investigation treats a broad selection of cultural artifacts such as film, fiction, and visual arts read in the context of demographic alterations and urban-planning agendas to identify a nostalgic turn that, Sark argues, differs from *Ostalgie* and *Westalgie*. Rather, the nostalgia for Babylon responds to "the systematic gentrification and rebranding of the city throughout the 1990s and 2000s, the gradual disappearance of its open spaces, and the increasing impossibility of utopian dreams, desires, and longing for alternative modes of existence and creativity in a globalized and reconstructed city." Sark's chapter resonates with the examinations of several other contributions, particularly with Lynn Kutch's treatment of critical antigentrification comics and the contributions that probe the reconfigurations of spaces and historical sites. Sark's intervention that conceptualizes cultural shifts in Berlin may well map onto and illuminate other urban situations.

No individual narrative embodies the underbelly of Berlin society as saliently as the autobiographically inspired story of Christiane F. Hers is the life story unfolding in Berlin's subcultural milieu, seemingly out of sight and untouched by processes of gentrification. In "Taking a Walk on the Wild Side: Berlin and Christiane F.'s *Second Life*," Susan Ingram examines the second life of this most iconic Berlin subcultural figure, the drug addict best known for her 1979 autobiographical *Wir Kinder vom Bahnhof Zoo* (*We Children of Bahnhof Zoo*) and the film based on the book. Ingram's chapter establishes the centrality of Christiane Felscherinow's life story to Berlin's current incarnation and the global reach of its urban aesthetic and imaginary. Seeking to understand the appeal of drug culture within the urban cultural imaginary, Ingram reads Felscherinow's 2013 follow-up autobiography *Mein zweites Leben* (*My Second Life*) together with two other autobiographies from the drug milieu: Sven Marquart's 2014 *Die Nacht ist Leben* (*The Night Is Life*) and Michael W. Clune's *White Out: The Secret Life of Heroin* (2013). Felscherinow's autobiographies, Ingram shows, are central to creating and maintaining the image of Berlin as a "poor but sexy" nightlife capital and as a subcultural space where one may "walk on the wild side." But they also arguably confirm Christiane F.'s status as an undeterred nonconformist who continues to escape the confines of strict bourgeois norms and refuses to submit to the dictates of the capitalist marketplace. It is thus that Ingram identifies Felscherinow, the marginalized underground drug addict, as a prototypical Berlinerin.

Countering mainstream notions of *Bildungsbürgertum* (educated bourgeoisie), Lynn Kutch argues against the marginalization of comics as a trivial art form. In the chapter titled "Representations and Interpretations of 'The New Berlin' in Contemporary German Comics," Kutch persuasively demonstrates the pivotal role of comics artists in shaping the creative and sociocritical environment of Berlin. In fact, comics are seeing a revival in Berlin, which hosts an annual comics festival and other events to promote it. Kutch analyzes the visual and textual strategies deployed by comics artists Ulli Lust and Tim Dinter to address urban planning, marketing trends, gentrification, and other issues of concern to the everyday life of Berliners to show comics' critical engagement with the city. Berlin comics, Kutch convincingly demonstrates, enrich our understanding of the New Berlin. Comics expose its contradictions and failures, as well as its charm and appeal. By reading the comics in the context of Clare Colomb's study of Berlin's urban development and branding and marketing strategies, Kutch shows how the artists challenge its official images as the city of prosperity under the tutelage of marketing experts. Their work points to the shadow side of gentrification that displaces people through high rent and real-estate prices, destroys neighborhoods and communities, and yields few benefits for average Berliners and even for the very creative class that is supposed to be driving Berlin's economic growth.

Simon Ward's "Reconfiguring the Spaces of the 'Creative Class' in Contemporary Berlin" heads off the volume's next section titled "Spaces, Monuments, and the Appropriation of History." In it, he takes up contemporary art in Berlin as well, considering shifting urban planning politics in relation to artists and a youngish, relatively newly arrived slice of Berlin citizenry, most of whom participate in what is often called the

New Economy. Ward builds upon Sharon Zukin's work on contemporary modes of artistic production that emphasize ways of doing over ways of seeing; through their connection to specific sites of production and display, such art practices influence the urban spaces that house them. In Berlin, as in other global cities, artists and artistic practices are thus ambivalently implicated in the enrichment of daily life and in the gentrification of which *Zwischennutzung* of abandoned sites for artistic purposes is a part. Ward focuses on several projects meant to facilitate studio space for artists—*ID-Studios, BLO-Studios* and *Funkhaus*, showing how these projects have variously negotiated the pressures and possibilities that the market and city government brought to bear. Finally, Ward uses the example of the mixed-use project of *Allianz bedrohter Berliner Atelierhäuser* (Alliance of Threatened Berlin Studio Spaces—AbBA), which is in turn inspired by a nonprofit *ExRotaprint,* to show how diverse sets of stakeholders mobilize against their impending displacement. Ward sees these projects as models offering the potential of a sustained resistance to the homogenization and flexibilization of the creative class. By advocating for the distinct needs of studio artists, Ward argues, these groups decelerate the process by which transitional artist spaces increase commercial property values only to catch the eyes of real-estate investors.

Zwischennutzung—the term denoting the temporary, transitional use of buildings and lots—seems, too, an appropriate way to describe how historical meaning is assigned within the vast memoryscape that defines contemporary Berlin that is examined in the other contributions in this article grouping. Selective and provisional, memory is made relevant to the task at hand. Stakeholders compete for particular interpretations of German history, contingent perspectives that are temporarily concretized in the use of historical sites and the remembrance, narration, and memorialization of events. Not only are the physical uses of historical sites contested, but the meanings attached to and constructed around them are as well.

Stefanie Eisenhuth and Scott E. Krause maintain that the city government has thus far not developed a cohesive strategy on how to exhibit Berlin's shattered past. Examining the complexities of creating an urban memoryscape in Berlin, the chapter "Negotiating Cold War Legacies: The Discursive Ambiguity of Berlin's Memory Sites" focuses on three historical sites linked to Cold War memories—Checkpoint Charlie, the former Ministry of State Security, and Tempelhof Field. These historical sites profit from the boom in tourism, rising interest in historical localities, and the longing for historical authenticity. They are urban capital, and as part of the "history industry," they play a major role in the constitution of historical meaning. Eisenhuth and Krause's chapter sheds light on the political, ideological, and institutional investments that shape these locations and their competitive struggle for funding and recognition. Their analysis shows how the discursive and material construction of memorial and historical sites is shaped by societal, political, and institutional negotiations taking place in the present. They conclude by pointing to the irony that after decades of having been perceived as the most un-German city, the New Berlin has risen to represent the focal point of German history and identity.

Like Eisenhuth and Kraus, Sarah Podoga and Rüdiger Traxler touch on the Berlin branding campaigns. Indeed, several contributions in our volume consider this striking and influential phenomenon. Podoga and Traxler consider the "Be Berlin" campaign and the initiatives of groups such as Berlin Partners in order to understand debates around monumentalization and memorialization in the city. Podoga and Traxler's "Branding the New Germany: The Brandenburg Gate and a New Kind of German Historical Amnesia" compares the possible meanings and deployments of the Brandenburg Gate and the planned National Freedom and Unity Memorial at the Humboldt Forum. They demonstrate how the Freedom and Unity Memorial may further simplify the vicissitudes of German history by accentuating an unequivocally positive interpretation that would also suggest a relentless march into a slick, shiny future. For them, this type of political myth-building, perhaps common in today's highly competitive attention economy, moves away from the Habermasian constitutional patriotism that has for decades informed a thoughtful engagement with the past, the present, and consideration of future action. Podoga and Traxler outline the complex cultural meaning of the Brandenburg Gate as a way of arguing for the benefits of employing this historically significant monument to represent the freedom and unity of a German people who have important responsibilities in the contemporary world.

Ayse N. Erek and Eszter Gantner come to similar conclusions about the simplification of the German past in their claim that a persistent focus on the present and the future helps to market the New Berlin. "Disappearing History: Challenges of Imagining Berlin after 1989" uses three case studies: the redevelopment of a former Jewish Girls' School, the "Be Berlin" campaign, and the promotion of the city as the global capital of contemporary arts. Erek and Gantner show how in each case history is selectively appropriated to increase Berlin's cultural capital. This practice glosses over complexities and exoticizes otherness to achieve its marketing goals. Both the medialization of the Girls' School redevelopment and the "Be Berlin" campaigns weight their narratives toward the present and the future, the former by emphasizing novel uses of the site and the latter by articulating what Berlin might be rather than what it has been. To further support their argument about the disappearance of history in the discursive production of Berlin today, Erek and Gantner consider Berlin's rebirth as an art city, outlining how Berlin has been purposely developed and touted as a global urban gallery on par with New York, at times its urban heritage appropriated with new uses. Such city marketing invested in contemporary artistic production also aims toward the present and the future in lieu of the past. Erek and Gantner explore the ways in which history has been disappearing in the urban imagineering processes of Berlin over the last twenty-five years and examine what replaces it and repositions this new capital nationally and globally.

As do Ward and Johanna Schuster-Craig, Barış Ülker uses the quickly changing Neukölln as an example for the ways in which societal and urban planning narratives are brought to bear upon and reworked by various stakeholders. In the next section, "Reimagining Integration," Ülker lays out an optimistic history of entrepreneurship and ethnic entrepreneurship with a focus on Berlin politics. "Governing through Ethnic Entrepreneurship" offers a case study of Rojda Jiwan, a Turkish-German immigrant who has built up and runs a successful healthcare business that serves its elderly population primarily born in Turkey in accordance with their specific cultural needs. Jiwan is also engaged in a variety of related activities to further the economic and social robustness of migrant communities in Berlin and has been variously recognized, for example with Berlin's integration prize in 2008. In 2010, she was Berlin's entrepreneur of the year. Ülker argues that, rather than simply adhering to definitions of ethnic entrepreneurship and to the precise objectives and mandates of the Berlin government's Neighborhood Management program, this businesswoman has successfully negotiated an iteration of ethnic entrepreneurship that expresses her multifaceted values and aims.

Schuster-Craig's exploration of Neukölln offers a differing perspective. Her work on the gentrifying area of Neukölln unpacks how the notion of "parallel societies" furthers racism in the media, public policy, and the general public. As with the creative classes that Ward in particular discusses, parallel-societies discourses can legitimate policies that privilege the individual inputs of certain actors while neglecting the efforts and aspirations of others. Schuster-Craig examines two very different projects based in Neukölln, a working-class neighborhood characterized by non-German (im)migrants and hipster transplants. She shows how Anna Faroqhi's comics/graphic novel *Weltreiche erblühten und fielen (Empires Rose and Fell)*, which was commissioned by Neukölln Cultural Commission and aims to articulate "simple stories" of the quarter's residents, and "Playing-in-the-Dark," a series of community conversations about racism curated by Philippa Ebéné and the *Werkstatt der Kulturen* (atelier of cultures), variously expose racist agendas. "Resisting Integration: Neukölln Artist Responses to Integration Politics" examines the contributions of these projects to the debate sparked by Thilo Sarrazin's book *Deutschland schafft sich ab* ("Germany does away with itself"). Pointing out the difficulties of creating a sustained resonance with these community-based projects in a media landscape that is seemingly more partial to the position articulated by Sarrazin, Schuster-Craig probes how publicity functions in heterogeneous societies to further and hamper public discourse on issues of multiculturalism.

Hila Amit's "The Revival of Diasporic Hebrew in Contemporary Berlin" focuses on another conception of alternative community in her examination of the political function of the attempts to revive the Hebrew language in the New Berlin. Leaving open the question whether such a revival is indeed taking place there, she examines the work of Tal Hever-Chybowski, a Hebrew activist and PhD student of history at Humboldt University, and Berlin-based Hebrew author Mati Shemoeluf within the historical context of Zionism and Jewish emigration. Amit explores how Hever-Chybowski and Shemoeluf undermine the connection drawn by Zionist thought between the Hebrew language and the land of Israel. Opposing the Zionist "blood" and "soil" connection, they seek to promote diasporic, nonhegemonic Hebrew as a deterritorialized language and culture functioning and developing outside the confines of Israeli borders. However, according to Amit, they maintain the Zionists' utopian aspirations to create a new and different culture. Amit reads this disassociation of Hebrew from the Israeli territory as an attack on the Israeli regime. Its effectiveness remains to be seen. For now, the promotion of Hebrew language and culture in Berlin remains a marginal phenomenon driven not only by a desire to resist but also by passion, grand pronouncements, and a measure of exaggeration. Yet, these reestablishment efforts might also speak to the recent endeavors to incorporate transnational narratives into Berlin's self-portrayals, showcasing ethnic and cultural diversity in shaping historical and promotional urban narratives.

As Eisenhuth and Krause and Podoga and Traxler have shown in their analyses, debates and public events influence how meanings are ascribed to the historical sites in which they are held, and, indeed, event culture plays an important role in promoting trans- and international narratives that speak to the self-definition of contemporary Berlin—as it does increasingly in other cities around the globe as well. In "The Eventification of Place: Urban Development and Experience Consumption in Berlin and New York City," Doreen Jakob traces the recent trend to link urban and economic development policies to the promotion of experiences. Within this experience economy, the production and consumption of products and places is transformed into "theater."[24] Berlin is the stage for a myriad of festivals aimed to attract cosmopolitan visitors. Marike Janzen's analysis of one of these high-profile events, the *internationales literaturfestival berlin (ilb)*, tests the notion of the fluidity of boundaries that Christiane Steckenbiller thematizes in Emine Sevgi Özdamar's fiction and asks how new non-German residents may truly weave their stories into the master narratives of Germanness.

In 2015, the annual *ilb*—one of the largest and most prestigious literary festivals in Germany—made the refugee condition its theme. It featured readings and discussions on the topic and the publication of a volume of short prose and poetry contemplating the fate of refugees and asylum seekers. Janzen problematizes *ilb*'s claim to globality in her chapter "Berlin's International Literature Festival: Globalizing the *Bildungsbürger*" by scrutinizing *ilb*'s approach to the theme of the refugee condition and exposing it as a self-interested investment into German *Bildung*. She investigates whether *ilb*'s support of German intellectual self-formation indeed productively expands notions of Germanness, posing the question in how far the festival's explicit and implicit indebtedness to the notion of *Bildung* and its fusion of education and citizenship leaves room for the non-citizens to represent themselves. The festival, Janzen argues, is an event where a privileged "globalness" is performed in a way that sharply circumscribes and thus contains the refugee voice. Rather than creating an international space for literature, reading, and debate, Janzen concludes, *ilb* reinforces the German national project of self-affirmation through *Bildung*. Janzen buttresses her argument with an analysis of Jenny Erpenbeck's 2015 novel *Gehen, ging, gegangen* (*Going, Went, Gone*), which was first presented publicly at the festival and which Janzen so fittingly identifies as mirroring *ilb*'s problematic approach to the theme of refugees and asylum seekers. Erpenbeck's novel focuses on the encounter of a Berlin *Bildungsbürger*—a retired professor of literature—with asylum seekers. The story is told from the perspective of the German professor, and while his experience and development in the course of the novel are posited as an affirmative contrast to the barriers and prejudices imposed on asylum seekers, the novel simultaneously undermines its goal to raise awareness about the plight of refugees. It does so, as Janzen's analysis shows, by privileging the white male German voice and by filtering the voices of non-citizens through it. This narrative form prevents, Janzen argues, non-citizens from being known and heard and turns the novel—like the *ilb*—into a self-motivated and self-involved project of *Bildung*. Thus, although Erpenbeck's novel does assert the refugee's agency and right to claim space within Berlin, it ultimately affirms a specifically German project of *Bildung* as the appropriate mode for the handling of the refugee crisis, one that, in the case of the novel, is taken on by the *Bildungsbürger*. Janzen concludes by identifying potential spaces and media through which refugee voices may be heard: *ilb*'s extra-festival series of events connected to *Berlin liest,* where citizen and non-citizen Berliners read texts and engage in discussions, and the radio programs such as the "Refugee Radio Network." These and other initiatives provide hope that the voices of refugees and asylum seekers will be heard and will garner attention.

Christiane Steckenbiller explores Berlin as a fictionalized transnational cityscape through her close reading of Özdamar's final installment of the 2006 *Istanbul-Berlin-Trilogie, Seltsame Sterne starren zur Erde* (2003). In "Transnational Cityscapes: Tracking Turkish-German Hi/Stories in Postwar Berlin," part of our final grouping titled "Berlin Memoryscapes of the Present," Steckenbiller argues that Özdamar's novel compels its reader to understand the New Berlin as a product of over fifty years of migration history. Situated in Berlin, the novel writes across cities, nations, borders, cultures, and time, presenting urban space as a lived and embodied experience to be explored and inhabited through everyday practices. Highlighting the entwinement of spatiality and memory, Steckenbiller draws on critical geography to expose the layers and textures of Berlin's multifaceted land- and memoryscape shaped by shifting realities and memories that invest city narratives with multiple cultural, political, and symbolic meanings. As Steckenbiller shows, Özdamar's *Seltsame Sterne* is indicative of the efforts of a new generation of Germans with migrant backgrounds to inscribe transnational narratives into the German master narrative. The novel also draws attention to Berlin's legacy as a diverse, cosmopolitan space of transcultural interaction that importantly contests and rewrites accounts of Germanness. Özdamar's work consistently emphasizes the fluidity of borders and boundaries, illustrating how already in the 1970s both East and West Berlin were deeply transnational and transcultural cityscapes and, Steckenbiller argues, prefigure the vibrant and diverse postmigrant culture—expressed also in its theater scene—that is emerging in Berlin today.

While people of Turkish heritage have long been integral to West Berlin and the New Berlin, Israeli Jewish (im)migrants are newly shaping the transnational cityscape. Hadas Cohen and Dani Kranz's and Amit's ethnographically informed contributions present complementary insights into the Israeli Jewish diaspora. Both highlight how Israeli Jewish emigration contradicts the ideological and political project of Zionism and the Israeli state, marking the emigrant as a traitor while exposing them to various levels of discouragement and reproaches from the Israeli state and society. In "Israeli Jews in the New Berlin: From Shoah Memories to Middle Eastern Encounters," Cohen and Kranz argue that while Jewish Israeli identity is constructed around memories of the Shoah and while these collective, transgenerational memories shape their initial experience of the New Berlin, it is current Israeli social and geopolitical issues, in particular the ongoing Israeli-Palestinian conflict, that ultimately shape the self-understanding and experiences of the Israeli emigrants. Berlin, Cohen and Kranz conclude from their fieldwork, provides an escape from the constraints and conflicts that dominate life in Israel. They find that Israeli emigrants stress their dissatisfaction with the intrusion of religion into the private sphere and with the political stalemate surrounding the Middle East conflict. For them, Berlin is a place of the present and the future rather than the past.

As Cohen and Kranz's contribution and most others here suggest, temporally palimpsestic layerings imbue Berlin topographies with complex and contested meanings; they may similarly garner the elusive mystique of authenticity. In his investigation of the angelic in Wim Wenders's classic *Der Himmel über Berlin* (aka *Wings of Desire*) (1987) and the vampiric in Dennis Gansel's more recent *We Are the Night* (2010), Peter Gölz picks up on the notion of authentic places as glossed by Jennifer Jordan. Jordan points out that such sites are not ontologically authentic; rather, they gain authenticity through their claim to having hosted important events.[25] Several of our studies obliquely address memorials and memorialization through such a notion of authenticity; here, Gölz investigates how two fiction films deploy geographical authenticity for distinct ends. Gölz writes that "the reflective, thoughtful, passive angels of the past and the hedonistic, action-driven consumer vampires of the present complement each other.... They depict the city's history both as a dialogue with a past that is always present and as an unmediated existence among (and out of) the ruins of the previous century." Yet, it would seem that Gansel's film gestures toward erasure and cooptation. Gölz describes how the vampire film presents Berlin's history in a punctuated form that nearly elides the period of the Wall that gives a raison d'être to Wenders's story of angels. *Der Himmel über Berlin* invites viewers to engage with *Vergangenheitsbewältigung* (working through the fascist past) through its extensive, lyrical deployment of overdetermined sites of militarism and war such as the *Gedächniskirche* (Kaiser Wilhelm Memorial Church) and the *Siegessäule* (Victory Column). Gansel's *We Are the Night,* in contrast, depicts and seemingly valorizes a self-focused and instrumentalizing vampirization of weighty Berlin histories, celebrating the night-lifestyle that emerged in and upon urban sites that are now beginning to signify profitable accumulation of capital. This more contemporary film resonates with what Ingram reads in the autobiographies of Felscherinow, Marquart, and Clune as allegorical alternatives to and individualistic rebellion against the productivity that the new metropolis demands.

Complementing the notion of the vampirization of Berlin, Andre Schütze examines the cinematic tradition of the "uncanny Berlin" as inscribed in four recent action films/thrillers: Paul Greengrass's *The Bourne Supremacy* (2004), the European coproduction Jaume Collet-Serra's *Unknown* (2011), Farhan Akhtar's Indian blockbuster *Don II* (2011), and Ryoo Seung-wan's South Korean *The Berlin File* (2013). In these films, the German metropolis no longer holds a peripheral status but is portrayed as an international city with global communication and transportation connectivity. Although the physical Wall has disappeared and faded into memory, for Schütze it reasserts itself and its concomitant history through its very absence. Material absence turns into uncanny presents, and the New Berlin remains haunted by its history of violence and division. It is the stage for the protagonists' crisis of identity, loss and recovery of memory, flight from and fight with shadowy enemies, and dealings with uncertainty and danger. Past and present are inextricably intertwined. As Schütze shows, the protagonists' emplacements in and engagements with the city are not driven by rational knowledge or an understanding of Berlin's history or current status but rather by strong senses of emotional discontent. Against the backdrop of Berlin's continuing reputation as the world's historic capital of terror, crime, and struggle for political domination, the films, Schütze proposes, utilize the New Berlin not primarily to stage the struggle of the individual in a vast metropolis but to show new post–Cold War struggles in which the individual is pitted against anonymous organizations that are no longer connected to the city or to unambiguously identifiable economic and ideological interests and political powers.

While Berlin's iterations are in some ways unique, they resonate with global patterns of action and thought that are radically and even violently shaping our world. With this volume we aim to shed light on both the New Berlin's specificity and its global resonance today. We share our contributors' appreciation of the historic and cultural complexity of this city, as well as their unease about certain recent developments foreboding a future of urban growth dominated by market logics. In bringing together a multitude of perspectives and voices, we seek to reflect and cultivate the multitude that is Berlin. It is our hope that the critical import of our contributors' multifaceted and nuanced analyses will reshape our understanding of the intricacies of Berlin's current status as a global city and initiate debates, while evoking solutions to questions about how to create inclusive, equitable, and just urban communities.

Acknowledgments

The editors would like to thank Kathrin Spiller and Elena Kennedy for their professionalism, generosity, and patience in assisting with the preparation of this manuscript. We also gratefully acknowledge support from the McGill Social Sciences and Humanities Research Fund.

Karin Bauer is professor of German Studies at McGill University and the former editor of Seminar: A Journal of Germanic Studies. Publications include Adorno's Nietzschean Narratives: Critiques of Ideology, Readings of Wagner and Everybody Talks about the Weather: We Don't, as well as articles in critical theory and contemporary German literature and culture.

Jennifer Ruth Hosek (PhD Berkeley; post-doctorate Stanford) is associate professor of German at Queen's University, affiliated with Film, Gender, and Cultural Studies. Work includes Sun, Sex, and Socialism: Cuba in the German Imaginary, the documentary Rodando en La Habana: bicycle stories, articles on a range of topics, and the telecollaborative platform www.linguaelive.ca.

Notes

1. Christine Hentschel, "Postcolonializing Berlin and the Fabrication of the Urban," *International Journal of Urban and Regional Research* 39, no. 1 (2015): 83.
2. Saskia Sassen, *Cities in a World Economy* (Thousand Oaks, CA, 2006), 114.
3. Johannes Novy and Claire Colomb, "Struggling for the Right to the (Creative) City in Berlin and Hamburg: New Urban Social Movements, New 'Spaces of Hope'?" *International Journal of Urban and Regional Research* 37, no. 5 (2013): 1816.
4. Karen Till, *The New Berlin: Memory, Politics, Place* (Minneapolis, 2005), 8.
5. David Harvey, *Spaces of Hope* (Edinburgh, 2000).
6. Andreas Huyssen, "The Voids of Berlin," *Critical Inquiry* 24, no. 1 (1997): 62.
7. "Construction about to Kick Off at Areal Tacheles," posted by pwr development GmbH, March 22, 2016, accessed March 13, 2017, http://www.pwrdevelopment.com/en/construction-about-to-kick-off-at-the-tacheles-site/.
8. E.g., Johannes Fabian. *Time and the Other: How Anthropology Makes Its Object* (New York, 1983).
9. Huyssen, "Voids of Berlin," 59.
10. Henri Lefebvre, *The Production of Space,* trans. Donald Nicholson-Smith (Oxford, 1991), 39.
11. Ibid., 38–39.
12. Alan Latham, Derek McCormack, Kim McNarama, and Donald McNeil, *Key Concepts in Urban Geography* (New York, 2009), 111.
13. Ibid., 12.
14. Andreas Huyssen, *Present Pasts: Urban Palimpsests and the Politics of Memory* (Palo Alto, 2003), 84.
15. Ibid., 81.
16. J. Hillis Miller, *Topographies* (Palo Alto, 1995), 3.
17. Ibid., 6.
18. Michel de Certeau, *The Practice of Everyday Life* (Berkeley, 2011), 93.
19. Jeffery Peck, "Struggling with the Creative Class," *International Journal of Urban and Regional Research* 29 (2005): 761.
20. Fiona Allon, "Ghosts of the Open City," *Space and Culture* 16, no. 3 (August 2013): 300.
21. Karin Bauer and Jennifer R. Hosek, "Narrating the New Berlin: Sight, Sound, Image, Word," *Seminar: A Journal of Germanic Studies* 51, no. 4 (2015): 293.
22. David Harvey, "The Right to the City," *New Left Review* 53 (September–October 2008): 23–40.
23. Mike Davis, *Planet of Slums* (New York, 2007).
24. Doreen Jakob, "The Eventification of Place: Urban Development and Experience Consumption in Berlin and New York City," *European Urban and Regional Studies* 20. no. 4 (October 2013): 447–59.

25. Jennifer Jordan. *Structures of Memory: Understanding Urban Change in Berlin and Beyond* (Palo Alto, 2006).

Bibliography

Allon, Fiona. "Ghosts of the Open City." *Space and Culture* 16, no. 3 (2013): 288–305.

Bauer, Karin, and Jennifer R. Hosek. "Narrating the New Berlin: Sight, Sound, Image, Word." *Seminar: A Journal of Germanic Studies* 51, no. 4 (2015): 293–300.

"Construction about to Kick Off at Areal Tacheles." Posted by pwr development GmbH, March 22, 2016. Accessed March 13, 2017. http://www.pwrdevelop ment.com/en/construction-about-to-kick-off-at-the-tacheles-site.

Davis, Mike. *Planet of Slums*. New York: Verso, 2006.

de Certeau, Michel. *The Practice of Everyday Life*. Berkeley: University of California Press, 2011.

Fabian, Johannes. *Time and the Other: How Anthropology Makes Its Object*. New York: Columbia University Press, 1983.

Harvey, David. "The Right to the City." *New Left Review* 53 (2008): 23–40.

———. *Spaces of Hope*. (Edinburgh: Edinburgh University Press, 2000).

Huyssen, Andreas. *Present Pasts: Urban Palimpsests and the Politics of Memory*. Palo Alto: Stanford University Press, 2003.

———. "The Voids of Berlin." *Critical Inquiry* 24, no. 1 (1997): 57–81.

Jakob, Doreen. "The Eventification of Place: Urban Development and Experience Consumption in Berlin and New York City." *European Urban and Regional Studies* 20, no. 4 (2013): 447–59.

Jordan, Jennifer A. *Structures of Memory: Understanding Urban Change in Berlin and Beyond*. Palo Alto: Stanford University Press, 2006.

Latham, Alan, Derek McCormack, Kim McNamara, and Donald McNeil. *Key Concepts in Urban Geography*. New York: Sage, 2009.

Lefebvre, Henri. *The Production of Space*. Translated by Donald Nicholson-Smith. Oxford: Blackwell, 1991.

Miller, J. Hillis. *Topographies*. Palo Alto: Stanford University Press, 1995.

Novy, Johannes, and Claire Colomb. "Struggling for the Right to the (Creative) City in Berlin and Hamburg: New Urban Social Movements, New 'Spaces of Hope'?" *International Journal of Urban and Regional Research* 37, no. 5 (2013): 1816–38.

Peck, Jeffery. "Struggling with the Creative Class." *International Journal of Urban and Regional Research* 29, no. 4 (2005): 740–70.

Till, Karen E. *The New Berlin: Memory, Politics, Place*. Minneapolis: University of Minnesota Press, 2005.

PART I

Contesting Gentrification: Subculture to Mainstream

CHAPTER 1

Cultural History of Post-Wall Berlin

From Utopian Longing to Nostalgia for Babylon

Katrina Sark

> A lot of longing is projected onto this city, which remains a city, but also becomes a projection screen for everything that the name attracts. And Berlin is filling itself again with image-campaigns that imply new economic energies and well-known promises that communicate only one message: new here, different here. That difference is still under construction. It is still sought daily and sometimes caught. Berlin accomplishes this easily because it reminds us of so much, because it was so much, and has still so much to reveal.
> —Petra Sorg and Henning Brüns

As the editors of the short essay and fiction compilation *Sehnsucht Berlin* (*Berlin Longing*, 2000)[1] recognize in their preface, the changes Berlin underwent in the 1990s and 2000s were accompanied by a significant amount of projected longing and simultaneously by forward-looking urban and cultural image and identity construction. These two modes of reflection and construction define post-Wall Berlin and much of its cultural production. In this chapter I argue that contemporary Berlin is characterized by what I call "nostalgia for Babylon"—for the pre-gentrified Berlin voids and subcultures of the early 1990s. This nostalgia marks a shift from the established *Ostalgie* and *Westalgie* that manifested in literature, memoirs, photography, films, and exhibitions of the post-*Wende* years. Nostalgia for Babylon is a Berlin-specific phenomenon that hinges on utopian desires for creativity, new modes of living, and alternative social and cultural communities, unleashed in the voids of the 1990s by artists, musicians, filmmakers, and writers who began forging the subcultural scenes and cultural wealth that have transformed contemporary Berlin into a cultural capital. In this volume, Susan Ingram also refers to Berlin as the "*de facto* (sub)cultural capital of Europe" (quoting Enis Oktay) with a "cultural life beyond the mainstream," which contributed to its status as a "nightlife destination" and its "subcultural popularity." I argue that this popularity was forged in the pre-gentrified voids and ruins of the Babylonian Berlin of the 1990s.

Nostalgia for Babylon began to manifest itself in art, literature, and films produced in Berlin after reunification, specifically after the major (re)construction was complete, and after Klaus Wowereit adopted the creative city agenda and branding campaigns upon his second reelection as mayor in 2008. Nostalgia for Babylon does not simply aim to *restore* (to use Svetlana Boym's terminology) or recreate a disappearing past (as *Ostalgie* and *Westalgie* had done), but rather to *reflect* on the creative possibilities the spatial and economic voids made possible, as well as their effects on the new, reconstructed, and rebranded Berlin. Nostalgia for Babylon is evident in multiple memoirs, short stories, and essays that look back onto Berlin's creative scenes of the 1990s, as well as in many post-Wall Berlin documentary films, art projects, and photography collections, such as *Berlin Wonderland* (2014), discussed further by Simon Ward in this volume. My goal in this chapter is to map out a cultural-historical chronology of Berlin's transformation from a "city of voids" (as Andreas Huyssen calls it) in the aftermath of the *Wende,* to what *Time* magazine referred to in November 2009 as "Hip Berlin: Europe's Capital of Cool," celebrating its many subcultural scenes and its globally recognized and consumed cultural output. Understanding the ways in which this transformation came about, the various economic, political, and cultural forces at play, as well as the cultural and collective consequences of such rapid and significant change manifested through nostalgia and protest allows us to grasp not only the contemporary cultural history of Berlin but also the ways in which we reinvent cities and culture in the "creative economy" of late capitalism. Post-Wall nostalgia is merely one lens through which these transformations can be traced; urban branding and topographical transformations others. But we cannot really grasp the cultural history and cultural meaning of contemporary Berlin without understanding the roots and significance of its nostalgic expressions and its collective utopian longing and desires.

I divide the city's cultural history into two phases: pre-1999 Berlin Babylon (as filmmaker Hubertus Siegert called it)[2] and post-1999 New Berlin (a name introduced by the Berlin Partner marketing agency for its urban branding campaign shortly before the government move from Bonn to Berlin). As German cultural studies scholars including Barbara Mennel have noted, 1999 marked the year in which nostalgia (in the form of *Ostalgie* and *Westalgie*) resurfaced in German culture. I take this argument further, analyzing the ways in which Berlin's nostalgic turn emerged in response to the systematic gentrification and rebranding of the city throughout the 1990s and 2000s, the gradual disappearance of its open spaces, and the increasing impossibility of utopian dreams, desires, and longing for alternative modes of existence and creativity in a globalized and reconstructed city. The New Berlin after 1999, while heralded as open, free, and creative by the Berlin Partner, proved to be a less fertile ground for utopian dreams than East and West Berlin, or the Babylonian city of voids of the early 1990s. The examples of Berlin literature, film, and contemporary art produced during Berlin's reconstruction that I bring together came to be regarded as the "Babylonian chorus of competing opinions"[3] and demonstrate a vital mix of utopian and nostalgic longing that is at the core of nostalgia for Babylon. This nostalgia emerged as a reaction to Berlin's waves of urban transformations, in which ongoing gentrification and city branding feed and sustain a perpetual sense of longing and point to the unmaterialized and unlived utopian desires that erupted after the fall of the Wall. I examine post-Wall Berlin cultural production in relation to key historical events, social and political changes, as well as urban transformations that spurred multiple nostalgic waves. In an attempt to define and describe the current phenomenon that I understand as nostalgia for Babylon, I look closely at the differences between these nostalgic waves and the collective longing that continues to fuel them. I begin with a cultural-historical overview of post-Wall Berlin, and include my cultural analysis of how these changes were represented in films, documentaries, literature, and art, and I cross-reference my analysis with other German cultural scholars who have attempted to understand post-Wall Berlin and its culture.

The Babylonian Berlin of the 1990s has been continuously mythologized—as demonstrated by the authors and photographers of *Berlin Wonderland: Wild Years Revisited 1990–1996,* a volume of testimonies and photographs that accompanied a photo exhibition, edited and curated by Anke Fesel and Chris Keller in 2014, and discussed further in this volume by Simon Ward in regards to Berlin's cultural memory, its spaces of *Zwischennutzung* (transitional use), and the eventual displacement of its artists by the creative economy. In today's post-reconstructed and post-gentrified city, the voids and open spaces originally occupied by the artistic communities and subcultural scenes have been largely replaced by commercial real estate. As Ward notes in his chapter in this volume, quoting David Harvey (2002), culture and oppositional movements form in "transitional spaces," of which Berlin had more than plenty in the 1990s, and most of which have now been subsumed by capitalist ventures or remain dormant (as the current slumber state of *Tacheles*—the former artists' community mentioned in Karin Bauer and Jennifer Hosek's introduction). In order to unpack and understand the collective mythologizing attempts that underlie the cultural phenomenon of nostalgia for Babylon, we have to grasp how different Berlin of the early 1990s was from its contemporary reconstruction. The years 1989 to 1999 in Berlin were largely characterized by the removal of the Wall from the city's core and the creation of vast open spaces and voids in its place, followed by extensive reconstruction projects and economic and demographic shifts in response to the *Bundestag*'s vote in 1991 to transfer the capital from Bonn to Berlin. This time was accompanied by debates about memory, history, and borders,[4] as well as by urban marketing campaigns that aimed to construct a new image for the reunified city, attract tourism, and generate revenue and investments. After the creation of Berlin Partner, the marketing agency responsible for capital city marketing, and the initial series of events in 1994 around Potsdamer Platz labeled *Baustellensommer* (summer of construction sites), Berlin's branding gradually evolved into the elaborate and much-cited campaign series *Schaustelle Berlin* (exhibition site Berlin) that spanned from 1996 to 2005.[5] The first ten years after reunification were also characterized by massive institutional reorganizations, as the Berlin Senate merged the administration of all cultural institutions (museums, theaters, opera houses, concert halls, galleries, etc.) of the former East and West Berlin. What distinguished representations of Berlin at this time was the iconoclastic, self-ironizing symbol of its construction-crane-filled skyline. In 1994 construction at Potsdamer Platz began—the symbolic ground zero of post-Wall reconstruction—charged with contentious debates about reappropriations of this space. That same year, filmmaker Hubertus Siegert began filming the various construction sites in Mitte for his documentary film *Berlin Babylon* (2001), which shows Berlin as an uninhabitable city of voids and construction sites, with only one reference to its vibrant cultural scenes—the Love Parade. Also in 1994 the German

Figure 1.1. Palace of the Republic. Permission Katrina Sark.

federal government canceled the subsidies that made up 30 percent of the city's budget.[6]

Along with the mass exodus of many former East and West Berliners,[7] as well as the increased unemployment throughout the 1990s,[8] the city's income tax revenues dropped, all contributing to the massive debt accumulation and eventually to Mayor Wowereit's 2003 proclamation of Berlin as "poor but sexy."[9] In her contribution to this volume, Susan Ingram points out that this was also the title of two works on the New Berlin, by Agata Pyzik (a nonfiction volume) and Geoff Stahl (an edited collection). In 1995 Johannes Gross coined the term "Berlin Republic" to signal the changes that would accompany the government move to Berlin[10] and promise a hopeful future based on values of democracy and freedom. Characterized by both spatial and ideological openness, as well as by immense creativity and establishment of subcultural scenes, this period was marked by utopian imaginaries that can be traced in music, art, photography, and films produced in Berlin at this time. As Dimitri Hegemann, the founder of *Tresor* techno club, explained in the documentary film *Sub Berlin: The Story of Tresor* (2009):

> It was a kind of anarchy that was so favorable for subcultural movements and cultural activists because during that time, in the two years between 1990 and 92/93, the authorities had other problems than closing down illegal clubs. It was paradise![11]

This celebratory anarchic spirit of the early 1990s is precisely what some Berliners, including Hegemann (as can be seen in the documentary film *In Berlin* from 2009), have become nostalgic for in the new, gentrified Berlin.

The Babylonian practices of largely unregulated mobility, creativity, experimentation, artistic and entrepreneurial appropriation of spaces and voids began to taper off and fragment with the arrival of the New Berlin. The year 1999 marked the tenth anniversary of the fall of the Berlin Wall and the completion of major construction projects such as the *Reichstag,* the government quarters, and Potsdamer Platz. It was the year the federal government moved from Bonn to Berlin, and thus the official start of the Berlin Republic in the new capital, made explicit by the city marketing campaign announcing its arrival ("Das neue Berlin ist da!"). In the same year, nostalgia resurfaced in German cultural production—first in the form of *Ostalgie,* as in Thomas Brussig's short novel *Am kürzeren Ende der Sonnenallee (At the Short End of Sun Alley,* 1999), followed by Leander Haußmann's filmic adaptation that same year, and subsequently by *Westalgie,* in works such as Florian Illies's *Generation Golf* (2000) and Sven Regener's *Herr Lehmann* trilogy (2001–8), the first part of which was adapted by Leander Haußmann in 2003.[12] The works draw extensively on references to lifestyles and products that marked the affluent society of West Germany and the subsidized, leisurely existence of West Berlin in the late 1980s and early 1990s. The proliferation of these popular texts point to the nostalgic undercurrents of reunified Berlin, characterized by what Linda Shortt identified as "the dynamics of memory contests."[13] Moreover, two dominant streams become apparent in the course of the two decades after reunification in Berlin culture: namely, utopian desires and nostalgic longing. Brad Prager, in an essay on the "Re-emergence of Utopian Longing in German Cinema," provides a useful summary of the history of utopian desire in German culture and more recently in German film. Prager identifies utopian impulses in Tom Tykwer's *Heaven* (2002) and in Yüksel Yavuz's *Kleine Freiheit (A Little Bit of Freedom,* 2002) as manifested in romantic relationships rather than in landscapes of division and reunification.[14] This search for utopian ideals in relationships corresponds with David Clarke's reading of the 1990s post-reunification films, such as Tom Tykwer's *Run Lola Run* (1998) and Wolfgang Becker's *Das Leben ist eine Baustelle (Life Is All You Get,* 1997), which he describes as set in the Deleuzian *espace quelconque* or "any-space-whatever" of the postmodern, empty, alienating landscape of post-Wall Berlin, where the only possibility of meaning, identity, and belonging can be found in interpersonal connections and relationships.[15]

Furthermore, Barbara Mennel demonstrates links between the utopian aspirations of the West Berlin squatting and revolt culture, the subsequent "lack of utopia" in the Berlin Republic, and the nostalgic impulses of post-*Wende* films, such as *Was tun, wenns brennt?* (*What to Do in Case of Fire,* 2002) and *Herr Lehmann* (2003).[16] She identifies the "nostalgia for a leftist West German past" in these films marked not by the revolt era of 1968 but rather by the "lesser-known, anarchist, and creative alternative scene of West Berlin's 1980s."[17] This *Westalgie* is part of what she describes as the "nostalgic turn" in popular cinema,[18] which in part emerged as a countermeasure to the numerous literary and cinematic manifestations of *Ostalgie,* as identified in *Sonnenallee* (1999) and *Good Bye, Lenin!* (2003)—both of which prescribe a union of friendship or romance as the solution to the protagonist's respective experiences of loss. As the cultural historian Svetlana Boym asserted, "[T]he twentieth century began with a futuristic utopia and ended with nostalgia,"[19] noting that utopian and nostalgic longing are indeed closely linked. Thus, Berlin's nostalgic turn can be seen as having emerged in response to the systematic reconstruction and gentrification of the city, the gradual disappearance of its open spaces, and the increasing impossibility of utopian dreams, desires, and longing for alternative lifestyles in a more globalized city based on a new "creative economy" (as discussed by Ward and others in this volume). By the second decade after reunification, with the arrival of the New Berlin, the most common denominator among all the films of the nostalgic turn, such as *Good Bye, Lenin!* and even popular films such as *Sommer vorm Balkon* (*Summer in Berlin,* 2005), was an acute sense of longing, which in mainstream cinema is often resolved through interpersonal relationships. Thus, many of the post-reunification films reveal a gradual shift from collective utopian ideas, previously found in a community or ideology, to a more individual sense of utopia, found in a private union between like-minded individuals, where the idea of utopian possibilities of existence could still be kept alive.

I argue that 2009 marked another shift within the nostalgic turn with the emergence of nostalgia for Babylon, as the year marked the twentieth anniversary of the fall of the Berlin Wall with an internationally broadcast celebration, titled "Fest der Freiheit" (Festival of Freedom), bringing together state leaders, former East and West Berliners, and a whole generation of Berliners who had come of age with no firsthand experience of pre-unified Berlin. Along with numerous exhibitions dedicated to the theme of reunification,[20] personal testimonies and narratives of how the fall of the Wall shaped people's lives were collected and presented in the media.[21] Many of the German films released that year were documentary films, including *In Berlin, The Invisible Frame* (2009), and the commissioned *Deutschland 09*—a compilation of both fiction and nonfiction short films by Germany's leading filmmakers. Unlike the feature films that focused on interpersonal relationships, many of these documentary films featured elements of nostalgia for Babylon with a critique of the reconstruction, gentrification, and commercialization of urban space. In order to understand what this nostalgia means and how there can even be nostalgia for spatial emptiness and voids (in which multiple creative subcultures emerged in the 1990s), we first have to examine the process of transformation of Berlin's divided Mitte, which had remained culturally uneventful, "wie ein Dornröschenschloss" (as sleeping beauty's castle), until 1989, as Ulrich Gutmair observed in his memoir *Die Ersten Tage von Berlin: Der Sound der Wende* (*The First Days of Berlin: The Sound of Reunification,* 2013).[22] We also have to look closely at the thwarted hopes and utopian desires of artists and entrepreneurs of the post-*Wende* pioneer phase in the early 1990s.

The first few years following the fall of the Wall, from 1990 to about 1994, were a time of seemingly limitless possibility, mobility, and creativity, when "property ownership was unclear and public authorities didn't yet work properly,"[23] which is crucial for understanding both utopian and anarchic impulses and the subsequent nostalgic turn. In his memoir, Gutmair described this time as a "turbulent transition, marked by constant demonstrations, art happenings, and parties," confirming that in the vacuum between the political systems something was emerging that was close to what the "utopians of the nineteenth century called anarchy, an order that seemed to function almost without authority."[24] Today it may be hard to imagine what the sudden openness and freedom manifested by the fall of the Wall meant for people on either side of the Iron Curtain. Throughout the 1970s and 1980s, each of the cities had fostered vibrant underground cultural scenes in music, art, film, and fashion, made subversive and avant-garde, radical and rebellious by the opportunities (and subsidies), restrictions and lack of mobility imposed by the Wall. Within the avant-garde scenes of both East and West Berlin, the emerging punk culture expressed the rebellious and anarchic sentiments during the last decades of the Cold War. Marco Wilm's documentary film *Comrade Couture: Ein Traum in Erdbeerfolie* (*Comrade Couture: A Dream in Strawberry Foil,* 2009) captured this punkish, anarchic creativity of East Berlin's Prenzlauer Berg district of the 1980s, its underground fashion scene, as well as the protagonists'—including photographer Robert Paris, mentioned in Ingram's contribution to this volume—subsequent nostalgic sentiments and attempts to recapture the past feelings and creativity that have been subdued in the new, gentrified Berlin. Similarly, Ulrich Gutmair, who had moved to West Berlin in October 1989, only a month before the Wall fell, remained haunted by the disappearance not of West Berlin but of the Babylonian landscape of "Brachen" (voids), the Love Parade, and the artists' community at *Tacheles,* with the graffiti on its facade asking Berliners "How long is now?"—which for him summed up the spirit of *Wende* and the city in transition.[25]

In his memoir, Gutmair laments the disappearance of the Babylonian city that created the "art scene" and the "excessive party culture" (which Susan Ingram discusses further in this volume as "subcultural hedonism"), the fact that the former anarchy has become a marketing ploy to lure tourists, investors, and entrepreneurs, and that the early nineties seem like a dream, reflected in the "sound of reunification" comprised of breakbeats, house and techno, but also of construction noise.[26] These sentiments of loss of a particular subcultural creative freedom that erupted in the empty and abandoned spaces of Berlin's pre-reconstructed Mitte can be found in numerous memoirs, novels, short fiction, art, and documentary films produced after 2009.

After the initial euphoria of unity subsided, Berlin was not yet a very safe "place to be," with high unemployment, population mobility, and

Figure 1.2. *Tacheles*: How Long Is Now? Permission Katrina Sark.

urban ruins (akin to that in Detroit over the last two decades, which Peter Gölz discusses in relation to the "ruinification" of Berlin after re-unification in this volume)[27]; violent outbursts against foreigners in the former East; Eastern European mafia mobility; and the drug scene form-ing around Berlin's vibrant nightlife (detailed in Ingram's interpretation of the techno and punk memoirs). This often gloomy and unsafe at-mosphere influenced the mood of many films set in post-Wall Berlin, such as *Ostkreuz* (1991), *Das Leben ist eine Baustelle* (*Life is All You Get*), *Nachtgestalten* (*Nightshapes*; 1999), and later *Knallhart* (*Tough Enough*; 2006) and *We Are the Night* (*Wir sind die Nacht*, 2010)—discussed in Gölz's contribution to this volume. The West Berlin city officials in charge of reunited Berlin sought to cover and fill the empty spaces and aban-doned buildings as quickly as possible, creating subsidies for corporate investors and interim-use leases for buildings whose future had not yet been determined. Federal officials in charge were busy establishing in-stitutions such as the *Treuhand*, responsible for appropriating and selling former GDR industry and manufacturing businesses, while the Berlin Senate was subsidizing investors and selling off real estate in the city center to Daimler, Sony, and other multinational corporations. In this tur-bulent period, subcultural creative communities also began to emerge, fueled precisely by the temporary lag in regulations of property owner-ship laws for the empty industrial buildings in the formerly East districts of Mitte, Prenzlauer Berg, Friedrichshain, and along the Spree River. (Ste-fanie Eisenhuth and Scott H. Krause's chapter examines developments at what is now called the Mediaspree.) In addition to topographical trans-formations, vibrant nightlife, and avant-garde creativity, the Babylonian Berlin of the 1990s was also marked by migrant cultures, multicultur-alism, and linguistic transitions. The Russian-born author Wladimir Ka-miner described the first few years after the dismantling of the Wall as the "gold rush years" in his autobiographical collection of short stories, *Russendisko* (2000; *Russian Disco*), vividly restaged by director Oliver Ziegenbalg in collaboration with Kaminer for the film adaptation in 2012.[28] Since relocating from Moscow in 1990, Kaminer has been writ-ing about the transformations in post-Wall Berlin and contributing to its diverse music scene with his *Russendisko* events, having established himself as a Russian DJ before becoming a Berlin author. The social mobility spurred by the fall of the Wall brought not only Russians and Eastern Europeans to Berlin but also West Germans and Western Euro-peans who contributed to the transformation of reunified Berlin into the techno capital of the world.

The Love Parade, perhaps more than any other cultural movement of the 1990s, symbolized utopian dreams in the reunified Berlin Babylon. In her autobiography *The Beauty of Transgression: A Berlin Memoir* (2011), artist, musician, fashion designer, and author Danielle de Picciotto, who was a co-founder of the Love Parade, described the gradual transformation of the gloomy, melancholy, and rebellious West Berlin into the post-reunification "party metropolis" during the techno revolution. De Picciotto and her then-partner DJ Motte (Matthias Roeingh), owner and DJ at the well-known club *Turbine Rosenheim,* traveled to London in 1988 to visit a rave club and came back to Berlin to stage the first Love Parade on Kurfürstendamm in West Berlin in the summer of 1989, only a few months before the Wall fell. In the next few years, the techno wave and the Love Parade expanded and captured not only national but global imaginations, and gradually replaced the anarchic punk culture of the 1980s with a colorful and playful style of techno and electro music and fashion culture in the 1990s. De Picciotto described the first Love Parade as "true anarchy" that consisted of a "small truck, a record player, and crowds of policemen" which had "managed to traumatize the whole city."[29] She contends that this techno utopia allowed the city to earn "millions thanks to the Love Parade, finally having something to attract thousands of fun-loving tourists, spending much more money in clubs, bars, hotels, and stores than those who went to see the somber historic landmarks" and also functioned as a cultural platform, allowing artists, DJs, and musicians to "originate projects within the event, promoting the idea that art and music can have a social influence."[30] But much like the new reconstructed Berlin, the Love Parade, which was originally registered as a political demonstration, soon became commercialized and stripped of its original anarchic spirit of celebrating individuality and freedom. De Picciotto and Motte have moved on to other artistic endeavors. Significantly, de Picciotto was featured as one of the protagonists of the documentaries *In Berlin* and *Sub Berlin,* while both Kaminer and Motte appear in *Mauerpark* (2011), speaking out against the systematic gentrification and urban transformation of the city, which Ward discusses in this volume to be the consequence of capital's need to "destroy a location's uniqueness." As representatives of the Babylonian Berlin, they all comment on the gradual disappearance of Berlin's voids and the ultimate threat to creative subcultures and artistic communities.

Svetlana Boym identified Berlin between 1989 and 1999 as characterized by "both the euphoria and anxiety of transition," noting that "at

Figure 1.3. Kastanienallee Squat. Permission Katrina Sark.

that time, East German police no longer had power over the city and West German police had not yet taken control, so Berlin's abandoned center became a kind of utopian commonwealth of alternative culture with Oranienburger Straße at its core."[31] It was in this mixed atmosphere of endings and beginnings, transitions and dismantling, openness and yet unforeseen future structures that the techno movement and its many artistic and entrepreneurial ventures erupted in the voids, and continue to echo to this day.[32] During her visit to Berlin in 1998, Boym noted that "the participants of the parade crisscrossed the former territory of the Wall with happy indifference, as if walking in a weightless cosmic zone, shaking to a subdued Techno beat."[33] It is precisely this "weightless cosmic zone" temporarily occupied and reinvented by the techno movement that later became the object of nostalgia for Babylon. De Picciotto's account of Berlin's "Babylonian state of life" in the early 1990s that was about nonconformity and "breaking down boundaries, building new bridges, discovering something untouched, unnamed, unpredictable," carried out by a group of "ever-changing, multilingual pioneers," is inextricably linked with the creative scene of West Berlin and is not without hints of *Westalgie* for the "feelings of community" that existed among the members of the art and music scenes established in the 1980s.[34] Throughout the second half of her book, de Picciotto expressed her difficulties adjusting to the increasingly fragmented and commercialized life in the New Berlin and identified the initial closure of the White Trash Fast Food restaurant and the Tresor nightclub in 2005 and 2006, as well as the subsequent repopulation of Berlin by "hipsters," as an end of an era.[35] Despite her sense of increasing "displacement" and the fear of losing the very values of "liberty of the mind" and artistic expression that have been forged in the experimental years of the early 1990s, she found hope in the uncompromising music of Einstürzende Neubauten (and in her romantic union with band member Alexander Hacke, also a protagonist of *In Berlin*), which, for her, kept the utopian dream of nonconformity alive in the New Berlin. At the end of the book, she concludes,

> I had been watching the surface of the city changing and not under-
> stood that the truth lies beyond the facade. As long as I stayed close
> to this character trait, maintaining my sense of integrity and inquisi-
> tiveness, the city I had known when I first arrived in the 1980s would
> continue existing as a metaphor, and I could find happiness anywhere.
> I finally understood that happiness did not require living in a certain
> city but having a certain state of mind.[36]

In her attempt to come to terms with the New Berlin, de Picciotto constructed a metaphor of a "Berlin state of mind" to encapsulate her utopian dreams. She described her transference of utopian ideals from a geographical and temporal location to a metaphorical state of mind, which she linked with nonconformity and individuality. This transference from collective to individual utopian possibilities became especially acute after the completion of the major construction projects at Potsdamer Platz (1998) and the government quarters (1999), the arrival of the New Berlin, and following the years of the financial scandal and crisis that lead to the election of Mayor Klaus Wowereit (SPD) in 2001.[37] Just as Gutmair, Hegemann, Motte, and other members of the techno movement (and several other protagonists of *In Berlin*), de Picciotto presents the Babylonian Berlin that has disappeared in the New Berlin with a sense of longing and nostalgia to which most creative people who came to reunified Berlin in the early 1990s can relate. This disappearance and nostalgia are strongly tied to the urban spaces in Mitte that have been utterly transformed and gentrified, as well as to the gradual fragmentation and displacement of artistic communities and scenes out of the new, gentrified neighborhoods.

Another key element of the Babylonian Berlin was its active protest culture; its treatment in sociological and urban studies,[38] as well as film and literature, also suggest links between utopian and nostalgic long-

Figure 1.4. LinienStraße Squat. Permission Katrina Sark.

ings. While German feature films of the 1990s and early 2000s envision the possibilities of utopian impulses and escapes through romantic relationships, documentary films, such as Hito Steyerl's *Die leere Mitte* (*The Empty Middle,* 1998), and short fiction, for example Inka Bach's "Besetzer" ("Squatters," 1997), recorded the ephemeral and short-lived protests of the young squatters at Potsdamer Platz in June 1990, actively opposing Daimler-Benz's acquisition and reconstruction of the former death strip. Both Steyerl and Bach were interested in borders, physical and symbolic, as well as in the border crossers from Eastern Europe who made their living at the unlicensed bazaars and souvenir stands in the voids.[39] Steyerl's film shows the protests of unemployed German construction workers, who demonstrated (not always peacefully) against Chancellor Helmut Kohl's employment of low-wage foreign laborers, even in projects as symbolically and economically significant as the reconstruction of the *Reichstag.* Her film documents the transformation of Potsdamer Platz from marginality to centrality,[40] and the contested claims to these spaces now divided by the less visible walls of class boundaries and the metal fences of capital. In the final segment of Steyerl's film, entitled *Utopie,* the female voiceover narrator informs us that in "June 1990, the squatters announced the founding of a Socialist Republic in the death strip. Afterwards their traces are lost." The squatters' utopian vision of a "Free Socialist Republic at Potsdamer Platz," where people who are expats of both East and West Berlin can come together and live an alternative lifestyle, is juxtaposed and visually superimposed with images of construction of the *Infobox* (a documentation center for the future design of Potsdamer Platz erected in 1995) at Leipziger Platz. This superimposition signals that the 1990s and early 2000s marked the gradual eradication of the West Berlin squatting culture, which has largely been replaced by the branding culture and the creative economy of the New Berlin. The film presents a rather bleak portrait of the Berlin Republic under construction yet ends on a hopeful, perhaps even utopian note, referencing Siegfried Kracauer's quote narrated over images of holes in the chipped Berlin Wall: "There are always holes in the wall we can slip through and the unexpected can sneak in." Thus, the film ends with the hope that possibilities of escape and change exist in the cracks of established systems of domination. The Wall, itself a former symbol of oppression, is reappropriated by Steyerl as a projection screen of utopian possibilities of freedom and escape. As Brad Prager reminds us, utopian impulses tell us more about the present than about the future,[41] and Steyer's film, Bach's short fiction, and the techno memoirs remind us to look for the seeds of these unfulfilled desires and collective longing not only in the Babylonian Berlin of the 1990s but also in the post-gentrified New Berlin, where the unlived utopian ideas began to be transformed into nostalgia.

Gentrification became a key factor in the transformation of Berlin Babylon into the New Berlin. In the conclusion of her discussion of *Was tun, wenns brennt?*, Barbara Mennel refers to the post-*Wende* social mobility of squatters from the formerly West Berlin neighborhood of Kreuzberg to East Berlin's Prenzlauer Berg:

> At the happy end, the characters find themselves at the new center of Berlin, having left behind Kreuzberg. This move reflects part, but not all, of the real story of the generation of squatters from the 1980s.... A great many of those involved in the alternative movement in Berlin left Kreuzberg after unification and moved to Prenzlauer Berg in the former East. By bypassing the 1990s, the film avoids confronting the role played by the former squatters, who displaced East Berlin working-class residents of Prenzlauer Berg and, through their departure, turned Kreuzberg into a neighborhood of primarily Turkish-Germans, branded by the media and politicians as "a Turkish ghetto."[42]

Of course, today Kreuzberg is no longer a "Turkish ghetto," and Prenzlauer Berg no longer houses West Berlin squatters. In the process of the city's transformation into a reunified capital, the population of Prenzlauer Berg, Mitte, and Friedrichshain by West Berlin squatters, which is also explored in Peter Schneider's novel *Eduards Heimkehr* (*Eduard's Homecoming,* 1999), became a short-lived phenomenon, as they were replaced by West German and Western European young urban professionals a decade later. As Sebastian Lehmann, the editor of *Lost in Gentrification* (2012), a collection of short fiction about the New Berlin, noted, "gentrification devours her own children"[43] by displacing them when the rents become unaffordable. Many contributors to this anthology identify different waves of gentrification in Berlin and simultaneously attempt to mythologize their own role in the history of Berlin's transformation into a cultural capital with titles such as, "We Built This City, We Built This City on Rock'n'roll." In fact, these authors are several generations of gentrification waves away from the initial, creative "pioneer phase" that endowed the city with its "cultural capital"[44] and its vibrant subcultural scenes. On the one hand, their critique that "a city has also to provide for those who contribute less to the gross national income: unemployed, immigrants, retired and low-income earners, and many others. A city cannot act as a profit-oriented corporation or an investment fund"[45] articulates what is a general discontent of both old and new Berliners with the governance practices of the New Berlin. On the other hand, the stories collected in Lehmann's book reveal that the young generation of new Berliners seems to be less concerned with the welfare of minorities and marginal groups than they are with their own comforts and stability. They are part of what de Picciotto referred to as the "hipsters" whose arrival in the New Berlin marked the end of an era for her and the previous generations of creative Berliners. Maik Martschinkowsky's short story "Gentrivacations," as well as other works in this collection, present the New Berlin's systematic gentrification with humor and irony, poking fun both at the leisure-seeking new Berliners and the city marketing discourse that has entered the vernacular communication of Berliners, evoked by the construction worker who orders the "occupying" leisure-seeking Berliners blocking him from doing his job to go and "be Berlin!" somewhere else.[46]

Post-Wall Berlin authors can be divided between those who moved to Berlin before 1999 and identify themselves as the creative pioneers and those who moved there after 1999, often not by choice but due to corporate relocation to the new capital, seeing their aim to "civilize"[47] and repopulate Berlin's new and reconstructed Mitte. Increasingly, the members of the latter group produce works that satirize their experiences in the new but still "barbaric" Berlin; for example, the authors of the two volumes edited by Claudius Seidl, the former culture editor of

Spiegel who relocated to Berlin in 2001, titled *Hier spricht Berlin: Geschichten aus einer barbarischen Stadt* (*This Is Berlin Speaking: Stories from a Barbaric City,* 2003) and *Schaut auf diese Stadt: Neue Geschichten aus dem barbarischen Berlin* (*Look at this City: New Stories from the Barbaric Berlin,* 2007). The short texts in these volumes are often written in the first person, primarily by West Germans with full-time corporate jobs and company cars, who often complain about everything that is "wrong" with Berlin in comparison to Hamburg or Munich.[48] They find Berlin "uninhabitable,"[49] full of construction and renovation sites, too noisy, with too many unemployed people who have no money but too much time,[50] and who don't seem to understand why they—the working professionals—are always in a hurry and expect better service. As Seidl's volumes and other works set in the New Berlin attest, utopian aspirations have either been replaced by satire (Kaminer, Brussig) or by nostalgias (*Ostalgie, Westalgie,* and nostalgia for Babylon).

Along with literature and film, contemporary art from this time also demonstrates a mix of utopian and nostalgic longing. In time for the commemorations of the twentieth anniversary of the fall of the Berlin Wall in 2009, the *Berlinische Galerie* put on an exhibition titled "Berlin 89/09: Art Between Traces of the Past and Utopian Futures" (2009–10), which featured numerous works of art depicting Berlin's spatial transformations, utopian ideas, and nostalgic longing. Perhaps the most utopian conceptual work in the exhibition, titled *Baut Tatlin* (*Build Tatlin,* 1993), was by Norbert Kottmann, who set up and photographed a sign in the empty voids of Potsdamer Platz, advocating the construction of the unbuilt tower proposed by the Russian avant-garde architect Vladimir Tatlin in 1919 for a "Monument to the Third International" that symbolized a "breakthrough into a new age—albeit a failed breakthrough."[51] Kottmann's sign proposed the tower to be used as the "Parliament Building for the United Nations of Euroasia," thus transforming the voids of Potsdamer Platz into a site for architectural and social utopias and simultaneously capturing "something of the sense of social optimism that was generated and became widespread with the fall of the Berlin Wall, the reunification of Germany, and the accompanying end of the Cold War."[52] Kottmann's art project demonstrated a great deal of irony, not only proposing to build a monumental structure associated with Soviet communism amid the future headquarters of Western capitalist corporations, albeit repurposing it from celebrating communist ideology to housing the UN parliament, but also juxtaposing a tower that was never built with both the temporary emptiness of the site and the corporate towers to be erected there in the next years. Interestingly, I. M.

Figure 1.5. *Deutsches Historisches Museum.* Permission Katrina Sark.

Pei's annex to the *Deutsches Historisches Museum* at Under den Linden includes a glass stairwell structure that resembles Tatlin's utopian tower, thus a version of Tatlin's design made it into Berlin's gentrified Mitte.

Echoing the appropriation of Potsdamer Platz by the squatters who wanted to proclaim a socialist republic in its voids in Steyerl's film, Kottmann's tower also hints at the utopian dreams projected onto this space in the form of a modernist tower of Babel—an ancient symbol of uncompleted building projects and utopian grandeur.

Another example of utopian art presented at the *Berlinische Galerie* in 2009 was Tobias Hauser's photographs of his 2002 art project, titled *Walden am Leipziger Platz,* a reconstruction of the legendary wooden cabin of the American philosopher Henry David Thoreau, originally built in 1845 in the woods near Walden Pond, close to Concord, Massachusetts. Dwarfed against the backdrop of the now-completed skyscrapers at Potsdamer Platz and by the surrounding emptiness at Leipziger Platz, the reproduced cabin underscored the scale and disconnection of the new skyscrapers from their surroundings at the time. Hauser's art project coincided with the twenty-first World Congress of Architecture, which was held in Berlin in 2002,[53] perhaps drawing attention to the discrepancies between the architectural visions of investors and the various utopian dreams of local inhabitants. Both the form and the concept of the wooden cabin are not without hints of nostalgia for a simplicity of time and space, just as the regulation of both was reinstated in the former death strip. The breakthrough into a new age, and a new millennium, seems to have been achieved, as the completed towers (of the capitalist Babylon) attest, yet the fragmented emptiness around them has not yet been filled. The temporary presence of the wooden cabin underscores the paradoxes inherent in this site: the layers of histories and the unlived utopian desires projected onto it. These desires cannot be repressed, but they have been culturally transformed into nostalgic longing. This nostalgia became more apparent as the construction of Potsdamer Platz was completed. By 2009, one of *In Berlin*'s protagonists, Peter Schneider, pointed out the significance of the layers behind the now-completed and commercialized urban spaces (like Potsdamer Platz) and expressed his own nostalgia for the voids of Berlin.

As these art works, fiction and documentary films, and literary texts attest, Berlin's post-Wall culture has been marked to a great extent by two dominant streams of utopian and nostalgic longing. Berlin's reconstruction came to be regarded as the "Babylonian chorus of competing opinions" that started with the debates "regarding the future layout of Potsdamer Platz,"[54] which came to symbolize one of the most contested spaces of the New Berlin. Its reconstruction has preoccupied much of the literature,[55] as well as a whole range of documentary and feature films of the 1990s and 2000s. Moreover, transformations in the nostalgic turn leave us with the question: What does it mean to have a different type of nostalgia—not *Ostalgie* or *Westalgie*—manifested in Berlin culture and documentary films after 2009? As this chapter has demon-

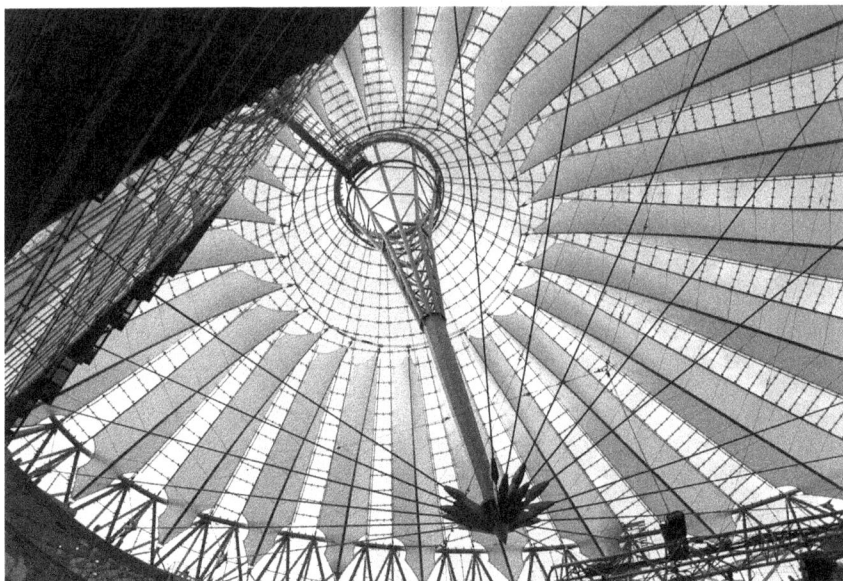

Figure 1.6. Potsdamer Platz, Sony. Permission Katrina Sark.

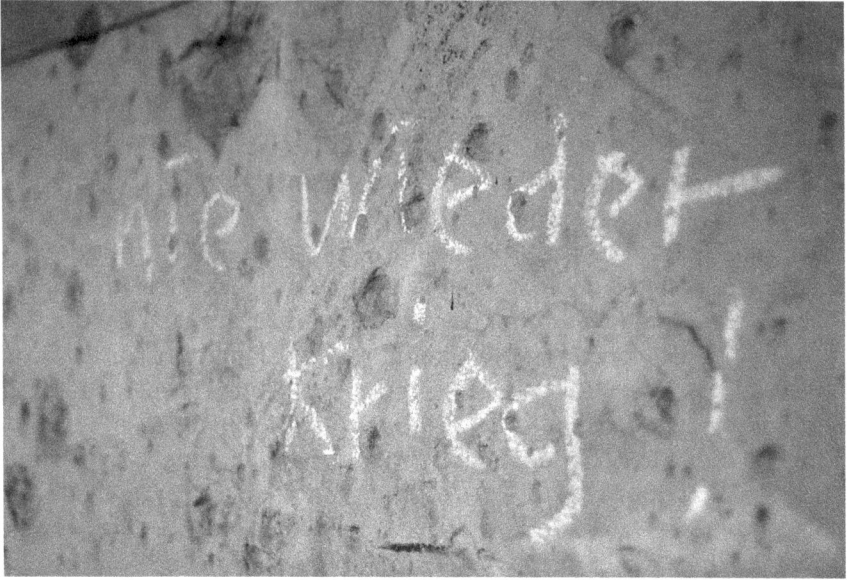

Figure 1.7. Bullet Holes. Permission Katrina Sark.

strated, nostalgia for Babylon emerged as a reaction to Berlin's rapid gentrification and branding projects. It is also evident that nostalgia has more to do with the present (marked by gentrification and artistic displacement) than the past. By 2009, nostalgia for Babylon began to manifest itself in Berlin documentary films, art and photography exhibitions, and memoirs of artists who created Berlin's subcultural scenes. What these multiple nostalgic turns in Berlin culture tell us about the New Berlin is that the waves of transformation, gentrification, and branding feed and sustain a perpetual sense of longing and point to the unlived utopian dreams and desires that erupted there during Berlin's Babylonian years. Thus, nostalgia for Babylon is also an attempt to reexamine the construction, conceptualization, gentrification, and branding of the New Berlin as a cultural capital that has still not found the balance between supporting cultural communities and creativity and selling off and fragmenting the very spaces in which this culture can be cultivated.

Katrina Sark currently teaches at the University of Victoria. She specializes in cultural analysis, cultural history, media and gender studies, and fashion cultures. She is the coauthor of *Montréal Chic: A Locational History of Montreal Fashion* (2016), and *Berliner Chic: A Locational History of Berlin Fashion* (2011). See her blog: http://suitesculturelles.wordpress.com/.

Notes

1. Petra Sorg and Henning Brüns, eds., *Sehnsucht Berlin* (Tübingen, 2000), 7. Translation is my own.
2. *Berlin Babylon,* directed by Hubertus Siegert (Düsseldorf, 2001), DVD.
3. Guido Fassbender and Heinz Stahlhut, eds., *Berlin 89/09: Art between Traces of the Past and Utopian Futures* (Berlin, 2010), 81.
4. See Pierre Nora, "Between Memory and History: Les Lieux de Mémoire," *Representations* 26 (1989): 7–24; Andreas Huyssen, *Present Pasts: Urban Palimpsests and the Politics of Memory* (Palo Alto, 2003); Karen E. Till, *The New Berlin: Memory, Politics, Place* (Minneapolis, 2005); Janet Ward, *Post-Wall Berlin: Borders, Space and Identity* (New York, 2011).
5. See Claire Colomb, *Staging the New Berlin: Place Marketing and the Politics of Urban Reinvention Post-1989* (New York, 2012), 77–78.
6. Ibid., 223.
7. See Janet Ward, "Berlin, the Virtual Global City," *Journal of Visual Culture* 3, no. 2 (2004): 245. For more population numbers, see *Amt für Statistik Berlin-Brandenburg* 2013, accessed May 1, 2013, http://www.statistik-ber lin-brandenburg.de/basiszeitreihegrafik/Zeit-Wanderungen.asp?Ptyp=400 &Sageb=12007&creg=BBB&anzwer=8.
8. Stefan Krätke, "City of Talents? Berlin's Regional Economy, Socio-Spatial Fabric and 'Worst Practice' Urban Governance," *International Journal of Urban and Regional Research* 28, no. 3 (2004): 512.
9. See Colomb, *Staging the New Berlin,* 222.
10. Margit M. Sinka, "Heinz Bude's Defining Construct for the Berlin Republic: The Generation Berlin," in *Berlin: The Symphony Continues; Orchestrating Architectural, Social, and Artistic Change in Germany's New Capital,* ed. Carol Anne Constabile-Heming, Rachel J. Halverson, and Kristie A. Foell (Berlin, 2004), 194.
11. *Sub Berlin: The Story of Tresor,* directed by Tilmann Künzel (2009). Dimitri Hegemann tells the story of finding the basement of the former Wertheim department store vault and opening the *Tresor Club* in 1991 without any legal permission from the Senate.
12. Anthony Enns, "Post-Reunification Cinema: Horror, Nostalgia, Redemption," in *A Companion to German Cinema,* ed. Terri Ginsberg and Andrea Mensch (West Sussex, 2012), 115–16.
13. Linda Shortt, "Reimagining the West: West Germany, Westalgia, and the Generation of 1978," in *Debating German Identity since 1989,* ed. Anne Fuchs, Kathleen James-Chakraborty, and Linda Shortt (Rochester, NY, 2011), 156.
14. Brad Prager, "Glimpses of Freedom: The Reemergence of Utopian Longing in German Cinema," *The Collapse of the Conventional: German Film and Its Politics at the Turn of the Twenty-First Century,* ed. Jaimey Fisher and Brad Prager (Detroit, 2010), 369.
15. David Clarke, "In Search of Home: Filming Post-Unification Berlin," *German Cinema since Unification,* ed. David Clarke (London, 2006), 151–80.

16. See Barbara Mennel, "Political Nostalgia and Local Memory: The Kreuzberg of the 1980s in Contemporary German Film," *Germanic Review* 82, no. 1 (2007): 62.
17. Ibid., 57.
18. Ibid., 61.
19. Svetlana Boym, *The Future of Nostalgia* (New York, 2001), xiv.
20. See Andreas Ludwig, "Representations of the Everyday and the Making of Memory: GDR History and Museums," in *Remembering the German Democratic Republic: Divided Memory in a United Germany,* ed. David Clarke and Ute Wölfel (New York, 2011), 50.
21. "Erzählen Sie Ihre Mauergeschichte!" (Tell Us Your Wall Story!) was the title of a public art project by Anne Peschken und Marek Pisarsky conceptualized for the twentieth-anniversary celebrations, in which a large mobile buoy traveled across the city to the places along the now-invisible Wall, where people's stories took place, and displayed their personal narratives in their original setting.
22. Ulrich Gutmair, *Die Ersten Tage von Berlin: Der Sound der Wende* (Stuttgart, 2013), 10.
23. Fassbender and Stahlhut, *Berlin 89/09,* 152.
24. Gutmair, *Die Ersten Tage von Berlin,* 17.
25. Ibid., 27.
26. Ibid., 23–24.
27. Stuart Braun, "Danielle de Picciotto: Detroit is the New Berlin," *Deutsche Welle,* November 21, 2013, accessed March 19, 2016, http://www.dw.com/en/danielle-de-picciotto-detroit-is-the-new-berlin/a-17241866.
28. "Commentaries," *Russendisko,* directed by Oliver Ziegenbalg (Berlin, 2012), DVD.
29. Danielle de Picciotto, *The Beauty of Transgression: A Berlin Memoir* (Berlin, 2011), 57.
30. Ibid., 58.
31. Boym, *The Future of Nostalgia,* 175–76, 204. *Tacheles* is located in Oranienburger Straße.
32. Ibid., 175.
33. Ibid., 174.
34. de Picciotto, *The Beauty of Transgression,* 261–62.
35. Ibid., 263–64.
36. Ibid., 277.
37. Colomb, *Staging the New Berlin,* 225–26.
38. See Matthias Bernt, Britta Grell, and Andrej Holm, eds., *The Berlin Reader: A Compendium on Urban Change and Activism* (Bielefeld, 2013).
39. Inka Bach, "Squatters," in *Berlin Tales,* trans. Lyn Marven (Oxford, 2009), 116. Originally published in German: "Besetzer," in *Bahnhof Berlin,* ed. Katja Lange-Müller (München, 1997).
40. See Barbara Mennel, "Shifting Margins and Contested Centers: Changing

Cinematic Visions of (West) Berlin," in *Berlin: The Symphony Continues: Orchestrating Architectural, Social, and Artistic Change in Germany's New Capital*, ed. Carol Anne Costabile-Heming, Rachel J. Halverson, and Kristie A. Foell (Berlin, 2004), 41–59.

41. Prager, "Glimpses of Freedom," 360, 380.
42. Mennel, "Political Nostalgia and Local Memory," 73.
43. Sebastian Lehmann and Volker Surmann, eds., *Lost in Gentrification: Groß-stadtgeschichten* (Berlin, 2012), 17.
44. Ibid., 12.
45. Ibid., 19. The notion of the city as corporation was also satirized in Wladimir Kaminer, *Ich bin kein Berliner: Ein Reiseführer für faule Touristen* (München, 2007), 212.
46. Maik Martschinkowksy, "Gentrivacations," in *Lost in Gentrification: Groß-stadtgeschichten*, ed. Sebstian Lehmann and Volker Surmann (Berlin, 2012), 110–13. In this short story, two students who recently moved to Berlin set out to spend a day in a beach bar by the river, along the *Mediaspree* construction sites, and find that the beach bar has been replaced by a construction site overnight. In mock protest, they decide to spread out their beach towels in the middle of the construction sands, only to be forcefully removed by a tractor, whose driver mockingly greets them with the slogan: "Be Berlin!"
47. Claudius Seidl, ed., *Schaut auf diese Stadt: Neue Geschichten aus dem barbarischen Berlin* (Köln, 2007), 13.
48. Claudius Seidl, ed., *Hier spricht Berlin: Geschichten aus einer barbarischen Stadt* (Köln, 2003), 1.
49. Ibid., 15.
50. Nils Minkmar, "Marktwirtschaft," in *Hier spricht Berlin*, ed. Claudius Seidl (Köln, 2003), 120–21.
51. Fassbender, *Berlin 89/09*, 109.
52. Ibid., 109.
53. Ibid., 127.
54. Ibid., 81.
55. See Katharina Gerstenberger's examination of the literary texts that deal with Potsdamer Platz after reunification in *Writing the New Berlin: The German Capital in Post-Wall Literature* (Rochester, NY, 2008).

Bibliography

Bach, Inka. "Squatters." In *Berlin Tales*, edited by Helen Constantine, 106–24. Translated by Lyn Marven. Oxford: Oxford University Press, 2009.

Berlin Partner für Wirtschaft und Technologie GmbH. "Berlin—eine Stadt mit Profil." *sei.berlin.de*. Accessed February 21, 2015. http://www.sei.berlin.de/kampagne.

Boym, Svetlana. *The Future of Nostalgia*. New York: Basic Books, 2001.

Brussig, Thomas. *Am kürzeren Ende der Sonnenallee.* Frankfurt: Fischer Verlag, 2005.

Bude, Heinz. *Generation Berlin.* Berlin: Merve Verlag, 2001.

Clarke, David. "Capitalism Has No More Natural Enemies: The Berlin School." In *A Companion to German Cinema,* edited by Terri Ginsberg and Andrea Mensch, 134–54. West Sussex: Wiley-Blackwell, 2012.

——, ed. *German Cinema since Unification.* London: Continuum, 2006.

Clarke, David, and Ute Wölfel, eds. *Remembering the German Democratic Republic: Divided Memory in a United Germany.* New York: Palgrave Macmillan, 2011.

Colomb, Claire. *Staging the New Berlin: Place Marketing and the Politics of Urban Reinvention Post-1989.* London: Routledge, 2012.

Constabile-Heming, Carol Anne, Rachel J. Halverson, and Kristie A. Foell, eds. *Berlin: The Symphony Continues; Orchestrating Architectural, Social, and Artistic Change in Germany's New Capital.* Berlin: Walter de Gruyter, 2004.

——. *Textual Responses to German Unification.* Berlin: Walter de Gruyter, 2001.

De Picciotto, Danielle. *The Beauty of Transgression: A Berlin Memoir.* Berlin: Gestalten, 2011.

Diez, Georg. "Der Wind." In *Schaut auf diese Stadt: Neue Geschichten aus dem barbarischen Berlin,* edited by Claudius Seidl, 108–10. Cologne: Kiepenheuer & Witsch, 2007.

——. "Staatsmacht." In *Hier spricht Berlin: Geschichten aus einer barbarischen Stadt,* edited by Claudius Seidl, 17–19. Cologne: Kiepenheuer & Witsch, 2003.

Enns, Anthony. "Post-Reunification Cinema: Horror, Nostalgia, Redemption." In *A Companion to German Cinema,* edited by Terri Ginsberg and Andrea Mensch, 110–33. West Sussex: Wiley-Blackwell, 2012.

Erb, Andreas, ed. *Baustelle Gegenwartsliteratur: Die neunziger Jahre.* Opladen: Westdeutscher Verlag, 1998.

Fassbender, Guido, and Heinz Stahlhut, eds. *Berlin 89/09: Art between Traces of the Past and Utopian Futures.* Berlin: Berlinische Galerie, 2009.

Fesel, Anke, and Chris Keller, eds. *Berlin Wonderland: Wild Years Revisited 1990–1996.* Berlin: Gestalten, 2014.

Fierl, Bruno. *Berlin baut um—Wessen wird die Stadt? Kritische Reflexionen 1990–1997.* Berlin: Verlag für Bauwesen, 1998.

Finger, Evelyn. "Mehr Revolution wagen!" *Die Zeit,* July 9, 2009.

Fisher, Jaimey, and Barbara Mennel, eds. *Spatial Turns: Space, Place, and Mobility in German Literary and Visual Culture.* Amsterdam: Rodopi, 2010.

Fisher, Jaimey, and Brad Prager, eds. *The Collapse of the Conventional: German Film and Its Politics at the Turn of the Twenty-First Century.* Detroit: Wayne State University Press, 2010.

Fuchs, Anne, Kathleen James-Chakraborty, and Linda Shortt, eds. *Debating German Identity since 1989.* Rochester, NY: Camden House, 2011.

Gehler, Michael. *Three Germanies: West Germany, East Germany, and the Berlin Republic.* Translated by Anthony Mathews. London: Reaction Books, 2011.

Gerhardt, Christina. "Transnational Germany: Hito Steyerl's Film *Die leere Mitte* and Two Hundred Years of Border Crossings." *Women in German Yearbook* 23 (2007): 205–23.

Gerstenberger, Katharina. "Play Zones: The Erotics of the New Berlin." *German Quarterly* 76, no. 3 (2003): 259–72.

———. *Writing the New Berlin: The German Capital in Post-Wall Literature.* Rochester, NY: Camden House, 2008.

Gerstenberger, Katharina, and Jana Evans Braziel, eds. *After the Berlin Wall: Germany and Beyond.* New York: Palgrave Macmillan, 2011.

Gutmair, Ulrich. *Die ersten Tage von Berlin: Der Sound der Wende.* Stuttgart: Tropen, 2013.

Hobbs, Robert. "Marking Time: Frank Thiel's Photographs." In *A Berlin Decade 1995–2005,* by Frank Thiel, 15–30. Ostfildern: Hatje Cantz Verlag, 2006.

Huyssen, Andreas. "Diaspora and Nation: Migration into Other Pasts." *New German Critique* 88 (2003): 147–64.

———. *Present Pasts: Urban Palimpsests and the Politics of Memory.* Palo Alto: Stanford University Press, 2003.

———. "The Voids of Berlin." *Critical Inquiry* 24, no. 1 (1997): 57–81.

Illies, Florian. *Generation Golf.* Frankfurt: Fischer Verlag, 2000.

Kaminer, Wladimir. *Ich bin kein Berliner: Ein Reiseführer für faule Touristen.* Munich: Goldmann, 2007.

———. *Liebesgrüße aus Deutschland.* Munich: Goldmann, 2011.

———. *Russendisko.* Munich: Goldmann, 2000.

———. *Schönhauser Allee.* Munich, Goldmann, 2001.

Kohlhaase, Wolfgang. *Sommer vorm Balkon.* Berlin: Aufbau Taschenbuch Verlag, 2005.

Krätke, Stefan. "City of Talents? Berlin's Regional Economy, Socio-Spatial Fabric and 'Worst Practice' Urban Governance." *International Journal of Urban and Regional Research* 28, no. 3 (2004): 511–29.

———. "Creative Cities and the Rise of the Dealer Class: A Critique of Richard Florida's Approach to Urban Theory." *International Journal of Urban and Regional Research* 34, no. 4 (2010): 835–53.

Krätke, Stefan, and Renate Borst. *Berlin: Metropole zwischen Boom und Krise.* Opladen: Leske und Budrich, 2000.

Ladd, Brian. *The Ghosts of Berlin: Confronting German History in the Urban Landscape.* Chicago: University of Chicago Press, 1997.

Lehmann, Sebastian, and Volker Surmann, eds. *Lost in Gentrification: Großstadtgeschichten.* Berlin: Satyr Verlag, 2012.

Martschinkowksy, Maik. "Gentrivacations." In *Lost in Gentrification: Großstadtgeschichten,* edited by Sebastian Lehmann and Volker Surmann, 110–13. Berlin: Satyr Verlag, 2012.

Mennel, Barbara. "Political Nostalgia and Local Memory: The Kreuzberg of the 1980s in Contemporary German Film." *Germanic Review* 82, no. 1 (2007): 54–77.

——. "Shifting Margins and Contested Centers: Changing Cinematic Visions of (West) Berlin." In *Berlin: The Symphony Continues: Orchestrating Architectural, Social, and Artistic Change in Germany's New Capital,* edited by Carol Anne Costabile-Heming, Rachel J. Halverson, and Kristie A. Foell, 41–59. Berlin: Walter de Gruyter, 2004.

Minkmar, Nils. "Marktwirtschaft." In *Hier spricht Berlin: Geschichten aus einer barbarischen Stadt,* edited by Claudius Seidl. Cologne: Kiepenheuer & Witsch, 2003.

Moos, David. "Utopian Construction? The Work of Frank Thiel." In *A Berlin Decade 1995–2005,* by Frank Thiel, 9–13. Ostfildern: Hatje Cantz Verlag, 2006.

Nora, Pierre. "Between Memory and History: Les Lieux de Mémoire." *Representations* 26 (Spring 1989): 7–24.

——. "From Lieux de Mémoire to Realms of Memory." In *Realms of Memory: Rethinking the French Past,* edited by Pierre Nora and Lawrence D. Kritzmann. New York: Columbia University Press, 1997.

Prager, Brad. "Glimpses of Freedom: The Reemergence of Utopian Longing in German Cinema." In *The Collapse of the Conventional: German Film and Its Politics at the Turn of the Twenty-First Century,* edited by Jaimey Fisher and Brad Prager, 360–85. Detroit: Wayne State University Press, 2010.

Purdy, Daniel. "Berlin Mitte and the Anxious Disavowal of Beijing Modernism: Architectural Polemics within Globalization." In *After the Berlin Wall: Germany and Beyond,* edited by Katharina Gerstenberger and Jana Evans Braziel, 249–72. New York: Palgrave Macmillan, 2011.

Regener, Sven. *Herr Lehmann.* Munich: Goldmann, 2003.

Schneider, Peter. *Berlin Now: The Rise of the City and the Fall of the Wall.* Translated by Sophie Schlondorff. London: Penguin Books, 2014.

——. *Der Mauerspringer.* Hamburg: Rowohlt, 1982.

——. *Eduards Heimkehr.* Reinbeck: Rowohlt, 1999.

Seidl, Claudius, ed. *Hier spricht Berlin: Geschichten aus einer barbarischen Stadt.* Cologne: Kiepenheuer & Witsch, 2003.

——, ed. *Schaut auf diese Stadt: Neue Geschichten aus dem barbarischen Berlin.* Cologne: Kiepenheuer & Witsch, 2007.

Shortt, Linda. "Reimagining the West: West Germany, Westalgia, and the Generation of 1978." In *Debating German Identity Since 1989,* edited by Anne Fuchs, Kathleen James-Chakraborty, and Linda Shortt, 156–69. Rochester, NY: Camden House, 2011.

Sinka, Margit M. "Heinz Bude's Defining Construct for the Berlin Republic: The Generation Berlin." In *Berlin: The Symphony Continues; Orchestrating Architectural, Social, and Artistic Change in Germany's New Capital,* edited by Carol Anne Constabile-Heming, 187–204. Berlin: Walter de Gruyter, 2004.

Sorg, Petra, and Henning Brüns, eds. *Sehnsucht Berlin.* Tübingen: Konkursbuch Verlag Claudia Gehrke, 2000.

Starkman, Ruth A., ed. *Transformations of the New Germany.* New York: Palgrave Macmillan, 2006.

Thiel, Frank. *A Berlin Decade 1995–2005*. Ostfildern: Hatje Cantz Verlag, 2006.
Till, Karen E. *The New Berlin: Memory, Politics, Place*. Minneapolis: University of Minnesota Press, 2005.
Ward, Janet. "Berlin, the Virtual Global City." *Journal of Visual Culture* 3, no. 2 (2004): 239–56.
———. *Post-Wall Berlin: Borders, Space and Identity*. New York: Palgrave, 2011.
Zukin, Sharon. *Landscapes of Power: From Detroit to Disney World*. Berkeley: University of California Press, 1991.

Filmography

Berlin Babylon. Directed by Hubertus Siegert. 2001. Düsseldorf: Philip-Gröning-Filmproduktion, SUMO Film, 2012. DVD.
Comrade Couture: Ein Traum in Erdbeerfolie. Directed by Marco Wilms. 2009. Berlin: Looks Filmproduktion, 2009. DVD.
Das Leben ist eine Baustelle. Directed by Wolfgang Becker. 1997. Berlin: X-Filme Creative Pool, Westdeutscher Rundfunk, ARTE, 2012. DVD.
Der Himmel über Berlin / Wings of Desire. Directed by Wim Wenders. 1987. Berlin and Paris: Reverse Angle Library and Argos Films, 2009. DVD.
Deutschland 09: 13 kurze Filme zur Lage der Nation. Directed by Fatih Akin, Wolfgang Becker, et al. 2009. Berlin: Herbstfilm Produktion, 2009. DVD.
Die leere Mitte. Directed by Hito Steyerl. 1998. Munich: Produktion Hochschule für Fernsehen und Film, 1998. DVD.
Good Bye, Lenin! Directed by Wolfgang Becker. 2003. Berlin: X-Filme Creative Pool, 2003. DVD.
Herr Lehmann. Directed by Leander Haußmann. 2003. Berlin: Boje Buck Produktion, 2004. DVD.
In Berlin. Directed by Michael Ballhaus and Ciro Cappellari. 2009. Berlin: ARTE, Cine Plus, RBB, 2009. DVD.
The Invisible Frame. Directed by Cynthia Beatt. 2009. New York: Icarus Films, 2009. DVD.
In weiter Ferne, so nah! Directed by Wim Wenders. 1993. Berlin: Road Movies, 2000. DVD.
Lola rennt. Directed by Tom Tykwer. 1998. Berlin: X-Filme Creative Pool, Westdeutscher Rundfunk, ARTE, 1999. DVD
Mauerpark. Directed by Dennis Karsten. 2011. Berlin: Filmblut Productions, 2011. DVD.
Nachtgestalten. Directed by Andreas Dresen. 1999. Berlin: ARTE, Mitteldeutscher Rundfunk, Ostdeutscher Rundfunk Brandenburg, 2005. DVD.
Russendisko. Directed by Oliver Ziegenbalg. 2012. Berlin: Black Forest Films, Seven Pictures, 2012. DVD.
Sommer vorm Balkon. Directed by Andreas Dresen. 2005. Berlin: Peter Rommel Productions, X-Filme Creative Pool, 2007. DVD.

Sonnenallee. Directed by Leander Haußmann. 1999. Berlin: Ö-Film, Sat.1, Boje Buck Produktion, 2012. DVD.

Sub Berlin: The Story of Tresor. Directed by Tilmann Künzel. 2009. Berlin: Film-lounge Production, 2012. DVD.

Was tun, wenns brennt. Directed by Gregor Schnitzler. 2001. Munich: Claussen and Wöbke Filmproduktion GmbH, Deutsche Columbia TriStar Filmproduktion, 2002. DVD.

Wir sind die Nacht. Directed by Dennis Gansel. 2010. Munich: Constantin Film Verleih, 2011. DVD.

CHAPTER 2

Taking a Walk on the Wild Side
Berlin and Christiane F.'s Second Life

Susan Ingram

Berlin may be "a city of multiple temporalities and of diverse modalities: virtual and actual, divided and united, built and destroyed, repaired and rebuilt, living in a perpetual *mise en scene* of its own history, a history it both needs and fears, both invests and disowns,"[1] but the city's reputation has come to rest to a great extent on cultural life beyond the mainstream. "Poor but sexy," former mayor Klaus Wowereit's well-known bon mot about Berlin, which makes a number of appearances in this volume, was the title of not one but two books published in 2014. Agata Pyzik chose it for her reflections on *Cultural Clashes in Europe East and West* (her book's subtitle), while Geoff Stahl collected ten contributions about Berlin's much-vaunted lifestyle culture under the same title, subtitling the volume *Reflections on Berlin Scenes.*[2] The afterlife of Wowereit's phrase speaks to the city's status as "*de facto* (sub)cultural capital of Europe."[3] As Stahl's volume illustrates, this part of the city's cultural topography involves topics such as "Turkish gay clubs, queer filmmaking, record labels, the legendary Russendisko, electronic music festivals, the city's famous techno scene, [and] the clandestine dimensions of its nighttime club culture."[4] That this particular modality has firmly established itself in the global cultural imaginary is addressed in Enis Oktay's catchily titled contribution to Stahl's volume, "The Unbearable Hipness of Being Light: Welcome to Europe's New Nightlife Capital,"[5] and acknowledged by the editors of this volume in the introduction. Katrina Sark theorizes this subcultural mystique in terms of a nostalgia for Berlin Babylon, the period after the fall of the Wall in which the reunited city was experienced as a canvas of possibility.

Contributing to the solidification of Berlin's (sub)cultural reputation have been a number of autobiographical accounts by key players associated with the underground scenes that have been influential in the making of the city's gritty allure. Punk diva Nina Hagen's *Bekenntnisse* (*Confessions*) were published in 2010; Danielle de Picciotto, cofounder of the Love Parade and long-time partner of Einstürzende Neubauten's Alexander Hacke, produced *The Beauty of Transgression: A Berlin Memoir* in 2011 (see Sark in this volume for a discussion of it); Christiane Felscherinow, *the* child of *Bahnhof Zoo* and Germany's best-known junkie, published *Christiane F.: Mein zweites Leben* (*My Second Life*) in 2013; and Sven Marquart, bouncer at the fabled Berghain nightclub and a respected photographer, came out with *Die Nacht ist Leben* (*The Night Is Life*) in 2014.[6] Of the group, Felscherinow's memoir has had by far the greatest reach, having already, according to her publisher, been translated into thirteen languages (Hagen's is the only other text in the group to have thus far enjoyed translation—into French). What I am interested in connecting here are the ongoing appeal and resonance of Felscherinow's life story and Berlin's appeal as a nightlife destination.[7] The character of Christiane F. that has emerged from Felscherinow's recounting of her life story may be prototypical for the city's "poor but sexy" reputation, yet the drug usage she is emblematic of remains a taken-for-granted, while underanalyzed, aspect of Berlin's cultural topography. Drug-taking is one of the key aspects of the historical distance between the two films Gölz analyzes in this volume. What changes from the melancholic male angels in *Wings of Desire* to the hedonism of the female vampires in *We Are the Night* is the latter's consumption-driven lifestyle. As he quotes, the trio's credo is "We eat, drink, *sniff coke,* and fuck as much as we like. But we never get fat, pregnant *or hooked*" (italics added). If, as Schütze claims at the outset of his contribution to this volume, one of the allures of the New Berlin's topography that makes it attractive globally is its dangers, then the role that drug consumption plays in fostering an atmosphere of wild abandon deserves to be taken seriously, as I do here.

By reading Felscherinow's *Second Life* together with, first, Marquart's *The Night Is Life,* the memoir of someone from Berlin's nightlife who is not a drug addict, and then with Michael W. Clune's 2013 *White Out: The Secret Life of Heroin,*[8] the memoir of a drug addict not from Berlin, I seek here to determine the contours and textures of Felscherinow's life writing that make it so phenomenally popular and in how far they are related to Berlin's equally phenomenal subcultural popularity. After establishing the centrality of drug addiction to Felscherinow's popularity,

I proceed to demonstrate the way it is woven together with celebrity in her *Second Life*. Likening herself to Ariadne, Felscherinow offers her life story as a thread out of the contemporary labyrinth of capitalist consumption. However, in doing so, she herself remains trapped. Drawing on work that tackles the deep involvement of Western modernity in narcotics and intoxication, such as Hermann Herlinghaus's work on narcoepics and Lynn Hunt's on the rewriting of world history, I confirm, just as Katharina Gerstenberger did in 2003, that the female body remains a powerful representation of Berlin.[9] I also note the tragic consequences that this representation has had for the actual physical body of the female arguably most intimately connected with the city's topography in the global imaginary.

Christiane Felscherinow first reached prominence in 1978 when, as a teenager, she told her story to *Stern* reporters Horst Rieck and Kai Hermann, who were investigating the trial of a man who paid underage girls with heroin in return for sex.[10] The initial two-hour interview session famously turned into two months and an unexpected bestseller:

> The journalists painstakingly transcribed Christiane's story over the course of two months, transforming her words into autobiography, with several additional sections written by Christiane's mother and one section written by a managing pastor of a Berlin youth center. *Wir Kinder vom Bahnhof Zoo* was first published in *Stern* as a serial; the writers later decided to collect the stories into book form. But when they initially searched for a publisher, they met with some resistance: "Known publishers declined to print the book because they did not believe it could be a commercial success. Therefore *Stern* magazine decided to publish the whole story as a book," Hermann said in a recent statement.[11]

By 1981, 1.3 million copies of *Wir Kinder vom Bahnhof Zoo* had been sold. Dubbed the "Bibel der Turnschuhgeneration" (the bible of the sneaker generation),[12] it was turned into *Christiane F.: Wir Kinder vom Bahnhof Zoo,* an award-winning film directed by Uli Edel and marketed as "the image of a generation."[13] Felscherinow became a media darling who struggled both with her drug addiction and with the celebrity status that came with the success of Rieck and Hermann's book and Edel's film. Intermittently she made appearances on talk shows, and inevitably the question of her drug usage came up.[14] Exemplary of this tendency is the interview she did with Günther Jauch in 1989, during which he comments, "They say one falls back into one's old ways, takes drugs again, can never free oneself from them—are you clean today or is the question too stupid and simply posed?" She replies, "Well, for me it's a question of where being clean really starts," and she goes on to argue about the unfairness and hypocrisy of alcohol and cigarette consumption being tolerated and drug consumption criminalized.[15]

Felscherinow has not been able to stay out of the headlines. As Yager puts it, "Every few years, Berlin newspapers run a where-is-she-now story on Christiane F."[16] In 2008, Felscherinow was involved in a dramatic drug-related episode, as a result of which the courts took her son away from her and the media set out to track her down for interviews, and where else would they start looking but at the contemporary center of the drug scene? In 2011, Patrick Wengenroth put on a musical based on her story at the *Berliner Schaubühne*, with drug-themed songs by Udo Lindenberg such as "Schneewittchen" ("Snow White") and "Riskante Spiele" ("Risky Games") substituting for the Bowie music that featured prominently in Edel's film so that it would appeal to Lindenberg's fans, a demographic thought more likely to attend such a musical than Bowie fans.

The release in 2013 of her second book was Felscherinow's attempt to quell rumors and provide her side of the story since the hopeful, and unrealistic, ending of Edel's film, and likely also to capitalize on the success of Bowie's comeback in January of that year.[17] That the thrust of her story again aimed at garnering understanding and support for drug addiction is clear from the sections written by her coauthor, Sonja Vukovic. These five chapters are interwoven with Felscherinow's and serve to recap and situate Felscherinow's story in the larger landscape of opiate dependency in Germany and users' struggles for state support for methadone withdrawal, something Vukovic researched at length. In her first chapter, for example, which comes after Felscherinow has introduced the main elements of her story as she sees it and pointed out that "No one was interested in the real story,"[18] Vukovic provides a societal perspective on the "Mythos Christiane F," emphasizing that the "sorrows of young Christiane F were celebrated as enlightenment about a part of German society, whose existence up until then had been denied."[19] Similarly, in her epilogue, with which the book closes, Vukovic sums up what she has learned about the German drug scene during her work with Felscherinow, namely that it is very complex: "Through my work with her and through the talks I held for the factual chapters in this book with experts who work with drug addicts and on the medical side of addiction, I became aware of how complex the theme of opiate dependency actually is. It's not the case that all junkies are the same."[20] One also finds this message on a poster for the F. Foundation that grew out of the collaborative work on *Second Life*: "We live in a society that worships intoxication and despises addicts."[21] The F. Foundation was established as an "intersection of research, politics and society" ("Schnittstelle zwischen Forschung, Politik und Gesellschaft") to try to establish a more positive, preventative way of dealing with drugs and addiction:

> The rehabilitating of her myth and what ended up being four years of working with Christiane changed the way all those involved saw society's values and structures, the question of legal and illegal addictions—and therefore legal and illegal addicts—the question of decisions and chances of those affected and their relations so much that together they initiated the founding of the *F. Foundation*.[22]

As the foundation declared in announcing its founding, it stands for "feeling instead of taking drugs."[23]

As though proving the need for the F. Foundation, the German-language media continue to sensationalize Felscherinow's story. They badgered her so much during the interviews she gave to publicize *Second Life* that she made a point of withdrawing temporarily from the public realm, including the internet, leaving Vukovic to do the publicity for the book.[24] In the summer of 2015, Felscherinow hit the headlines again, this time for an incident that occurred while she was walking her dog around the Hermannplatz. That she had announced in the *Exberliner* as part of the early publicity she did for the memoir that "[y]ou'll find me around Hermannplatz because my methadone doctor is there" gives credence to her belief that she was attacked because of her celebrity: "I'm sure they simply wanted to steal my dog and hassle me because I'm Christiane F."[25] As Vukovic dryly notes in the memoir's epilogue, "It has been a long time since Christiane Felscherinow read something good about herself in the press."[26]

Part of the reason for the popularity of Felscherinow's second book as well as the ongoing popularity of her life story is that it fits nicely into Berlin's "walk on the wild side" mythology. Putting *Second Life* in dialogue with Berghain bouncer Marquart's *The Night Is Life* takes us to the core of Berlin's subcultural appeal—that it promises a supposedly temporary escape from the mundane dreariness of everyday life, whether via drugs or clubbing. Indeed, these two memoirs were displayed together on the main floor of Dussmann's, one of Berlin's main, not to mention largest, bookstores, surrounded by titles such as *Berlin* on Vinyl, Verbrechen in Berlin (Crimes in Berlin), and Berlin Wonderland: Wild Years Revisited (which is discussed by both Ward and Sark in this volume). Both Marquart and Felscherinow could be described in the same way that the Berliner Zeitung did Marquart: as "ein Chronist der Unangepassten" (a chronicler of misfits). Indeed, the two have much in common. Both were born in 1962 (Marquart in February, Felscherinow in May); both grew up amid Berlin's urban blight: Marquart in Pankow in the East, while Felscherinow moved to the Gropiusstadt social housing project in West Berlin when she was six. Both come from broken families and show understanding in their coauthored life stories (Marquart's is with Judka Strittmatter) for their young parents and the difficult circumstances that drove them to divorce. Both begin their books with a significant moment and an important relationship: Marquart's begins with a photo shoot of an elderly woman experiencing the onset of Alzheimer's-like symptoms and a New Year's Eve celebration with his "Seelenkameraden" (soulmate), fellow photographer Robert Paris— they are "Helden in einer verfallenen Stadt" (heroes in a decaying city), the title of his first chapter. Felscherinow's starts with meeting the dog of the Greek lover with whom she spent seven years on an "Insel der Hoffnung" (island of hope), the title of her first chapter. Both quickly lead to the scenes in which they became enmeshed: Marquart gravitates to the queer underground and ends up being a key player in the Berlin Babylon mythos on account of his Berghain connections; Felscherinow, even while in Greece, finds herself drawn to drugs and fellow addicts. In other words, both depict themselves as finding their own third way, the kind of way that Bowie announced, and stood for, in the 1970s with hits such as "Rebel Rebel" and "Heroes," and, thirty years later, that the female vampires choose in We Are the Night. As Patrick Wengenroth puts it, Bowie was "a symbol of freedom, so as to say: I've got it all under control. Today I'll do a lot of drugs and tomorrow I'll only drink mineral water. I can change myself like a chameleon, but at the same time I'm completely myself."[27] The comparison with Marquart drives home the specific quality that marks Felscherinow's life story. Whereas he is the one framing situations with his camera and letting people into magical realms, she never has anything around her under control, at least not for very long.

Felscherinow uses the struggle for control to great effect as a structuring device for her Second Life. It opens on the Greek island of Paros, from which, as she notes, one can watch the ferries that in the distance travel to "the neighboring island of Naxos … on which Ariadne was left forgotten after she helped handsome Theseus slay the Minotaur."[28]

Felscherinow draws on Greek mythology to convey her own feelings of abandonment, and at one point she explains her empathy for people who feel the world is against them: "Because I know only too well how it feels to trust someone and be rejected."[29] If, as Vukovic claims to have learned, "work on addiction is work on relationships,"[30] then one has to attend to the type of relationships that are related in terms of abandonment. When Felscherinow meets Bowie by chance in the Berlin nightclub the *Dschungel* two years after the filming of *Wir Kinder vom Bahnhof Zoo,* for example, he flies her to his next concert and then leaves her to find her own way back to Berlin.[31] In contrast, abandonment is never an issue in Felscherinow's romantic relationships. She is the one who chooses to leave the handsome Greek Panagiotis, who cheated on her with his brother's girlfriend.[32] She also leaves Sebastian, her son Phillip's father and seven years her junior, when their son is nine months old.[33] Moreover, in the cases when her romantic partners leave her, she depicts them as understandable consequences of her inability to free herself from her drug-related lifestyle. Gode Benedix, the boyfriend with whom she originally traveled to Greece, eventually leaves her because he has had it with her antics: "A year later things with Gode were really over. He'd had it with me—quite rightly."[34] The seventeen-year-old Alexander Hacke is similarly let down by the infidelities that were a part of her drug-oriented lifestyle: "Today I think that I cheated because I suspected that Alex would too. I knew that he wasn't ok with my relapse. I knew that our relationship couldn't be saved. He was too young for such headgames. He would leave me for another. And that's what happened."[35] Felscherinow is equally pragmatic about getting into relationships that are unlikely to succeed ("I always fall in with people who deceive and cheat me")[36] simply because "I have, for example, a deep-seated problem with not being able to be alone,"[37] which she later reiterates: "I am afraid of being alone,"[38] further asking, "can one imagine how alone we were?"[39]

Felscherinow's ability to understand and contextualize both her own problems and those of others is remarkable. Vukovic confirms that "the intensity and speed with which Christiane sometimes took in her surroundings and would be gobsmacked by all of the impressions; that is, besides her great love of animals, an important characteristic."[40] However, it is in her ability to articulate that understanding in a down-to-earth manner that Felscherinow really shines. After detailing some of the rather unappetizing personal habits of the inhabitants of the institution in which her friend Felix lives and in which she sometimes stays, she notes:

That's simply because they never learned any norms. Most of them
had always had too much or too little of everything: too little attention
from mother, too much bodily attention from mother's new boyfriend;
too little protection from their parents' problems, too much inner emptiness; too many bad examples, too few chances to do better; too little
money to play with other kids in a club, or too much money, from the
clutches of which one could only free oneself through rebellion.[41]

These insights are, of course, based on personal experience. As she so-
berly notes in her final chapter, "Toxitus," "Much that has happened to
me and much of what I am today is grounded to a great extent in my
childhood."[42] Vukovic notes in the epilogue that follows that Alice Miller
diagnosed Felscherinow's early drug use in her 1980 *For Your Own
Good* (*Am Anfang war Erziehung*) as "a kind of self-therapy,"[43] which
she undertook to tame the confused love-hate feelings she had for her
father. Felscherinow seems to have taken the lessons of Miller's writings
about her to heart. Her candid recounting of her relationship with both
of her parents (her father has lived for many years in Thailand,[44] while
she broke with her mother after she gave a lengthy interview with *BZ*
in 2008[45]) demonstrates that, "for many children, it feels better to understand the fallibility of their parents rather than to despair about it."[46]
While deeply personal, Felscherinow's insights, like her work with Vukovic, allow her story to become generalizable, part of a larger societal
critique.

To see that this type of critique is not inherent to the addiction memoir genre, I turn next to analyses of the work of Michael W. Clune. An
English professor at Case Western Reserve in Cleveland, Clune's insights
into addiction are compounded in his more recent memoir *Gamelife*,[47]
which brings the phenomenology of video games as an addictive phenomenon into dialogue with the heroin usage that features in his 2013
memoir *White Out*. In exploring how Clune was able to come clean
of heroin and manage his gaming, Ian Bogost attributes it to Clune's
coming to grips with the way "dope disrupts memory, making every
moment the same."[48] Noting that "Clune calls heroin addiction a 'memory disease,'" Bogost shows that in doing so, Clune recognizes the way
that dope disrupts memory's function of keeping things in the past: "For
Clune, each time he takes heroin is 'still as new and fresh as the first
time.' Doping is pure repetition, the eternal return of the same for no
reason other than to repeat itself."[49] Clune is able to recognize that a
"memory disease traps you in time, making all moments, past and present, identical. Junkies aren't just strung out; they're out of phase with
ordinary space-time."[50] Bogost links this "bad kind of habit"[51] to video

games such as *Super Mario Bros.*, whose purposeless repetition he sees as functioning similarly. To escape this addiction, one must, as Clune did but Felscherinow has never been able to do, create new forms of repetition: "He attends Narcotics Anonymous meetings, which help him understand and avoid the simple triggers that lead to relapse, like deliberately thinking about taking the freeway onramp that leads home rather than to the dope spot."[52]

As we have seen, Felscherinow rejects this level of personal fault-finding in her *Second Life*. Whenever she narrates a relapse, and an uncharitable reading would see the memoir as one long chain of relapses, the circumstances are made clear. Often relapses are brought about by the circles in which she finds herself: "I was staying with Rick and his girlfriend, and my good intentions quickly evaporated";[53] other times it is the result of being confronted with something awful that has happened to her: "To distract myself from the sadness and anger at myself, I went again to the scene."[54] Unlike Clune, then, Felscherinow experiences taking drugs not as something personal but as something inherently social: not all trips are like the first time, and junkies are not all the same either—"Und dabei ist Junkie nicht gleich Junkie" (junkies are not all the same). She understands drug-taking not as a series of repetitions but as an act bound up in larger social forces, at least as far as the circumstances that lead to consumption, the consumption itself, and the consequences are concerned: "[T]he problem is often not only the heroin but the social surroundings ... I'm talking here not only about addiction but also the other things that lead you again and again into dependency."[55] This understanding is also reflected in the space she makes for Vukovic's research in her memoir and the work of the F. Foundation she fosters in order to access the larger historical and social context that makes addiction a powerful social barometer rather than an individual curse that can be dealt with through proper self-disciplining.

The shift that Felscherinow draws attention to, from addiction to dependency, is similar to the one that Hermann Herlinghaus makes in his more theoretical considerations of the transnational narrative formations that emerged during the 1980s and 1990s in Latin American literature, film, music, and testimony. Just as Felscherinow has mobilized her life story in order to win support for those whose life circumstances make it difficult to free themselves from drug dependency, Herlinghaus seeks to get "beyond the efforts of numerous modern writers and artists to approach the phenomenon of hallucination/altered states of mind as creative transgression."[56] Wresting the concept of intoxication away from "a certain Christian morality, from a powerful pharmacological dis-

course, as well as from the propaganda related to the 'war on drugs,'"
Herlinghaus finds that it "leads us to both the borders and the heart
of the influential and perplexing notion of the modern Western subject in its constitution as 'contained' subjectivity [... and therefore also
to] highly charged cultural, 'moral,' biopolitical, and geopolitical questions."[57] Specifically, he suggests

> a conceptual and genealogical mapping for that which attains legibility
> today as an enabling condition, not of a disenchanted, secular world,
> but of a dark dialectic of capitalism through which low-level ecstasy,
> coupled with the market-driven dream of "happiness" in one world,
> contrasts with increasing exploitation and stigmatization in the nearby
> other world.[58]

What Felscherinow's second memoir makes clear is that there is another such world of exploitation and stigmatization much closer than
some suspect. In the chapter on her friendship with Anna Keel, wife
of the founder of the Diogenes publishing house, for example, she relates how, during the second year that she spent living with the Keels in
Zürich, Anna grew curious about Platzspitz, a large, open-air drug scene
near the train station that Felscherinow later described in an interview
as "like Disney World for junkies."[59] Felscherinow immediately invited to
take Anna there: "Let's go, I'll show it to you. You have your own Bahnhof Zoo here."[60]

Another scholarly attempt to write drugs into modern history, Lynn
Hunt's *Writing History in the Global Era,* emphasizes the neural effects
brought about by the import of exotic spices and stimulants into Europe in the seventeenth and eighteenth centuries. She goes so far as
to argue that a "physiology of *dependence* alongside the economics of
demand fueled the early stages of globalization" and "that democracy
and capitalism took the place of kings and seigneurs thanks – in large
part – to a colossal release of dopamine. ... Revolutionaries channeled
the biochemical energy imbibed in the market to galvanize their political energy in the streets of Paris. Revolutions were fought on the terrain
of armies, ideas, and neurons."[61] Herlinghaus not only concurs but also
draws attention to the colonial and geopolitical dimensions of this history and how

> the reverse side of the psychoactive revolution has been marked by
> concern with fostering an increasingly sophisticated, capital-intensive
> workforce in industrial and postindustrial contexts, versus the massive
> exploitation and narcotic numbing of preindustrial or early industrial

labor in which drugs like opium, coca, nicotine, and alcohol were crucial ingredients for maintaining the functioning of the labor treadmill. The complementary side of this dynamic has been marked by the "society of the spectacle's" taking a major hold on the psychopathological regulation of subjectivity in contemporary Western life.[62]

Herlinghaus details how the argument is prefigured in Benjamin's *Arcades Project,* "Surrealism" essay, and writings about hashish, which establish that "the actual, that is, the *cultural,* power of bourgeois rationalism, in a wide sense, consisted of its 'cunning' capacity to activate passions, emotions, and dreams from beneath its 'clean,' discursive surfaces."[63]

The dynamic of activating passions, emotions, and dreams that draw attention to the myth of this clean, bourgeois surface is precisely what gives Felscherinow's telling of her life story its strength. It also points us in the direction of the role that Berlin's subcultures have helped the city to play in the new Germany and the new Europe. The phenomenon of "Berlin capitalism" is explored by Anja Schwanhäusser in Stahl's *Poor But Sexy* volume and by a number of contributors in this volume. Drawing on Angela McRobbie's work on London's dance/rave culture, which shows how it "as a mass phenomenon has strongly influenced the shaping and contouring, the energising and entrepreneurial character of the new cultural industries,"[64] Schwanhäusser demonstrates how Berlin's subcultural hedonism functions similarly as "a training ground for capitalist consumption practices."[65] Parties prove to be key moments in the organization of the techno underground, and drugs are "inextricably linked to the party experience."[66] Schwanhäusser's fieldwork revealed a number of paradoxes involving drug use that Felscherinow also relates, with liberation referring to both producing, "as a non-commercial DIY happening," and consuming the experience. The promotion of "consumption values like spending money, style and pleasure fulfillment" is necessary as it helps to create "perfect neoliberal individuals that have freed themselves from any dogma, thus nurturing the free floating of money, goods, ideas, styles, etc."[67]

Felscherinow emerges from a comparison with Berlin's subcultural excesses as a prototypical, yet also self-consciously imperfect, neoliberal individual, which helps to explain the fascination with her attempts to negotiate the demands of neoliberal society, particularly on women. As the best-known junkie in Germany, if not the world, she is an archetypal consumer who cannot stop herself from consuming; however, the substances she consumes render her unfit for any type of regimented productivity, of which her wise investment of the profits of her early celebrity have in any case spared her the need. While she acknowledges that, "ok, I've always spent my money on dope,"[68] she defends herself twofold: first, with the argument that it is but one of many forms of conspicuous consumption ("But other people invest the same amount in a car or plastic surgery. Otherwise I'm very frugal"[69]); and second, that she has the money to spend and does not need to run up debts or steal ("I had enough money; that wasn't the problem"[70]). Her intuitive assessment that society worships intoxication and despises addicts points to the tensions she understands herself to embody: on the one hand is the ongoing profit-driven spectacularizion of her story in the media; on the other are the support and understanding she receives from her large and equally vocal fan base, who empathize with her desire for both privacy and the decriminalization of her lifestyle. Her ability to reflect on the competing reactions that her story continues to give rise to also accounts for the respect and empathy she receives. Vukovic comments that "the perceptiveness with which the young Berlinerin studies her own demise, and the self-confidence with which she regards her fate, giving no one except herself the blame, explains perhaps the fondness that the public quickly shows her."[71] In her honest and self-reflexive self-presentation, Felscherinow offers the public an identificatory model that they can at once relate to with their own addictive impulses and weaknesses and aspire to for her candor. At the same time, as a contemporary Ariadne, she finds herself abandoned on the bedrock of the popular press and cannot avoid serving as an ideal celebrity foil for those interested in blaming victims and reveling in their downtroddenness.

A 2013 *Deutschland Akut* interview that Felscherinow participated in revolved around the question of the relevance of her first book: "But how relevant is *The Children of Bahnhof Zoo* today? Is it right that the book, 35 years after its appearance, is still a mandatory read in many German schools? What does Christiane F.'s story have to say to young people today besides romanticizing drugs and providing misery voyeurism?"[72] In light of the discussion here, one would encourage *The Children of Bahnhof Zoo* to be read in tandem with Felscherinow's *My Second Life* so that the larger issues that are addressed in Vukovic's *Sachkapitel*, which situate Felscherinow's story in the context of how the German state deals with opiate dependency and specifically the difficulties in providing adequate facilities for those trying to use a substitute to kick their habit, counteract the romanticizing, voyeuristic appeal of Felscherinow's storytelling prowess. It is noteworthy that media such as *Deutschland Akut* reject such an approach, preferring to capitalize on her appeal rather than delve into the sociopolitical causes and consequences that her *Second Life* and the work of her F. Foundation are trying to raise awareness of.

So what can we learn about the cultural topographies of the New Berlin given the fate of Felscherinow and her life writing? The difficulty she has had in circumnavigating the treacherous terrain of media relations is indicative of the forces with which the city's "walk on the wild side" image has also had to contend and to which it must be understood in relation. Part of Berlin's success with the Easyjetset and its status as Europe's "new nightlife capital" is that it, like both Bowie and Felscherinow, has found ways to capitalize on the fact that the tendency for bourgeois rationality "to activate passions, emotions, and dreams from beneath its 'clean,' discursive surfaces" has called forth a lifestyle culture to not only meet but to commodify desires for what precisely lies beneath. Felscherinow's *Second Life* makes one appreciate much about this phenomenon: the level of control that Bowie's changes via costumes and styling allowed him to exercise, even in dying;[73] the physical risks and tolls that a life of drug-taking entails; and the challenge of imagining where else such a story could be based, could make possible a life story told with such attentiveness to the social and subcultural ramifications. While it is true that much of the memoir takes place elsewhere—in Greece, Zürich, California, and the failed attempt to flee with her son to Holland, which resulted in his being taken away from her, it is nonetheless to Berlin to which Felscherinow constantly returns, and returns us, reminding us that the city served as Simmel's model for modern metropolitan stimulation, against which individuals have had to find forms of resistance in order not to be leveled by and, as Simmel put it, "used up in the social-technological mechanism."[74] In her lucid, candid, and courageous refusal to give in to forms of publicity-driven self-disciplining, Felscherinow proves to be a prototypical Berlinerin, whose ongoing highs and lows confirm for us that the female body continues to be "the surface on which the contradictions and tensions of the New Berlin become visible."[75]

Susan Ingram is associate professor in the Department of Humanities at York University, Toronto. She is the editor of Intellect Book's *World Film Locations* volume on Berlin and of its Urban Chic series, and coauthor of volumes on Berlin, Vienna, and Los Angeles (forthcoming). Her research focuses on European modernity and its legacies.

Notes

1. Thomas Elsaesser, "Sonnen-Insulaner," in *Memory Culture and the Contemporary City: Building Sites,* ed. Uta Staiger, Henriette Steiner, and Andrew Webber (New York, 2009), 37.
2. Agata Pyzik, *Poor but Sexy: Culture Clashes in Europe East and West* (Hants, 2014); Geoff Stahl, *Poor, but Sexy: Reflections on Berlin Scenes* (Bern, 2014). For my review of the latter, see *Topia: Canadian Journal of Cultural Studies* 33 (Spring 2015): 226–29.
3. Enis Oktay, "The Unbearable Hipness of Being Light: Welcome to Europe's New Nightlife Capital," in *Poor, but Sexy: Reflections on Berlin Scenes,* ed. Geoff Stahl (Bern, 2014), 8.
4. Stahl, *Poor, but Sexy,* back cover.
5. Oktay, "Unbearable Hipness of Being Light," 211–25.
6. One could also include the autobiographies of fashion models Veruschka and Uschi Obermeier in this group. While admittedly more of a stretch, both do have connections to Berlin's scenes. Since moving to Berlin in 2006 from New York, Vera Lehndorff has been an active member of the city's burgeoning artistic community, beginning with her role in *Prater,* directed by Ulrike Ottinger (Vienna, 2007), while Obermaier's reputation as a 1968 icon is based on having been a member of Berlin's radical *Kommune 1* in addition to her relationships with the likes of Keith Richards. Keith Richards's *Life* is indicative of the fact that these co- or ghostwritten autobiographies are part of a larger global trend.
7. I would like to acknowledge, and offer my profound thanks, to the graduate students in the University of Minnesota's Department of German for inviting me to give the keynote at their 2015 conference on "Transformations: Growth, Decay, Remains," and to Nichole Neumann, in particular, for her outstanding organization and hospitality. The gathering and its thematics proved most propitious in helping me to locate the material for this chapter in Berlin's larger history of transformation.
8. Michael W. Clune, *White Out: The Secret Life of Heroin* (Center City, MN, 2013).
9. Katharina Gerstenberger, "Play Zones: The Erotics of the New Berlin," *German Quarterly* 76, no. 3 (2003): 259–72.
10. The English and German Wikipedia entries for "Christiane F." both provide good overviews of Felscherinow's early experiences.
11. Matia Burnett, "Station to 'Station': The Rebirth of a Foreign Cult Classic," *Publisher's Weekly,* December 20, 2012, http://www.publishersweekly.com/pw/by-topic/childrens/childrens-book-news/article/55212-station-to-station-the-rebirth-of-a-foreign-cult-classic.html.
12. The reference appeared in the April 3, 1981, issue of *Die Zeit.* See Franziska Gerlach, "Übersetzen als Kulturaustausch—Belletristik—Felscherinow, Christiane—Goethe-Institut," May 2012, http://www.goethe.de/ins/se/prj/uar/fin/bel/fel/de9394812.htm.

13. This phrase was the tagline for one of the English-language posters for the film. It can be found at https://en.wikipedia.org/wiki/Christiane_F._–_We_Children_from_Bahnhof_Zoo, but is sadly not available for reproduction on account of copyright issues.

14. A collection of interviews with Felscherinow is available at C. Conner, "Christiane F.—Interviews, Berichte, Film 'Wir Kinder Vom Bahnhof Zoo,'" accessed February 28, 2016, https://www.youtube.com/playlist?list=PLMFRn FegTKScvBzIsIk_FCnfjrT8_WNQh.

15. The clip is available at https://www.youtube.com/watch?v=XMp-Nj4GAjU. Unless otherwise noted, all translations are mine.

16. Jane Yager, "Revisiting Seedy West Berlin with Christiane F. and Patricia Highsmith," October 8, 2013, http://janeyager.com/2013/10/08/revisiting-seedy-west-berlin-with-christiane-f-and-patricia-highsmith/.

17. See Susan Ingram, "Bowie's Berlin: Where We Are Now," *Descant* 45, no. 3 (Fall 2014): 228–38, for a discussion of that comeback.

18. Christiane Felscherinow, *Mein zweites Leben: Autobiographie* [*My Second Life*] (Berlin, 2013), 55. "Die wahre Geschichte hat niemanden interessiert."

19. Ibid., 60. "Die Leiden der jungen Christiane F. wurden gefeiert als Aufklärung über einen Teil der deutschen Gesellschaft, dessen Existenz man bis dahin geleugnet hatte."

20. Ibid., 321. "Durch die Arbeit mit ihr und durch die Gespräche mit Experten aus Drogenhilfe und Suchtmedizin, die ich für die Sachkapitel in diesem Buch führte, wurde mir bewusst, wie komplex das Thema der Opiatabhängigkeit tatsächlich ist. Und dabei ist Junkie nicht gleich Junkie."

21. The story of the F. Foundation's formation is available on its website. "Entstehung der F. Foundation," *F. Foundation,* accessed June 5, 2016, http://www.f-foundation.org/die-stiftung/entstehung-der-f-foundation/. "Wir leben in einer Gesellschaft, die dem Rausch huldigt und den Süchtigen verachtet."

22. Ibid. "Die Aufarbeitung ihres Mythos und die insgesamt vierjährige Arbeit mit Christiane veränderten den Blick aller Beteiligten auf die Werte und Strukturen der Gesellschaft, auf die Frage nach legalen und illegalen Süchten—und damit legalen und illegalen Süchtigen —auf die Frage nach Entscheidungen und Chancen von Betroffenen und Angehörigen so sehr, dass sie gemeinsam die Gründung der F. Foundation initiierten."

23. "Fühlen statt fixen," *Tip Berlin,* accessed February 28, 2016, http://www.tip-berlin.de/kultur-und-freizeit/fuhlen-statt-fixen.

24. There is a gap of over a year on the Facebook page for "Christiane Felscherinow" from January 26, 2014, to March 12, 2015.

25. The first announcement was in Ines Montani and Walter Crasshole, "Christiane's Second Life," *Exberliner* January 22, 2014, http://www.exberliner.com/features/people/christianes-second-life/. The more recent response can be found in Angie Pohlers, "Christiane F.: Das war ein Raubüberfall auf mich," *Der Tagesspiegel,* July 22, 2015, http://www.tagesspiegel.de/berlin/polizei-justiz/nach-rangelei-in-berlin-neukoelln-christiane-f-das-war-ein-

raubueberfall-auf-mich/12089228.html. "Ich bin mir sicher, die wollten einfach meinen Hund stehlen und mich fertig machen, weil ich eben Christiane F. bin."

26. Felscherinow, *Mein zweites Leben,* 321. "Es ist lange her, dass Christiane Felscherinow über sich selbst etwas Gutes in der Presse las."

27. "Fixen, Drogen, Babystrich—die Angstlust funktioniert," *Stern* February 15, 2011, http://www.stern.de/kultur/kunst/wir-kinder-vom-bahnhof-zoo-fixen-drogen-babystrich-die-angstlust-funktioniert-1654174.html. "[E]in Symbol für Freiheit. So nach dem Motto: Ich habe das alles im Griff. Heute nehme ich ganz viele Drogen und morgen trinke ich nur Mineralwasser. Ich kann mich verwandeln wie ein Chamäleon, aber gleichzeitig bin ich immer total ich selbst."

28. Felscherinow, *Mein zweites Leben,* 15. "Nachbarinsel Naxos ... auf der Ariadne vergessen wurde, nachdem sie dem schönen Theseus geholfen hatte, den Minotaurus zu töten."

29. Ibid., 255. "[W]eil ich selbst nur zu gut weiß, wie es sich anfühlt, wenn man sich jemandem anvertraut und zurückgewiesen wird."

30. Ibid., 322. "Suchtarbeit ist Beziehungsarbeit."

31. Ibid., 101–2.

32. Ibid., 30–32.

33. Ibid., 47, 211.

34. Ibid., 196. "[E]in Jahr später war es mit Gode endgültig vorbei. Er hatte die Schnauze voll von mir—zu Recht."

35. Ibid., 132. "Heute denke ich, dass ich fremdgegangen bin, weil ich ahnte: Auch Alex würde es tun. Ich wusste, er kam mit meinem Rückfall nicht klar. Ich wusste, das mit uns war nicht mehr zu retten. Er war zu jung für so einen Psychoscheiß. Er würde mich für eine andere verlassen. Und so kam es dann auch."

36. Ibid., 226. "Ich falle immer wieder auf Menschen herein, die mich betrügen und bestehlen."

37. Ibid., 206–7. "Bei mir zum Beispiel ist es das tief sitzende Problem, nicht allein sein zu können."

38. Ibid., 271. "Ich habe Angst vor dem Alleinsein."

39. Ibid., 306. "Kann man sich vorstellen, wie allein wir waren?"

40. Ibid., 320. "Die Intensität, mit der Christiane manchmal blitzschnell ihre Umgebung wahrnimmt, und von all diesen Eindrücken auch oft schrecklich aufgerieben ist, das ist neben ihrer großen Tierliebe wohl ein bedeutender Wesenszug."

41. Ibid., 272. "Das liegt einfach daran, dass sie Normen nie kennengelernt haben. Die meisten von ihnen hatten immer auf irgendeine Art zu viel oder zu wenig von allem: zu wenig Aufmerksamkeit der Mutter, zu viel körperliche Zuneigung des neuen Freundes der Mutter; zu wenig Schutz vor den Problemen der Eltern, zu viel innere Leere; zu viele schlechte Vorbilder, zu wenig Chancen, es besser zu machen; zu wenig Geld, um in einem Verein mit den

anderen Kindern zu spielen, oder zu viel Geld, aus dessen Umklammerung man sich nur durch Rebellion befreien konnte."

42. Ibid., 305. "Vieles, was mir passiert ist, und viel von dem, was ich heute bin, liegt zum großen Teil in meiner Kindheit begründet."

43. Ibid., 320. "eine Art Selbsttherapie."

44. Ibid., 204.

45. Ibid., 77.

46. Ibid., 320. "Für viele Kinder fühlte es sich besser an, die Fehlbarkeit ihrer Eltern zu verstehen, statt daran zu verzweifeln."

47. Michael W. Clune, *Gamelife* (New York, 2015).

48. Ian Bogost, "In the Habit," *Los Angeles Review of Books,* September 20, 2015, https://lareviewofbooks.org/article/in-the-habit/.

49. Ibid.

50. Ibid.

51. Ibid.

52. Ibid.

53. Felscherinow, *Mein zweites Leben,* 131. "Ich wohnte bei Rick und seiner Freundin, und meine guten Vorsätze waren schnell verflogen."

54. Ibid., 203. "Um mich abzulenken von der Traurigkeit und der Wut auf mich selbst, ging ich wieder auf die Szene."

55. Ibid., 206–7. "Das Problem ist oft nicht nur das Heroin, sondern das soziale Umfeld ... ich rede hier nicht nur von der Sucht, sondern auch von anderen Dingen, die dich immer wieder in die Abhängigkeit führen."

56. Hermann Herlinghaus, "In/Comparable Intoxications: Walter Benjamin Revisited from the Hemispheric South," *Discourse* 32, no. 1 (2010): 17.

57. Ibid.

58. Ibid., 29.

59. Max Daly, "'I Will Die Soon—I Know That': Meeting the Real Christiane F.," *Vice,* December 10, 2013, http://www.vice.com/en_ca/read/christiane-felscherinow-interview.

60. Felscherinow, *Mein zweites Leben,* 153. "Komm mit, dann zeige ich es dir. Ihr habt hier auch euren Bahnhof Zoo."

61. Larry S. McGrath, "From the Globe to the Brain and Back," *Los Angeles Review of Books*, October 1, 2015, https://lareviewofbooks.org/review/from-the-globe-to-the-brain-and-back. Italics added.

62. Herlinghaus, "In/Comparable Intoxications," 27–28.

63. Ibid., 19.

64. Angela McRobbie, "Clubs to Companies: Notes on the Decline of Political Culture in Speeded Up Creative Worlds," *Cultural Studies* 16, no. 4 (2002): 519.

65. Anja Schwanhäusser, "Berlin Capitalism: The Spirit of Urban Scenes," in *Poor, but Sexy: Reflections on Berlin Scenes,* ed. Geoff Stahl (Bern, 2014), 116.

66. Ibid., 112.

67. Ibid., 113, 117.

68. Felscherinow, *Mein zweites Leben,* 149. "Okay, für mein Dope habe ich immer Geld ausgegeben."
69. Ibid., 149. "Aber andere Menschen investieren dieselbe Summe in ein Auto oder in Schönheitsoperationen. Ansonsten bin ich sehr sparsam."
70. Ibid., 15. "Geld hatte ich genug, das war nicht das Problem."
71. Ibid., 59–60. "[D]er Scharfsinn, mit dem die junge Berlinerin ihren eigenen Verfall beobachtet, und das Selbstbewusstsein, mit dem sie auf ihr Schicksal blickt, indem sie niemand anderem die Schuld gibt, außer sich selbst, erklären vielleicht die Sympathie, die die Öffentlichkeit ihr schnell entgegenbringt."
72. "Deutschland Akut 27.11.2013—Nach den 'Kindern vom Bahnhof Zoo,'" YouTube video, accompanying text, posted by Schmidt Media, November 28, 2013, https://www.youtube.com/watch?v=bSqIo3XgR3w. "Doch wie relevant sind *Die Kinder vom Bahnhof Zoo* heute? Ist es richtig, dass das Buch noch immer—35 Jahre nach seinem Erscheinen—in zahlreichen deutschen Schulen zur Pflichtlektüre gehört? Was kann die Geschichte der Christiane F. heute noch jungen Menschen sagen, abseits von Drogen-Romantik und Elends-Voyeurismus?"
73. "Changes," from the *Hunky Dory* album of 1971, went on to become one of Bowie's best-known songs and has come to be seen as a manifesto "for his chameleonic personality, the frequent change of the world today, and frequent reinventions of his musical style throughout the 1970s." David Buckley, *Strange Fascination—David Bowie: The Definitive Story* (London, 1999), 116. Further substantiation of this tendency being associated with Bowie is in the failure of his song "No Control"; see Nicholas P. Grego, *David Bowie in Darkness: A Study of 1. Outside and the Late Career* (Jefferson, NC, 2015), 195. For an analysis of the retro stylings of Bowie's 2013 single about Berlin, "Where Are We Now?," see Ingram, "Bowie's Berlin."
74. Georg Simmel, "Die Grossstädte und das Geistesleben," in *Die Grossstadt. Vorträge und Aufsätze zur Städteausstellung,* ed. Theodore Petermann (Dresden, 1903), 9: 185–206, http://gutenberg.spiegel.de/simmel/essays/grosstad.htm. "[I]n alledem wirkt das gleiche Grundmotiv: der Widerstand des Subjekts, in einem gesellschaftlich-technischen Mechanismus nivelliert und verbraucht zu werden."
75. Gerstenberger, "Play Zones," 260.

Bibliography

Bauer, Karin, and Jennifer R. Hosek. "Narrating the New Berlin: Sight, Sound, Image, Word." *Seminar: A Journal of Germanic Studies* 51, no. 4 (2015): 293–300.

Bogost, Ian. "In the Habit." *Los Angeles Review of Books,* September 20, 2015. Accessed March 13, 2017. https://lareviewofbooks.org/review/in-the-habit.

Buckley, David. *Strange Fascination—David Bowie: The Definitive Story.* London: Virgin, 1999.

Clune, Michael W. *Gamelife.* New York: Farrar, Straus, and Giroux, 2015.

———. *White Out: The Secret Life of Heroin.* Center City, MN: Hazelden, 2013.

Daly, Max. "'I Will Die Soon—I Know That': Meeting the Real Christiane F." *Vice,* December 10, 2013. Accessed March 14, 2017. http://www.vice.com/en_ca/read/christiane-felscherinow-interview.

De Picciotto, Danielle. *The Beauty of Transgression: A Berlin Memoir.* Berlin: Gestalten, 2011.

Elsaesser, Thomas. "Sonnen-Insulaner." In *Memory Culture and the Contemporary City: Building Sites,* edited by Uta Staiger, Henriette Steiner, and Andrew Webber, 32–51. New York: Palgrave Macmillan, 2009.

Felscherinow, Christiane, with Sonja Vukovic. *Mein zweites Leben: Autobiographie.* Berlin: Deutscher Levante Verlag, 2013.

"Fixen, Drogen, Babystrich—die Angstlust funktioniert." *Stern,* February 15, 2011. Accessed March 12, 2017. http://www.stern.de/kultur/kunst/wir-kinder-vom-bahnhof-zoo-fixen-drogen-babystrich-die-angstlust-funktioniert-1654174.html.

"Fühlen statt fixen." *Tip Berlin.* Accessed February 28, 2016. http://www.tip-berlin.de/kultur-und-freizeit/fuhlen-statt-fixen.

Gerlach, Franziska. "Übersetzen als Kulturaustausch—Belletristik—Felscherinow, Christiane—Goethe-Institut." Accessed September 5, 2015. http://www.goethe.de/ins/se/prj/uar/fin/bel/fel/de9394812.htm.

Gerstenberger, Katharina. "Play Zones: The Erotics of the New Berlin." *German Quarterly* 76, no. 3 (2003): 259–72.

———. *Writing the New Berlin: The German Capital in Post-Wall Literature.* Rochester, NY: Camden House, 2008.

Hagen, Nina. *Bekenntnisse.* Munich: Pattloch, 2010.

Herlinghaus, Hermann. "In/Comparable Intoxications: Walter Benjamin Revisited from the Hemispheric South." *Discourse* 32, no. 1 (2010): 16–36.

———. *Narcoepics: A Global Aesthetics of Sobriety.* New York: Bloomsbury, 2013.

Ingram, Susan. "Berlin: The Scenes Beat Goes On." *Topia: Canadian Journal of Cultural Studies* 33 (Spring 2015): 226–29.

———. "Bowie's Berlin: Where We Are Now." *Descant* 45, no. 3 (2014): 228–38.

Lehndorff, Vera, and Jörn Jacob Rohwer. *Veruschka: Mein Leben.* Cologne: DuMont, 2011.

Marquart, Sven. *Die Nacht ist Leben: Autobiographie.* Berlin: Ullstein Verlag, 2014.

McGrath, Larry S. "From the Globe to the Brain and Back." *Los Angeles Review of Books,* October 1, 2015. Accessed March 12, 2017. https://lareviewofbooks.org/review/from-the-globe-to-the-brain-and-back.

McRobbie, Angela. "Clubs to Companies: Notes on the Decline of Political Culture in Speeded Up Creative Worlds." *Cultural Studies* 16, no. 4 (2002): 516–31.

Montani, Ines, and Walter Crasshole. "Christiane's Second Life." *Exberliner,* Janu-

ary 22, 2014. Accessed March 12, 2017. http://www.exberliner.com/features/
people/christianes-second-life/.

Obermaier, Uschi, and Anna Cavelius. *Expect Nothing! Die Geschichte einer un-
gezähmten Frau.* Munich: Riemann, 2013.

Oktay, Enis. "The Unbearable Hipness of Being Light: Welcome to Europe's New
Nightlife Capital." In *Poor, but Sexy: Reflections on Berlin Scenes,* edited by
Geoff Stahl, 211–25. Bern: Peter Lang, 2014.

Pohlers, Angie. "Christiane F.: Das war ein Raubüberfall auf mich." *Der Tagesspiegel,* July 22, 2015. Accessed March 12, 2017. http://www.tagesspiegel.de/
berlin/polizei-justiz/nach-rangelei-in-berlin-neukoelln-christiane-f-das-
war-ein-raubueberfall-auf-mich/12089228.html.

Pyzik, Agata. *Poor but Sexy: Culture Clashes in Europe East and West.* Hants:
Zero Books, 2014.

Schwanhäußer, Anja. "Berlin Capitalism: The Spirit of Urban Scenes." In *Poor,
but Sexy: Reflections on Berlin Scenes,* edited by Geoff Stahl, 103–21. Bern:
Peter Lang, 2014.

Simmel, Georg. "Die Grossstädte und das Geistesleben." In *Die Grossstadt. Vorträge und Aufsätze zur Städteausstellung,* edited by Theodore Petermann
(Dresden, 1903), 9: 185–206, http://gutenberg.spiegel.de/simmel/essays/gr
osstad.htm.

Stahl, Geoff, ed. *Poor, but Sexy: Reflections on Berlin Scenes.* Bern: Peter Lang,
2014.

Yager, Jane. "Revisiting Seedy West Berlin with Christiane F. and Patricia Highsmith." *Jane Yager,* October 8, 2013. Accessed March 12, 2017. http://janey
ager.com/2013/10/08/revisiting-seedy-west-berlin-with-christiane-f-and-
patricia-highsmith/.

CHAPTER 3

Representations and Interpretations of the New Berlin in Contemporary German Comics

Lynn Marie Kutch

In a country such as Germany, where the distinction between high art and pop art persists, exploring Berlin's cultural and social contours as reflected in comics could seem especially problematic. The recent proliferation of traditionally pop-culture comics and graphic novels that treat conventionally high-culture themes such as literature, fine art, social change, and politics provides a curious platform for analyzing aspects of artistic engagement and criticism in the capital city. In September 2013 as part of the *internationales literaturfestival berlin (ilb)*, German comics artists, graphic novelists, and their publishers created the *Comic-Manifesto* to acknowledge formally the ideological divide between valuations of low and high cultural products. The signatories of this document "demand that the comic be afforded the same respect as literature and the visual arts."[1] Advocates argue that comics artists, like their counterparts in other artistic fields, play a pivotal role in the creative and sociocritical landscape that has developed in Berlin amid a rapidly changing social and economic environment. The present study contributes to the as-yet-small but growing scholarly field that treats the serious and analytical side of comics by exploring the medium's aptitude to, among many other things, "celebrate and legitimize dominant values and institutions in society" or to "critique and subvert the status quo."[2] In this chapter, I perform close readings and analyses of selected Berlin comics from Ulli Lust's 2008 *Fashionvictims, Trendverächter: Bildkolumnen und*

Minireportagen aus Berlin (Fashionvictims, Trends Despisers: Pictorial Newspaper Columns and Mini-reportages from Berlin) and Tim Dinter's 2011 *Lästermaul & Wohlstandskind: Neue Berliner Geschichten* (Scandalmonger & Child of Prosperity: New Berlin Stories). The first level of analysis concerns techniques peculiar to the comics field that the artists deploy in their commentary on aspects of the "New Berlin," and the second level considers the specific contributions that each artist makes to critical conversations about the effects of Berlin's urban planning and marketing trends on the city's inhabitants, and especially on artists. Lust and Dinter both use the multimodal comics medium to scrutinize the visual legitimacy of Berlin's official image advanced in promotional campaigns. Not surprisingly, the resulting pictorial rendition or documentation of the New Berlin differs between the two artists. While Lust presents isolated "snapshots" of everyday life seemingly from an outside observer's perspective, Dinter's commentary emerges through conversations between two recurring characters: disgruntled Berliners who attempt to find their way in a New Berlin that has arisen around them. Despite these differences in artistic approach, Lust and Dinter—as producers of and commentators on culture—each incorporate cooperating visual and verbal tools of contradiction, paradox, irony, and humor in order to engage in critical discussions of urban development, consumerism, commercialism, and image campaigns specific to the New Berlin.[3]

Defining the New Berlin

Each contributor to this volume has framed and defined the term "New Berlin" from a range of historically, artistically, and socioeconomically defined angles. I supplement the information found in other chapters by offering a brief discussion of documented origins and some contemporary connotations of the "New Berlin." The background I offer here illuminates some of the concepts and trends with which, as I will argue, Lust and Dinter critically interact in their comics art. Since the 1990s, politicians, urban planners, authors, and artists have understood the latest iteration of the "New Berlin" in a variety of contexts. The label commonly refers to a Berlin that has not only experienced significant rebuilding and redesign during that time period but has also been and continues to be a carefully staged and marketed global city, oftentimes developing independently of its citizens and especially artists who theoretically, but not always practically, play a central role in the city's emergent character. In this volume, Ayse N. Erek and Eszter Gantner describe the significance of artists and the professional art arena for a reenvisioned Berlin: "[F]rom the middle of the 1990s onward, the growing art scene has played an increasingly important role in the process of reimagining it." Erek and Gantner, in this volume, go so far as to claim that "[a]rt replaces history as the city's master discourse." While that certainly seems to be true, it is also true that artists' production has often competed with, or at least has existed parallel to, city marketing campaigns whose interests, as Sarah Pogoda and Rüdiger Traxler argue in this volume, "reduce Berlin's discursive playing field to a site of urban icons," which are often recognizable, and thus highly marketable, architectural features such as the Brandenburg Gate, the Victory Column, or Alexanderplatz. Indeed artists—and as I will argue in this chapter, comics artists—also act as interpreters of these marketed icons right along with targeted consumers.

Although the proliferation of these marketing campaigns since reunification would make the "New Berlin" seem like a recent development, the designation (traced to an architectural journal dated 1929) has been repeatedly implemented and repurposed: "every successive political regime since the nineteenth century envisioned a 'new' Berlin different from that of its predecessors" to refer to a city eager to reshape or even drastically change its identity.[4] This consistent desire to redesign, restructure, and "reimage" comes as no surprise given Berlin's extensive history of collapse and renewal. Historically Berlin has consistently stood for upheaval and massive transformation, but the changes and trends since reunification in 1990 differ significantly from those that occurred during other time periods in Berlin's turbulent yet fascinating history. For example, Berlin had to rebuild physically after wartime defeats and destruction, but in the early 1990s the New Berlin was the capital city in need of extensive renovation and rebuilding as a result of the positive developments associated with reunification. Reflecting Berlin's image of constant and seemingly endless construction, New Berlin's innovations in tourism, such as *Schauplätze* (venues), combine the emblem of the omnipresent construction crane with twenty-first-century mass-marketing techniques that promote these sites as interactive tourist attractions. Gary L. Catchen comments on the symbolic value of the construction vehicles in his essay "*Gedächtnis* and *Zukunft,* Remembrance and the Future: A Photo Essay": "The myriad of cranes, pointing in all directions, symbolizes the construction of new architecture, the signpost for the new Berlin spanning from the immediate present well into its future."[5] With this positive potential in mind, official image-promotion campaigns begun in the 1990s aimed to showcase these locations, to bring residents and visitors into direct contact with rebuilding projects, and to emphasize a forward-looking confident attitude of growth.

Designers intended campaigns, such as *Schauplätze—20 Jahre Berlin im Wandel* (Venues—20 Years of Berlin in Transition), to celebrate "the twentieth anniversary of the fall of the Wall in terms of several showcased sites of urban renovation."[6] In Janet Ward's words, however, these showplaces amounted to little more than "self-obsessed displays of the city's current and future shape."[7] Concurrent with this far-reaching urban transformation, as Katrina Sark argues in this volume, a nostalgia for what she terms "Babylon," or a utopian desire for creativity, emerged among artists as a reaction to the official marketing. Specifically, artists used their craft to critique reconstruction, gentrification, and commercialization of urban space. A key question that emerged, and that the comics artists under consideration here have also addressed, concerns where, how, and whether the individual fits into these vast landscapes of construction cranes and imagined future buildings.

Speaking about cities in general, Lawrence J. Vale and Sam Bass Warner Jr. address the correlation between sweeping waves of rebuilding, accompanying promotional tools, and local reactions to those methods as "the interplay between the physical stuff of planners and architects and the social experience and outlooks of image makers and their audiences."[8] The dynamic they describe consists of a number of stakeholders: those crafting and distributing the message and those receiving and interpreting it. In this case, although Lust and Dinter as artists should, according to campaigns that brand Berlin as the artistic metropolis, theoretically have the power to craft and distribute messages, their artistic renderings suggest that they perhaps more often receive and interpret the marketing messages right along with other consumers. As interpreters and critics of city marketing products, they use their comics art as a method of gauging the perceived effectiveness, ineffectiveness, or even absurdity of the campaigns. These promotional ideas define Berlin using an index of criteria, including the artists' scene, diversity and history, but also rebuilding and construction. In speaking about architecture and iconography that continues to emerge in the New Berlin, Pogoda and Traxler state in this volume that "the growing complexity of social reality amplifies the need for correspondingly dimensioned elements." By contrast, however, the present chapter explores what happens when an artistic element of seemingly lesser dimension voices critique within the bound frame of a comic and how that compressed message can be read as social comment on the New Berlin.

A 2014 cartoon by German comic artist Götz Wiedenroth not only helps us to understand how the New Berlin concept corresponds to more general theories of urban space—significant for Berlin because of official aspirations of joining New York and London as world cities—but also offers insight into artistic and social countermovements in which Berlin comics artists have participated and continue to participate. Wiedenroth deploys the distinctive comics-artistic techniques of visual and rhetorical exaggeration to portray the officially projected or imagined hyperbolic effect of increased tourism and building campaigns on native Berliners unwillingly and uncomfortably caught between factions of architects, developers, and image-makers. The single panel shows an outdoor café with two customers covered in dust emitted by a nearby construction site, shown only in silhouette behind them (see figure 3.1).

Figure 3.1. Götz Wiedenroth, "Urlaub. Hotel. Baustelle in der Nachbarschaft," *Karikamur-Karikatur!—Wiedenroth,* September 19, 2014, www.wiedenroth-karikatur.blogspot.de.

Against this backdrop, the pair receives dirt-covered "Eis mit Krokant und Streuseln"[9] from a waitress who is also covered in debris.[10] The cartoon does not directly mention the prevalence of marketing campaigns such as *Schaustelle Berlin* or its motto "Entdecken, was dahinter steckt" (Discover, what's behind it all).[11] Nonetheless, readers familiar with this and similar campaigns, or those who live in the German capital, may detect Wiedenroth's ironic criticism of the initiative, which one Berlin business leader explained in these rosy terms: "Bauarbeiten stehen nicht nur für Lärm, Staub und Umleitungen, sondern vor allem für die Zukunft unserer Stadt."[12] The details of Wiedenroth's single-panel comic intimates, however, that campaigns and marketing ideas like *Schaustelle Berlin,* which "promotes a vision of a *future city* to *locals* through tourism practices," has apparently not awakened in this representative cartoon couple the intended excitement about the city's present construction and future development.[13] Specifically, the comic's composition draws the reader's eye to the couple in the foreground whose simultaneously surprised and complacent facial expressions indicate their greater concern yet reluctant acceptance of their immediate ice cream toppings as an unavoidable side effect of Berlin's building projects.

This superficially simple comic panel operates within the tradition of ideology and comics, which examines why and how comics "challenge and/or perpetuate power differences."[14] Wiedenroth's comic in particular critiques the status quo and decisions often reached by dominant institutions, such as the city of Berlin's administration. Moreover, its reduced yet highly expressive and communicative form demonstrates the comic medium's elasticity and range, which Lust and Dinter also display. In particular, Wiedenroth's one-panel comic reveals ways that the comics artist can manipulate the visual medium in order to build a complex and multilayered critique. Many of the contemporary Berlin comics artists, for example, thematize two coexisting components of global urban character, which scholars have identified, and which are also represented locally in Berlin, as Anne Marie Broudehoux articulates. She envisions urban space as consisting of two distinct parts. First is the "the *physical* image of the city," or "the actual city itself, as it is produced, lived and experienced by people on an everyday basis and represented in a series of visual symbols, physical places, and social characteristics."[15] Second, Broudehoux identifies the "*rhetorical* image of the city — the 'idea' or conceptual image of the city as it is imagined and represented in collective consciousness."[16] Each in distinctive ways, Wiedenroth, Lust, and Dinter's comics critique the incompatibility of these two levels by way of verbal and visual exaggeration and irony.

Wiedenroth's comic suggests that happenings of actual day-to-day life do not fit seamlessly inside the rhetorical city image that politicians, economists, and city planners endorse. For example, the construction of the future city, marked by the outlines of two construction cranes in action, problematically interferes with ordinary Berliners' routine summertime visit to the *Eiscafe*.

While general definitions of urban theory, such as those mentioned above that divide cities into physical and rhetorical components, certainly pertain to contemporary Berlin, the capital city's turbulent twentieth-century history sets it apart from other global metropolises. A nearly universal fascination with World War II history and East German history continues to influence tourism and image campaigns. Despite this enduring, and economically measurable, curiosity, the current marketing and branding climate in Berlin is marked by a "desire to transcend the defining power of the Nazi past and to achieve political and cultural normalization."[17] Janet Ward suggests that this drive for normalization also closely connects to Germany's divided past, within which "each of the two parts [had] to reinvent itself as an artificially holistic entity with a symbolic identity."[18] Since reunification, the lingering images of Berlin as the former symbolic site of the Cold War and the physical site of the Berlin Wall, along with the 1990s construction surge has "turned the city into a laboratory for changing German identity."[19] In this volume, Erek and Gantner attribute the experimental and laboratory quality of the New Berlin to a deliberate redirection of perception to the positive and beloved values of the Weimar Republic, which essentially calls for rewinding past a divided Germany or Germany of the Third Reich. That desired return to a particular era in the past contrasts other current notions of a forward-looking construction of Berlin as the future world metropolis. Claire Colomb argues that Berlin's reimaging "emerged with a *visibility* and *intensity* rarely witnessed in other (European) cities" and describes the nature of the campaign: "In order to support the city's transformation into an invoked 'European metropolis,' local policymakers had to break with the negative images associated with the city's tormented past, reinvent and transmit a new image of the city to three main target groups: potential tourists, visitors and investors."[20] Paradoxically, some actual visual product designs that belong to this reinvention draw upon historically loaded images or places but manipulate them to represent aspects of the New Berlin. Berlin comics art follows this same principle of incorporating "grafische Zitate," or graphic quotations, but uses them to build an ironic or humorous critique of the Berlin that results from opposing or at least incompatible marketing ideas.[21]

The following two examples from prominent image campaigns illustrate ways that these campaigns not only visually quote but also recontextualize recognizable, yet historically charged, images for promotional purposes. First, a series of posters originally unveiled on May 23, 1999, features the newly refurbished *Reichstag* building's glass cupola, through which visitors were able to walk for the first time on that date. Notably, the *Reichstag* building itself is barely or not at all visible on the posters.[22] The designers implemented the strategy of reversing past negative associations with the historical structure and instead emphasized its updated status as a visual emblem for a forward-looking and transparent New Berlin Republic. A second key visual emblem of the New Berlin is Potsdamer Platz, which the Berlin Wall had dissected. Since reunification, the square has been the site of major rebuilding and development projects. As a way of physically connecting viewers to the future conceptual image of the city often visible only in the form of unfinished construction, *Infoboxes* allow passersby to watch ongoing construction. Colomb argues that the major rebuilding of Potsdamer Platz and the nearly fanatical attention to it represents "the search for a restoration of a sense of *continuity* in reunified Berlin."[23] From the perspective of city planners and image marketers, reclaiming physical images and recasting rhetorical associations result in communicating a convincingly positive image of the new city. This particular and sustained focus on certain parts or aspects of Berlin leads to "a fragmenting of urban space into 'represented' and 'non-represented' space" as "place marketers always have to select and single out specific sites and landmarks."[24] As is commonly the case during times of major national and social change, artists participate in this process of environmental evaluation that manifests itself, and differentiates itself, through particular thematic approaches and aesthetics. And nearly all of them, including Lust and Dinter, observe and render the non-represented space, in which ordinary Berliners, and the artists who render them, reside.[25]

Berlin and Comic Art

In addition to the forms of artistic expression that might immediately spring to mind, such as literature, visual art, and even architectural art, comics art production in Berlin has grown significantly during the decades since Germany's reunification. In fact, as with the timing for physical reconstruction in Berlin and ideological image campaigns, the decade of the 1990s "marks a chronological point from which the local comic scene started to come together and find a new orientation."[26] Likewise in the area of literature, some contemporary Berlin authors, for example, have tried to "capture [Potsdamer Platz's] dimension in experimental language or inventive metaphors."[27] Comics artists similarly operate within systems of experimentation and creative invention. By contrast, however, they draw upon a multimodal and multimedial collection of artistic tools. Similar to the public reimaging or "graphically quoting" well-known images such as the *Reichstag*, Potsdamer Platz, or neighborhood-specific architecture, comics artists also reference images from promotional campaigns or the New Berlin commercial or consumer culture, subsequently redesign them in their comics, and use these reimagings as tools for their critique. In this way, the artistic responses of Berlin comics artists to public and marketed iconography becomes clear. The artists essentially answer image with image. In addition to building upon existing visual vocabulary to establish their critiques, Berlin comics artists enhance their levels of critique by developing their own visual language: "The characters rant away in dialect, the artists play around with a great deal of local features and the contemporary goings on in the city are sharply poked fun at."[28] Analogous to the stylistic breadth that authors and artists demonstrate, subject matter and aesthetic impressions also vary greatly among comics artists.

In spite of the medium's seemingly singular dimensionality, its visual aspect delivers an additional level of complexity that requires the meticulous process of analysis commonly used for reading literature. Indirectly addressing the German cultural divide to which the authors of the *Comic Manifesto* vehemently reacted, American comics scholar Charles Hatfield comments on the preconception that reading comics represents a lesser form of reading: "Yet it is by no means clear that comics are universally regarded as a *reading* experience"; and he also cites a tradition that "links comics with illiteracy and the abdication of reading as a civilized (and civilizing) skill."[29] Jens Meinrenken confronts these long-standing notions in his observations on the 2013 *Comics aus Berlin* exhibit, which could not "replace actually reading comics," but could "encourage people to read them."[30] Meinrenken declares, "If we manage this feat [of exhibiting comics], then the exhibition has fulfilled its most important task: to carry the comics into the hearts of a literarily and artistically demanding audience."[31] The present chapter also has the similar task of highlighting the literariness and artistic quality of New Berlin comics, and thus attempting to propel them into the realm of works of art that deliver highly literate and literary social critique.

The works of the artists under consideration here, Tim Dinter and Ulli Lust, employ differing aesthetic forms, each of which focuses their readers' attention on their criticism of particular aspects of the New Berlin inside a single frame or a single strip. Thus their work becomes analogous to Berlin's *Infoboxes,* or large elevated structures overlooking construction sites in Berlin, from which tourists and Berliners alike can focus on the logistics and challenges of the construction process. In terms of this purpose, Lust's and Dinter's work could on the one hand fit into the category of comics journalism, which Kristian Williams has defined as "serious nonfiction comics about current events."[32] Amy Kiste Nyberg defines comics journalism as essentially a form of New Journalism, which "introduces fiction techniques into nonfiction writing, [posing] a challenge both to journalism and literature [and] blurring the distinctions between fact and fiction."[33] On the other hand, these comics do not necessarily fulfill comics journalism's criterion of taking a serious tone.[34] Nonetheless, as with comics journalism, the boundaries between fiction and nonfiction blur in Lust's and Dinter's comics because the narrative techniques that the comics artists use blur boundaries between the "non-fictional" *Alltagsreporter* and the "fictional" *Erzähler.* Specifically, the *Alltagsreporter* or "everyday/daily reporter" who neutrally conveys certain facts, simultaneously operates as the *Erzähler,* or "storyteller" who often supplies additional information as well as subtle and often humorous suggestions for interpretation. Lust presents her readers with a series of single-paneled cartoons that largely leave interpretation up to the reader (she also offers multipaneled strips in the volume, but I concentrate here on the single-panel comics), while Dinter provides more explicit and elaborated commentary in the form of a comic strip story with a beginning, middle, and end. In what follows, I will analyze specific ways that each of these artists supplements his or her role as a comic artist with that of documentarian, storyteller, and cultural critic. In doing so, I will examine ways that Lust and Dinter depict how everyday Berliners, and in particular artists, fit into the big-city politics and policies that as artists they were supposed to have a hand in creating or at least maintaining. Instead, their comics intimate they seem to view themselves against a backdrop being created around them while they also interpret that backdrop.

Flaneursjournalistin Ulli Lust

In his foreword to Lust's *Fashionvictims,* fellow Berlin comic artist Kai Pfeiffer uses the terms *Flaneursjournalist* and *Alltagsspion* (Strolling

Journalist and Spy into Everyday Life) to describe Ulli Lust, who presents her scenes of Berlin as "Blitzpsychogrammen"[35]: "[ihre] Geschichten stellen sich mitten im Satz ein und sind meist schon vorüber, bevor dem ungeübten Lauscher klar wird, dass soeben wieder eines der begehrten *vollständigen Fragmente* vorbei gehuscht ist."[36] As Pfeiffer's word choices imply, and as the appearance of Lust's comics confirm, the stories happen quickly and focus on a single captured moment, with an implied surrounding context that the viewer can interpret using aspects of New Berlin marketing politics. Similar to a careful reading of a poem or other literary text, Lust's audience also reads and analyzes every aspect of the visual composition, as well as the interaction between word and image. Her comics operate on a system of illustrative reduction, but they offer the viewer only fragments of full conversations and thus only carefully selected portions of critical commentary, which the readers must supplement with their interpretations. Lust's Berlin comics demonstrate specifically ways that comics artists can use this concentrated, reduced form to respond to complex Berlin-specific issues as they develop and evolve.

One such example, and a common theme found in many of Lust's strips, is the topic of Berlin's new urban tourism. This trend describes tourists who experience the city "beyond the officially stated tourist attractions, strolling through the 'ordinary' but diverse and lively neighborhoods, eager to consume 'authentic local amenities.'"[37] This new form of tourism distinguishes itself from the enclavic or bubble tourism that "concentrate[s] on iconic architecture and events with little friction with 'normal' life in the city."[38] Thus, the everyday activities that Lust conveys take on significance as markers for the real and "off-the-beaten track areas" of the city.[39] Additionally, she suggests in her compositions, often dense with renderings of various individual personalities, that this blending and overlapping of neighborhoods makes it nearly impossible to distinguish between tourist, resident, transplant, and native. With a physical layout that mirrors that of a postcard, her comic panels allude both to traditional tourism as well as to this new brand of tourism and its intensified focus on the seemingly ordinary moment of the Berliners inadvertently yet undoubtedly affected by building and tourism trends. In her role as *flaneur,* Lust emphasizes the place of the artist conceptualizing and capturing the ordinary citizen within her comic frames.

The worldwide proliferation of serious comics art, as opposed to the kind often found at train station kiosks, has generated volumes of books that detail how to read comics.[40] While I incorporate many of those methods here, comics scholarship has also begun to forge new territory by merging theory from other disciplines with the practice of reading comics. In addition to standard techniques for reading comics that Hatfield and Scott McCloud, among others, have articulated, readers of comic art can also draw upon methods of interpreting the messages of parallel genres, such as literature and photography, especially examples of those that have to do with Berlin. In his article on Berlin writers who attempt to or even achieve similar social commentary with their literature, Bastian Heinsohn presents a reading of these fiction works as "counterrepresentations" or as voices of a "counterdiscourse" against the "globalized Berlin envisioned by urban planners, investors and politicians."[41] Focusing on two Berlin novels from the early 2000s, Heinsohn examines the emphasis on the Berlin local who "creates a literary counterspace against the corporate nature of the new streetscape."[42] Lust and Dinter treat similar topics as those found in these and other novels, which offer snapshots "of spaces in flux during the process of post-Wende gentrification and [analyze] effects of that gentrification on the communities that occupy such spaces."[43] One such effect, which will be discussed in more detail below, is the documented crisis of studio space, on which Simon Ward elaborates in his chapter in this volume.

Given the topic discussed in this chapter of reading visual cues in the New Berlin, it is productive to integrate and adapt methods for reading street scenes or photographs of urban scenes. In her article "Commercial Discourses, Gentrification and Citizens' Protest: The Linguistic Landscape of Prenzlauer Berg, Berlin," Uta Papen establishes and elaborates on the concept of "linguistic landscapes" and comments on their communicative function. Papen lists examples of competing linguistic elements, such as commercial signs, protest banners, evidence of community initiatives, street art, and graffiti, all of which exist in any urban space.[44] For the New Berlin, however, as she argues, the linguistic landscape is a "motor fueling the process of change" and one that contains "productive signs," such as shop names, that convey the area's character to private investors and potential residents.[45] In the context of Berlin comics, one can apply these techniques of reading visual evidence to reading the comics medium, discovering how these linguistic landscapes are shown, what the artist emphasizes, and what the reader observes or interprets. Unlike observing the signs firsthand on the corner of a Berlin street, or looking at photographs or satellite images, analyzing comic images requires viewers to remember that they are looking at a graphic version of an artist's mental snapshot, designed visually and verbally, and stylized according to individual artistic approach.

Although Lust's comics treat a range of social issues, I will concentrate here on the criticism of the pervasive and even destructive consumerism as shown in her comic-art street scenes. Important to mention is that just because she presents and seems to criticize themes such as consumerism at the expense of pure art, and displacement of artists because of that consumerism, that does not mean that she does not find herself to be a part of, or even a beneficiary of, that growing consumerism. One particular comic demonstrates the artist's visual quotations, or deployment and adaptation of images seen in other contexts, such as the official image campaigns explained above or consumer logos. Lust reiterates these recognizable images as a way to advance a statement about the "purposing" of Berlin's neighborhoods into economy-boosting shopping hubs. The comic panels show residents of the New Berlin negotiating a larger, internationally commercialized atmosphere, yet still attempting to cope locally with the official push to elevate Berlin into the category of global metropolis and to attract tourists. This official campaign stands in sharp contrast to the perceptions of the actual residents, which Henning Füller and Boris Michel discuss in their article "Stop Being a Tourist": "The growing influx of tourists was evoked [at a public community forum] for all kinds of problems in Kreuzberg [including] a changing commercial structure and the rise in housing costs."[46] Lust's single untitled panel divided in two addresses these opposing sides (see figure 3.2). In the top half, the artist's drawing shows trendy boutiques housed in a historic Prenzlauer building, an image that mirrors actual economic development in the New Berlin.[47] Decorative flags (whose appliques take on the look of coats of arms with reimagined and repurposed shapes and emblems) hang from a building with discernible *Berliner Altbau* architecture, a "quoted" Berlin image and symbol of a changing Berlin. On the flags, Lust duplicates shop names such as "Glück der Erde"[48] and "Glaube und Wahrheit."[49] All of these elements together count as examples of Papen's system of "productive signs," which contribute to an area's aesthetic value and ensuing sense of commercialization.[50] The visual cues not only situate this trendy shopping street in one of Berlin's gentrified neighborhoods, but they also establish the social critique that both panels cooperate to deliver, as explained in the following paragraph.

The lower panel shows a young couple at a café, but they appear small in comparison to a sign hanging on the building and a sandwich board in the panel's foreground. Here, Lust demonstrates her aptitude for inventing comic scenery that layers elements plucked from Berlin's real cityscape. In particular, she emphasizes competing script types and fonts in order to build her social comment with carefully selected visual moments.[51] For example, she provides a graphic quotation of the mar-

Prenzlauer Berg: Sinnstiftung beim Kauf von
Gummistiefeln oder Kuchen.

Figure 3.2. Ulli Lust, *Fashionvictims, Trendverächter: Bildkolumnen und Minireportagen aus Berlin* (Berlin, 2008), 14.

keting letters written in different styles and displayed on varying sizes of poster board strung across the building that display the name of the popular Berlin shop "Kauf dich glücklich."[52] Although the font that "Kauf dich glücklich" chose (which takes on the look of a ransom note), and maybe even the scene, are not completely Lust's original creations, her method of composing them together allows her to address the popular themes of estrangement, displacement, and fragmentation in the wake of urban redevelopment, also incidentally prevalent themes in litera-ture that Heinsohn identifies.[53] In the foreground on a blackboard-style sandwich board, the words "Liebe Waffeln Eis"[54] appear in an elegant cursive script. The equal sizing of all three words suggests a sense of equality between the abstract concept of love and the tangible waffles and ice cream available for purchase. As is common in advertising, the words convince the consumer that buying something material results in attaining spiritual satisfaction. This particular cartoon, however, helps the viewer reread common theories of advertising with Berlin-specific criteria, specifically that this satisfaction is also linked to the new and improved Prenzlauer Berg area of the New Berlin. Although Lust's drawing contains ample visual elements that help to advance a socially critical reading, she also provides a caption, thus emphasizing the multilayered aspects of comics. The caption underlines her original take and critique on what could be a neutral comic replica of a Berlin street scene: "Prenzlauer Berg: Sinnstiftung beim Kauf von Gummistiefeln oder Kuchen."[55] This verbal supplement to the comic amplifies the comic's use of irony by suggesting that the image campaigns and economic policies continue to experience great success. It is not entirely clear, however, whether her comic characters are tourists or native/resident Berliners. If the man and woman belong to the former, then the targeted group does in fact gain satisfaction in Berlin's new commercial culture. If they are native Berliners, then the panel suggests that they have bought into the idea of gaining satisfaction by purchasing and consuming goods in a neighborhood in which drastic economic and social changes have occurred.

By contrast, in another single-panel comic, Lust provides a snapshot of an early morning group of clearly nontourist Berlin residents inside a car on the U2 subway line, a setting quite different from the bustling and energetic shopping street scenes above.[56] Karein Goertz and Mick Kennedy discuss the symbolic nature of Berlin's subway, which Lust has translated into comic form: "The train line cuts through Berlin to expose views into the city's private spaces and unofficial views of the public face of government, commerce and culture. The city becomes a complex surface of activities and interactions that are usually dismissed as anomalous in conventional representations of the urban."[57] Similarly Lust presents a subway train that highlights Colomb's non-represented space (see figure 3.3). The scenery consists of a diverse cross-section of people riding the U2 at 7:30 on a typical weekday morning. Located underground and far from any flashy commercialism, this comic panel displays much more subdued elements of a linguistic landscape, with far fewer hints of consumerism and more overtures to the non-represented class. School bags and purses, used every day for the same purpose, replace shopping bags that celebrate a one-time find. One barely visible sign indicates a handicapped seat and another small sign forbids bicycles on the subway. Through the sketched figures' vacant facial expressions and the averted gazes, Lust conveys to her reader common urban themes of alienation and anonymity, which, according to goals

— Aus der Gesellschaft —

Morgens um 7 Uhr 30 in der U2: Durch den Wagen tönt
inbrünstiger Gesang. Das müde Publikum sieht kaum auf,
um nicht dem Blick des Kleingeld heischenden
Sängerknaben zu begegnen.
Jedoch, heimlich in seiner Kabine verborgen, singt
völlig unentgeltlich der Fahrer Schlager a capella.
Er erwartet keinen Applaus und
bekommt auch keinen. [kp]

Figure 3.3. Ulli Lust, *Fashionvictims, Trendverächter: Bildkolumnen und Minireportagen aus Berlin* (Berlin, 2008), 32.

of Berlin's image campaigns, would have no direct connection to quite opposite intended developments on street level.

In line with criteria for comics journalism, which can easily vacillate between the realistic and the symbolic, this sample from Lust's collection contains the added effects of a jagged white shape indicating fluorescent light much too bright for this early morning crowd. Additionally a smooth white thick ribbon containing the chorus of the 1968 chanson "Für mich soll's rote Rosen regnen"[58] in large cursive letters cuts through the center of the panel from the top.[59] The typically German *Schlager* style song being sung underground challenges the projected idea of Berlin as the burgeoning global metropolis above ground. Similar to a newspaper photograph that demands a caption, Pfeiffer provides one. Unlike the often matter-of-fact verbal information that accompanies a journalistic photograph, however, this one imbues the scene with an element of wry humor while also intensifying the feelings of separateness and alienation among the travelers:

> Morgens um 7 Uhr 30 in der U2: Durch den Wagen tönt inbrünstiger Gesang. Das müde Publikum sieht kaum auf, um nicht dem Blick des Kleingeld heischenden Sängerknaben zu begegnen. Jedoch, heimlich in seiner Kabine verborgen, singt völlig unentgeltlich der Fahrer Schlager a capella. Er erwartet keinen Applaus und bekommt auch keinen.[60]

In this example, both the comic form and the style of the caption are greatly reduced, demonstrating that Lust, like many other comic artists in Berlin today, "demonstrates just as often a love of irony as [of] serious criticism," as Meinrenken notes.[61] Moreover, as I have argued here, Lust's deployment of irony directly contributes to her system of social criticism. In this instance, Lust draws upon the realistic and symbolic to render and interpret images of competing stakeholders in this urban space: the modern workforce, the driver at the helm, and the influence of *Schlagerkultur* on the driver's and the passengers' moods. If "global" indicates a lack of distinctiveness, as many scholars would argue, then the typically German style of music definitively steers this comic back to Berlin. In her article "Ausgrabungen in der Global City," Saskia Sassen advances the theory that Berlin does not belong to an accepted network of global cities.[62] Lust's comic, which highlights specifically Berlinesque visual and verbal elements, would seem to support, in its direct comic style, this failure of achieving a global designation.

As a subset of the commentary discussed thus far, Lust has developed a series of comics titled "Terrarium" that provides stylized snapshots of shopping centers: the same shopping centers, as Ward points out in his chapter to this volume, that were formerly studio space for Berlin's creative class. With her signature irony, Lust points up an incongruity between the perfectly dressed salespeople, cleaning crew, and security personnel and the clientele: "Das angelockte Publikum wirkt dagegen oft wie ein Designproblem."[63] On the one hand, "city politicians and city public relations work together to produce and sell a certain image of a global, or at least globally important city."[64] On the other hand, the shopping center setting exemplifies "shifting urban terrain," and the "increasing incomprehensibility, facelessness and artificiality" of the space.[65] In a collection of single-panel comics, a format that Williams credits with the ability to "incorporate a complex sequence of events, an entire history, into a single composition," Lust configures a variety of visual markers that enable the verbal and the visual to combine into examples of striking social comment.[66] In this comic series, Lust presents snapshots of Berliners in terrarium-like vessels, enclosed glass settings that provide conditions necessary for sustaining life but that nonetheless come across as extremely artificial. Recognizable logos and other examples of the urban linguistic landscape add ornamentation that serves the comics' larger critical function. Throughout "Terrarium," Lust features single captured scenes from the many monochromatic shopping centers and indoor malls that have sprouted up in Berlin since the 2000s, such as the *Gesundbrunnencenter* in Wedding, the *Ring Center,* as well as the many *Passagen.*

In one single-panel comic titled "Spree Center," Lust provides elements of a rich linguistic landscape as well as visual indicators that point to the inauthenticity—that is, the "unnaturalness"—of these invented marketplaces.[67] Here, the ubiquitous and highly identifiable *Tchibo* coffee brand logo functions as a title emblazoned across the top of the panel. The reader gazes through a large glass window behind which two middle-aged men whose vastly different clothing choices (one cowboy, one more typical for a man their age) suggest an artificially constructed multiculturalism. They enjoy their *Tchibo* coffee, surrounded in the café by the company's current promotional items. In the foreground outside the window, the viewer sees two small fountains, on which the coffee drinkers, and probably the comic reader, have fixed their gaze. Engrossed in the man-made fountains, one of the men declares: "Da weiß man endlich wieder, wofür man schuftet."[68] Although the visual style would seem to convey the neutral tone of newspaper photographs, Lust's panels offer a carefully designed blend of verbal and visual elements that help to deliver an ironic comment on Berlin's manufactured consumer culture. "Spree Center," which comes across as highly ironic given the name of Berlin's magnificent, culturally significant river as compared to the puny, man-made fountain, offers visual and verbal evidence that the New Berliner, having adjusted to this non-natural environment, has become content or complacent, feeling compelled to sense either personal accomplishment or resignation.

Much of Lust's comic art in *Fashionvictims* takes on the look of journalistic photographs, snapped at unplanned times so as to show the ordinariness of everyday life in the New Berlin. For as indiscriminate and neutral as the photograph seems, however, as Nyberg argues, "[t]he camera is never objective—from the choice of subject to the way an image is framed to its reproduction, images are a representation of reality, rather than a 'window' on the world."[69] Similarly, Lust's comics are equally as nonobjective because of the layered comic composition. Although her drawings are taken from life, and perhaps even from snapshots, Lust has chosen to use the comic medium to enable her critical voice, one that seems to say, in part, as Koolhaas formulates it: the "city can no longer be understood without shopping."[70] For as cliché as that may sound, Lust shows that these clichés are alive and well as one walks through the New Berlin and surveys its newly marketed landscape. Lust's style of developing these photograph-like drawings, which force the reader to interpret messages about the New Berlin, clearly positions her as the *Alltagsspion* or *Flanuersjournalistin* mentioned above, gazing into these scenes, regarding them and considering their meanings right along with her audience, who also consider their placement in this new city.

Tim Dinter

Tim Dinter's comic form contrasts Lust's common single-panel style in that he tells mini-stories in comic strips, which ran in the *Berliner Tagesspiegel* from 2006 to 2010. Rather than a constantly shifting focus from an outsider's perspective on ordinary Berliners walking down the street, riding the subway, or shopping, Dinter's strips consistently feature the same two characters, a pair of friends who experience and try to cope with the steady changes in the capital city: "[E]r ist, von irgendwo, ... nach Berlin gekommen," "[S]ie ist schon eine echte Berlinerin."[71] With their often contentious relationship and their inability to agree on any issue, the two friends stand for current Berlin types—one native, one transplant—whose personal and professional backgrounds cause them both to view contemporary debates and living conditions with varying degrees of annoyance. Like other Berlin artists, including Lust, Dinter takes up the themes of urban development, consumerism, and commercialism that have overrun the city in the opinion of many residents. Also in line with other Berlin cartoonists, Dinter designs the visual and verbal to interact to produce a narrative irony. Whereas Lust positions the artist outside the comic frame as observer, creator, and interpreter of the image, Dinter centralizes the artist in his strip through the character of "he." Significantly, "he" does not always directly talk about his artist's existence. Instead, he indirectly comments on the relationship between the artist and the New Berlin, particularly as the two relate in terms of art and the artist's role as a "catalyst for change in public space" (see Ward's discussion of Zukin in this volume).

One strip amplifies the negative aspects of transformed urban spaces and possible negative consequences. In the strip "Stille Zeit,"[72] "she" tells about the nice quiet Christmas she had "ganz ohne Zugereiste"[73] and without the "Konsumterroristen!,"[74] whom they observe loaded down with shopping bags in the ubiquitous shopping centers.[75] When a couple of "typische Unterschichten-Spackenguerilla"[76] throw some fireworks in "his" and "her" direction as they walk down a Berlin city street, the two characters discuss ways that they actually view this incident in a positive light. Just this premise alone of turning the situation of randomly lit and thrown fireworks into something constructive would seem to offer ample ironic criticism. As is typical for Dinter, however, he intensifies the humor even more and guides his criticism in the unexpected direction of underscoring the quarrelsome interactions between native East Berliners, which "she" represents, and the transplant West Berliners, which "he" represents. The consumer terrorism, or the result of her family and friends' shopping for "her," has left "her" with a collection of useless Christmas gifts, which "she" states "she" will exchange for fireworks. Her criticism is that "he" would have nothing to exchange because his people thoughtlessly and unimaginatively only give money as gifts. Their initially common displeasure with the consumer culture evolves into an East/West-based argument about the New Berliner's proper behavior amid a landscape of fellow Berliners, now reunified, misbehaving. In contrast to Lust's observations of the city's inhabitants in terrarium-like settings, Dinter's addition of dialogue provides an extra dimension by which to read the experiences of these Berliners within a constructed *Heimat*.

"Innere Werte"[77] displays some of the artist's most innovative storytelling and clever social critique by combining identifiable visual motifs with abstract concepts of the New Berlin (see figure 3.4).[78] When "he" poses the question of what should be on his Christmas list, "she" suggests a new hoodie so that he does not always wear the same one. "He" answers in gender-specific terms that also refer to the prevalent consumerism that results in unwilling fashion victims: "Nein. Bloß wir sind keine Modeopfer und wir müssen auch nicht ständig etwas Neues anziehen."[79] As part of this discussion, involving one friend's very personal comment on another's clothing choices, "he" also tries to establish himself as an artist as contrasted with the New Berlin consumer; and yet the comic strip's irony succeeds at expressing something opposite:

Figure 3.4. Panels from Tim Dinter, "Innere Werte," in *Lästermaul & Wohlstandskind: Neue Berliner Geschichten* (Berlin, 2011), 48.

perhaps that they reject what is happening around them with a certain resigned acceptance. Moreover, "he" tries to disassociate himself from the demands of the new city, and any of its up-and-coming districts or neighborhoods, by calling his hoodie a "mobiles Zuhause."[80] A subsequent stylized portrait of "him" as Charlie Brown provides a visually recognizable backdrop for his single-hoodie rationale: "Hast du Charlie Brown schon mal mit einem anderen Pulli gesehen?"[81] Here, Charlie Brown functions as an identifiable icon, which "possesses a unique recognizable, marketable feature" (see Pogoda and Traxler in this volume). The fact that Dinter chooses an American comic character as an icon suggests, like Lust, a push toward globalization. That he chooses Charlie Brown indicates that this push falls short.

Similarly, "he" offers another loaded graphic quotation as "she" appears as one of the female *Simpsons* characters. "She" directs "her" accompanying comment to "him," but because it appears in the same frame with "her" *Simpsons* character, it ends up being associated with "her": "Das ist 'ne Comicfigur, außerdem total unsexy."[82] Here, Dinter alludes to a different aspect of Berlin image campaigns, as popularized in a speech for the delegates to the SPD convention in 2001 by former Berlin mayor Klaus Wowereit: "Berlin ist arm, aber sexy."[83] With his worn hooded sweatshirt, "he" is clearly not doing his part to uphold the sexy part of this description. As the conversation about voluntarily neglected physical appearance persists, Dinter not only continues with the gendered theme by turning to "his" letting his facial hair grow, but adds place specificity as well, hinting at internal arguments among Berliners and reviving the East/West arguments referenced above regarding quality of life in various quarters: "Ah ja, die Männer wuchern zu wie die Bären, aber von den Frauen wird erwartet, makellos und unbehaart zu sein. Scheiß Mitte-Männer-Körperhaar-Revival!"[84] Because Lust's panel style invites mere observation, it would appear that her subjects contentedly take advantage of shopping opportunities or simply sip contemplatively their *Tchibo* coffee. Dinter's addition of dialogue, by contrast, has his nontourist Berliners voice their passionate opinions about changes over which they feel they have no control but about which they have to offer comment.

Another urban issue that often materializes in gentrified cities regards not only the transplantation but also the displacement of the creative class in Berlin as well as the related implication for artists living in Berlin, as Ward argues in this volume. For example, the theoretically elite creative class connects much more with other precarious labor because "tensions between capital investors and cultural producers" eliminate, Ward notes, studio space in favor of commercial or high-rent residential space. In some of his strips, Dinter seems to address the phenomenon and calls attention to the fact that the material for his comics emerges from his own life experiences as an artist: "[E]r bedient sich da, wie er zugibt, aus seiner Biographie."[85] Dinter belongs to the group of creative professionals who moved to Berlin for its opportunities while his character embodies highly exaggerated characteristics that typify the idealized New Berlin artist, which investors have exploited, according to Ward in this volume, by seeking "to use a cachet of conventional conceptions of the artist for marketing purposes." Dinter directly addresses and enters into dialogue with the Berlin urban social phenomenon known as the "creative class," comprised of "creative professionals, employed bohemians and freelance artists"; but he also incorporates the ensuing critique and debunking of this term.[86] The concept in general often has to do with the creative work that this group accomplishes within a certain geographic area. Theorists, most notably Richard Florida, have linked the creative presence to economic prosperity and other social developments: "[T]he driving force is the rise of human creativity as the key factor in our economy and society. Both at work and in other spheres of our lives, we value creativity more highly than ever, and cultivate it more intensely."[87] Dinter moved to Berlin in 1994, which means that he had established his studio well before other creative professionals had begun moving to the city in the 2000s. And yet, it could be argued that he has still experienced the displacement of artists that accompanied the crisis of studio space that Ward documents in his contribution in this volume. In the strip "Manche nennen es Idylle, wir nannten es Atelier,"[88] "he" relays to his readers a brief history of local changes that "he" observed firsthand from the window of his studio. As with his other strips, the character's voice takes on a noticeably critical tone when he describes how these changes have affected this section of town and "him" personally as well.[89] This is the only strip in the collection in which Dinter uses black and white, lending the story a historical look that serves the strip's biographical purpose. It is also one of very few strips largely devoid of dialogue. Instead, extensive exposition and description accompany each panel.

The first color panel shows Dinter's character along with a fellow artist working in shared office space: "Damals stand die ehemalige Kita leer und niemand interessierte sich dafür. Also wurde sie für fast zehn Jahre unser Atelier. Bis jetzt."[90] With this reference to an empty childcare space, Dinter addresses the long-standing statistic of a negative German birth rate, with the distinction in 2015 of being the lowest in the world.[91] The next panel offers a visual counterargument to these statistics—it shows a happy young couple with a baby stroller: "Aber schon damals begann sich die Umgebung zu verändern."[92] Dinter then indexes these changes with specialized terms and knowledge that could just as well be found in a sociological study. Dinter's visual and verbal irony makes it clear that he presents an artistic take on the developments. For example, in one panel the two main characters discuss gentrification: "'Was ist eigentlich Gentrifizierung?' 'Keine Ahnung. Ich nehm noch'n Soja Latte.'"[93] In the scenario that this minimalist dialogue establishes, the artists do indeed, if even unwittingly or unwillingly, contribute to their area's economic growth. In a moment of self-referentiality, "he" as an artist views himself as an extra, merely a dispensable statistic in the large number of artist types. With the perspective from inside his studio looking out his open window onto the street, he observes: "Und irgendwann blieben die Sonntagsspaziergänger vor unserem Fenster stehen, dann kamen die Touristen. Wir wurden Berlinstatisten."[94] The dialogue that accompanies this panel evidences Dinter's awareness of the creative-class concept, as well as its proven untrustworthiness as a sustainable idea. One tourist asks in English: "Are you the Creative Class?" while the other asks: "Can I take a picture?"[95] "His" comment on this sociological notion becomes clear in a subsequent panel when he addresses creativity: "Die Menschen aber, die vor zehn Jahren noch hier wohnten, sind verschwunden, und mit ihnen der ursprüngliche und interessante Charakter der Gegend."[96] After mentioning the investors, new hotels, and "absurd" marketing schemes, the last panel, returning to color, shows "him" standing with a single cardboard box: "Ich will eigentlich nicht in den Wedding."[97] As the small cardboard box of possessions suggests, "he" nonetheless has been displaced, having to move to the Wedding section of Berlin because his current residence has become too "veredelt"[98] for him to afford.

Symbolically representative of this nonacceptance of the New Berlin's urban policies and marketing, a recurring motif in Dinter's strips is that of illness or physical discomfort.[99] For Dinter, these symptoms come across as allergic reactions to the dominant "creativity, diversity, tolerance, vibrancy and hipness," the "buzzwords that have been used in Berlin's changed place marketing since the early 2000s."[100] Paradoxically, "he" and "she" represent and want to embrace manifestations of those very buzzwords while they at the same time exhibit adverse physical reactions to the concepts. In other words, the characters place themselves into trendy situations that subsequently affect their personal health. The strip "Sommer Ghetto" shows "him" and "her" in an artificial beach area in the middle of Berlin, an example of Berlin's trend of *Zwischennutzung,* or temporarily repurposing small urban pockets (see figure 3.5).[101] The oversized opening panel frames the beach with the ICE train, high rises, and cranes signaling the city's still ongoing construction.[102] The beach represents a design and marketing feat that the characters feel compelled to enjoy as citizens of this New Berlin. Here, Dinter uses his cartoon not only to discuss but also to vehemently question these new urban spaces that entrepreneurs have bought, designed, and marketed with specific visions for a renewed and vibrant future city.[103] As the comic demonstrates, however, residents do not always have the desired positive reactions to their city's transformation.

The strip presents two of Berlin's would-be consumers—"he" and "she"—discussing the advantages and disadvantages of this artificially generated venue. As is characteristic for this collection of comic strips, the discussion quickly escalates into a heated argument between the two. "He" says: "Tja, man kann nicht alles haben. Das hier ist jedenfalls

Figure 3.5. Panel from Tim Dinter, "Sommer Ghetto," in *Lästermaul & Wohlstandskind: Neue Berliner Geschichten* (Berlin, 2011), 10.

besser als in verrauchten Clubs abzuhängen—und viel gesünder."[104] Dinter ironically comments on the blossoming party scene by having his comic figures assess these more pleasant options that have come along since the proliferation of clubs and the citywide indoor smoking ban.[105] "She" vehemently responds to his commentary on the state of urban public health by ironically mentioning cultural markers of dialogues about the health of the New Berlin: "Hat grad 'n Vogel in deine Bionade gekackt? Früher hat man Lungenkrebs bekommen, heute kriegt man auch noch Hautkrebs dazu."[106] The final panel shows "her" slumping in her chair with a nasty case of sunburn as "she" asks the wait staff for "Zwei Eimer, Sangria!"[107] As is characteristic for Dinter, he artfully incorporates contradiction and paradox to construct the strip's visual and verbal punch lines. Trying to enjoy the amenities of the New Berlin, where according to the comic strip one can find better opportunities for relaxation than in other European vacation spots, elicits an unhealthy physical reaction in the nontourists who try to take advantage of these new imposed amenities.

Dinter continues with the visual portrayal of the theme of physical illness or discomfort throughout his collection as proof of visceral reactions not necessarily to various urban developments and to urban life in the German capital, but to their attempting and usually failing to adapt to the externally imposed conditions. In the strip "Acht Stunden,"[108] "she" and "he" discuss the difficulties of getting eight hours' sleep amid all-night dance clubs and a twenty-four-hour commercial scene. As the two silhouetted figures frame the window of a twenty-four-hour *döner* (Turkish-style gyro) shop, "she" uses this opportunity to educate "him" about the original Berliners in the eastern part: "Hier sind wir Nachtschwärmer und Morgenmuffel und keine Frühaufsteher und Abends-bald-Schlappmacher wie im Westen."[109] Dinter adds exaggerated visual elements to underscore differences in their appearances: "his" half-closed eyes and worsening color versus "her" fully wide-awake look. This changes in the last panel for "her" when "she" dejectedly looks at the ground and says: "Du hast's gut—ich krieg schon seit langem kein Auge mehr zu" to "his" proclamation: "Ich muss los.... Sonst penn' ich noch auf der Straße ein."[110] The seemingly simple, even inane, storyline and everyday dialogue serve a larger criticism of imposed urban transformations and the Berliners' sometimes involuntarily adverse reactions to them. In another strip about sleep patterns, "Am Puls der Zeit,"[111] Dinter, similar to other Berliner cartoonists, once again "plays around with local features" and offers one central graphic quotation to create his Berlin-specific comics.[112] The *Welt-Zeit-Uhr* (World

Time Clock) on Alexanderplatz provides a meeting place immediately recognizable to Berliners and tourists. This time, the argument between the two characters results from "his" forgetting that they have switched to daylight savings time, causing "him" to be an hour late, ironically even at this location "am Puls der Zeit." The decision to inaugurate daylights savings time is certainly not a new one decided by current Berlin politicians or architects of marketing campaigns. Because Dinter now has his comic figures debate a decision that has been around for a century, yet still presumably affects their personal well-being and health, Dinter alludes to another of his recurring themes: the loss of youth or showing noticeable signs of physical aging among members of the New Berlin's creative class.

The comics discussed above allude to a change in condition or aging to which the comic figure can no longer adjust physically, as one can when one is younger, to changes in sleep or eating habits: "[I]ch muss meinen Rhythmus einhalten."[113] In the strip "So jung kommen wir nicht mehr zusammen,"[114] "he" and "she" discuss their loss of youthful characteristics, as portrayed subtly by drawings of wilted flowers and much more directly with a sketch of anti-aging cream, a glass of water with Alka-Seltzer, and glimpses of the two characters in the mirror, which reveal wrinkles, bloodshot eyes, and a few extra pounds: "Nee, der Spaß ist schon lange vorbei ... 37 ist fast schon 40, fühlt sich aber an wie 60."[115] As with his other strips, this one also displays a keen sense of irony and humor, as shown through the strip's closing dialogue:

> *Er*: So allmählich vermisse ich meine Jugend.
> *Sie*: Du willst doch nicht wieder Pickel und Dauererektion?
> *Er*: Nee, aber so ausgebrannt und verschwendet wie jetzt?
> *Sie*: Mach was draus, schreib doch ein Buch über deinen Verlust deiner Jugend. Besser noch, einen autobiographischen Comic![116]

With the characteristic ironic humor and visual exaggeration that threads throughout Dinter's strips, along with the succinct yet expressive dialogue, Dinter's alter ego abandons youth, perhaps not entirely by choice, for the life of the artist interested in using his comic art to document and comment on the New Berlin's reality.

Concluding Remarks

In a 2014 interview, Dinter spoke about the ability of comics to document reality in the same way that photography manipulates that same reality: "People think that a photograph is objective, but actually a photo can very easily lead people to adopt a specific point of view and to often make false assessments about an event."[117] He also addresses similar stereotypes about sketched drawings that affect their reception: "At the same time, people tend to be very critical of a drawing and see it as a very personal statement."[118] The analysis of the work of these two Berlin comics artists has shown that they impart their specific perception and imagining of the city, offering their personal graphic statements on the events they observe. Both Lust and Dinter create drawings based in part on photographs they have taken of the venues. On the one hand, this technique speaks to a need for authenticity; but on the other hand, their artistic manipulation of the photographic material calls the need for authenticity into question, and shifts the focus to the deliberately critical aspect of the work. If the photographs document the politics of urban development, then the artistic manipulation speaks to individuals' successes or struggles in this New Berlin, reflecting, as Colomb states, that the "politics of urban development [are] closely related to politics of collective identity."[119] Sociologists have written about the *Infoboxes* and the *Schaustelle* campaign by which "visitors are given physical and mental spaces to form and develop their own interpretation of the urban landscape on display."[120] Likewise, Lust and Dinter produce parallel physical and mental spaces, which they in turn offer their readers as tools to develop interpretations and advance criticism of New Berlin's urban landscape.

In this chapter, I have discussed the distinctive approaches that these two artists have taken to their critical renderings of policies and results of these policies that have influenced the New Berlin. Similar to the comics artist that Johanna Schuster-Craig discusses in her chapter in this volume, Lust and Dinter also "create a differentiated portrayal of individuals" by "including as many individual stories as possible."[121] Lust's style generally leaves more up to interpretation while Dinter provides the detail of a narrative that conveys a more clearly stated point of view. Comic artists, just like authors or painters, display individual styles. Differences between Lust and Dinter and how they approach themes of the New Berlin, however, could also relate to the years in which the artists created and published their strips. For example, Colomb discusses the "spectacularization of the built environment" prevalent in the early 2000s.[122] Relatedly, much of Lust's work concentrates on the newly built shopping centers and stylized, even artificial, indoor marketplaces and endless *Passagen*. Later in the 2000s, when Dinter worked on and published his strips about a struggling and frustrated artist in the New

Berlin, the city experienced a shift in the marketing emphasis. At that time, it revolved less around promoting built environments and more around attracting creative people, or the creative class, in order to boost economic growth.[123] Although many studies have shown that the infusion of a creative class rarely, if ever, leads to desired or predicted economic growth,[124] Lust and Dinter have shown through their comic art something that Colomb articulates: "[A]rtists can subvert meaning or throw light on the hidden and the unrepresented in the official imaging process."[125] In speaking generally about the imaging of Berlin, Andrew Smith describes it in a way that also aptly describes Lust's and Dinter's modification of the official imaging campaigns: a "process of brokering the best metaphor, in ways that will shift or consolidate public sensibilities or invent the possibility for new kinds of place attachments."[126] The connections that each artist's renditions establish to place also constitute a chief difference between the artists. Lust deals mostly in permanent and singly purposed shopping centers, but Dinter bases many of his stories and criticism on the temporary places, such as the bazaars, techno clubs, and pop-up urban beaches. In both cases, however, the graphic representations refer to the place, or perhaps more accurately the search for place that the artist embodies in this changing landscape.

The Wiedenroth comic panel mentioned at the beginning of this article to explain the dynamics and trends in the New Berlin can also aid in underscoring the key difference between Lust's and Dinter's artistic approaches concerning how they view a scene and how they convey that scene to a viewer. Lust would observe the *Eiscafe* from afar and perhaps enhance it with a wry caption or a bit of dialogue between the two patrons. Dinter would have his alter ego Berlin artist patronize the *Eiscafe* and also order the ice cream with the oddly crunchy topping. As opposed to a one-line caption, however, the protagonist would engage in a lengthy conversation about this new culinary convention, positioning himself somewhere between repulsion and the inevitable need to take part in this new trend, even if it would adversely affect his health like so many things in the New Berlin threaten to do.

Highlighting their individual styles within the collective urban environment in their prolific comic collections, Lust and Dinter provide their own answers to the central questions that reside at the intersection of comics and ideology, including the ability of comics to challenge or perpetuate power differences or their purpose of celebrating or critiquing dominant values and policy.[127] Because they attack and confront contemporary issues with their art, they, along with other Berlin writers, artists, and comics artists, have demonstrated credible reasons why, as the 2013 *Comic Manifesto* demanded, comics should be afforded the same respect as literature and the visual arts.

Lynn Marie Kutch is professor of German at Kutztown University of Pennsylvania. She has published on German crime fiction, drama pedagogy, and German-language comics and graphic novels. She received the AATG's best article prize for her article in *Die Unterrichtspraxis/ Teaching German* on teaching and assessment models using graphic novels.

Notes

1. "The Comic-Manifesto: COMICS ARE ART," *internationales literaturfestival berlin,* accessed March 1, 2016, www.literaturfestival.com/archiv/sonderpr ojekte/comic/manifest.
2. Matthew P. McAllister, Edward H. Sewell, and Ian Gordon, *Comics and Ideology* (New York, 2001), 2.
3. For an example of comic art taking on the weighty issue of parallel societies and Berlin's politics of integration, see Johanna Schuster-Craig's discussion of Faroqui and Kolland's *Weltreiche erblühten und fielen* in this volume.
4. Claire Colomb, *Staging the New Berlin: Place Marketing and the Politics of Urban Reinvention Post-1989* (London, 2012), 177.
5. Gary L. Catchen, "*Gedächtnis* und *Zukunft,* Remembrance and the Future: A Photo-Essay," in *Berlin: The Symphony Continues; Orchestrating Architectural, Social, and Artistic Change in Germany's New Capital,* ed. Carol Anne Costabile-Heming, Rachel J. Halverson, and Kristie A. Foell (New York, 2004), 13.
6. Die Senatsverwaltung für Stadtentwicklung, "10 Jahre Schaustelle Berlin," *Berlin.de,* accessed February 3, 2016, https://www.berlin.de/rbmskzl/aktu elles/pressemitteilungen/2005/pressemitteilung.46015.php.
7. Janet Ward, "Re-Capitalizing Berlin," in *The German Wall: Fallout in Europe,* ed. Marc Silberman (New York, 2011), 80. See Schuster-Craig's chapter in this volume for a related analysis of the "parallel" societies and cultures that develop as a result of localized image campaigns, marketing, and gentrification.
8. Lawrence J. Vale and Sam Bass Warner Jr., *Imaging the City: Continuing Struggles and New Directions* (New Brunswick, NJ, 2001), xiii.
9. "Ice cream with brittle and sprinkles." Unless otherwise noted, translations are my own.
10. Götz Wiedenroth, "Urlaub. Hotel. Baustelle in der Nachbarschaft," *Götz Wiedenroth: Feine Zeichnungen und Karikaturen. Fotos,* September 19, 2014, https://wiedenroth.wordpress.com/2014/09/page/2/.
11. "Discover what is behind it, i.e. what it has to offer."

12. Senatsverwaltung für Stadtentwicklung, "10 Jahre Schaustelle Berlin," *Berlin.de.* "Construction sites do not only stand for noise, dust, and detours but rather primarily for the future of the city."

13. Emphasis in original. Karen E. Till, "Construction Sites and Showcases: Mapping 'The New Berlin' through Tourism Practices," in *Mapping Tourism,* ed. Stephen P. Hanna and Vincent J. Del Casino (Minneapolis, 2003), 52.

14. McAllister et al., *Comics and Ideology,* 2.

15. Emphasis in original. Anne Marie Broudehoux, *The Making and Selling of Post-Mao Beijing* (London, 2004), 26.

16. Emphasis in original. Ibid.

17. Katharina Gerstenberger, *Writing the New Berlin: The German Capital in Post-Wall Literature* (Rochester, NY, 2008), 1.

18. Janet Ward, *Post-Wall Berlin: Borders, Space and Identity* (New York, 2011), 279.

19. Gerstenberger, *Writing the New Berlin,* 1.

20. Emphasis in original. Colomb, *Staging the New Berlin,* 6.

21. Tobias Witte, "'Im Westen nichts Neues': Ist das noch ein Comic? Eickmeyers mutige Adaption des Klassikers," *texte und bilder,* May 31, 2014, http://www.texteundbilder.com/tag/im-westen-nichts-neues-comic/.

22. Colomb, *Staging the New Berlin,* 176–77.

23. Emphasis in original. Ibid., 158.

24. Ibid., 144.

25. In this chapter, I focus on the opposition between Berlin tourists and native Berliners who have little or no say in how their city has changed. It is also important to consider how various ethnic groups experience this process. For an examination of topics such as integration, see Schuster-Craig's chapter in this volume.

26. Jens Meinrenken, Mona Koch, and Ulrich Schreiber, eds., *Comics aus Berlin* (Berlin, 2013), 12.

27. Gerstenberger, *Writing the New Berlin,* 164.

28. Meinrenken et al., *Comics aus Berlin,* 24.

29. Emphasis in original. Charles Hatfield, *Alternative Comics: An Emerging Literature* (Jackson, MS, 2005), 33.

30. Meinrenken et al., *Comics aus Berlin,* 10.

31. Ibid.

32. Kristian Williams, "The Case for Comics Journalism," *Columbia Journalism Review* 43, no. 6 (2005): 52.

33. Amy Kiste Nyberg, "Theorizing Comics Journalism," *International Journal of Comic Art* 8, no. 2 (2006): 106.

34. Ibid., 98.

35. "Lightning-fast psychological profiles."

36. Emphasis in original. Kai Pfeiffer, foreword to *Fashionvictims, Trendverächter: Bildkolumnen und Minireportagen aus Berlin,* by Ulli Lust (Berlin, 2008), 8. "Her stories start in the middle of a sentence and are largely over before

the inexperienced eavesdropper realizes that yet again one of the desired *complete fragments* has also just whizzed by."

37. Henning Füller and Boris Michel, "'Stop Being a Tourist!': New Dynamics of Urban Tourism in Berlin-Kreuzberg," *International Journal of Urban and Regional Research* 38, no. 4 (2014): 1314.

38. Ibid., 1305.

39. Robert Maitland, "Everyday Life as a Creative Experience in Cities," *International Journal of Culture, Tourism and Hospitality Research* 4, no. 3 (2010): 176.

40. The list of books defining the aesthetics of comic art and how to read comic art critically continues to grow—and there are too many to list here. Some titles that continue to top the list of practitioner guides on reading comics are Scott McCloud's *Understanding Comics,* Will Eisner's *Comics and Sequential Art: Principles and Practices from the Legendary Cartoonist,* and Charles Hatfield's *Alternative Comics: An Emerging Literature.*

41. Bastian Heinsohn, "Protesting the Globalized Metropolis: The Local as Counterspace in Recent Berlin Literature," in *Spatial Turns: Space, Place, and Mobility in German Literary and Visual Culture,* ed. Jaimey Fisher and Barbara Mennel (Amsterdam, 2010), 189.

42. Ibid.

43. Ibid., 190.

44. Uta Papen, "Commercial Discourses, Gentrification and Citizens' Protest: The Linguistic Landscape of Prenzlauer Berg, Berlin," *Journal of Sociolinguistics* 16, no. 1 (2012): 59.

45. Ibid., 57.

46. Füller and Michel, "Stop Being a Tourist!," 1304.

47. Lust, *Fashionvictims, Trendverächter,* 14.

48. "Heaven on Earth."

49. "Belief and truth."

50. Papen, "Commercial Discourses," 57.

51. For a theory about the role that commercial signs and street art play in the discursive reconstruction of a gentrified Kreuzberg, see Uta Papen, "Signs in Cities: The Discursive Production and Commodification of Urban Spaces," *Sociolinguistic Studies* 9, no. 1 (2015): 1–26.

52. Lust, *Fashionvictims, Trendverächter,* 14. "Shop yourself happy."

53. Heinsohn, "Protesting the Globalized Metropolis," 195.

54. "Love, waffles, ice cream."

55. Lust, *Fashionvictims, Trendverächter,* 14. "Prenzlauer Berg: Finding meaningfulness while buying rubber boots or cake."

56. Ibid., 32.

57. Karein Goertz and Mick Kennedy, 2004. "Tracking Berlin: Along S-Bahn Linie 5," in *Berlin: The Symphony Continues; Orchestrating Architectural, Social, and Artistic Change in Germany's New Capital,* ed. Carol Anne Costabile-Heming, Rachel J. Halverson, and Kristie A. Foell (New York, 2004), 95.

58. "It Should Rain Red Roses for Me."
59. Lust, *Fashionvictims, Trendverächter,* 32.
60. Ibid. "Mornings at 7:30 am in the U2: fervent singing rings throughout the car. The tired audience barely looks up, so as not to catch the glance of the choir boy looking for change. Yet, the subway driver, hidden away in his cabin, sings Schlager a cappella free of charge. He doesn't expect applause and he doesn't get any."
61. Meinrenken et al., *Comics aus Berlin,* 26.
62. Saskia Sassen, "Ausgrabungen in der Global City," in *Berlin Global City oder Konkursmasse?,* ed. Albert Scharenberg (Berlin, 2000), 14–26.
63. Lust, *Fashionvictims, Trendverächter,* 59. "[T]he enticed audience often seems like a design problem."
64. Heinsohn, "Protesting the Globalized Metropolis," 191.
65. Ibid., 199.
66. Williams, "Case for Comics Journalism," 54.
67. Lust, *Fashionvictims, Trendverächter,* 61.
68. Ibid. "Now you finally know what you work so hard for."
69. Nyberg, "Theorizing Comics Journalism," 102.
70. Rem Koolhaas et al., "Shopping: Harvard Project on the City," in *Mutations,* ed. Rem Koolhaas et al. (Bordeaux, 2000), 127.
71. Harald Martenstein, foreword to *Lästermaul und Wohlstandskind: Neue Berliner Geschichten,* by Tim Dinter (Berlin, 2011), 5. "[H]e came from somewhere else … to Berlin." "She is a true Berlinerin."
72. "Quiet Time."
73. "Entirely without out-of-town guests."
74. "Consumer terrorists."
75. Tim Dinter, *Lästermaul und Wohlstandskind: Neue Berliner Geschichten* (Berlin, 2011), 22.
76. "Typical low-class idiotic urban guerillas."
77. "Intrinsic Values."
78. Dinter, *Lästermaul und Wohlstandskind,* 48.
79. Ibid. "It's just that we're not fashion victims and we don't have to keep changing our outfits."
80. "Transportable home."
81. Ibid., 49. "Have you ever seen Charlie Brown with a different sweater?"
82. Ibid. "That's a cartoon character. Besides totally unsexy."
83. Wolfgang Kumpfe, "Arm, sexy, schwul, mutig—dit ist Berlin," *Der Tagesspiegel,* August 26, 2014, http://www.tagesspiegel.de/berlin/klaus-wowereit-die-besten-zitate-arm-sexy-schwul-mutig-dit-is-berlin/10610608.html.
84. Dinter, *Lästermaul und Wohlstandskind,* 49. "Oh yeah, men can grow as hairy as bears but women are expected to be flawless and hairless. Shitty Mitte [a part of Berlin in the former East] men body hair revival!"
85. Martenstein, foreword to *Lästermaul und Wohlstandskind,* 5. "He makes use of, as he admits, his biography."

86. Sjoerdje van Heerden and Marco Bontje, "What about Culture for the Ordinary Workforce? A Study on the Locational Preferences of the Creative Class in Prenzlauer Berg, Berlin," *Journal of Urban Affairs* 36, no. 3 (2014): 469.
87. Richard Florida, *The Rise of the Creative Class: And How It's Transforming Work, Leisure, Community, and Everyday Life* (New York, 2002), 4.
88. Dinter, *Lästermaul und Wohlstandskind,* 104–5. "Some Call It Idyll, We Called It Studio."
89. Ibid.
90. Ibid. "At that time, the former daycare center was empty and no one showed any interest in it. So for almost ten years it became our studio. Until now."
91. Louis Doré, "Germany Replaces Japan as Country with World's Lower Birth Rate," *Independent,* May 30, 2015, http://www.independent.co.uk/news/world/europe/germany-s-birth-rate-lowest-in-the-world-according-to-study-10286525.html. Dinter's collection also features the strip "Schwangerei," where the characters discuss the epidemic of pregnant women in Mitte. Dinter, *Lästermaul und Wohlstandskind,* 34–35.
92. Dinter, *Lästermaul und Wohlstandskind,* 104. "But even back then the area had been starting to change."
93. Ibid. "'What exactly is gentrification?' 'No clue. I'll take another soy latte.'"
94. Ibid. "And at some point the Sunday strollers remained standing in front of our window, then came the tourists. We have turned into Berlin extras."
95. Ibid., 104–5.
96. Ibid., 105. "But the people who lived here ten years ago have disappeared, and with them the original and interesting character of the area."
97. Ibid. "I really don't want to go to Wedding."
98. "Refined, cultivated."
99. According to Gerstenberger, the city as body is a common motif in literature of the New Berlin. She discusses relationships between cities and bodies, blurring boundaries between physical and metaphorical bodies, mostly dealing with deformities. See Gerstenberger, *Writing the New Berlin,* 53.
100. Colomb, *Staging the New Berlin,* 143. Dinter's collection also includes "offiziell KRANK," which features a "graphic quotation" of Carl Spitzweg's *Der arme Poet.* See Dinter, *Lästermaul und Wohlstandskind,* 70–71.
101. Colomb, *Staging the New Berlin,* 243.
102. Dinter, *Lästermaul und Wohlstandskind,* 10–11.
103. In contrast to the artificial beach and corresponding to the graphic quotations that Berlin architecture offers, Dinter's collection also includes "Zurück in die Vergangenheit," in which the characters discuss the wasteful spending associated with renovating the *Stadtschloss* and also in devising slogans, such as "Be Berlin," which do not fit in with these initiatives to renovate old buildings rather than constructing new ones for less money

and a more modern appeal. See Dinter, *Lästermaul und Wohlstandskind,* 76–77.

104. Dinter, *Lästermaul und Wohlstandskind,* 11. "Well you can't have everything. This is definitely better than hanging around in smoky clubs—and much healthier."

105. Dinter also devotes a comic, "Rauchen kann erregen," to the smoking ban. See Dinter, *Lästermaul und Wohlstandskind,* 18–19.

106. Dinter, *Lästermaul und Wohlstandskind,* 11. "Did a bird take a crap in your organic drink? You used to get lung cancer, now you get skin cancer on top of it."

107. Ibid. "Two buckets of sangria!"

108. "Eight Hours."

109. Ibid., 16. "Here we're night owls and not morning people and not early risers and not already exhausted in the evening like in the West."

110. Ibid., 17. "You're lucky—I haven't been able to sleep for a long time." "I have to go. ... Otherwise I'll fall asleep right here on the street."

111. "The Latest Trends," but also in this context at the "pulse point of time," as indicated by the location at the World Time Clock.

112. Meinrenken et al., *Comics aus Berlin,* 24.

113. Dinter, *Lästermaul und Wohlstandskind,* 16. "I have to keep my natural rhythm."

114. "We're Not Getting Any Younger," or "You Only Live Once."

115. Ibid., 56. "Naw, the fun has been over for a long time ... 37 is almost 40, but feels more like 60."

116. Ibid., 57.
    He: I'm really starting to miss my younger days.
    She: You're not saying you want to go back to pimples and a permanent erection?
    He: No, but so burned out and wasted like we are now?
    She: Make something out of it, why don't you write a book about the loss of your youth. Better yet, an autobiographical comic!"

117. Katerina Oikonomakou, "Tim Dinter, 'Comics Are a Good Way of Documenting Reality,'" *Berlin Interviews: Conversations with Artists and Thinkers, in the Most Exciting European Capital.* September 18, 2014, http://berlininterviews.com/?p=1337.

118. Ibid.

119. Colomb, *Staging the New Berlin,* 4.

120. Ibid., 205.

121. See Schuster-Craig's contribution to this volume.

122. Colomb, *Staging the New Berlin,* 216.

123. Ibid., 265.

124. Many studies have refuted Florida's claims, and statistics from around 2012 prove the shortcomings of this theory. For example, in the 2000s, 30 percent of social scientists and 40 percent of artists are unemployed in Berlin;

see Adam Ozimek, "Richard Florida Is Wrong about Creative Cities," *Forbes,* May 23, 2012, http://www.forbes.com/sites/modeledbehavior/2012/05/23/richard-florida-is-wrong-about-creative-cities/#7374cde07e42. Florida himself has "conceded the limits" of the theory; see Joel Kotkin, "Richard Florida Concedes the Limits of the Creative Class," *The Daily Beast,* March 20, 2013, http://www.thedailybeast.com/articles/2013/03/20/richard-florida-concedes-the-limits-of-the-creative-class.html.
125. Colomb, *Staging the New Berlin,* 300.
126. Andrew Smith, "Conceptualizing City Image Change: The 'Re-Imaging' of Barcelona," *Tourism Geographies* 7, no. 4 (2005): 399.
127. McAllister et al., *Comics and Ideology,* 2.

Bibliography

Broudehoux, Anne-Marie. *The Making and Selling of Post-Mao Beijing.* London: Routledge, 2004.

Catchen, Gary L. "*Gedächtnis und Zukunft,* Remembrance and the Future: A Photo-Essay." In *Berlin: The Symphony Continues; Orchestrating Architectural, Social, and Artistic Change in Germany's New Capital,* edited by Carol Anne Costabile-Heming, Rachel J. Halverson and Kristie A. Foell, 13–40. New York: Walter de Gruyter, 2004.

Colomb, Claire. *Staging the New Berlin: Place Marketing and the Politics of Urban Reinvention Post-1989.* London: Routledge, 2012.

Constabile-Heming, Carol Anne, Rachel J. Halverson, and Kristie A. Foell, eds. *Berlin: The Symphony Continues; Orchestrating Architectural, Social, and Artistic Change in Germany's New Capital.* Berlin: Walter de Gruyter, 2004.

Dinter, Tim. *Einführung in die Semiotik.* Munich: Wilhelm Fink, 2002.

———. *Lästermaul und Wohlstandskind: Neue Berliner Geschichten.* Berlin: avant-verlag, 2001.

Doré, Louis. "Germany Replaces Japan as Country with World's Lower Birth Rate." *Independent,* May 30, 2015. Accessed March 12, 2017. http://www.independent.co.uk/news/world/europe/germany-s-birth-rate-lowest-in-the-world-according-to-study-10286525.html.

Eisner, Will. *Comics and Sequential Art: Principles and Practices from the Legendary Cartoonist.* New York: W. W. Norton, 2008.

Fisher, Jaimey, and Barbara Mennel, eds. *Spatial Turns: Space, Place, and Mobility in German Literary and Visual Culture (Amsterdamer Beiträge zur neueren Germanistik).* Amsterdam: Rodopi, 2010.

Florida, Richard. *Cities and the Creative Class.* New York: Routledge, 2005.

———. *The Rise of the Creative Class: And How It's Transforming Work, Leisure, Community, and Everyday Life.* New York: Basic Books, 2002.

Füller, Henning, and Boris Michel. "'Stop Being a Tourist!': New Dynamics of Urban Tourism in Berlin Kreuzberg." *International Journal of Urban and Regional Research* 38, no. 4 (2014): 1304–18.

Gerstenberger, Katharina. *Writing the New Berlin: The German Capital in Post-Wall Literature*. Rochester, NY: Camden House, 2008.

Goertz, Karein, and Mick Kennedy. "Tracking Berlin: Along S-Bahn Linie 5." In *Berlin: The Symphony Continues; Orchestrating Architectural, Social, and Artistic Change in Germany's New Capital,* edited by Carol Anne Costabile-Heming, Rachel J. Halverson, and Kristie A. Foell, 93–118. New York: Walter de Gruyter, 2004.

Hatfield, Charles. *Alternative Comics: An Emerging Literature*. Jackson: University Press of Mississippi, 2005.

Heinsohn, Bastian. "Protesting the Globalized Metropolis: The Local as Counterspace in Recent Berlin Literature." In *Amsterdamer Beiträge zur neueren Germanistik, Spatial Turns: Space, Place, and Mobility in German Literary and Visual Culture (Amsterdamer Beiträge zur neueren Germanistik)*, edited by Jaimey Fisher and Barbara Mennel, 189–210. Amsterdam: Rodopi, 2010.

internationales literaturfestival berlin. "The Comic-Manifest: COMICS ARE ART." Accessed March 1, 2016. www.literaturfestival.com/archiv/sonderprojekte/comic/manifest.

Koolhaas, Rem, Tae-Wook Cha, Chuihua Judy Chung, Jutiki Gunter, Daniel Herman, Hiromi Hosoya, Sze Tsung Leong, et al. "Shopping: Harvard Project on the City." In *Mutations,* edited by Rem Koolhaas et al., 124–83. Bordeaux: ACTAR, 2000.

Kotkin, Joel. "Richard Florida Concedes the Limits of the Creative Class." *Daily Beast,* March 20, 2013. http://www.thedailybeast.com/articles/2013/03/20/richard-florida-concedes-the-limits-of-the-creative-class.html.

Kumpfe, Wolfgang. "Arm, sexy, schwul, mutig—dit ist Berlin." *Der Tagesspiegel,* August 26, 2014. Accessed March 12, 2017. http://www.tagesspiegel.de/berlin/klaus-wowereit-die-besten-zitate-arm-sexy-schwul-mutig-dit-is-berlin/10610608.html.

Lust, Ulli. *Fashionvictims, Trendverächter: Bildkolumnen und Minireportagen aus Berlin*. Berlin: avant-verlag, 2008.

Maitland, Robert. "Everyday Life as a Creative Experience in Cities." *International Journal of Culture, Tourism and Hospitality Research* 4, no. 3 (2010): 176–85.

McAllister, Matthew P., Edward H. Sewell, and Ian Gordon. *Comics and Ideology*. New York: Peter Lang, 2001.

McCloud, Scott. *Understanding Comics: The Invisible Art*. Northampton, MA: Kitchen Sink Press, 1993.

Meinrenken, Jens, Mona Koch, and Ulrich Schreiber, eds. *Comics aus Berlin*. Berlin: Vorwerk 8 Verlag, 2013.

Nyberg, Amy Kiste. "Theorizing Comics Journalism." *International Journal of Comic Art* 8, no. 2 (2006): 98–112.

Papen, Uta. "Commercial Discourses, Gentrification and Citizens' Protest: The Linguistic Landscape of Prenzlauer Berg, Berlin." *Journal of Sociolinguistics* 16, no. 1 (2012): 56–80.

———. "Signs in Cities: The Discursive Production and Commodification of Urban Spaces." *Sociolinguistic Studies* 9, no. 1 (2015): 1–26.

Peck, Jeffery. "Struggling with the Creative Class." *International Journal of Urban and Regional Research* 29, no. 4 (2005): 740–70.

Pfeiffer, Kai. "Vorwort." In *Fashionvictims, Trendverächter: Bildkolumnen und Minireportagen aus Berlin,* by Ulli Lust, 7–8. Berlin: avant-verlag, 2008.

Sassen, Saskia. "Ausgrabungen in der Global City." In *Berlin Global City oder Konkursmasse?,* edited by Albert Scharenberg, 14–26. Berlin: Karl Dietz Verlag, 2000.

Senatsverwaltung für Stadtentwicklung. "10 Jahre Schaustelle Berlin." *Berlin.de.* Accessed February, 3, 2016. Accessed March 12, 2017. https://www.berlin.de/rbmskzl/aktuelles/pressemitteilungen/2005/pressemitteilung.46015.php.

Smith, Andrew. "Conceptualizing City Image Change: The 'Re-Imaging' of Barcelona." *Tourism Geographies* 7, no. 4 (2005): 398–423.

Smith, Neil. "Gentrification, the Frontier, and the Restructuring of Urban Space." In *Readings in Urban Theory,* edited by Susan S. Fainstein and Scott Campbell, 229–46. Chichester: Wiley-Blackwell, 2011.

Till, Karen E. "Construction Sites and Showcases: Mapping 'The New Berlin' through Tourism Practices." In *Mapping Tourism,* edited by Stephen P. Hanna and Vincent J. Del Casino Jr., 51–78. Minneapolis: University of Minnesota Press, 2003.

Vale, Lawrence J., and Sam Bass Warner Jr., eds. *Imaging the City: Continuing Struggles and New Directions.* New Brunswick, NJ: Center for Urban Policy Research, 2001.

van Heerden, Sjoerdje, and Marco Bontje. "What about Culture for the Ordinary Workforce? A Study on the Locational Preferences of the Creative Class in Prenzlauer Berg, Berlin." *Journal of Urban Affairs* 36, no. 3 (2014): 465–81.

Ward, Janet. *Post-Wall Berlin: Borders, Space and Identity.* New York: Palgrave, 2011.

———. "Re-Capitalizing Berlin." In *The German Wall: Fallout in Europe,* edited by Marc Silberman, 79–98. New York: Palgrave Macmillan, 2011.

Wiedenroth, Götz. "Urlaub. Hotel. Baustelle in der Nachbarschaft." *Götz Wiedenroth: Feine Zeichnungen und Karikaturen. Fotos,* September 19, 2014. Accessed March 14, 2017. https://wiedenroth.wordpress.com/2014/09/page/2/.

Williams, Kristian. "The Case for Comics Journalism." *Columbia Journalism Review* 43, no. 6 (2005): 51–55.

Witte, Tobias. "'Im Westen nichts Neues': Ist das noch ein Comic? Eickmeyers mutige Adaption des Klassikers." *texte und bilder,* May 31, 2014. Accessed March 12, 2017. http://www.texteundbilder.com/tag/im-westen-nichts-neues-comic/.

PART II

Spaces, Monuments, and the Appropriation of History

CHAPTER 4

Reconfiguring the Spaces of the "Creative Class" in Contemporary Berlin

Simon Ward

The impact of gentrification has been particularly tangible in Berlin since the turn of the century. Elsewhere in this volume, Johanna Schuster-Craig investigates how these tensions manifest themselves in terms of the "integration" debate in the specific district of Neukölln and how cultural production has sought to address these issues. Linking to the contribution of Katrina Sark on the cultural history of post-Wall Berlin in this volume, but focusing on the conditions of production rather than on production itself, the present contribution analyzes how gentrification impacts the availability of spaces for cultural production across the city, ultimately illustrating how this particular problem is now being seen in relation to the integration of marginalized groups into the city.

In 2014, a book titled *Berlin Wonderland* commemorated the early years of *Tacheles,* an artist collective that had gathered, in the immediate post-unification period, in an abandoned building, a former department store in the center of what was East Berlin. *Berlin Wonderland* presented a relatively ordered archive of photographs and testimony of the years from 1990 onward when, as the book's preface described it,

> in East Berlin, entirely new dimensions of freedom arose—political, social and cultural. Empty buildings that had been quietly decaying were occupied by new inhabitants. Cultural projects and artists from all over the world moved in. With a spirit of improvisation, imagination and creativity, they laid claim to an intermediate zone whose open spaces

became meeting points for the most diverse of people. Suddenly the possibilities seemed immense.[1]

This publication was significant for two related reasons. First, the book represents the kind of nostalgic longing that Sark analyzes in her contribution to this volume, translating this period of cultural activity in Berlin into the realm of cultural memory, as if there was a felt need to preserve not only the period but also the possibilities represented—in that both were under threat of vanishing. It curated the activities of those years into a series of categories (e.g., "City as Stage," "Wild Gangs") that describe a model of cultural activities in an intermediate space and time—what has become known as *Zwischennutzung* (transitional use).[2] Second, the publication appeared at a time when such a model of productive, imaginative collective action was subject to severe economic pressure as the difficult situation regarding studio provision for artists in Berlin reached the crisis point that is the focus of this article.[3]

The multifarious activities at *Tacheles* (artistic production and exhibition, bar, cinema, etc.) can be read as an example of what Sharon Zukin described as a new view of art focused on a "way of doing" rather than a distinctive "way of seeing," which had emerged in the wake of Fluxus and similar international avant-garde art movements of the 1960s.[4] For Zukin, in this form of art, site and product become largely synonymous and with it a definition of the role of art as a catalyst for cultural and social change in collective public space. Such an art also redefines the boundaries of the space in which the artist works and operates, as well as his or her relationship to other users of public space.

Well before the current crisis around studio space emerged, a *Spiegel* online article published in October 2007 reported a new study that suggested Berlin was poised for a boom driven by the "creative class."[5] The study, conducted by the Berlin Institute for Population and Development and financed by the nonprofit Robert Bosch Stiftung, based its work on the theory of growth potential developed by Richard Florida. Florida's 2003 book *The Rise of the Creative Class* identified the "creative core of this new class," which includes "scientists and engineers, university professors, poets and novelists, artists, entertainers, actors, designers and architects."[6] Martha Rosler has observed that Florida's coupling of "artists and bohemians with all kinds of IT workers and others not remotely interested in art or bohemia, has been identified by many observers—perhaps especially those involved in the art world—as a glaring fault."[7] Florida's coupling of artists with other creative laborers indicates that they share, up to a point, in the process of urban regeneration. In her 1982 study *Loft Living: Culture and Capital in Urban Change*, Sharon Zukin laid out a theory of urban change in which artists and the entire visual art sector—including those spaces that were run by artists themselves—were a key engine for the repurposing of the postindustrial city. Crucial to Zukin's analysis was the eventual displacement of those artists, a development not of interest to Florida.

As we shall see, the discourse in Berlin around the "creative class" and in particular the spaces and milieus in which they work is certainly informed by Florida, albeit negatively in that his refusal to acknowledge the specificity of artists in constructing an amorphous "creative class" prepares the ground for the process of displacement that Zukin described. That kind of displacement is viewed less critically by John Montgomery, who in 2005 asserted that "the days of funding endless self-serving 'community arts action' groups, of seeing art as a proxy for social work, should soon be over."[8] Clare Colomb and Johannes Novy's discussion of recent connections between collective artist production and social protest in Hamburg and Berlin offers a strong counternarrative.[9]

This chapter argues that there is a reconfiguration of the "creative class" going on in Berlin at the present moment, around the dividing line between the "artist" and other creative workers. This contemporary reconfiguration reimagines how the artist relates not to the high earners identified by Florida but to workers who are less privileged and whose earning levels place them at risk from rent rises, and who can be described as members of a "culture precariat" (Kulturprekariat), a term that will be delineated in more detail below. The chapter argues that the prime driver of that reconfiguration is the contemporary crisis regarding spaces for cultural production in Berlin in recent years, a crisis that has thrown into question the model that has been predominant in Berlin since the early 1990s. By considering a series of contemporary studio spaces, this chapter elucidates a differentiated understanding of the relationship between capital investors and cultural producers, as well as new models of what constitutes the space of cultural production, a model that is becoming increasingly important at the time of writing.

The year 2014, the same year Berlin Wonderland was published, was a year of crisis for sites of cultural production in the city, as tensions between capital investors and cultural producers made them visible. Anna Pataczek introduced her series of articles in the Tagesspiegel that year with an ominous description of the situation:

> Berlin is the most important place for the creation of new art, we are told. But the space available is becoming ever scarcer. Studios and workshops are being pushed out, to make way for residential accommodation.[10]

In line with the Zukin model of displacement, Pataczek's article outlined the repurposing of a series of postindustrial spaces that had been (temporarily) used for artistic purposes. Among these was the site of the former *Schultheiss* brewery in Moabit (in the former West of the city), which had been bought by the investor Harald G. Huth in order to be reconfigured as a shopping center.[11] Another example was a former piano factory, the *Mengerzeile* in Alt-Treptow. These artists had celebrated their anniversary in 2013, but that year saw the death of the owner, who, as a benefactor, had hoped to gift it to the artist collective. The factory was in fact sold off, and with a plan in place to convert it to residential accommodation, an ongoing battle of the studios continues at this point of writing.

The BLO-Studios (named after the *Betriebswerk Lichtenberg Ost,* the railway depot built on the site between 1881 and 1894) were presented by Pataczek in 2014 as a potential beacon of resistance in the situation. The BLO-Studios are situated at a location that is by no means central—Lichtenberg is to the east of the more fashionable district of Friedrichshain, and the former railway depot, unsurprisingly, finds itself on the wrong side of every track that funnels into Lichtenberg before the final stretch toward Alexanderplatz and the city center. The site was "discovered," four years after its closure, in February 2003 by Thomas Seyffert und Daniel Rabe, who had been taking part in a project organized by the self-stylized "self-organized social-cultural center" RAW-Tempel e.V.[12] RAW-Tempel itself took shape from 1999 onward on the former railway repair site "Franz Stenzer," which had closed in 1995. Indeed, in the anniversary frenzy that seems to have consumed the cultural scene in Berlin in 2014, RAW-Tempel also celebrated fifteen years of "cultural activity" (*Kulturarbeit*) in that year.

Also in 2014, a ten-year rental contract with the *Deutsche Bundesbahn* (German Federal Railway Company) ended, and renewal negotiations that same year did not appear to be going well. The demands of the railway company included threats of a 120 percent increase in rent prices in order to mirror other—residential—rents in the area, thus illustrating one of the key tensions between capital investors, who do not always see the need to respect the different requirements and possibilities of cultural producers in reflecting upon what constitutes a "market price." This dispute is not yet resolved. Another plan mooted at the time rejected artistic use altogether and sought to use the site for the relocation of the S-Bahn museum from Potsdam-Griebnitzsee. The rhetoric around this suggestion (which came from the Christian Democratic Union party) emphasized that the "location" was in an "interesting space for development" in the city, an "attractive residential area with varied character."[13] This kind of rhetoric fits neatly into the Zukin model of displacement that comes with urban regeneration.

The same CDU proposal also highlighted the restructuring of the area north of the Frankfurt Allee, focusing on the reconfiguration of the former buildings of the Ministry for State Security (Stasi, MfS) as a "campus of democracy."[14] Regeneration here was linked to the democratization of the material legacy of the Stasi, here with the former Operative Technical Sector building in the formerly restricted area in Alt-Hohenschönhausen beyond Friedrichshain, being transformed into the Intelligence Department Studios.

The opportunity to develop this area emerged as a result of the Berlin regional government divesting itself of the physical inheritance of the GDR state. The three buildings here that were formerly part of the Stasi infrastructure were bought in 2009 by the Immonen Group, a "real estate investment and development company," founded in 2007, and "operating in Berlin."[15]

The group expressly claims to have been influenced by the ideas of Richard Florida, devoting a page of their website to the theory of the "creative class" and its benefits to the city ("Berlin's economic growth and real estate development has proven it right!").[16] They claim that they "have successfully led innovative and unique projects that contribute to and benefit from the diversified horizon of creativity and growth in Berlin."[17] Indeed the ID-Studios is one of four (very different) projects described on their website, and the only one specifically related to artistic production. The others include a large area of land situated in Alt-Hohenschönhausen, which will offer 140,000 cubic meters of diverse real estate, including mixed residential, commercial, and service areas, gastronomy, and hotels. This is a project from which, they claim, "the city district and all of Berlin will profit as an example of modern urban development."[18] Another project is a 3,000-cubic-meter *Jugendstil* monumental hotel built in 1903, which is being developed into a multipurpose hotel, spa, and residential complex.

The ID-Studios is currently one of Berlin's largest studio complexes. Compared to the fifty artists housed at BLO-Studios, ID-Studios contains around 250 artists, of whom many are sculptors (which gives an indication of the size of the studios available). The relationship between capital investors and cultural producers is less antagonistic here, as questions of ownership/tenancy, and contractual relations, have been very clear from the start. Indeed Ariel Levin, spokesperson for the group, has highlighted the creation here of a "little artist city."[19] This disconnection of artistic production from wider social processes is clearly in the interest of capital investors who are seeking to use the cachet of conventional conceptions of the artist for marketing purposes. While there is little that is strikingly original about the other development projects described above, the ID-Studios is somewhat different, in that traces of the past are not entirely erased here. Under the GDR regime, the site was responsible for the development, production, and maintenance of all espionage equipment including wiretapping devices, cameras, camouflage, and monitoring instruments. Levin has noted that this former space of Stasi technical experimentation has now become a site of artistic experimentation.

In fact, the Immonen Group trades on the unique historical authenticity of the location (right next to the Berlin-Hohenschönhausen Stasi memorial site), observing that it had retained many of the historical features, focusing on the "charm of the GDR [sic]" in the maintenance of large-scale doors, the lifts, and even the showers "with their algae-blue tiling from 1985."[20] A large space, originally built to provide soundproof 'interview" rooms for the Stasi, had been retained for future use as gallery space.

In 2002, David Harvey reflected on the motivations of capital investors at such transitional spaces, obliged as they were to "support forms of differentiation and allow divergent and to some degree uncontrollable local cultural developments that can be antagonistic to its own smooth functioning."[21] According to Harvey, "it is within such spaces that all manner of oppositional movements can form even presupposing, as is often the case, that oppositional movements are not already firmly entrenched there. The problem for capital is to find ways to co-opt, subsume, commodify and monetize such cultural differences just enough to be able to appropriate monopoly rents therefrom."[22] In Harvey's account, culture and opposition flourish as an unintended consequence of capital's need to not totally destroy a location's uniqueness, which is the basis for the generation of what Harvey terms "monopoly rents." Hence capital can even support "transgressive" cultural practices precisely because this is one way in which a space can be marketed as original, creative, and authentic as well as unique. The ID-Studios project profits from the notion of the authenticity of the site, but by engaging with its tenants as individual artists, it undoes any sense of the collectivity that Harvey imagines in a model that belongs to the *Tacheles* pattern discussed above.[23]

While this strategy of marketing the past is foregrounded at this former Stasi site, the former Broadcasting House (*Funkhaus*) of the GDR, the world's biggest connected building (on a 50,000-cubic-meter area), has not traded so explicitly on its historical legacy. It had served from 1956 until 1990 as the premises of the East German broadcasting services in Berlin before being sold off to the Israeli property entrepreneur Albert Ben David through Keshet GmbH. Under the slogan "Space for Their Ideas" the Keshet GmbH & Co. rented out the rooms of Block A as studios and workshops for mostly young artists from winter 2011–12 onward. In that sense, it fit in with the general growth of "creativity" in this rather distant, southeastern corner of the city. Indeed the area around the *Funkhaus* was identified as a crucible of creativity in an article in the *Berliner Zeitung* in 2012. This was evidenced by the presence not only of artists but also the thousands of students nearby at the new campus for the *Hochschule für Technik und Wirtschaft* (College for Technology and Economy) at Wilhelminenhof. This development was marked from 2008 onward by the "Kunst am Spreeknie" (Art at the Bend in the River Spree) festival, which crucially involved not only artists but also design students from the HTW who exhibited fashion designs as well as that sine qua non of the contemporary creative industry, the computer game.[24]

In the summer of 2015 it was revealed that ownership of the *Funkhaus* had passed to the entrepreneur Uwe Fabich. Fabich was presented in the *Berliner Kurier* as a "real-estate phantom" who does not allow himself to be photographed.[25] If Fabich might then appear as the "invisible hand" of capital, he nevertheless possesses the very concrete biography of a forty-one-year-old, having studied business management in Berlin, Hong Kong, and New York and worked in London for Deutsche Bank. Interviews with Fabich have certain elements in common in the discursive construction of this figure. These representations emphasize his casual dress sense, but also his background in finance; they also present him as a developer of potential spaces in the city, as he had bought the *Postbahnhof* in the Oranienburger Straße (previously the location of the C/O photo gallery, and a few hundred yards from the *Tacheles* site), and descriptions of him emphasize a speed and tempo that we might easily associate with finance capitalism.[26]

In terms of monopoly rent, the historical authenticity of the *Funkhaus* does in fact play an important role in Fabich's vision for the site. Interviews reiterate the story he tells of his "discovery" of the building—by boat from the Spree. Fabich makes it clear that one of his aims is to recreate this moment of discovery by establishing a ferry route that would bring an audience (of cultural consumers) to the *Funkhaus*. Here, as it were, we can ourselves "discover" culture; at the core of Fabich's vision is a lifestyle experience that the *Funkhaus* offers, cut off as it is from the main cultural circuits and infrastructural routes of the city.

Fabich's initial interventions in the site have been interesting. Block A of the *Funkhaus* is a five-story building, and the top story, previously housing offices grander but in structure similar to those that had been transformed into studios on the floors below, has been reconfigured into a large, open space. Viewed skeptically, the creation of such a fungible space would obviously lend itself to a form of residential "loft living" in due course.

The *Funkhaus* currently combines production and exhibition, as seen in the "Arcadia Unbound" group exhibition that ran in early September 2015 at the *Funkhaus*, after Fabich had taken over the running of the site. One of the co-organizers of this exhibition was the artist Janine Eggert, who had moved to the *Funkhaus* from the former *Schultheiss* brewery in Moabit when those studio spaces were repurposed in 2014. Eggert described the *Funkhaus* as an "abandoned, forgotten idyll that we are trying to reawaken back to new life through art."[27] The artists here clearly work with a notion of the uniqueness of the space and of artistic production as mode of engagement with the space. Sibylle Jazra, another co-curator, claimed that the exhibition sought to create a dialogue between the architecture and the art, so that, for example, the two large broadcast studios were used for audio and video works. The authenticity of the location guarantees the "authenticity" and significance of the artist creations, some of which, as with Ingo Gerken's *BIG EASY,* playfully interact with the building's existing forms.

The press release highlighted the variety of different architectural forms and features:

> Such as long curved hallways, spiral staircases, columned halls, and various textured surfaces of marble and wood.… "Arcadia Unbound" especially generates an opportunity of dialogue & tense confrontation of artwork on environment. This particular and unusual architecture leads to a new and extraordinary emphasis on the artworks.[28]

The press release's claim that the "exhibition breaks deliberately with the rules of a White Cube" does not sound particularly groundbreaking; indeed the Berlin newspaper *taz* described the exhibition as "sympathetic, but not exactly visionary," despite the presence of several renowned international artists among the participants.[29] While some reviews favorably considered the relationship between the installations and their setting, more important was perhaps the "amazing" nature of the location (as iHeartBerlin described it on their Facebook page).[30]

To return to Harvey's arguments about the operations of "monopoly rent" in this context, the situation at the *Funkhaus* demonstrates that it is not only capital that thrives on the assertion of the unique "authenticity" of locations, but rather cultural production here that also co-opts the past. As one blogger, Rea McNamara, describes it, here there is the "still lingering *ostalgie* (nostalgia for the East) that looms largely in the collective unconsciousness of many *wahlberliners* [by-choice Berlin inhabitants]."[31] McNamara claims that "until its capitalist makeover is complete, the *Funkhaus* Berlin remains a unique site of discourse between the loaded built environment of the East and the booming culture of the city's present."[32] What McNamara does not recognize is that this site of interaction is precisely part of the makeover process, where cultural production and consumption are sited in a particular unique and authentic (or "amazing") location. This process already buys into the logic of the ultimate decoupling of artists from other forms of creative production, which are understood as complicit with the "capitalist makeover."[33]

These three locations illustrate different aspects of the relationship between the capital investor and cultural producers: conflict in the case of the BLO-Studios; incorporation within the investor project at the Studios-ID; and an emerging complicity in the marketing of the space at the *Funkhaus*. The term "Arcadia," and its gloss by Eggert, is fascinating here. It has no political connotations, and any sense of a utopian perspective is subsumed within the pastoral trope. "Arcadia Unbounded" is a significant construction of the space as "apolitical" but also "free" in the sense that it is not affected by the constraints of society.

All three situations invoke, in different ways, the assumption that the space of the "artist" is a sacrosanct space, something that has also, up to now, been visible on an institutional level in the city. Since 1993 the Berlin Senate has funded an "artists' studio" program, which has played an important role as an enabler of artistic production in Berlin. The program, run through the *berufsverband bildender künstler* (Professional Association of Visual Artists, hereafter *bbk*) offers financial support to artists, covering part of their studio rent at certain locations throughout Berlin, and has supported over a thousand artists over the past two decades. The *bbk* website contains a wide range of documentation relating to the Studio Program, including video interviews with the major players in the program as well as with artists who have benefitted from it.[34] The image composition employed in these videos is significant as, by filming the artists individually in their studios, it decouples them from any sense of a broader or collective context. This separation is underlined by the interview of the artists themselves, as they consistently highlight the importance of an appropriate individual "studio space" as a space of creation, one that is also close to the Berlin art world; for Birgit Brenner, studio space is separated from the misogynist capital processes of the art market, while for Stefan Saffer it is a crucial space of production that ultimately benefits those who "steal and profit" (Saffer's words) from it.[35]

The crisis of studio space was documented in an article in the Berlin listings magazine *tip* from 2014.[36] The author of that article, Constanze Suhr, followed a group of artists from the aforementioned *Mengerzeile* complex in search of new studio space, bringing to the fore some of the considerable problems that they, and the *bbk*, faced in finding locations that were appropriate both in terms of dimensions and amenities and also in terms of infrastructural connections to the city. This problem has been addressed on a theoretical level by the Berlin collective *raumlabor*, in their project "Art City Lab," which produced a publication of that name in 2014. While they look in this project at various existing models of "reuse" of existing buildings, in Berlin but also beyond, perhaps the most striking proposal they investigate is the flexible use of prefabricated units that can be installed at low cost in small, unused spaces within the inner city.[37]

Beyond the presentation of these alternative models, *raumlabor* also staged a discussion on the concept of studio space among interested parties (cultural producers and facilitators) in Berlin. This discussion brought to light an important distinction in addressing questions larger than simply the studio space of the artist, as expressed in a significant disagreement between Florian Schmidt, the director of the *bbk*'s artist studio program, and one particular curator, Adrienne Goehler. Goehler argued strongly for understanding artists within the broader context of the *Kulturprekariat*, which includes independent designers and architects who suffer from a great deal of instability due to the nature of their professions. Goehler suggested that the focus on studio space was an "oversimplification."[38] Schmidt, on the other hand, was particularly concerned with preserving a clear, qualitative distinction between visual artists and other creative and cultural professionals since, in Schmidt's view, "art is indeed a profession, but it's usually not considered a trade. … If we could agree that the visual arts operate beyond the market …, then these special requirements are a good tool for arguing that we can't ignore."[39]

The significance of this focus on the "artist's studio" becomes clear when we consider that, in September 2015, the Berlin Senate produced proposals to reconfigure the Studio Program. Under these plans, the Studio Program would evolve into a general program for the provision of space for "artists and creatives" ("*Künstler und Kreative*"). In addition, a conversation between Florian Schmidt, the *bbk* commissioner, and the cultural administrators suggested they were planning a move toward "interdisciplinary and creative collaboration" in "flexible spaces," signaling the end, as Schmidt saw it, of "professionally usable spaces for professional artists."[40] This discursive shift is crucial, for it seems to indicate a "homogenization" of the perception of "creative space" in line with the kind of coupling enacted by Richard Florida.

The concluding section of the article investigates a different conception of studio space that is emerging in Berlin, which allows us to consider a contemporary reconfiguration of the "creative class" in a way that is not simply defined by the description of that class provided by Richard Florida.

In 2007, the nonprofit ExRotaprint was founded in order to bring new life into the former premises of a printing press manufacturer in Berlin-Wedding. The area had been earmarked for sale to an Icelandic real-estate investment trust, but when this fell through, the company managed to agree to a deal whereby it was granted tenancy rights for the next hundred years. ExRotaprint had its origins in a *bbk* studio building in the vicinity that could no longer contain all the artists who wanted to work there. The philosophy behind ExRotaprint rejects the idea of a traditional studio building with a monocultural tenant structure (as can be seen in the three models discussed above), but rather seeks to promote the site as an "urban interface in the everyday life of Wedding."[41] Daniela Brahm, one of the members of the company, participated in the aforementioned *raumlabor* discussion and underscored the importance of small-scale solutions, suggesting that solidarity with small-scale craftsmanship and trade operators was important, emphasizing, again in contrast to Florian Schmidt, the similarities between such forms of productions.[42]

The "authenticity" of the former printing works is derived not from its historical significance (or the marketing thereof) but from an ongoing set of interactions with the locality. ExRotaprint is home to a variety of ventures that address the socially marginalized—a school for truants, an initiative focusing on qualifications for the long-term unemployed, as well as carpentry shops, silk-screening workshops, offices for architects and designers, as well as twenty-five studio spaces for artists. In addition, there is a canteen that functions as a local meeting point and site of encounter. The project thus represents an attempt to solve the tension "between supporting cultural communities and creativity and selling off and fragmenting the very spaces in which this culture can be cultivated," which Sark analyzes elsewhere in this volume. It does this by seeking to integrate itself into the development of this economically—and culturally—challenged district, reconfiguring here what constitutes the "creative class" not as a distinct social grouping but as a model whereby artistic workers are interconnected with other forms of "precarious" labor and existence in the district.[43]

This model can also be seen in the emergence of the *Allianz bedrohter Berliner Atelierhäuser* (Alliance of Threatened Berlin Studio Spaces—hereafter AbBA), a collective formed to call on the government to free up unused buildings to activate a production center for the arts, culture, and social affairs. Focused on the space that professional artists require, this collective's main purpose is not an explicit sociopolitical agenda. Nevertheless, in the public statements of the AbBA, they explicitly invoke the model enacted at ExRotaprint, citing it, as well as other locations such as the *Zentrum für Kunst und Urbanistik* (Center for Art and Urbanism) in Moabit. What these projects have in common, according to AbBA, is that they are lively sites of artistic, social and *long-term* production and encounter for society as a whole.[44]

Doris Kleilein has commented on the way the AbBA collective demonstrates a level of professionalization in terms of organization and communication by alternative stakeholders that enables them to negotiate directly with the likes of Berlin's Finance Senator.[45] Striking too is the plan proposed by the AbBA to deal with its current object of interest, the former government *Haus der Statistik* (House of Statistics). As a GDR-legacy building, the site belongs to the Federal State, and the Senate has proposed two alternative models for the space: first, the demolition of the building and its replacement by a largely high-rent residential and business quarter that would ultimately exclude artists; second, the use of the existing building as a center for administrative activities related to the work of the Senate.

One of the principles behind the AbBA counterplan is a rejection of a classic gentrification model—in which the space is transitionally appropriated by artists in preparation for a general revaluation of the district—in favor of a more durable solution. This was embodied in the plan for the creation of social and cultural diversity at the *Haus der Statistik,* since all other buildings in the area were in private ownership or already rented out. Significant here, and visible in the plan, is the idea of integrating refugees into urban society, something discussed elsewhere by Schuster-Craig in this volume. Under the plan, 45 percent of the available space would be used for temporary accommodation for refugees; 25 percent would be used for "art and cultural purposes," providing work space for cultural producers, both native Berliners and those who have come there as refugees; 20 percent would provide space for educational and integrational projects for refugees; and the final 10 percent would be used as space for events.

The debate around the *Haus der Statistik* makes a key contribution to the discursive construction of the "creative class" in Berlin, in that it counters the categorical distinction between (visual/fine) artists and other creative producers. This distinction is ultimately founded on the (doubtless well-

Figure 4.1. AbBA-Plan for the *Haus der Statistik*. Source: *Haus der Statistik*, https://hausderstatistik.wordpress .com, accessed January 10, 2016.

founded) suspicion of Richard Florida's elision of artists with other creative producers, an elision that would lead to the ultimate disappearance of discrete studio spaces. In contrast, this project recalibrates the notion of the creative class and organizes that group spatially so that they might mutually support each other. The ultimate fate of the *Haus der Statistik* will in the end have much to say about the future of this potential reconfiguration of the creative class in Berlin.

Simon Ward is Associate Professor in German at Durham University (UK). He is the author of *Urban Memory and Visual Culture in Berlin: Framing the Asynchronous City, 1957–2012* (Amsterdam University Press, 2016), as well as a wide range of articles on German culture of the twentieth century.

Notes

1. Anke Fesel and Chris Keller, *Berlin Wonderland* (Berlin, 2014), 9. The publishing house, bobsairport, is a photographic agency founded in 2007 in Berlin by Fesel and Keller. Fesel and Keller came to Berlin in 1990 and became heavily involved in the scene at the Tacheles building in the center of Berlin in the early 1990s, albeit mostly in an organizational role.
2. On "transitional use," see, for example, Tanja Gallenmüller, *Mind the Gap: Zwischennutzung von Leerräumen am Beispiel des Quartiers Boxhagener Platz* (Mammendorf, 2004).

3. The ownership and development of *Tacheles* has itself been a long-term issue of debate. See, for example, Janet Stewart, "The Kunsthaus Tacheles: The Berlin Architecture Debate of the 1990s in Micro-Historical Context," in *Recasting German Identity: Culture, Politics and Literature in the Berlin Republic,* ed. Stuart Taberner and Frank Finlay (Rochester, NY, 2005).

4. Sharon Zukin, *Loft Living: Culture and Capital in Urban Change* (New Brunswick, NJ, 1982), 98.

5. "Economic Prospects Report: Berlin Tops Germany for 'Creative Class,'" *Spiegel Online,* October 10, 2007, http://www.spiegel.de/international/business/economic-prospects-report-berlin-tops-germany-for-creative-class-a-510609.html.

6. Richard Florida, *The Rise of the Creative Class: And How It's Transforming Work, Leisure, Community, and Everyday Life* (New York, 2004), 34.

7. Martha Rosler, "Culture Class: Art, Creativity, Urbanism," *e-flux* 21, no. 12 (2010), accessed September 10, 2015, http://www.e-flux.com/journal/culture-class-art-creativity-urbanism-part-i/.

8. John Montgomery, "Beware 'The Creative Class': Creativity and Wealth Creation Revisited," *Local Economy* 20, no. 4 (2005): 342.

9. Johannes Novy and Clare Colomb, "Struggling for the Right to the (Creative) City in Berlin and Hamburg: New Urban Social Movements, New 'Spaces of Hope'?," *International Journal of Urban and Regional Research* 37, no. 5 (2013): 1816–38.

10. Anna Pataczek, "Bedrohte Atelierhäuser in Berlin: Atelier ade," *Tagesspiegel,* September 12, 2014, http://www.tagesspiegel.de/berlin/bedrohte-atelierh aeuser-in-berlin-atelier-ade/10661700.html.

11. Huth is described as one of the "invisible giants" of the Berlin real-estate investment market in a *Welt* article in 2012. Dirk Westphal, "Die großen Bauherren des Berliner Monopolys," *Die Welt,* February 23, 2014.

12. "Geschichte des BW-BLO," *BLO-Ateliers,* accessed September 10, 2015, http://www.blo-ateliers.de/geschichte-betriebsbahnhof-lichtenberg-ost/.

13. Thuy Anh Nguyen, "Platzmangel: S-Bahn Museum will nach Lichtenberg," *Bezirks-Journal,* June 24, 2014. That the BLO, the largest independent art community in the East of the city, has survived (to date of writing) has been due in large part to the support it has received from the district administration.

14. "CDU will S-Bahn Museum nach Lichtenberg holen," CDU—Fraktion in der BVV Lichtenberg, May 27, 2014, http://www.cdu-fraktion-lichtenberg.de/meldungen/einzelansicht/article/cdu-will-s-bahn-museum-nach-lichten berg-holen.html.

15. "Über uns," Immonen Group, accessed August 10, 2015, http://www.immo nen-group.com. Unless otherwise noted, translations are my own.

16. Ibid.

17. Ibid.

18. Ibid.

19. Ibid.

20. Karolina Wrobel, "Industriebauten in der Genslerstraße ziehen internationale Künstler an," *Berliner Woche,* April 4, 2013, http://www.berliner-woche.de/neu-hohenschoenhausen/sonstiges/industriebauten-in-der-gensler strasse-ziehen-internationale-kuenstler-an-d25278.html.
21. David Harvey, "The Art of Rent: Globalization, Monopoly and the Commodification of Culture," *Socialist Register* 38 (2002): 108.
22. Ibid.
23. In an email exchange between the author and the painter Klaus Walter, who has his studio in Studios-ID, Walter emphasized the advantages of this setting in terms of being able to work in an undisturbed fashion. Klaus Walter, email message to author, February 18, 2016.
24. Karin Schmidl, "'Kunst am Spreeknie' lockt Kreative," *Berliner Zeitung,* July 11, 2015.
25. Marc Fleischmann, "Postbahnhof, Erdmann-Höfe, Wasserturm, Nalepastraße: Der neue Coup des Immo-Phantoms," *Berliner Kurier,* June 9, 2015.
26. Ibid.; see also Karin Schmidl, "Das größte Musikzentrum der Welt soll in Berlin entstehen," *Berliner Zeitung,* July 5, 2015; Thomas Loy, "Hollywood und Honecker zieht's in die Nalepastraße," *Der Tagesspiegel,* June 28, 2015.
27. Stephanie Wurster, "Ein vergessenes Idyll," *taz,* September 15, 2015, http://www.taz.de/!5229352/.
28. "About," *Arcadia Unbound,* accessed September 10, 2015, http://www.arcadia-unbound.de/index.php/about/.
29. Ibid.
30. iHeartBerlin.de's Facebook page, accessed December 10, 2015, https://www.facebook.com/iHeartBerlin.de/.
31. Rea McNamara, "Curating in a Loaded Void: Art in Berlin's Vacant Communist Architecture," *Art F City* (blog), September 18, 2015, http://artfcity.com/2015/09/18/curating-in-a-loaded-void-art-in-berlins-vacant-communist-architecture/. On Berlin-specific *Ostalgie* and nostalgia, see Sark's contribution to this volume.
32. Ibid.
33. In an email exchange between the author and Joachim Seinfeld, one of the artists who has a studio in the *Funkhaus,* Seinfeld expressed uncertainty about the situation going forward, as it seemed as if Fabich was looking to retain a few "serious" artists and rent the rest of the space to "creatives" (Seinfeld's term). Joachim Seinfeld, email message to author, February 20, 2016.
34. "Artist Interviews," *The Berlin Studio Program,* accessed July 10, 2015, http://www.berlin-studio-program.de/artist-interviews/.
35. "Das Berliner Atelierprogramm: Stefan Saffer," YouTube video, 0:43, posted by Berlin Studio Program, October 9, 2013, https://www.youtube.com/watch?v=lAVg-p2XtCc.
36. Constanze Suhr, "Atelierhäuser in Berlin," *tip-Berlin,* September 19, 2014.
37. raumlabor berlin, *Art City Lab* (Berlin, 2015), 73–105.
38. Ibid., 160.

39. Ibid., 162.
40. Florian Schmidt, "Stellungnahme," *Kulturwerk des bkk berlin,* accessed August 30, 2015, http://www.bbk-kulturwerk.de/con/kulturwerk/upload/ateliers/2015-08-20_Stellungnahme_AB_zu_HH_2016-17_FINAL.pdf.
41. raumlabor berlin, *Art City Lab,* 41.
42. Ibid., 162–63.
43. Ibid., 38–41. See Ülker in this volume for a case study of how "ethnic entrepreneurship" engages with similar challenges of economic restructuring within the management of neighborhoods.
44. "Arbeitsplätze für Künstlerinnen und Künstler (erhalten!)—bezahlbar, langfristig, vielfältig, innerstädtisch," *AbBa,* accessed January 12, 2016, http://abbanetzwerk.tumblr.com. Emphasis mine.
45. Doris Kleilein, "Die letzte Insel," *Bauwelt* 6 (2016): 2.

Bibliography

"About." *Arcadia Unbound.* Accessed September 10, 2015. http://www.arcadia-unbound.de/index.php/about/.

"Arbeitsplätze für Künstlerinnen und Künstler (erhalten!)—bezahlbar, langfristig, vielfältig, innerstädtisch." *AbBa.* Accessed January 12, 2016. http://abbanetzwerk.tumblr.com.

"Artist Interviews." *The Berlin Studio Program.* Accessed July 10, 2015. http://www.berlin-studio-program.de/artist-interviews/.

Colomb, Claire. *Staging the New Berlin: Place Marketing and the Politics of Urban Reinvention Post-1989.* London: Routledge, 2012.

"Economic Prospects Report: Berlin Tops Germany for 'Creative Class,'" *Spiegel Online,* October 10, 2007. Accessed March 12, 2017. http://www.spiegel.de/international/business/economic-prospects-report-berlin-tops-germany-for-creative-class-a-510609.html.

Fesel, Anke, and Chris Keller, eds. *Berlin Wonderland: Wild Years Revisited 1990–1996.* Berlin: Gestalten, 2014.

Fleischmann, Marc. "Postbahnhof, Erdmann-Höfe, Wasserturm, Nalepastraße: Der neue Coup des Immo-Phantoms." *Berliner Kurier,* June 9, 2015. Accessed March 12, 2017. http://www.berliner-kurier.de/kiez-stadt/postbahnhof—erdmann-hoefe—wasserturm—nalepastrasse-der-neue-coup-des-immo-phantoms,7169128,30905714.html.

Florida, Richard. *Cities and the Creative Class.* New York: Routledge, 2005.

———. *The Rise of the Creative Class: And How It's Transforming Work, Leisure, Community, and Everyday Life.* New York: Basic Books, 2002.

Gallenmüller, Tanja. *Mind the Gap: Zwischennutzung von Leerräumen am Beispiel des Quartiers Boxhagener Platz.* Mammendorf: Pro-Literatur-Verlag, 2004.

Harvey, David. "The Art of Rent: Globalization, Monopoly and the Commodification of Culture." *Socialist Register* 38 (2002): 93–110.

———. *Spaces of Hope.* Edinburgh: Edinburgh University Press, 2000.

Kleilein, Doris. "Die letzte Insel," *Bauwelt* 6 (2016): 2.

McNamara Rea. "Curating in a Loaded Void: Art in Berlin's Vacant Communist Architecture." *Art F City* (blog), September 18, 2015. Accessed March 12, 2017. http://artfcity.com/2015/09/18/curating-in-a-loaded-void-art-in-berlins-vacant-communist-architecture/.

Montgomery, John. "Beware 'The Creative Class': Creativity and Wealth Creation Revisited." *Local Economy* 20, no. 4 (2005): 337–43.

Novy, Johannes, and Claire Colomb. "Struggling for the Right to the (Creative) City in Berlin and Hamburg: New Urban Social Movements, New 'Spaces of Hope'?" *International Journal of Urban and Regional Research* 37, no. 5 (2013): 1816–38. Accessed August 10, 2015. doi:10.1111/j.1468-2427.2012.01115.x_.

Pataczek, Anna. "Bedrohte Atelierhäuser in Berlin: Atelier ade." *Der Tagesspiegel,* September 12, 2014. Accessed March 12, 2017. http://www.tagesspiegel.de/berlin/bedrohte-atelierhaeuser-in-berlin-atelier-ade/10661700.html.

raumlabor berlin. *Art City Lab.* Berlin: Jovis Verlag, 2015.

Rosler, Martha. "Culture Class: Art, Creativity, Urbanism." *e-flux* 21, no. 12 (2010). Accessed September 10, 2015. Accessed March 12, 2017. http://www.e-flux.com/journal/culture-class-art-creativity-urbanism-part-i/.

Schmidl, Karin. "Das größte Musikzentrum der Welt soll in Berlin entstehen." *Berliner Zeitung,* July 5, 2015.

———. "'Kunst am Spreeknie' lockt Kreative," *Berliner Zeitung,* July 11, 2015. Accessed March 12, 2017. http://www.berliner-zeitung.de/berlin/schoenew eide—kunst-am-spreeknie—lockt-kreative,10809148,16590224.html.

Schmidt, Florian. "Stellungnahme." *Kulturwerk des bkk berlin.* Accessed August 30, 2015. http://www.bbk-kulturwerk.de/con/kulturwerk/upload/ate liers/2015-08-20_Stellunghahme_AB_zu_HH_2016-17_FINAL.pdf.

Stewart, Janet. "The Kunsthaus Tacheles: The Berlin Architecture Debate of the 1990s in Micro-Historical Context." In *Recasting German Identity: Culture, Politics and Literature in the Berlin Republic,* edited by Stuart Taberner and Frank Finlay, 51–66. Rochester, NY: Camden House, 2005.

Suhr, Constanze. "Atelierhäuser in Berlin." *tip-Berlin,* September 19, 2014, http://www.tip-berlin.de/kultur-und-freizeit/atelierhauser-berlin.

Westphal, Dirk. "Die großen Bauherren des Berliner Monopolys." *Die Welt,* February 23, 2014.

Wrobel, Karolina. "Industriebauten in der Genslerstraße ziehen internationale Künstler an." *Berliner Woche,* April 4, 2013. Accessed March 12, 2017. http://www.berliner-woche.de/neu-hohenschoenhausen/sonstiges/industrie-bauten-in-der-genslerstrasse-ziehen-internationale-kuenstler-an-d25278.html.

Wurster, Stefanie. "Ein vergessenes Idyll." *taz,* September 17, 2015. Accessed March 12, 2017. http://www.taz.de/!5229352/.

Zukin, Sharon. *Loft Living: Culture and Capital in Urban Change.* New Brunswick, NJ: Rutgers University Press, 1982.

CHAPTER 5

Negotiating Cold War Legacies
The Discursive Ambiguity
of Berlin's Memory Sites

Stefanie Eisenhuth and Scott H. Krause

Berlin's history has never been more fun. Today, tourists can indulge in eating a typical East German *Softeis* at the East Side Gallery, buying a Soviet military hat at the former Checkpoint Charlie border crossing, imagining Hitler's last hours in his bunker at the parking lot that replaced it, driving around in an old Trabi, spending a few uneasy minutes in a former Stasi prison's cellar, and walking through a GDR passport control cabin at the *Tränenpalast*. Berlin's numerous historic places seem to form a gigantic open-air museum of twentieth-century history, offering pleasure-seeking travelers an amalgam of history and entertainment. While city trips have soared by 58 percent within the last five years across the globe,[1] Berlin has emerged as one of Europe's most popular tourist destinations: with an expected 30 million overnight stays in 2015, the city now competes with the numbers of Paris and London. Given the German capital's reputation for being "poor but sexy" (Klaus Wowereit), one might expect that many locals would welcome this development as it brings not only people but also revenue to the city. However, the increasing influx of tourists has spawned considerable criticism and even anti-tourist sentiments,[2] illustrating a broader conundrum. On the one hand, more and more European cities complain about a negative impact of tourism such as the "Disneyization"[3] of historic neighborhoods: several Italian heritage protection organizations have already asked UNESCO to put Venice on its list of endangered world heritage; Barcelona is suing homestay sites such as Airbnb after thousands of locals took to the streets protesting against "binge tourism." On the other hand, all these cities also benefit from popular interest in their history, and they also provide the necessary infrastructure to cater to tourists' needs—often by simplifying and "spectacularizing history" as Ayse N. Erek and Eszter Gantner argue in this volume.

Moreover, cash-strapped Berlin exemplifies a second trend in which historical authenticity has become a powerful currency. The notion of having to preserve localities with a dark past for commemorative and educational purposes is a recent phenomenon.[4] Since the 1970s, history workshops[5] made local historical remnants visible again by searching for the forgotten or suppressed past of their immediate surroundings, thus turning seemingly insignificant spots into significant sites of commemoration. Due to an increased longing for "authenticity,"[6] these places are nowadays ascribed a certain aura of truthfulness, and their preservation enables visitors to approach the past not only intellectually but also emotionally.[7] This "pathos of authenticity,"[8] however, obscures the fact that "'place' is variously 'made up'—not only in rooted locations but also through memory and imagination and the various media that enable them."[9] By assigning historical meaning to previously ignored localities, they become part of a group's heritage and a potential destination for visitors. Already in 1990, Ashworth and Tunbridge described the phenomenon of the tourist-historic city: as an urban resource, "heritage ... supplies a major 'history industry' which shapes not merely the form but the functioning and purpose of the 'commodified' city."[10] Ascribing this phenomenon only to the work of a so-called heritage industry, however, ignores the "communicative construction" of a heritage site.[11] According to Jennifer Jordan, it is mostly due to four forces that a place is being remembered: first, so-called "memorial entrepreneurs"; second, past and current use of the site at stake; third, public versus private landownership; fourth, public attention and appreciation.[12] Various actors contribute to this process of urban "imagineering" in order to establish and promote a certain image or reputation of a city.[13] A dark past can thereby turn from a stigma into a competitive advantage.

Studying the architectural *Ghosts of Berlin*, Brian Ladd has highlighted that "contradictory images shape contemporary decisions about architecture, planning, and preservation."[14] Within the discourses of urban "imagineering," buildings or places matter "because they are the symbols and the repositories of memory."[15] However, Berlin as an incoherent and often contradictory site of memory still complicates the process of memorializing the Cold War era, even twenty-six years after German reunification: "The Wall and other monuments recall controversial deeds, mostly of the recent past, deeds that prevent any consensus about the sort of things that monuments are supposed to embody, such as national identity or a common ideal."[16] Yet, the ghosts of the past and an uncertainty about the future were already haunting Berlin before the year 1989 added another historical layer to the city's texture.[17] To this day, the city's various names—Westberlin, West-Berlin, Berlin (West), Ost-Berlin, Berlin–Capital of the GDR, Greater Berlin—carry distinct and competing historic associations. Moreover, the political East-West rivalry engendered myths that propagandists on both sides polished into narratives: Berlin was a showcase of the West and the East, the capital of socialist Germany as well as a bulwark against it, a hotspot as well as a forgotten relic of the Cold War. The many competing Berlin narratives—also discussed by Sarah Pogoda and Rüdiger Traxler in this volume—highlight how historical authenticity in present-day Berlin derives from competing discursive constructs.[18] The selective appropriation of historical tropes from Berlin's rich—and often horrific—past opens the possibility for a compartmentalization of history around the colliding interests in the "tourist-historic city."

Using the three currently most heavily contested sites as case studies, this chapter will discuss decisive aspects of the multifaceted process of creating an urban memoryscape in Berlin. It will highlight who tries to have an impact on what is being remembered, how, and to what purpose.

First, the debate about the former border crossing point Checkpoint Charlie illustrates the local struggle for interpretational sovereignty over the city's recent history. Second, the discussion about the future of the former headquarters of the GDR's Ministry for State Security (Stasi) located at Normannenstraße reveals different opinions regarding the appropriate forms of dealing with "shadow places."[19] Third, debates on the memorial landscape of the former *Tempelhof* Airport uncover the geographic layering of competing historical memory tropes in Berlin, as well how local inhabitants couch their interests in their own historic interpretations. Taken together, this chapter will demonstrate the discursive nature of memorial sites. No matter how dark a place's past has been, if and how that place is being remembered depends entirely on societal negotiations and present needs.

Checkpoint Charlie: Negotiating Who Won the Cold War

Few places illustrate Berlin's troubled relationship with its past as plainly as the former Checkpoint Charlie border crossing. Opened as a crossing point for Allied personnel, diplomats, and foreign citizens after the erection of the Wall, the October 1961 standoff between American and Soviet tanks cemented its place as an epicenter of the Cold War. Countless period pieces, such as most recently Steven Spielberg's *Bridge of Spies,* reinforce this status to this day. Its reputation attracts a steadily increasing stream of tourists from across the world. Instead of a death strip, tourists now encounter *Döner* stands; vendors peddling (presumably fake) pieces of the Berlin Wall have long replaced GDR border guards; and students supplement their income by posing for pictures in American and Soviet uniforms at the congested thoroughfare.[20]

While few local stakeholders are content with the current status of Checkpoint Charlie, the decades-long quest to commemorate the Cold War past appropriately has elicited political passions from bygone eras. Checkpoint Charlie demonstrates the imprint left in Berlin by the victorious powers of World War II, first as wartime Allies, then as competing partisans in the Cold War, occupying Berlin from 1945 until 1990. Moreover, the site's geographical centrality and popularity upsets the commemorative status quo that has artificially compartmentalized these politically delicate memories. After reunification, the *Alliierten-museum* (Allied Museum) opened in the former US Outpost Theater in suburban Zehlendorf. Its permanent exhibition "How Enemies Became Friends" seeks to celebrate cultural bonding between West Berliners and Western Allied forces in the face of the Communist enemy. Less than twenty years after its inauguration, the *Alliiertenmuseum*'s permanent exhibition still carries the air of victory and nostalgia for the Western comrades in arms. Visitors are mostly comprised of middle-aged West Berliners and Allied veterans on vacation. The other Allied force in Berlin, the Soviet Union, was consoled with its own, smaller German-Russian Museum located at the former Capitulation Museum (a branch of the Central Museum of Armed Forces Moscow since 1967 until the new museum opened in 1995) in Karlshorst. Its exhibition highlights the sacrifices of the Soviet population and army during World War II, while sidestepping the controversial policies the USSR pursued during the Cold War.

This institutional setup separating Eastern and Western sensibilities has created a vacuum that has been filled by a Cold War relic retrofitted into a shrine. In 1962, anti-GDR activist Rainer Hildebrandt opened his own private exhibition next to Checkpoint Charlie highlighting the suffering wrought by the Berlin Wall. Since then, the exhibition has been expanded significantly. Although the Wall itself has long come down, the institutional structure of the *Mauermuseum* (Wall Museum) has not changed. Since Hildebrandt's death, his widow has added hagiographic sections celebrating the museum's founder variously as Resistance fighter against Hitler, thorn in the side of the GDR regime, and global human rights activist. Today, this private exhibition with no scholarly advisory board continues to hold a commanding position at the former Checkpoint Charlie. Ascribed historical authenticity and symbolism attract visitors to this downtown intersection, regardless of this shadow place's educational offerings.

In 2009, politicians and academics proposed opening a new Cold War Museum at this location to prevent the site's irrevocable transformation into a "Snackpoint Charlie."[21] A diverse cast ranging from Czech dissident and later president Václav Havel to former West Berlin mayor Hans-Jochen Vogel to former US secretary of state Lawrence S. Eagleburger sought to offer a state-of-the-art educational opportunity to the masses of visitors interested in the Cold War.[22] A first temporary exhibition on site has met immediate success.[23] However, self-appointed custodians of West Berlin's Cold War heroics attacked the new Cold War museum project as if it had been concocted by Communist functionaries determined to distort history. Gunnar Schupelius, commentator of the (in)famous tabloid *B.Z.*, accused organizers of a biased approach to history: "At Checkpoint Charlie, one has to point out who was the aggressor after 1945: ... The Soviets [and] the SED under Walter Ulbricht. It is as simple and brutal as that. ... Who wants us to sweep the Communist atrocities under the carpet?"[24] The Christian Democratic Union (CDU), one of Berlin's governing parties, has picked up on this sentiment, fearing that the new museum would "downplay Soviet guilt." To rule out such interpretations, CDU members have alternatively suggested moving the *Alliiertenmuseum* to the vacated *Tempelhof* Airport of 1948/49 Airlift fame.[25]

Yet contextualization is not marginalization but the chance to move beyond the dichotomy of two antagonistic camps in narrating the Cold War. In a city littered with costly, at times megalomaniacal projects, misplaced thrift has jeopardized the Cold War Museum. After years of legal and political wrangling, the City of Berlin finally secured a desired plot for the Museum in December 2015 at the intersection of the former border crossing. In return, the city permitted the real-estate owner to construct Germany's first "Hard Rock Hotel."[26] This municipal deal gives the city the opportunity to educate its citizens and visitors on Cold War history by presenting a fresh perspective that highlights the internal volatility within the blocs and the exchanges between them to explain the conflict's remarkably peaceful conclusion. Any plausible history of the

Cold War needs to portray the two belligerent camps behind it. This does not mean moral equation of both sides, but dispassionate analysis of internal developments and disputes within the blocs. For instance, a hagiographic narrative of the West cannot sufficiently explain the GDR's terminal crisis. The Cold War's conclusion rather derived from a complex amalgam consisting of long-term developments that resulted in the overall erosion of the Eastern bloc, the formation of opposition groups, the mass exodus in the summer of 1989, and finally the ever-growing demonstrations in the fall and winter of 1989/90.[27] Conversely, Berlin served as the focal point not only of the Cold War but also of German postwar rehabilitation.[28] Both momentous developments were not insulated but rather coalesced uniquely in Berlin, where anti-Communist passions galvanized West Berliners productively toward a stable democracy. The political vitriol attached to the intersection's redevelopment might continue as long as the issue is framed as which side won the Cold War. It mirrors and even extends almost forgotten conflict lines that a new generation intends to overcome. But as long as those who fought the Cold War still shape public debates, agreement on a coherent narrative in the once divided city seems impossible. However, the redevelopment of Checkpoint Charlie anchored around a state-of-the-art museum would not only satisfy the curiosity of tourists but offer the chance for a new generation to narrate the Cold War in a way that incorporates the perspectives of East and West, bringing its impact on present-day Europe into view.

The "Campus for Democracy": Preserving vs. Recoding Space

At the height of the Peaceful Revolution, thousands of GDR citizens stormed the headquarters of the Ministry for State Security (MfS or Stasi) on January 15, 1990, to prevent its officers from continuing their work and from destroying their records.[29] In September of the same year, several members of the GDR opposition occupied parts of the building again and successfully forced the East and West German governments to include the Stasi records in the German Reunification Treaty.[30] Many records on surveillance and repression thus survived, and the government agency of the Federal Commissioner for the Records of the State Security Service of the former German Democratic Republic (BStU) was created to balance transparency over the Stasi's deeds with the privacy rights of its victims. Since then, the BStU has added an impressive outreach program to educate the public on the regime's repressive apparatus. The approaching expiration date in 2019 of parts of the Stasi Records Law (*Stasi-Unterlagen-Gesetz,* StUG) has initiated a debate regarding the overall future of the BStU as it had been considered a temporary institution from its inception. The possible dissolution of one of the biggest and internationally most prominent actors in the field of German memory politics has alarmed many other institutions that are shaping Germany's historical-political education. While some are eagerly hoping for a redistribution of the BStU's funds, others fear that the proposed transferal of the MfS files to the Federal Archive would turn the Stasi's victims into regular archival users without adequate support. Searching for a compromise, Federal Commissioner Roland Jahn has proposed turning the former Stasi headquarters at Berlin's Normannenstraße[31] into a Campus for Democracy—a venue that would simultaneously serve as an archive, as a place to commemorate the Stasi's victims, and as a center for historical-political education. This way, the Stasi records could stay in their traditional place (even if the Federal Archive was in charge of handling them), and the half-abandoned compound could be converted to a new use. Jahn highlighted the multilayered nature of the former headquarters in an interview on this project[32]: it is a place that represents not only repression but also the Peaceful Revolution. The Stasi Record Law, which has already enabled over 3 million individuals to read the files compiled on them, results from the courageous protests of the East German opposition movement. Jahn therefore insisted that the site also symbolizes the overcoming of dictatorship, the enlightenment of a previously oppressed population, and the ability to teach lessons about power mechanisms and surveillance.[33] Referring to the Human Rights Center in Cottbus,[34] he underlined that a historically burdened place allows people to address urgent questions of the present and should thus be actively used as a venue to debate and shape a democratic society.

Several architects, students, and other supporters have in the meantime developed ideas for the proposed Campus for Democracy. A first concept included the already existing exhibition State Security in the SED Dictatorship at the *Stasi Museum* (building #1), and the Stasi archive (building #7, #8 and #9) as well as the currently vacant former dining facility (building #22) and the former supply sector (building #18). Under the plan, the dining facility will be transformed into an information center with a library, a bookshop, a conference room, and a café. The supply sector—which contains several meeting rooms and a movie theater—will provide space for events. The Union of the Associations for the Victims of Communist Tyranny,[35] an umbrella organization for thirty different victim associations, has its office in building #1. The plans also included the archive of the GDR opposition (Robert Havemann Association, RHG).[36] After a protracted struggle to secure funding for a move, the RHG will soon reopen its doors within the compound.

Presented in January 2015 at a public event dedicated to the twenty-fifth anniversary of the dissolution of the Stasi, this concept initiated a heated debate about the appropriate use of the ambivalent locality. Besides the broader controversy about suitable forms of commemorating the Stasi's victims while simultaneously mediating history in a way that appeals especially to younger generations, the underlying assumptions regarding space and authenticity are quite revealing. While most panelists agreed on the overall importance of preserving the former headquarters, the idea by a group of students caused an outcry: in order to draw young people, they had suggested to turn the roof of building #18 into a beach bar that could then be used as an "idea lab." Two panelists applauded the idea, as it would turn a site that had been a symbol of suppression and surveillance for decades into a new forum for ideas and participation. Other panelists, however, insisted that such a dark place could only be used as a memorial site that focuses on commemoration and historical education. Fearing a rapid "touristification" and "eventization," they warned against any obfuscation of the buildings' painful past through what they perceived as a disrespectful use of this "authentic place." The proponents responded by insisting that historical education should not only please a certain intellectual elite; instead, these "shadow places" should inspire and encourage everyone to reflect on the present and develop ideas for the future—whereby people would appropriate historically burdened space and positively reinterpret it.[37]

In November 2014, an Expert Commission on the Future of the Agency of the BStU was appointed in order to make suggestions regarding the imminent transformation. Their suggestions have to take into account the StUG, the overall German Memorial Site Concept (*Gedenkstätten-konzept des Bundes*), and the future of the former MfS headquarters.

In April 2016, the commission's report broadly endorsed Jahn's vision. It recommended to the *Bundestag* to dissolve the BStU and delegate the responsibility for all its archival holdings to the Federal Archives (even though the records would remain in situ). A new Dictatorship and Resistance Foundation (*Stiftung Diktatur und Widerstand*) would be put in charge of coordinating the different facilities and NGOs and Normannenstraße. The BStU's research branch is intended as a spinoff for an independent Research Institute on GDR State Security in a Comparative Perspective (*Forschungsstelle DDR-Staatssicherheit in vergleichender*

Perspektive). The office of the federal commissioner would be rebranded as the Federal Commissioner for Examining the SED Dictatorship and its Consequences.[38] Several journalists, politicians and historians opposed these ideas quite strongly, interpreting them as an attempt to put an end to the process of coming to terms with the past or even to whitewash the SED regime.[39] While the debate is still going on, parts of the compound (building #15, the former offices of the Stasi's foreign espionage) are now used as a refugee camp, and those in favor of the campus are trying to create a fait accompli: the Federal Government has recently repurchased the former dining facility, and a new information center along with a library and a café is supposed to open in 2019.[40]

The ongoing debate about the future of the Stasi headquarters highlights how a certain aura gets ascribed to historically burdened localities. Many observers feel as if the past of these "shadow places" imposes certain parameters for future usage. In this view a semi-abandoned compound seems more appropriate and dignified than an experimental rooftop venue that may draw younger people to these places. However, the authenticity ascribed to these shadow places and the ideas of what would be the appropriate reuse result from societal negotiation. Whether such a site of oppression becomes a memorial site or a creative forum for political education depends on present needs and beliefs, on the kind of role society ascribes to historical sites. Moreover, material motives further fuel these clashes for interpretational sovereignty between different "memorial entrepreneurs:" The German Memorial Site Concept binds together memory and place. For any memorial initiative, it is more likely to get a permanent institutional funding if its activities are tied to an "authentic" site. Yet veterans of the GDR opposition have not been able to establish their own memorial sites, since they met clandestinely in private living rooms or the cellars and backrooms of churches. Hence appropriating former sites of oppression that entail guaranteed federal funding enables them to break the cycle of annual grant applications and the related financial uncertainty.

Tempelhofer Freiheit: Appropriating the Past for the Future

Few spaces in Berlin embody the city's contradictory incarnations during the twentieth century like the *Tempelhofer Feld*. Before World War I, the vast field had been used as a recreational area, a parade ground for the Prussian army, and a practice area for aviation enthusiasts. The *Tempelhof* Airport terminal, however, is a reminder of the Nazis' attempt to alter Berlin's cityscape through an imposing and allegedly "Germanic" architectural style. Since the 1920s, Nazi propaganda had diligently nurtured the perception of Berlin as a depraved metropolis foreign to the rest of the country to legitimize the "Fight for Berlin" that culminated in the street violence of the early 1930s.[41] After the Nazis' seizure of power, Berlin NSDAP *Gauleiter* Goebbels sought to transform the diverse metropolis into a Nazi stronghold—partly to improve his own standing among the party leadership. In order to Nazify the city, Goebbels turned to architecture that met Hitler's approval and hurriedly undertook major construction projects. The party imposed itself onto the cityscape with pompous projects such as Hitler's Chancellery and underground bunker, the Olympic Stadium for the 1936 Games, and Ernst Sagebiel's *Reichsluftfahrtministerium*, or Ministry of Aviation. The terminal building for the new *Tempelhof* Airport designed by the same Sagebiel was the largest Nazi construction project that neared completion.[42] The sprawling complex paved over the grounds of the infamous *KZ Columbia-Haus,* a first-generation concentration camp in which the Nazis had imprisoned and tortured their enemies since the first days of their rule. During the war, the new terminal became a production hub for the German war effort where forced laborers and inmates from satellite camps toiled under degrading conditions.[43]

In the postwar era, this Nazi regime vestige experienced a most unlikely rebranding, being linked with "freedom."[44] Despite the ubiquitous destruction wrought by years of aerial bombardment and the Battle of Berlin in April 1945, this building had survived the war nearly unscathed. Following the Potsdam Agreement, the US Office of Military Government (OMGUS) took control of the airport in July 1945 and used it as the main supply base for the American occupation in Berlin. During the 1948–49 Berlin Airlift, it shed the glaringly incriminating legacies of the most recent past to become firmly associated with the stubborn insistence on liberal democratic values in the Cold War, reflecting the image of the truncated Western half-city it served.

This transmogrification derived from a transatlantic campaign. Together, West Berlin Social Democratic politicians and American occupation officials presented West Berlin as "the Outpost of Freedom" against Communist encroachment, celebrating *Tempelhof* Airport as hub of the Airlift and a symbol for German-American bonding.[45] Veteran West Berlin journalist Peter Bender has wryly pointed out the American-led Airlift's two dimensions. Besides the "technical, organizational, and humanitarian brilliance" of the logistical feat, the Airlift had an even larger propagandistic effect: "If President Truman would have employed a public relations firm with staging the containment of Communism, it would have needed to invent the Airlift."[46]

Truman did not stage the Berlin crisis that precipitated the Airlift, but his local allies capitalized on *Tempelhof* as spatial confirmation of German democratic rehabilitation in the Cold War. Moreover, they promoted *Tempelhof* as the core of the "Outpost of Freedom" in a fifteen-year-long public relations campaign. Immediately after the Soviets had lifted their blockade, Mayor Ernst Reuter inaugurated the hastily re-named *Platz der Luftbrücke,* or Airlift Square, in the shadow of Sagebiel's terminal: "We have put a year behind us that will go down in history. Not only in the history of this city, in the history of Europe, but in the history of the world. Our valiant resistance has encouraged the world to help us, and the world has come to our assistance."[47] Besides triumphal rhetoric after enduring nine months of continued hardship, Reuter offered his constituents a comprehensive vision for democratization: understanding West Berlin as bastion of militant democracy lent Berliners political relevance in the Cold War, recognition as victims of Communism that increasingly displaced unsettling questions of culpability for the Nazis' crimes, and a blueprint for democratic reconstruction. In light of these stakes, the city of West Berlin and the US Mission Berlin institutionalized an Airlift commemoration that was anchored around *Tempelhof* Airport for years to come.[48]

Throughout the Cold War decades, *Tempelhof* served both as an US Air Force base and a city airport. However, the advent of the jet age during the 1960s prompted most major airlines to move their operations to *Tegel* Airport. The limited traffic ensured that modern mass aviation did not compete with the heroic myth of *Tempelhof.* A *Rosinenbomber,* or candy bomber (a vintage DC-3 in US Air Force livery), that offered scenic flights around Berlin's airspace for decades reinforced this myth, but it also served as an indicator for *Tempelhof*'s enduring popularity. German reunification in 1990 gave the amalgamated city of Berlin the chance to restructure its transportation corridors. It rebuilt *Schönefeld* Airport, and together with the surrounding state of Brandenburg, re-united Berlin decided to consolidate its three historic airports into one dubbed "Berlin-Brandenburg International." While the botched implementation of this venture continues to attract national and international ridicule, *Tempelhof* Airport was closed in 2008. While many Berliners welcomed the reduced noise pollution, a significant segment of former West Berliners mourned the airport that signified a lifeline to the "free world" during the days of division.

The end of aviation at *Tempelhof* opened vast tracts of real estate for redevelopment in Berlin's center. Yet the airport's landmark status and sheer scale put the city in a quandary regarding the site's future use. In characteristic Berlin fashion, the municipal Senate first introduced a temporary concept titled *Tempelhofer Freiheit* (Tempelhof Freedom), while exploring the options for the site's long-term use.[49] The terminal building has been opened to business startups and advertised as a concert venue.[50] The former airfield was opened into a large, nearly four-square-kilometer park that has meanwhile proved popular beyond expectations, attracting between 1.5 and 2 million visitors annually. While the new name was supposed to reference the site's multifaceted history and legacy, the park's most vocal users rather appreciated the freedom from commercial designs it offered and have wanted to preserve it as a space for creative experimentation.[51]

The open question of the field's future shape made it a centerpiece in political debates on the quality of life in Berlin that many saw as eroding with rising rents. In 2014, the grassroots initiative *100% Tempelhofer Feld* collected over 185,000 signatures to add a proposition to the ballots that would preserve municipal ownership and maintain the entire former airfield as the city's "green jewel."[52] Berlin voters approved this proposition in a citywide referendum over the Berlin Senate vision that planned the "circumspect development" of "affordable housing" on the site's "edges."[53] Popular resentment against the inability of Berlin urban politics to stem the gentrification of the city's central districts propelled the referendum's success. Ironically, the failure of plans to add rental units within the central *Ringbahn* perimeter coincided with drastically rising rents in the traditionally heavily immigrant neighborhood of Neukölln that was once in the airport's flight path and was now adjacent to the large park.

A year later, *Tempelhof* Airfield has not only become the site of the pursuit of urban utopias but also a stark reminder of the ongoing European refugee crisis. In October 2015, the surge of refugees entering the EU led the Berlin Senate to house 2,300 refugees in the terminal building on short notice. The city converted hangers into makeshift shelters, offering bunk beds divided only by sheets, but few sanitation facilities, with a shuttle service to off-site showers.[54] Under pressure to house hundreds of newly arrived refugees each day, the Berlin Senate unveiled plans to rapidly expand these shelters. Under these new plans, the city would build five housing halls, a dining hall, a kindergarten, and a school for up to 7,000 refugees on the site.[55] The desire of these refugees to find freedom from violence and persecution divided the local park activists. While many local Berliners have volunteered in the refugee shelters, activist group *100% Tempelhof* decried the recent plans of the Berlin Senate as "ghettos on the [air]field rather than integration in the city."[56]

These current disputes underscore *Tempelhof*'s relevance both as a mirror of the challenges facing the city and as a gauge for the city's creativity in finding solutions for them. While all stakeholders agree that the former airport should remain recognizable as such, the long-term visions for the site clash. While the city administration views the former airport as real estate available for development in a growing city, grassroots activists contend that preserving the property opens a unique space for relaxation and experimentation. While the city wants to shelter refugees there and engage with the historical memory attached to the site institutionally by bringing the *Alliiertenmuseum* to *Tempelhof,*[57] the activists see the airfield as an urban reserve of the noncommercial creativity that shaped the city during the 1980s and 1990s. However, the debate about *Tempelhof* Airport has drawn attention to its multilayered history. Just like in the 1970s and 1980s, when the history workshop movement started to literally unearth local history, Berliners realized the ambiguity of yet another historic site. Whether its future will be dominated by remembrance or recreation is still up to societal negotiation. Currently the place combines both, enabling visitors to first take part in a guided tour about the Third Reich or the Cold War and afterward enjoy a sunbath or have a BBQ right in front of the most monumental relic of Berlin's shattered past.

Not One but Many Berlins

The architectural traces of Berlin's past and its eclectic functionalization comprise a unique tableau that attracts visitors as it challenges locals. The contentious relationship between space and memory reflects the crosscurrents between global and local that had defined politics in Cold War Berlin. The twentieth century created a fractured urban memoryscape in which the fault lines run not only chronologically but also geographically due to the city's division during the Cold War. The unique arsenal of sites illuminates the discursive nature of heritage and authenticity, the competing interests that shape them, the contentious debates on the future of these historically fraught sites, and finally the opposing interpretations of twentieth-century history that animates these debates.[58] While all stakeholders seem to agree on the importance of preserving Berlin's "shadow places," it is hard to reach a consensus regarding their purpose and message. Private and public museums, nongovernmental initiatives, and numerous smaller commemorative projects compete not only for funding, attention, and visitors but also for interpretational sovereignty.

The city currently has over ten museums that display different aspects of the city's Cold War history.[59] In most of them, though, the city only serves as an example for the nation's division and the successful overcoming of it in 1989. Many Cold War oddities that were unique to Berlin have simply been forgotten; other remnants of the city's past experienced an intentional process of erasure. Especially during the 1990s, monuments were dismantled and streets renamed; some buildings were destroyed, while others are now being restored. In many cases, only gaps and voids or maybe a plaque serve as reminders of the past. Most people are aware of this process with regard to East Berlin. However, many of West Berlin's iconic places and characteristics are gone as well. Most of them disappeared slowly while others are about to disappear.[60]

Especially debates about the future of ambivalent places that are connected with several historic events or conflicting memories bring the politically charged disagreements over the past to the fore. Checkpoint Charlie, the Stasi compound, and *Tempelhof* Airport lend themselves to multiple interpretations. Competing understandings of the city's past engender fierce debates over which interpretation to privilege regarding these sites. Will casual tourists take away from Checkpoint Charlie that the Western side "won" the Cold War or that a decades-long global nuclear standoff could be ended peacefully by popular demand? Should the former MfS headquarters be preserved in its GDR condition as a memorial to its victims or should it house an outreach operation promoting the ideals of the civil society's Peaceful Revolution that brought the Stasi to its knees? What balance between the past and the future will the city strike at *Tempelhof*'s hulking hangars?

These complex issues centered on individual properties within the city illustrate how Berlin is not a coherent, unequivocal *lieu de mémoire*, but rather an arena of battlefields for interpretational sovereignty. According to Pierre Nora, a *lieu de mémoire* is "any significant entity, whether material or nonmaterial in nature, which by dint of human will or the work of time has become a symbolic element of the memorial heritage of any community."[61] It thus represents, establishes, and passes on a group's collective identity. This definition suggests why analyzing Cold War Berlin as a *lieu de mémoire* is rather problematic: there are many groups who remember Cold War Berlin quite differently. Despite

Nora's famous claim—"there are no longer any milieux de memoire, set-tings in which memory is a real part of everyday experience"—the ex-amples given have shown that the multifaceted experience of divided Berlin prevents the establishment of a coherent narrative of the city's history. According to Alexander Huyssen, the reunited city still is a "fas-cinating mix" of "presence and absence, memory and forgetting,"[62] a "text frantically being written and re-written."[63]

Memories of Cold War Berlin are still divided by time and space. East Berliners remember different things than West Berliners. West Germans remember different things than West Berliners. To one generation, the Wall was a constant reminder of the unnatural separation of their city and their country. To those generations of West Berliners that had never experienced the city without a wall and to those who moved there in the 1970s and 1980s, it was often just the annoying cause of delays when they wanted to go on holidays. To their East Berlin counterparts, the other half of the city was an imagined space mediated through ra-dio, television, or stories told by their parents, grandparents, or Western relatives.[64] The Wall has turned the city into a divided space of experi-ence and memory—at the same time it also provided the few shared memories East and West Berliners have. Being the only German city possessing both an Eastern and Western legacy, Berlin has often "been the center of discussion about diplomatic, pedagogical, and artistic re-sponses to Germany's troubled past."[65] This leaves Cold War Berlin in peculiar limbo regarding its place in Germany's cultural memory. On the one hand, aspects of the city's history are part of Germany's his-toriographical "master narrative." On the other hand, it has become a "cipher, an essentially empty space in which by chance as it were, a Cold War battle took place."[66] Despite the century-long tradition of complaining about Berlin being the most un-German city,[67] non-Berlin Germans' numerous jeers stemming from East and West Berlin's status as a "spoiled" showcase of each respective political system, and the very unique memories tied to living close to the Wall, the city is now ironi-cally the focal point of German history and is supposed to represent the overall German Cold War experience.[68]

Stefanie Eisenhuth is a research fellow at the History Department of Berlin's Humboldt University and at the Centre for Contemporary His-tory Potsdam. Her research interests include the history of West Berlin and the GDR, public history, and historical authenticity. Stefanie's cur-rent project examines the American occupation of West Berlin.

Scott H. Krause is a Leibniz-DAAD fellow at the Centre for Contemporary History Potsdam. He specializes in the cultural history of German-American relations and their political repercussions. His current project charts West Berlin's transformation from the capital of Nazi Germany to a symbol of freedom and democracy in the Cold War.

Notes

1. See "ITB World Travel Trends Report 2014/2015," accessed June 1, 2016, http://www.itb-berlin.de/media/itbk/itbk_dl_en/WTTR_Report_A4_4_Web.pdf.
2. See Henning Füller and Boris Michel, "'Stop Being a Tourist!': New Dynamics of Urban Tourism in Berlin-Kreuzberg," *International Journal of Urban and Regional Research* 38, no. 4 (2014): 1304–18.
3. See Alan E. Bryman, "The Disneyization of Society," *Sociological Review* 47, no. 1 (1999): 25–47; Frank Roost, *Die Disneyfizierung der Städte* (Opladen, 2000).
4. See Volkhard Knigge, "Vom Zeugniswert der authentischen Substanz für die Gedenkstättenarbeit," in *Denkmalpflege für die Berliner Mauer: Die Konservierung eines unbequemen Bauwerks; Beiträge zur Geschichte von Mauer und Flucht,* ed. Axel Klausmeier and Günter Schlusche (Berlin, 2011), 65–71.
5. The history workshops resulted from an international grassroots movement that intended to establish a more democratic approach: history "from below" with a local focus, written by academics and nonacademics alike. It is considered to be the beginning of what is nowadays called "public history."
6. Lionel Trilling, *Sincerity and Authenticity* (London, 1974); Susanne Knaller and Harro Müller, "Einleitung: Authentizität und kein Ende," in *Authentizität: Diskussion eines ästhetischen Begriffs,* ed. Susanne Knaller and Harro Müller (Paderborn, 2006), 7–16.
7. See Eva Ulrike Pirker et al., eds., *Echte Geschichte: Authentizitätsfiktionen in populären Geschichtskulturen* (Bielefeld, 2010).
8. Achim Saupe, "Authentizität, Version: 2.0," *Docupedia-Zeitgeschichte,* October 22, 2012, http://docupedia.de/zg/Authentizit.C3.A4t_Version_2.0_Achim_Saupe?oldid=106404.
9. Sharon Macdonald, *Memorylands: Heritage and Identity in Europe Today* (London, 2013), 98. See also Valentin Groebner, "Touristischer Geschichtsgebrauch. Über einige Merkmale neuer Vergangenheiten im 20. und 21. Jahrhundert," *Historische Zeitschrift* 296, no. 2 (2013): 408–28; Deepak Chhabra, Robert Healy, and Erin Sills, "Staged Authenticity and Heritage Tourism," *Annals of Tourism Research* 30, no. 3 (2003): 702–19; Sharon Macdonald, "A People's Story: Heritage, Identity and Authenticity," in *Touring Cultures: Transformations of Travel and Theory,* ed. Chris Rojek and John Urry (London, 1997), 155–75.

10. Gregory J. Ashworth and John E. Tunbridge, *The Tourist-Historic City* (London, 1990), 1f.

11. Bernhard Tschofen, "Antreten, ablehnen, verwalten? Was der Heritage-Boom den Kulturwissenschaften aufträgt," in *Prädikat Heritage: Wertschöpfungen aus kulturellen Ressourcen,* ed. Dorothee Hemme, Markus Tauschek, and Regina Bendix (Berlin, 2007), 28.

12. Jennifer A. Jordan, *Structures of Memory: Understanding German Change in Berlin and Beyond* (Stanford, 2006), 1–22.

13. Rolf Lindner, "The Imaginary of the City," in *The Contemporary Study of Culture,* ed. Bundesministerium für Wissenschaft und Verkehr/Internationales Forschungszentrum Kulturwissenschaften (Vienna, 1999), 289–94.

14. Brian Ladd, *The Ghosts of Berlin: Confronting German History in the Urban Landscape* (Chicago, 1997), 3–4.

15. Ibid. Ladd shows that what is being preserved and then advertised depends on whether one wants to define Berlin "as royal residence, as industrial and imperial powerhouse, as Nazi capital, as Cold War battleground," or as the vibrant post-Wall New Berlin.

16. Ibid., 11; See also Dirk Verheyen, *United City, Divided Memories? Cold War Legacies in Contemporary Berlin* (Lanham, MD, 2008).

17. See Krijn Thijs, "West-Berliner Visionen für eine neue Mitte: Die Internationale Bauausstellung, der 'Zentrale Bereich' und die 'Geschichtslandschaft' an der Mauer (1981–1985)," *Zeithistorische Forschungen / Studies in Contemporary History* 11, no. 2 (2014): 235–61.

18. For officially prescribed historical interpretations in political architecture, see Sarah Pogoda and Rüdiger Traxler's contribution to this volume.

19. Martin Sabrow, "Schattenorte," *Merkur* 69, no. 795 (2015): 77–84.

20. For an in-depth analysis of this phenomenon, see Sybille Frank, *Der Mauer um die Wette gedenken: Die Formation einer Heritage-Industrie am Berliner Checkpoint Charlie* (Frankfurt, 2009).

21. Kate Connolly, "Checkpoint Charlie's New Cold War with the Hot Dog Vendors," *The Guardian,* April 22, 2012, http://www.theguardian.com/world/2012/apr/22/checkpoint-charlie-hot-dog-vendors.

22. See "Aufruf zur Gründung eines 'Museums des Kalten Krieges—Teilung und Befreiung Europas,'" accessed June 1, 2016, http://www.bfgg.de/zentrum-kalter-krieg/zentrum-kalter-krieg.html.

23. Jula Danylow, "BlackBox Kalter Krieg: Ein Werkstattbesuch am Checkpoint Charlie," *Zeithistorische Forschungen / Studies in Contemporary History* 11, no. 2 (2014): 328–36.

24. Gunnar Schupelius, "Museum am Checkpoint Charlie abgelehnt," *B.Z.,* May 16, 2012, http://www.bz-berlin.de/artikel-archiv/museum-am-checkpoint-charlie-abgelehnt.

25. Timo Steppat, "Kalter Krieg am Checkpoint Charlie: Mehr Disneyland als Gedenken," *Cicero,* August 15, 2012, http://www.cicero.de/berliner-republik/mehr-disneyland-als-gedenken/51555.

26. Uwe Aulich, "Neues Museum und Hard Rock Hotel im Zentrum," *Berliner Zeitung,* December 8, 2015, http://www.berliner-zeitung.de/berlin/bebau ung-am-checkpoint-charlie-neues-museum-und-hard-rock-hotel-im-zen trum,10809148,32727332.html.

27. For a survey of the peaceful revolution, see Charles Maier, *Dissolution: The Crisis of Communism and the End of East Germany* (Princeton, 1997); Ilko-Sascha Kowalczuk, *Endspiel: Die Revolution von 1989 in der DDR* (Munich, 2009).

28. See Konrad Jarausch, "Die Teilung Europas und ihre Überwindung: Über-legungen zu einem Ausstellungskonzept für Berlin," *Zeithistorische Forschungen / Studies in Contemporary History* 5, no. 2 (2008): 263–69.

29. See Jens Schöne, "Die Besetzung der Staatssicherheit 1989/90: Vorausset-zungen und Abläufe. Ein Überblick," in *"Es lag was in der Luft": Die Beset-zungen der Bezirksverwaltungen des MfS/AfNS in Erfurt, Suhl und Gera,* ed. Hans-Joachim Veen und Peter Wurschi (Weimar, 2014), 9–27; Jens Gieseke, *The History of the Stasi: East Germany's Secret Police 1945–1990* (New York, 2014).

30. The occupant's demands can be found here: http://www.ddr89.de/ddr89/ texte/erklaerung34.html.

31. See the official database of monuments by the Berlin Senate Department for Urban Development and the Environment: http://www.stadtentwick lung.berlin.de/denkmal/liste_karte_datenbank/de/denkmaldatenbank/de tailansicht.php?id=12396.

32. Much of the information mentioned above and below is based on an inter-view with Roland Jahn conducted on November 8, 2016, at the BStU.

33. For further plans of the federal government to commemorate the Peaceful Revolution in a Freedom and Unity Memorial in the central Mitte district, see Pogoda and Traxler's contribution to this volume.

34. The *Menschenrechtszentrum Cottbus e.V.* is located at a former prison and was founded by former inmates. Its intention is to promote human rights based on historical education. http://www.menschenrechtszentrum-cott bus.de/.

35. UOKG—Union der Opferverbände Kommunistischer Gewaltherrschaft e.V., accessed June 5, 2016, http://www.uokg.de.

36. See BStU, "Campus für Demokratie—eine Ideenskizze," accessed June 1, 2016, https://www.bstu.bund.de/SharedDocs/Downloads/DE/jahn_campus.pdf.

37. Quotes are based on notes taken at the panel discussion.

38. See Deutscher Bundestag, "Bericht der Expertenkommission zur Zukunft der Behörde des Bundesbeauftragten für die Unterlagen des Staatssicher-heitsdienstes der ehemaligen DDR (BStU)," Drucksache 18/8050, April 5, 2016, https://www.bundestag.de/ausschuesse18/gremien18/bstu.

39. See Klaus-Dietmar Henke, "Gedächtnisverschiebung? Für eine kategoriale Asymmetrie bei der Auseinandersetzung mit der NS- und der SED-Zeit," *Zeitschrift für Geschichtswissenschaft* 65, no. 1 (2017): 54–65.

40. See Jutta Schütz, "Stasi-Zentrale wird Campus für Demokratie," *Der Tagesspiegel,* January 7, 2016, http://www.tagesspiegel.de/berlin/berlin-lichten berg-stasi-zentrale-wird-campus-fuer-demokratie/12802542.html.

41. Daniel Siemens, "Prügelpropaganda: Die SA und der Nationalsozialistische Mythos vom 'Kampf um Berlin,'" in *Berlin 1933–1945: Stadt und Gesellschaft im Nationalsozialismus,* ed. Michael Wildt and Cristoph Kreutzmüller (Munich, 2013), 33–50.

42. For an overview of the Nazis' construction in Berlin, see Matthias Donath, "Städtebau und Architektur," in *Berlin 1933–1945,* ed. Michael Wildt and Cristoph Kreutzmüller (Munich, 2013), 229–44.

43. For an overview of the site's use during National Socialism, see Berliner Geschichtswerkstatt, *Kein Ort der Freiheit: Das Tempelhofer Feld 1933–1945* (Berlin, 2012).

44. For another example of contradictory associations competing over one site, see the Brandenburg Gate in Pogoda and Traxler's contribution to this volume.

45. See Stefanie Eisenhuth and Scott H. Krause, "Inventing the 'Outpost of Freedom': Transatlantic Narratives and Actors Crafting West Berlin's Postwar Political Culture," in *Zeithistorische Forschungen / Studies in Contemporary History* 10, no. 2 (2014): 188–211.

46. Peter Bender, "Sterben für Berlin," in *Sterben für Berlin? Die Berliner Krisen 1948–1958,* ed. Burghard Ciesla, Michael Lemke, and Thomas Lindenberger (Berlin, 2000), 17.

47. "Einweihung des Platzes der Luftbrücke mit Redeausschnitt von Ernst Reuter," *RIAS,* June 25, 1949, DZ102443, Deutschlandradio Archiv, Berlin.

48. Günter Klein, "Vermerk über in den Vereinigten Staaten geführte Besprechungen, soweit sie Berlin betreffen," March 4, 1958, A6 1/WBA-BER-0085 Auslandsreisen USA 2.1958; England 3.1958, Willy-Brandt-Archiv im Archiv der sozialen Demokratie, Bonn; "Aufruf zur Unterstützung der Aktion 'Luftbrückendank,'" April 29, 1959, *RIAS Sammlungsgut,* Rundschreiben Geschäftsleitung, 1948–1959, Deutsches Rundfunkarchiv, Potsdam-Babelsberg. See Helmut Trotnow and Bernd von Kostka, eds., *Die Berliner Luftbrücke: Ereignis und Erinnerung* (Berlin, 2010).

49. Berliner Senatsverwaltung für Stadtentwicklung, Städtebauliche Planung: Tempelhofer Freiheit, accessed December 20, 2016, https://web.archive .org/web/20080325061621/http://www.stadtentwicklung.berlin.de/planen/ staedtebau-projekte/tempelhof/index.shtml; idem, "Zukunft—Tempelhofer Feld," March 5, 2008, http://www.stadtentwicklung.berlin.de/aktuell/presse box/archiv_volltext.shtml?arch_0803/nachricht2972.html.

50. Tempelhof Projekt GmbH, Eventlocation Flughafen Tempelhof, accessed June 18, 2017, http://www.thf-berlin.de/angebote/eventlocation/.

51. Rolf Lautenschläger, "Wo der Himmel über Berlin weit ist," *taz,* May 25, 2014, http://www.taz.de/Volksentscheid-Tempelhofer-Feld/!5042004/.

52. Elisabeth Meyer-Renschhausen, "Tempelhofer Freiheit für alle," *taz*, May 23, 2014, http://www.taz.de/Keine-Einhegung-der-Allmenden/!5041578/.

53. Die Landesabstimmungsleiterin Berlin, "Amtliche Information zum Volksentscheid über den Erhalt des Tempelhofer Feldes," May 25, 2014, 40–42, https://www.wahlen-berlin.de/abstimmungen/VE2014_TFeld/Broschüre_TempelhFeld.pdf.

54. "Berliner Flüchtlingsunterkunft: Im Shuttle-Bus zur Dusche," *Frankfurter Allgemeine Zeitung,* November 2, 2015, http://www.faz.net/aktuell/politik/berliner-fluechtlingsunterkunft-im-shuttle-bus-zur-dusche-13889567.html.

55. Thomas Loy and Sigrid Kneist, "Michael Müller: Notfalls 7000 Flüchtlinge nach Tempelhof," *Der Tagesspiegel,* January 8, 2016, http://www.tagesspiegel.de/berlin/fluechtlinge-in-berlin-michael-mueller-notfalls-7000-fluechtlinge-nach-tempelhof/12806236.html.

56. See the website of the grassroots initiative *100% Tempelhofer Feld,* accessed June 5, 2016, http://www.thf100.de.

57. Klaus Kurpjuweit, "Trotz Flüchtlingen: Alliiertenmuseum zieht nach Tempelhof," *Der Tagesspiegel,* November 14, 2015, http://www.tagesspiegel.de/berlin/alliiertenmuseum-in-berlin-trotz-fluechtlingen-alliiertenmuseum-zieht-nach-tempelhof/12586504.html.

58. See Andreas Huyssen, "The Void of Berlin," *Critical Inquiry* 24, no. 1 (1997): 75–81; Karen E. Till, *The New Berlin: Memory, Politics, Place* (Minneapolis, 2005).

59. *DDR-Museum, Kulturbrauerei, Tränenpalast, Hohenschönhausen, Bernauer Straße, Museum am Checkpoint Charlie, Black Box Kalter Krieg, Notaufnahmelager Marienfelde, Stasi-Museum, Alliierten Museum,* Story of Berlin, *Berliner Unterwelten.*

60. See Wilfried Rott, "Abschied von West-Berlin," *Bundeszentrale für Politische Bildung,* March 4, 2010, http://www.bpb.de/apuz/32893/abschied-von-west-berlin.

61. Pierre Nora, "From Lieux de Mémoire to Realms of Memory," in *Realms of Memory: Rethinking the French Past,* ed. Pierre Nora (New York, 1997), 1: xvii.

62. Andreas Huyssen, *Present Pasts: Urban Palimpsests and the Politics of Memory* (Palo Alto, 2003), 79.

63. Andreas Huyssen, "The Voids of Berlin," *Critical Inquiry* 24, no. 1 (Fall 1997): 57.

64. See David Barclay, "Westberlin," in *Erinnerungsorte der DDR,* ed. Martin Sabrow (Munich, 2009), 437.

65. Brian Ladd, "Epilogue: The View from Berlin," in *Beyond Berlin: Twelve German Cities Confront the Nazi Past,* ed. Gavriel D. Rosenfeld and Paul B. Jeskot (Ann Arbor, 2008), 298.

66. Paul Steege, "Finding the There There: Local Space, Global Ritual, and Early Cold War Berlin," in *Earth Ways: Framing Geographical Meanings,* ed. Gary Backhaus and John Murungi (Lanham, MD, 2004), 155–72.

67. See Daniel Kiecol, *Selbstbild und Image zweier Europäischer Metropolen: Paris und Berlin zwischen 1900 und 1930* (Frankfurt, 2001), 238–85; Daniel Kiecol, "Berlin und sein Fremdenverkehr: Imageproduktion in den zwanziger Jahren," in *Selling Berlin,* ed. Thomas Biskup and Marc Schalenberg (Stuttgart, 2008), 161–74.

68. "In our contemporary memorial landscape, Westberlin is something unique and unusual, because it is closely intertwined with the history of the GDR and our perception of the history of the GDR—despite never having been part of it." Barclay, "Westberlin," 432; See David E. Barclay, "Kein neuer Mythos: Das letzte Jahrzehnt West-Berlins," *Aus Politik und Zeitgeschichte* 65, no. 46 (2015): 37–42.

Bibliography

Abel, Andreas. "Das Havemann-Archiv bekommt weniger Geld," *Berliner Morgenpost,* January 3, 2016. Accessed March 13, 2017. http://www.morgenpost.de/berlin/article206879913/Das-Havemann-Archiv-bekommt-weniger-Geld.html.

Ashworth, Gregory J., and John E. Tunbridge. *The Tourist-Historic City.* London: Routedge, 1990.

"Aufruf zur Unterstützung der Aktion 'Luftbrückendank,'" April 29, 1959. RIAS Sammlungsgut, Rundschreiben Geschäftsleitung, 1948–1959. Deutsches Rundfunkarchiv, Potsdam-Babelsberg.

Aulich, Uwe. "Neues Museum und Hard Rock Hotel im Zentrum." *Berliner Zeitung,* December 8, 2015. Accessed March 14, 2017. http://www.berliner-zeitung.de/berlin/bebauung-am-checkpoint-charlie-neues-museum-und-hard-rock-hotel-im-zentrum,10809148,32727332.html.

Barclay, David. "Kein neuer Mythos: Das letzte Jahrzehnt West-Berlins." *Aus Politik und Zeitgeschichte* 65, no. 46 (2015): 37–42.

———. "Westberlin." In *Erinnerungsorte der DDR,* edited by Martin Sabrow, 431–40. Munich: C. H. Beck, 2009.

Bender, Peter. "Sterben für Berlin." In *Sterben für Berlin? Die Berliner Krisen 1948–1958,* edited by Burghard Ciesla, Michael Lemke, and Thomas Lindenberger, 11–24. Berlin: Metropol Verlag, 2000.

"Berliner Flüchtlingsunterkunft: Im Shuttle-Bus zur Dusche." *Frankfurter Allgemeine Zeitung,* November 2, 2015. Accessed March 14, 2017. http://www.faz.net/aktuell/politik/berliner-fluechtlingsunterkunft-im-shuttle-bus-zur-dusche-13889567.html.

Bryman, Alan E. "The Disneyization of Society," *Sociological Review* 47, no. 1 (1999): 25–47.

BStU. "Campus für Demokratie—eine Ideenskizze." Accessed March 14, 2017. https://www.bstu.bund.de/SharedDocs/Downloads/DE/jahn_campus.pdf.

Chhabra, Deepak, Robert Healy, and Erin Sills. "Staged Authenticity and Heritage Tourism." *Annals of Tourism Research* 30, no. 3 (2003): 702–19.

Connolly, Kate. "Checkpoint Charlie's New Cold War with the Hot Dog Vendors." *The Guardian,* April 22, 2012, sec. World news. http://www.theguardian .com/world/2012/apr/22/checkpoint-charlie-hot-dog-vendors.

Danylow, Jula. "BlackBox Kalter Krieg: Ein Werkstattbesuch am Checkpoint Charlie." *Zeithistorische Forschungen / Studies in Contemporary History* 11, no. 2 (2014): 328–36.

Deutscher Bundestag. "Bericht der Expertenkommission zur Zukunft der Behörde des Bundesbeauftragten für die Unterlagen des Staatssicherheitsdienstes der ehemaligen DDR (BStU)." Drucksache 18/8050, April 5, 2016. Accessed March 14, 2017. https://www.bundestag.de/ausschuesse18/gremien 18/bstu.

Die Landesabstimmungsleiterin Berlin. "Amtliche Information zum Volksentscheid über den Erhalt des Tempelhofer Feldes." 2014. Accessed March 14, 2017. https://www.wahlen-berlin.de/abstimmungen/VE2014_TFeld/Brosch üre_TempelhFeld.pdf.

Donath, Matthias. "Städtebau und Architektur." In *Berlin 1933–1945,* edited by Michael Wildt and Cristoph Kreutzmüller, 229–44. Munich: Siedler Verlag, 2013.

"Einweihung des Platzes der Luftbrücke mit Redeausschnitt von Ernst Reuter." RIAS, June 25, 1949. DZ102443. Deutschlandradio Archiv, Berlin.

Eisenhuth, Stefanie, and Scott H. Krause. "Inventing the 'Outpost of Freedom': Transatlantic Narratives and Actors Crafting West Berlin's Postwar Political Culture." *Zeithistorische Forschungen / Studies in Contemporary History* 10, no. 2 (2014): 188–211.

Frank, Sybille. *Der Mauer um die Wette gedenken: Die Formation einer Heritage-Industrie am Berliner Checkpoint Charlie.* Frankfurt: Campus Verlag, 2009.

Füller, Henning, and Boris Michel. "'Stop Being a Tourist!': New Dynamics of Urban Tourism in Berlin Kreuzberg." *International Journal of Urban and Regional Research* 38, no. 4 (2014): 1304–18.

Gieseke, Jens. *The History of the Stasi: East Germany's Secret Police 1945–1990.* New York: Berghahn Books, 2014.

Groebner, Valentin. "Touristischer Geschichtsgebrauch: Über einige Merkmale neuer Vergangenheiten im 20. und 21. Jahrhundert." *Historische Zeitschrift* 296, no. 2 (2013): 408–28.

Henke, Klaus-Dietmar. "Gedächtnisverschiebung? Für eine kategoriale Asymmetrie bei der Auseinandersetzung mit der NS- und der SED-Zeit." In *Zeitschrift für Geschichtswissenschaft* 65, no. 1 (2017): 54–65.

Huyssen, Andreas. *Present Pasts: Urban Palimpsests and the Politics of Memory.* Palo Alto: Stanford University Press, 2003.

———. "The Voids of Berlin." *Critical Inquiry* 24, no. 1 (1997): 57–81.

Internationale Tourismus-Börse Berlin. "ITB World Travel Trends Report 2014/ 2015." Accessed March 14, 2017. http://www.itb-berlin.de/media/itbk/itbk_ dl_en/WTTR_Report_A4_4_Web.pdf.

Jarausch, Konrad. "Die Teilung Europas und ihre Überwindung: Überlegungen zu einem Ausstellungskonzept für Berlin." *Zeithistorische Forschungen / Studies in Contemporary History* 5, no. 2 (2008): 263–69.

Jordan, Jennifer A. *Structures of Memory: Understanding Urban Change in Berlin and Beyond.* Palo Alto: Stanford University Press, 2006.

Kein Ort der Freiheit: Das Tempelhofer Feld 1933–1945. Berlin: Berliner Geschichtswerkstatt, *2012.*

Kiecol, Daniel. "Berlin und sein Fremdenverkehr: Imageproduktion in den zwanziger Jahren." In *Selling Berlin,* edited by Thomas Biskup and Marc Schalenberg, 161–74. Stuttgart: Franz Steiner Verlag, 2008.

———. *Selbstbild und Image zweier Europäischer Metropolen. Paris und Berlin zwischen 1900 und 1930.* Frankfurt: Peter Lang, 2001.

Klein, Günter. "Vermerk über in den Vereinigten Staaten geführte Besprechungen, soweit sie Berlin betreffen," March 4, 1958. A6 1/WBA-BER-0085 Auslandsreisen USA 2.1958; England 3.1958. Willy-Brandt-Archiv im Archiv der sozialen Demokratie, Bonn.

Knaller, Susanne, and Harro Müller, eds. "Einleitung: Authentizität und kein Ende," In *Authentizität: Diskussion eines ästhetischen Begriffs,* edited by Susanne Knaller and Harro Müller, 7–16. Paderborn: Wilhelm Fink Verlag, 2006.

Knigge, Volkhard. "Vom Zeugniswert der authentischen Substanz für die Gedenkstättenarbeit." In *Denkmalpflege für die Berliner Mauer: Die Konservierung eines unbequemen Bauwerks: Beiträge zur Geschichte von Mauer und Flucht,* edited by Axel Klausmeier and Günter Schlusche, 65–71. Berlin: Links Verlag, 2011,

Kowalczuk, Ilko-Sascha. *Endspiel: Die Revolution von 1989 in Der DDR.* Munich: C. H. Beck, 2009.

Kurpjuweit, Klaus. "Trotz Flüchtlingen: Alliiertenmuseum zieht nach Tempelhof." *Der Tagesspiegel,* November 14, 2015. http://www.tagesspiegel.de/berlin/alliiertenmuseum-in-berlin-trotz-fluechtlingen-alliiertenmuseum-zieht-nach-tempelhof/12586504.html.

Ladd, Brian. "Epilogue: The View from Berlin." In *Beyond Berlin: Twelve German Cities Confront the Nazi Past,* edited by Gavriel D. Rosenfeld and Paul B. Jeskot. 295–302. Ann Arbor: University of Michigan Press, 2008,

———. *The Ghosts of Berlin: Confronting German History in the Urban Landscape.* Chicago: University of Chicago Press, 1997.

Lautenschläger, Rolf. "Wo der Himmel über Berlin weit ist." *taz,* May 25, 2014. Accessed March 14, 2017. http://www.taz.de/Volksentscheid-Tempelhofer-Feld/!5042004/.

Lindner, Rolf. "The Imaginary of the City." In *The Contemporary Study of Culture,* edited by Bundesministerium für Wissenschaft und Verkehr/Internationales Forschungszentrum Kulturwissenschaften, 289–94. Vienna: Turia and Kant, 1999.

Loy, Thomas, and Sigrid Kneist. "Michael Müller: Notfalls 7000 Flüchtlinge nach Tempelhof." *Der Tagesspiegel,* January 8, 2016. Accessed March 14, 2017.

http://www.tagesspiegel.de/berlin/fluechtlinge-in-berlin-michael-muel
ler-notfalls-7000-fluechtlinge-nach-tempelhof/12806236.html.

Macdonald, Sharon. *Difficult Heritage: Negotiating the Nazi Past in Nuremberg and Beyond.* New York: Routledge, 2009.

———. *Memorylands: Heritage and Identity in Europe Today.* London: Routledge, 2013.

———. "A People's Story: Heritage, Identity and Authenticity." In *Touring Cultures: Transformations of Travel and Theory,* edited by Chris Rojek and John Urry, 155–75. London: Routledge, 1997.

Maier, Charles. *Dissolution: The Crisis of Communism and the End of East Germany.* Princeton, NJ: Princeton University Press, 1997.

Meyer-Renschhausen, Elisabeth. "Tempelhofer Freiheit für alle." *taz,* May 23, 2014. Accessed March 14, 2017. http://www.taz.de/Keine-Einhegung-der-Allmenden/!5041578/.

Nora, Pierre. "From Lieux de Mémoire to Realms of Memory." In *Realms of Memory. Rethinking the French Past,* edited by Pierre Nora and Lawrence D. Kritzmann. New York: Columbia University Press, 1997.

Pirker, Eva Ulrike, et al., eds. *Echte Geschichte: Authentizitätsfiktionen in populären Geschichtskulturen.* Bielefeld: transcript-Verlag, 2010.

Roost, Frank. *Die Disneyfizierung der Städte.* Opladen: Leske und Budrich Verlag, 2000.

Rott, Wilfried. "Abschied von West-Berlin." *Bundeszentrale für Politische Bildung,* March 4, 2010. Accessed March 14, 2017. http://www.bpb.de/apuz/32893/abschied-von-west-berlin.

Sabrow, Martin. "Schattenorte." *Merkur* 69, no. 795 (2015): 77–84.

Saupe, Achim. "Authentizität, Version: 2.0." *Docupedia-Zeitgeschichte,* October 22, 2012. Accessed March 14, 2017. http://docupedia.de/zg/Authentizit.C3.A4t_Version_2.0_Achim_Saupe?oldid=106404.

Schöne, Jens. "Die Besetzung der Staatssicherheit 1989/90: Voraussetzungen und Abläufe. Ein Überblick." In *"Es lag was in der Luft": Die Besetzungen der Bezirksverwaltungen des MfS/AfNS in Erfurt, Suhl und Gera,* edited by Hans-Joachim Veen und Peter Wurschi, 9–27. Weimar: Stiftung Ettersberg, 2014.

Schupelius, Gunnar. "Museum am Checkpoint Charlie abgelehnt." *B.Z.,* May 16, 2012. Accessed March 14, 2017. http://www.bz-berlin.de/artikel-archiv/museum-am-checkpoint-charlie-abgelehnt.

Schütz, Jutta. "Stasi-Zentrale wird Campus für Demokratie." *Der Tagesspiegel,* January 7, 2016, Accessed March 14, 2017. http://www.tagesspiegel.de/berlin/berlin-lichtenberg-stasi-zentrale-wird-campus-fuer-demokratie/12802542.html.

Senatsverwaltung für Stadtentwicklung und Umwelt Berlin. "Zukunft—Tempelhofer Feld," March 5, 2008. Accessed March 14, 2017. http://www.stadtentwicklung.berlin.de/aktuell/pressebox/archiv_volltext.shtml?arch_0803/nachricht2972.html.

Siemens, Daniel. "Prügelpropaganda: Die SA und der nationalsozialistische Mythos vom 'Kampf um Berlin.'" In *Berlin 1933–1945: Stadt und Gesellschaft im Nationalsozialismus,* edited by Michael Wildt and Cristoph Kreutzmüller, 33–50. Munich: Siedler Verlag, 2013.

Steege, Paul. "Finding the There There: Local Space, Global Ritual, and Early Cold War Berlin." In *Earth Ways: Framing Geographical Meanings,* edited by Gary Backhaus and John Murungi. 155–72. Lanham, MD: Lexington Books, 2004.

Steppat, Timo. "Kalter Krieg am Checkpoint Charlie: Mehr Disneyland als Gedenken." *Cicero,* August 15, 2012. Accessed March 14, 2017. http://www.cicero .de/berliner-republik/mehr-disneyland-als-gedenken/51555.

Thijs, Krijn. "West-Berliner Visionen für eine neue Mitte: Die Internationale Bauausstellung, der 'Zentrale Bereich' und die 'Geschichtslandschaft' an der Mauer (1981–1985)." *Zeithistorische Forschungen / Studies in Contemporary History* 11, no. 2 (2014): 235–61.

Till, Karen E. *The New Berlin: Memory, Politics, Place.* Minneapolis: University of Minnesota Press, 2005.

Trilling, Lionel. *Sincerity and Authenticity.* London: Harcourt Brace Jovanovich, 1974.

Trotnow, Helmut, and Bernd von Kostka, eds. *Die Berliner Luftbrücke: Ereignis und Erinnerung.* Berlin: Frank and Timme, 2010.

Tschofen, Bernhard. "Antreten, ablehnen, verwalten? Was der Heritage-Boom den Kulturwissenschaften aufträgt." In *Prädikat Heritage: Wertschöpfungen aus kulturellen Ressourcen,* edited by Dorothee Hemme, Markus Tauschek, and Regina Bendix, 19–32. Berlin: LIT Verlag, 2007.

Verheyen, Dirk. *United City, Divided Memories? Cold War Legacies in Contemporary Berlin.* Lanham, MD: Lexington Books, 2008.

CHAPTER 6

Branding the New Germany

The Brandenburg Gate and a New Kind of German Historical Amnesia

Sarah Pogoda and Rüdiger Traxler

On the symbolic date of November 9, 2007, the eighteenth anniversary of the fall of the Wall, the German *Bundestag* agreed to erect a "Freedom and Unity Monument" (FUM) in Berlin as a national monument commemorating both Germany's peaceful reunification in 1990 and, as the accompanying declaration itself stated, earlier nineteenth- and twentieth-century unification movements. Reading the events of 1989/1990 as fulfillment of Germany's long path to freedom and unity has become hegemonic in the last two decades: Norbert Lammert, president of the Parliament, characterized them as such a fulfillment in his opening address to the *Bundestag* session that approved the monument; Angela Merkel in her speech marking the nineteenth anniversary of German Reunification on October 3, 2009 described them similarly; and innumerable publications and media productions, among them Guido Knopp's influential television documentary *The Germans* (2008), have echoed such language. In recent decades, efforts to recast German identity from a history of guilt into a positive narrative of freedom and unity have intensified,[1] while more controversial discourses recollecting counternarratives have been increasingly neglected.

If the topos of freedom and unity has been central to narratives of German identity, then the FUM (despite the project's noncompletion) and its historical counterpart the Brandenburg Gate have been two key politicocultural elements in these narratives. This chapter focuses first on the highly charged interpretative disputes about the Brandenburg Gate, the public acceptance of which as the "genius loci" of German exceptionalism[2] has significantly diminished since the end of the 1990s. Then the chapter considers how the historiography of the FUM has altered, shifting from suggesting the complexity of German freedom and unity to expressing a positive and reductive interpretation of the recent German past. The planned FUM thus competes with the Brandenburg Gate.

In this context, reimagining German identity in connection with notions of freedom and unity has gone hand in hand with business interests, as international tourism has gained more and more importance for Berlin's economy: "Berlin stands for Freedom"[3] is one of the city's prime tourist slogans. Finally, the chapter gains additional perspective, first by using a form of visual semiotics that distinguishes between signs, icons, and symbols, and second by involving a previously neglected participant in the city's symbolic household, namely Berlin's marketing, whose interests reduce the discursive field to a site of urban icons.

The Symbolic Function of Political Architecture

To paraphrase Umberto Eco, architecture is a cultural phenomenon and as such serves to represent and mediate content.[4] In this function, architecture contributes significantly to social communication, perception, and the development of consciousness. The mediating function of architecture in sociopolitical communication processes is based both on established frameworks for physical experience in sociopolitical space and simultaneously—in Eco's terms—on mediatory elements in the process of social and political communication. It exceeds structural and aesthetic parameters.

We have no fundamental objection to a definition of architecture based upon its aesthetic or formal associations, i.e. as "the interaction of forms, materials, colors, and light in relation to a larger whole, which intensifies perception and particular spatial experience."[5] But architecture clearly functions well beyond the aesthetic or formal content of its design. According to Dietmar Schirmer, the "naive interpretation" of political architecture posits a "routine application of some simple and well-established schemes that identify architectural features more or less explicitly with political forms of domination and their legitimizing ideologies."[6] Such mapping seems to function, for instance, in historical examples of classical architecture, such as in the US capital. However, comparing, for instance, the Pentagon in Washington, DC, and Tempelhof Airport in Berlin, we are immediately confronted with the inadequacy of an architectural interpretation that is limited to the language of form: how could systemic differences between democracy (United States) and a dictatorial regime (Nazi Germany) be recognizable solely through exterior design?

For this reason, Christian Norberg-Schulz has based the need for symbols in architecture additionally on the notion that "the object world [is] highly complex and diverse," and those observing it need "a large number of different reference systems to describe it."[7] In regard to the specific nature of architecture, Norberg-Schulz explains:

> Usually a construction project includes functional, social and cultural poles. Its form is linked to these poles through various semantic relations. The same form (for example a column) can also be constituted in such a way that some elements respond to its physical environment and others to its symbolic environment. The semantic analysis of an architectural whole is therefore often a complex matter. We must reject in any event architectural theories that explain the relationship between task and means (i.e. Function → Form) by one principle only.[8]

The capacity of architecture to convey messages is by no means restricted to stylistic or iconographic elements, but its diversity only becomes apparent when thoroughly investigated. Both historic and modern political buildings, though first conceived in response to very specific political demands, have over the course of their existence acquired a variety of meanings. This complexity often makes the notion of signs unusable for analyzing how architecture communicates, as social reality cannot be subsumed by denotative typologies. Gerhard Göhler therefore introduces the term "symbols," and calls them "signs with surplus content."[9]

Symbols are not names or denotations. Rather, they present something in a way that means it still requires interpretation. In this sense, therefore, symbols are hermeneutic phenomena.[10] Their meaning depends on the interpretation that the recipient will perform.[11] The interpreter addresses the symbolic content and makes sense of it in his own individual way, which may differ from those of other interpreters. At the same time, symbols are not arbitrary in their content and interpretation. In grasping a symbolic meaning, interpreters from a given community are contextually bound to the symbols of that community, in that they share and reference its basic concepts and social conventions. Without that context, meaning would be lost. As a "selecting construct"[12] symbols communicate existing ideas that are not necessarily visually explicitly present. Indeed, it is the absence of denotative links between architectural form and content that enables the symbolic communication of any historical content. Architecture is intimately exposed to ongoing interpretive changes to content.

On the one hand, this polysemy makes the interpretation of architecture difficult. On the other, it enables a historical structure to be endowed with new, culturally contextualized meaning. It is this tension between context-dependent and context-independent interpretation that makes the symbol risky in terms of controlled political messaging. In contrast, icons reject all complexity, dissolving any incalculability in hermeneutic processes and enforcing a sole meaning. Thus, icons are powerful, univocal communicative tools, particularly in politically propagandistic contexts.

Neither the design of the Brandenburg Gate itself nor the design of its iconic representations offers any information about the historical complexity or the contemporary importance of the building as a symbol of freedom and unity. This is also because the architectural form of a gate does not necessarily suggest a memorial, but could simply be seen as a passageway. Nevertheless, no matter which functions a historical structure currently fulfills—whether symbolic or utilitarian—a knowledge of the original function is fundamentally important when interpreting its symbolic meaning. However, such knowledge needs to be communicated in order to facilitate reflection and elucidation, as will be shown using the Brandenburg Gate as an example. Having said that, it is important not to equate the symbolic meaning of a building with its architectural history.

National Memorial, Symbol, Event Location: The Brandenburg Gate in Contemporary Context

With the Brandenberg Gate, Carl Gotthard Langhans created not just a new architectural-aesthetic definition of Prussia but a monument to its political power. Although the building as a whole appeared in slim classical form, its detailed images were to carry a clear message: Hercules at the crossroads on the reliefs of the gateway passage; the victory of the virtuous Lapiths over the centaurs on the metopes; the god of war Ares and the strategist Athena in the side niches; and all this highly and visibly dominated by the goddess of victory, Nike, on both the Attica relief and the Quadriga.

Considering this martial iconography, it seems at first glance contradictory that King Friedrich Wilhelm II wanted to establish "Peace Gate" as the official term for this classical archetype.[13] After all, it is Nike, the goddess of victory, and not her mythical colleague Eirene, the goddess of peace, who is driving the Quadriga on top of the Brandenburg Gate. This is Nike returning home from war. Yet according to contemporary political understanding, peace was the "natural result of victory."[14] At the end of the eighteenth century—that "close of the Frederician epoch also marked by nearly continuous wars"[15]—the gate's artistic design represented a peaceful new beginning. Peace came with a "return to the humanistic and aesthetic values of Antiquity"—without, however, losing sight of "the glory of the Prussian ruling house" and "the glorification of the dynastic principle."[16] "The existing State order in Prussia" continued to be emphasized in this explosive time of epochal change between revolution and Napoleonic expansion.[17] The message of the icons was to "preserve this existing order by any means."[18] Thus, the goddess of victory driving the Quadriga becomes an "ambivalent 'peace goddess'."[19]

After Napoleon's looting of the Quadriga in 1806, the empty space on the Brandenburg Gate remained an unmistakable sign of Prussian humiliation for nearly ten years, before its reinstallation reestablished the original meaning of the victory of peace. The "patriotic procession" that carried the Quadriga in triumph from Paris back home to Berlin[20] in 1814 imbued the statue with its meaning of victory up until 1914. In hindsight, it can be said that herein lies the origin of this national site of remembrance, as the victory over Napoleon and the liberation of the German states from Napoleonic domination were later understood as a national achievement, presaging national unity: seeking freedom, the German nation united under the Prussian flag. From now on, the gate was no longer just the site where, in 1814, the Germans had overcome Napoleonic humiliation. With the visual impact of 1814, the Brandenburg Gate was established as the "Prussian and simultaneously German-national monument of the wars of liberation."[21] With this, the topos of freedom and unity became inseparably linked to Prussian supremacy. It was a topos that became performed reality in the victory marches held at the gate to commemorate the so-called unification wars of 1864, 1866, and 1871.[22]

Synthesizing aesthetics and popularity in 1814, the Brandenburg Gate functioned as the "backdrop for the most diverse historical events,"[23] and still does so today. As a political sign, it was familiar to the German public as "the central place of consecration"[24] for the founding of the German Empire in 1871. As such, it was the "representational element" in a political chain of events that legitimated the state.

Through ritualized use, the building became a central feature of the permanent "exhibition of imperial power,"[25] linking the idea of freedom to military supremacy. However, the gate received very little specific attention when ceremonial events were organized, as Demps says: "They understood it less as an architectural monument and more as part of a backdrop, a background that one could adorn with more or less effort according to taste and task."[26] The gate was used solely as a setting for staged political events; that is to say, solely as an icon. With Prussia about to claim a leading role in a united Germany, the gate's iconographic function was deployed to extend the chain of legitimation and identity. It was not the gate that wrote history in such moments: "[R]ather, the particular political circumstances forced it into conditions set by the politically powerful."[27]

In the Weimar Republic—after the military defeat and the change from monarchy to a republic—previous historical references faded from the spotlight. Langhans's art-historical gem was downgraded to just another "cultivated symbol [sic] of Berlin"[28]: the Weimar Republic could hardly maintain the operatic staging of the Wilhelminian era. National Socialist propaganda, however, began to use the Brandenburg Gate within the "logic of a memory site."[29] For the National Socialists, recourse to the historical practice of the monarchy was not in opposition to the "colossal aesthetics of National Socialist propaganda."[30] Thus, the notion of "the connection between Prussian monarchy and the German idea of Nation"[31] remained until May 1945—effectively outlasting all regime changes up to that point since the building was first erected.

In the face of Germany's postwar condition, however, the question arose as to what remained of this attribution of meaning. Was the gate now—relatively lightly damaged, although only small pieces of the once glorious Quadriga survived—solely the "sign of the victory and defeat of German arms," as Gustav Seibt defined it?[32] Indeed, the rigid semiotic straitjacket of meaning that defined the gate as a sign of power had become outdated. In the postwar years, the edifice was considered the sole remaining tie binding together a nation undergoing division, hence a symbol of unity. Its previous meaning of freedom and unity as a political sign—in the historical chain of legitimation Napoleon-Prussia-Bismarck—now continued symbolically only in the form of a memory site, counterfactual to the political realities post 1945. Indeed, the simultaneity of foreign victory and domestic defeat from 1806 now reappeared for the first time since 1814. Furthermore, this former emblem of the German nation-state's power was now situated exactly at the demarcation line of the Cold War. Such a moment of ambiguity in sociopolitical discourse made a hermeneutic extension of symbolic meaning not only feasible but also necessary.

Thus, between 1945 and 1961, with reference to the topos of national freedom and unity, the Brandenburg Gate was considered a "symbol of the transition between the two political systems in terms of overcoming division."[33] The still-open gate "illustrated" the connection between East and West and the "hope for an undivided Berlin."[34] This significance was strengthened both with the demonstration march of June 17, 1953, which took a route through the gate, and with the building's photographic representations, which found their way into the historical canon of the Federal Republic.[35]

After August 13, 1961, however, the gate was closed off behind the Berlin Wall, supplying "pictorial evidence"[36] of the divided nation. By means of a conceptual simplification, the former Prusso-German symbol both of power and of freedom and unity was now shaped into a putative symbol of division. The degree to which this attribution of meaning established itself in public discourse can be seen in post-*Wende* publications. For Helmut Börsch-Supan, for example,[37] the Brandenburg Gate *regained* its "symbolic value" of unity and freedom after 1989; and Norbert König expresses himself similarly:

> It was only with the opening of the gate that the fall of the Berlin Wall really came true. With a political ceremony, the gate was released from its role as a symbol of division. In its new symbolic function as a gate of reunification, and soon as a symbol of the "Berlin Republic" itself, the Brandenburg Gate developed surprisingly quickly.[38]

Without question, the entire visual association of November 9, 1989—the historical change from division to freedom and unity—is expressed in images at the Brandenburg Gate and of the people standing atop the Wall—even if the opening that night actually took place at other Berlin border crossings. Nevertheless, even commentators who were well aware of the complexity of meaning of the symbol and its relevance for narratives of freedom and unity expressed themselves along these lines. For instance, Friedrich Karl Fromme declared that, "through all the vicissitudes of history right from the beginning and through all temporally contingent interpretations," the true meaning of the Brandenburg Gate as the "symbol of unity and freedom" was recognizable.[39] His point makes it clear: symbols build relatively timeless frames that conserve, impart, and abandon particular meanings—such as freedom and unity—while interpretations by specific actors and public discourses are shaped and expressed within specific historical contexts. Today, the Brandenburg Gate is inscribed in the collective memory with iconographic images of November 9, 1989, embodying the topos of national freedom and unity. It also plays a central role in the hegemonic narrative of German national identity, while the once so predominant references to Prussian military supremacy have fallen into oblivion. This selective referencing, of course, simplifies the ambiguous German past, suggesting a teleological trajectory fulfilled by the peaceful revolution of 1989 (freedom) and the Reunification of 1990 (unity).

The Brandenburg Gate as Iconic Architecture

As Stefanie Eisenhuth and Scott H. Krause explore in their chapter on exhibiting the Cold War in twenty-first-century Berlin in this volume, Berlin gained in touristic popularity as an authentic place of German history not least because of 1989/1990. This might be due to the fact that the historical events that took place in Berlin fit extremely well into global narratives. This promotes Berlin for international tourism, as it is easy to identify with the city's history. International tourism brings pleasure-seeking travelers. According to Eisenhuth and Krause, this increases the risk of a Disneyfication of historical sites and commemoration. These authors note that whether "and how a place is being remembered depends entirely on societal negotiations and present needs." Further, Ayse N. Erek and Eszter Gantner, in their contribution to this volume, consider how economic demands and business stakeholders powerfully intervene in societal negotiations by branding historical sites as consumer products. The Brandenburg Gate exemplifies these assertions. It illustrates the competing efforts for "imagineering" history, for instance, by customizing history to guarantee that Berlin offers pleasure and fun. Now, this is where our analysis of the Brandenburg Gate as sign and symbol intersects with the concept of the urban icon.[40] The term "urban icon" emerges from a postindustrial urbanism that understands the city less as a place of production than as a place of consumption, whether the consumption be material or immaterial (commodities or meaning). In this way, it overlaps with the focus of city marketing. The notion of the icon, unlike symbol and sign, denotes a univocal mode of communication and understanding, as well as—simultaneously—expressing conditions of architectural production in the era of the attention economy (*Aufmerksamkeitsökonomie*)[41] and the culture of the spectacle.

Whereas symbols refer to a complex discourse of meaning, such as in the case of the Brandenburg Gate described above, icons refer to a simple, straightforward, and unambiguous meaning, such as in the case of the Brandenburg Gate's martial iconography, also described above. Consider also the bitten apple, the icon for Apple Inc. Having called this bitten apple an icon, we can also call it a symbol, referring to the complex and ambivalent digital age. This example shows that the same thing can be both icon and symbol—depending on the modes of perception and utilization. This is even the case when referring to the complex and ambivalent history of the nation-state of Germany. As touched on earlier in this chapter, whereas we used the term "icon" to describe the designated object in its unequivocal meaning, when we use the term "symbol" we describe the designated object in its complex and ambiguous meaning and in its capability of pointing self-reflexively to its own constructiveness. Certainly, the term "icon" is close to the term "sign." But the difference between "sign" and "icon" used in this essay is significant, since the sign is used within a semantic context, referring to hermeneutic processes, whereas the icon merely refers to a product from the toolkit of the visual marketing of Berlin and its architecture. The term "icon" is particularly helpful for considering the imagineering of urban topographies, as it points to the possibility of topographical visibility and obviation. An icon can be hypervisible in the urban landscape without entering public consciousness. An urban icon can thus be paradoxically visible and invisible at the same time.

True, the term "icon" has experienced an inflated usage, and these days almost anything may be advanced as an icon: a pop star, a fashion label, and, precisely, a building, be it historic (such as the Leaning Tower of Pisa) or purposely built as iconic architecture (like the Guggenheim Museum in Bilbao).[42] The consensus is that icons are phenomena that possess a unique, recognizable, marketable feature (*Alleinstellungsmerkmal*), and represent particular epochs, fashions, music styles, cities, and so forth. It is generally understood that urban icons such as the Leaning Tower of Pisa or the Guggenheim Museum in Bilbao mark their respective city and further its public acceptance.

The emotional mode of the reception of icons is key to this phenomenon. Icons are emotionally received; thus no intellectual argument takes place around them.[43] This mode of reception has its roots in the history of the icon. The original *Ikone* from which the anglicized *icon* stems is a devotional image used primarily in orthodox Christian practice. Christian icons produce an existential identification between their representation of the world—i.e. the divine—and the viewer. The emotional avowal of the icon is thus an unreflective avowal of the world-order of God and of the Church as God's earthly institution. In this affective conviction lies, moreover, an affirmation of the depicted immanent truth. The canonization of orthodox iconography (*Ikonenhaushalt*) is an affective didactics that fortifies authority.[44] This mechanism speaks to the topic at hand, as with it emerges the question of which affective identity-didactics Berlin's urban icons impart and whether a concomitant canonization and authority can be recognized.[45]

Of course, an important distinction must be made between Christian and urban icons. As per the argument above, urban icons follow marketing strategies and goals. These are difficult to pin down in terms of content, due to the involvement of multiple agents with diverse interests. Moreover, these strategies and objectives could then once again be relativized in terms of political discourses, similar to the situation described by Eisenhuth and Krause. A top-down canonization is therefore unlikely, although Erek and Ganter deliver a persuasive case for something of this kind in their analysis of the "be Berlin" marketing campaign initiated in 2008. A consolidation of the meaning of an icon through market dynamics can thus not be ruled out. Yet the affection of consumers for icons comes with an emotional affirmation of unequivocal allegiance, whether it refers to religious or to political authority. Therefore it can be assumed that, in the long run, staging the Brandenburg Gate or any other Berlin monument, such as the FUM, discussed below, as an icon and embedding it into marketing rationales will most likely impede rather than promote diversification of discourses on German national unity and identity.

The scholarly debate about urban icons becomes especially interesting when the mapping of icon and city is vague. As elaborated above, this is particularly the case with the Brandenburg Gate and its symbolic (not iconic) meaning. If one considers that the Brandenburg Gate, when perceived as a symbol, refers to Prussian hegemony and a militarily enforced nation-state, yet that the gate also stands for the "summer fairy tale" of the 2006 FIFA World Cup held in Germany, it becomes clear that the symbolic meaning limits the capability of the Brandenburg Gate to be an urban icon, as too many contradictions are involved. The complexity subverts its emotional reception, because the competing symbolic claims hamper straightforward affective attachment. Contradiction demands of each viewer either avoidance of this complexity or intellectual—not solely emotional—engagement, thus enforcing the hermeneutic process characteristic of symbols. It is possible for viewers to negate the objectively present contradictions in each subjective appropriation process by recognizing only those meanings and associations that fit seamlessly into their respective worldview or perception of the city. However, city marketing relies on common perceptions of cities, not on such individualized ones. It uses surveys and analyses of the public image from inside and outside the city. Therefore, such forms of individual knowledge production hinder the regulatory guidance of city marketing. There is little interest in producing and dispersing new meanings; instead, city marketing stresses and disperses extant meanings,[46] recognizable meanings—unambiguously iconic, as pinpointed by Erek and Gantner. Presumably, city marketing seeks to prevent complexity, which might transform the consumer into a citizen, who engages with the ambiguous national history and identity of Germany. From a consumer-friendly point of view, in the case of the Brandenburg Gate, a conversion of controversial cultural ideas and national identity into unambiguous meaning was required, as we will see in the following. As we will see, too, the age in which the construction of national identity was primarily led by national myths and politically driven image circulation is over. National discourse has long since become an economic enterprise driven by government and business. It is not enough that the capital cities of postindustrial nations just represent their own people and are a playground for domestic tourism: capital-city marketing operates globally, meaning that cities must also speak to an international public. However, despite this push for univocal understandings of the city through city marketing, intersectionalities and conflicting interests and strategies still do result, as national and international publics decipher cultural codes differently.

More than any other German city, Berlin must engage appropriately with these multiple tasks, as it is both an existing political center and an imaginary central point of the reunited nation. It must defend itself against German prejudices and offer an expansive identification screen, while simultaneously attracting international tourists and meeting their needs, expectations, and projections. At the same time, Berlin fosters an ambitious claim, as "marketing directors [see] the city on a par with New York or London—and market this image world-wide."[47] Yet, in order to promote the city to foreign investors, Berlin invests 2.9 million euros annually in the so-called Berlin Partner program alone. (Some 227 partner firms that—unlike the State of Berlin—are shareholders contribute that same amount again.)[48] Incidentally (or not), every one of these Berlin Partners includes a red-silhouetted Brandenburg Gate in their company logo and displays it prominently in the visuals of their main advertising campaigns. Also, all Berlin senate administration includes the same emblem, but blue-silhouetted, in all formal and informal publications.

City advertisers have attributed a unique quality to the Brandenburg Gate, one that, for example the Berlin television tower (*Alexanderplatz*

Fernsehturm), whose silhouette recalls those in other metropolitan cities, lacks, according to advertiser Erik Spiekermann, who developed the gate logo for Berlin's city administration in the early 1990s.[49] Thus, there is a shared interest to encourage the direct identification of Brandenburg Gate with Berlin. Addressing the complex history of the Brandenburg Gate is not intended; yet, to promote the accumulation of capital and to attract tourists and business partners, a glorified affirmation of the historical idealization of the topos freedom and unity functions as a form of self-advertisement for these national and multinational companies. Berlin campaigns accommodate these interests.

Erek and Gantner aptly describe the "be Berlin" campaign as the "disappearance" of history. To amplify their account: the disappearing of history in favor of global images and urban icons precipitates an increasing amnesia towards the symbolic meanings of the Brandenburg Gate among Berlin residents. This can be seen with the "be Berlin" campaign, which was directed at Berliners, who were to shape the city's identity.[50] Although the campaign aimed at capturing a personal, entirely subjective "Berlin feeling," it was always linked to the Berlin logo and its emblematic representation of the Brandenburg Gate. Also revealing is the fact that director Robert Thalheim's accompanying film presented Berlin ambassadors in their own neighborhoods, yet all segments featuring tourists were filmed in front of the Brandenburg Gate. Ironically, the Brandenburg Gate seems to have been transformed into a reciprocal icon through this filmic emplacement. Berliners identify tourists with the Brandenburg Gate just as tourists identify Berlin with the Brandenburg Gate. At the same time, Berliners do not necessarily identify themselves with the Brandenburg Gate. Seen through the perspective of the film, for Berliners, the Brandenburg Gate might just as well be forgotten. In this work on Berlin as a brand, a dialectic of forgetfulness emerges, a dialectic which renders the concept of societal negotiations proposed elsewhere in the present volume by Eisenhuth and Krause a little dubious.

The gate has now become an unambiguous, internationally recognized, must-see urban site. Perhaps unsurprisingly, the icon for the iPhone Cityguide Berlin app depicts the gate.[51] Berliners must recognize that they are living in an urban center which is being changed by city marketing—especially since the light rail stop *Unter den Linden* was renamed *Brandenburger Tor* in 2009. The gate is bound up with city marketing that above all promotes the "event" character of Berlin, advertising it as a young, entertaining, and even spectacular world of experience. Today, the concerns of Bernd M. Michael may sound surprising: in 2010 the advertising specialist characterized the Brandenburg Gate as "historically overburdened," and therefore unsuitable as a city emblem and urban icon.[52] Even though Michael did not further specify this overburdening, he must have been thinking of the historical conditions discussed above. Horst Hoheisel's 1997 artwork illustrates this historical overburdening by pushing it even further. Very few visitors are likely, however, to remember Hoheisel's projection of the gate of Auschwitz onto the Brandenburg Gate, demanding by means of this anti-monument the demolition of the former.[53] This art action set off a far-reaching, complex debate that today finds few resonances outside of academic discourse, having long since been outshone by the Festival of Lights—the extremely popular event illuminating Berlin's monuments.

These examples identify the crucial problem around national and global identity construction in Berlin: the interests of city marketing are at odds with remembrance and careful reflection. Having the Brandenburg Gate as a memorial to German national history meant foregrounding precisely the complex historical dimensions that Michael and Hoheisel problematized. Within a differentiated commemoration culture, the gate could hardly serve as an attractive icon for city advertising. The dominant dissemination of images by a city marketing that seeks to portray Berlin as the city of freedom, unity, and fun impedes societal discourses negotiating the symbolic meaning of the Brandenburg Gate in its full ambiguity, particularly in relation to national identity.

What are the consequences of reading German history as a teleology of freedom and unity? The question is, what role does the glorification of Berlin as the city of freedom and unity—with a concomitant failure to address the gate's historical complexity and the complex history of Germany—play in the reconstruction of post-reunification German identity? This question necessitates exploration of how economic interests relate to political ideas. The National Freedom and Unity Monument, its proposed name suggestively resonant, is an appropriate object of study for this question.

The National Freedom and Unity Monument: German History's Fortunate Turn

In 2007, eighteen years after the fall of the Berlin Wall, the *Deutsche Bundestag* decided to build a National Freedom and Unity Monument, consisting of two monuments, one in Leipzig—where the Monday Demonstrations in 1989 initiated the end of the GDR regime—and the other in Berlin at a site about a mile from the Brandenburg Gate. In April 2011 the winner of the architectural competition was chosen, but five years later, in April 2016, the Budget Committee decided to stop the project because of costs rising from 10 to 15 million euros. However, in February 2017, political leaders announced that the project would go ahead as planned.

Strikingly, only the initiators of the monument expressed disapproval at the 2016 decision to defund the project, whereas public protest was absent. Moreover, Monika Grütters, Federal Government Commissioner for Culture and the Media, made a plea for recognizing the Brandenburg Gate as the "real unity monument": "Like no other, this highly symbolic monument represents the division of the world into freedom and unfreedom and the joyful overcoming of this division. If had spoken in support of the Brandenburg Gate in a different way right from the start, maybe the desire for another monument would never have arisen."[54] Grütters's statement points to the original motivation and desire of the monument's initiators to design and erect a monument with a clear and explicit meaning—a desire that is worth considering in the context of this chapter. According to the wishes of its initiators, the FUM is to fulfill three tasks:

> It should not be a representative state monument, but a citizens' memorial. It should be a memorial that encourages an "upright gait" and civil courage, without which neither freedom, democracy, nor national unity can be gained or defended. It should have as a central focus human beings and citizenry, through whose personal engagement democracy lives. And it should express the liberating joy that the fall of the Berlin Wall triggered—a memorial of historic happiness and tears of joy.[55]

In sum, this memorial should encourage the production of popular political mythology.[56] The winning design managed to respond to these desires exemplarily well: the seesaw design invites visitors to realize the monument's message by accessing the platform in groups in order to keep this public space in balance. Being a mere spectator will not be sufficient to experience the monument, but visitors will become performers themselves, playfully animating the monument's message. The choreographer Sasha Waltz (Berlin), who cooperated with architect Johannes Milla and Partner (Stuttgart), promised visits of joy and happiness on this national playground.

We argue that these happy visits will come at the price of abandoning the complexity of the narrative discussed above of the long march to German freedom and unity that supposedly culminated in the uprising of autumn 1989. Waltz and Milla's design won, perhaps because its monumental engineering of joy and happiness is able to serve city-marketing objectives. In cases such as the FUM, promoting Berlin as the city of freedom and fun gets in the way of remembering the past. As a political process, this myth-building occurs in a manner favoring a positive interpretation of recent German history. The aspect of a civic memorial to the revolution "from below"[57] is relatively insignificant here.

Strikingly, the initiators did not intend the FUM to serve as a countermonument to the Brandenburg Gate; rather, within the framework of the national memorial landscape and culture of remembrance, it stands in relation to the Memorial to the Murdered Jews of Europe, a prototype of representations of historical guilt. This *Holocaust Mahnmal* (memorial of warning) impedes positive identification with the German past, yet it brings an affirmative identification with a German collective that the initiators sought and found in Waltz's design. In phrasing that avoids any differentiation—"We Germans"—the group's request to the German Federal Parliament, April 6, 2000, invoked the emotional world of a German *Gemeinschaft* (people's community):

> We Germans find monuments and memorials difficult.... The inability to celebrate and the inability to mourn belong together. They can also only be overcome together. Monuments of shame [sic] and of mourning, of pride and of joy are necessary foundation stones of the new Germany and the new federal capital....[58]

The initiators mistakenly conclude here that history can be divided into unambiguously positive and negative emotional states. This fallacy furthers the disregard of the Brandenburg Gate as a memorial to freedom and unity. Due to the concrete public utilization of the Brandenburg Gate since November 9, 1989, it is definitely possible to read it as a memorial to joy and happiness. What better than a multitude of cheerful soccer fans to suggest a positive and affirmative identification with the German nation? The same fallacy ignores the fact that the Brandenburg Gate also served as a "freedom and unity memorial of the peaceful revolution from below."[59] Where else than at the Brandenburg Gate did this metaphor of "freedom and unity" become reality on the night of the fall of the Wall, as the people stood in front of the Wall and gradually climbed to the top, making freedom and unity reality?[60] It is precisely this image that has etched itself into collective memory as the moment of freedom and unity, and even today it provokes goose bumps.

The initiators ignore the Gate's quality as a site of experience and its popularity, and they misrecognize this historically based, authentic site of memory as not just one of the "representative state monuments of national unity and free democracy."[61] The FUM initiators' elision of the concrete experiences of citizens at the Brandenburg Gate recalls the way the initiators of the Memorial to the Murdered Jews of Europe elided the historical sites in Berlin that were the places of persecution and deportation of Jews—for instance Track 17 at Grunewald train station. In a move similar to the German *Bundestag*'s joint motion stating that there was as yet no freedom and unity memorial to the peaceful revolution,[62] journalist and activist Lea Rosh took the position at the end of the 1980s that "Germany, the land of the perpetrators, the land of the inventors of this unique genocide, the murder of the Jews," had "not a single monument to memorialize the more than five million dead murdered by the Germans."[63]

The examples of the *Holocaust Mahnmal* and the FUM initiatives exemplify a pragmatic marketing strategy that also has a flattening effect on the landscape of memorialization and memory. Such major new architecture is generally legitimated using narratives based on the identification of a putative lack and the marking of a similarly putative need. Considerable discursive efforts are undertaken to exclude and simplify the meanings of existing sites and material realities. The artificial conceptions that result risk decontextualizing recollection for the viewing public as well. Remembrance is separated from actual historical sites and experiences and remains fixed at purely subjective levels, without making reflexive reference from individual experiences to the historical context.[64] When memorials are designed for absolutely specific purposes, the willingness to engage in controversial discourse is lost. The ability to think and reflect is replaced by a kind of sentimental historical didacticism.

Identity formation and collective remembrance do not follow an ideal of freedom when historical interpretations driven by elites supply content in readily consumable form. To echo Ernest Renan, national identity necessitates continual free discourse. According to Marko Demantowsky what the FUM involves—as intended by its initiators—is a "first-degree repository of symbolic meaning."[65] Demantowsky is referring to the monument's explicitness, lack of contradiction, and simplistic character.[66] In the face of such characteristics, Demantowsky is scathing about the prospects of didactic success for which the initiators and parliament hoped:

> Someone who, [...] erects a historical symbol of this kind and—as the
> initiators here—, justifies it with didactic arguments, impudently claim-

ing that he can demonstrate or even create a particular "historical consciousness", will be disappointed and will bring disillusionment.[67]

Demantowsky's point is clear: there should not be a brand-new invented symbol but a site with the force of authenticity in terms of its frame and location.[68]

The example of the Brandenburg Gate and the FUM demonstrates "how thoughtlessly and carelessly the city [of Berlin] treats the privilege of the historical site, perhaps also the responsibilities that arise from it."[69] In sum, as Schlögel says, Berlin's great potential for vitality and creativity is invested in "the invention of spaces and sites that have little to do with the history they are supposed to represent."[70] Accordingly, the "sites of the events themselves are ignored or marginalized."[71]

The Freedom and Unity Monument as a Liberating Memorial

The FUM is intended to express the "liberating happiness"[72] that the fall of the Wall brought, as Mausbach famously put it. Mausbach's statement draws together some of our findings. The joy about the fall of the Wall was certainly not a liberating one, but rather one of liberation or about liberation. In retrospect, the liberating effect might be characterized sarcastically as the joy of liberating Germans from the burden of finding a complex national identity in historical guilt.

The examination of discourses around national identity and its memory sites in Berlin reveals not liberation but rather a stabilization of associations leading to the standardization of certain political narratives. It also becomes clear that contemporary myths are imagineered. Contemporary myths are all too often neglected by the academic community and can thus be usurped by market forces with little resistance. Those involved in city marketing know how to snatch up, fulfill, and strengthen the desires that articulate themselves unconsciously in these narratives, while scholars reconstruct the dynamics and ideologies only decades later when they have turned into historical legends and myths. The fashioning of myth is—and this is a core finding of this article—no longer a societal effort or a political enterprise but rather the work of a firm that acts globally to create historicopolitical entertainment.

Visibility is a main objective of marketing efforts, as it facilitates visual representation of the city in today's highly competitive attention economy. Visibility requires large-scale projects such as the Memorial to the Murdered Jews of Europe and the FUM. Both memorials are easily captured in film and photography and shared via social media. Engagement with the memorial makes way for the iconic shot and the "selfie"; remembrance of the past gives way to the fun factor. True, this is a reasoning quite often used against the Memorial to the Murdered Jews of Europe, but whereas its architectural design causes unsettling experiences aiming to encourage further engagement, the FUM design lacks similar impulses. One could argue that the Brandenburg Gate similarly allows its use as a mere backdrop, as in the examples sketched above. However, the Gate comes with its authentic incorporation of the complex past in question, whereas the FUM could only really invoke its topographical setting (the Berlin *Schlossfreiheit*) in support of any claim to similar authenticity. Indeed, the reconstruction of the Berlin City Palace on the nearby *Schlossplatz* suggests that the proposed FUM's site is itself subject to intensive imagineering efforts that show a similar tendency toward a positive and simplifying identification with the Prussian past and German Empire.

In sum, the Brandenburg Gate above all lacks a vivid public discourse that facilitates social negotiations about what the German past is and how to remember it. Furthermore, we conclude that the debates around these memorials—if they take place at all—are market oriented. Stated differently, should the simplification, even banalization, of the Brandenburg Gate's meaning made possible by the gate's unambiguous iconization be contested in order to open it up to reflective discourse and political debate around national identity, beyond the soccer fan mile and the New Year's Eve party? Each of the actors considered here would certainly answer this question differently, yet if finally asked, the question might initiate much needed social negotiations.

Sarah Pogoda is lecturer in German at Bangor University (UK). Her research interests and publications include representations and performances of Germany in all arts in the nineteenth and twentieth centuries and Berlin as a capital city in German narratives. Her current research focuses on Christoph Schlingensief and his relation to the avant-garde.

Rüdiger Traxler, currently research consultant for education, science and research of the Christian Democratic Union at the Berlin House of Representatives, studied political science at Heidelberg University and Freie Universität Berlin, graduated as DPhil, and lectured in Germany and the United States. His academic research focusses on the communicative role of architecture.

Notes

Translated by Jennifer Ruth Hosek

1. Robert Meyer and Lutz Haarmann, "Das Freiheits- und Einheitsdenkmal, Die geschichtspolitische Verortung in de Ideengeschichte der Bundesrepublik," *Bpb: Bundeszentrale für politische Bildung,*" accessed January 10, 2017, http://www.bpb.de/geschichte/zeitgeschichte/deutschlandarchiv/53296/freiheits-und-einheitsdenkmal.

2. Klaus Schlögel, "Wir brauchen die Wippe nicht," *Die Welt,* May 28, 2011, http://www.welt.de/print/die_welt/vermischtes/article13399337/Wir-brauchen-die-Wippe-nicht.html.

3. "Tourismuskonzept Berlin: Handlungsrahmen 2011+," Senatsverwaltung für Wirtschaft, Technologie und Frauen (2011): 16, accessed October 26, 2015, http://www.dehoga-berlin.de/images/dehoga/005_daten_fakten/daten_fakten_pdf/tourismuskonzept_2011.pdf., 15. Translation by the authors of this chapter.

4. Umberto Eco, *Einführung in die Semiotik* (Munich, 2002), 295.

5. Claus Dreyer, "Politische Architektur als Bedeutungsträger: Ästhetik und Repräsentation," *Wolkenkuckucksheim* 6, no. 1 (2001), accessed May 9, 2015, http://www.cloud-cuckoo.net/openarchive/wolke/deu/Themen/011/Dreyer/dreyer.htm. Translation by the authors of this chapter.

6. Dietmar Schirmer, "Politik und Architektur, Ein Beitrag zur politischen Symbolanalyse am Beispiel Washingtons," in *Sprache des Parlaments und Semiotik der Demokratie: Studien zur politischen Kommunikation in der Moderne,* ed. Andreas Dörner and Ludgera Vogt (Berlin, 1995), 310. Translation by the authors of this chapter.

7. Christian Norberg-Schulz, *Logik der Baukunst* (Frankfurt, 1965), 179. Translation by the authors of this chapter.

8. Ibid.

9. Gerhard Göhler, "Der Zusammenhang von Institution, Macht und Repräsentation," in *Institution—Macht—Repräsentation, Wofür politische Institutionen stehen und wie sie wirken,* ed. Gerhard Göhler et al. (Baden-Baden, 1997), 33. Translation by the authors of this chapter.

10. Most relevant, see Gerhard Kurz, *Metapher, Allegorie, Symbol* (Göttingen, 2004), 85; Gerhard Göhler, "Symbolische Politik—Symbolische Praxis, Zum Symbolverständnis in der deutschen Politikwissenschaft," in *Was heißt Kulturgeschichte des Politischen? Zeitschrift für historische Forschung, Beiheft 35,* ed. Barbara Stollberg-Rilinger (Berlin, 2005), 65.

11. Göhler, "Der Zusammenhang von Institution, Macht und Repräsentation," 29.

12. Umberto Eco, *Zeichen: Einführung in einen Begriff und seine Geschichte* (Frankfurt, 1977), 130. Translation by the authors of this chapter.

13. See Jürgen Reiche, "Symbolgehalt und Bedeutungswandel eines politischen Monuments," in *Das Brandenburger Tor: Eine Monographie,* ed. Will-

muth Arenhövel and Rolf Bothe (Berlin, 1991), 270–316. Translation by the authors of this chapter.

14. Catalogue of an exhibition at the Prussian Academy of Arts, May 27, 1793, cited in Reiche, "Symbolgehalt und Bedeutungswandel," 274.

15. Michael S. Cullen and Uwe Kieling, *Das Brandenburger Tor: Ein deutsches Symbol* (Berlin, 1999), 12. Translation by the authors of this chapter.

16. Reiche, "Symbolgehalt und Bedeutungswandel," 274.

17. Rolf Bothe, "Edle Einfalt, falscher Friede," *Frankfurter Allgemeine Zeitung,* August 30, 1991. Translation by the authors of this chapter.

18. Ibid.

19. Ekkehard Schwerk, "Die verwickelte Wahrheit des gewandelten Wahrzeichens," *Der Tagesspiegel,* August 3, 1991. Translation by the authors of this chapter.

20. Gustav Seibt, "Das Brandenburger Tor," in *Deutsche Erinnerungsorte II,* ed. Etienne François and Hagen Schulze (Munich, 2009), 69. Translation by the authors of this chapter.

21. Ibid., 71.

22. See also Seibt, who points out "that anti-French, counterrevolutionary, and anti-Western turnaround that also colored the German concept of freedom: as meaning exterior freedom from foreign domination more than interior freedom." Seibt, "Das Brandenburger Tor," 71–72.

23. Cullen and Kieling, *Brandenburger Tor,* 40.

24. Laurenz Demps, *Geschichte Berlins, von den Anfängen bis 1945* (Berlin, 1987), 95. Translation by the authors of this chapter.

25. Ibid., 96.

26. Ibid., 95. E.g. the illuminated gate at the twenty-fifth anniversary of the commemoration of the 1870 Battle of Sedan on September 2, 1895.

27. Ibid., 97.

28. Reiche, "Symbolgehalt und Bedeutungswandel," 294.

29. Seibt, "Brandenburger Tor," 81.

30. Ibid., 80.

31. Ibid., 81.

32. Ibid.

33. Laurenz Demps, *Das Brandenburger Tor: Ein Symbol im Wandel* (Berlin, 2003), 83. Translation by the authors of this chapter.

34. Norbert König, "Die symbolische Bedeutung des Brandenburger Tores," in *Das Brandenburger Tor: Wege in die Geschichte. Tor in die Zukunft,* ed. Stiftung Denkmalschutz Berlin (Berlin, 2003), 130. Translation by the authors of this chapter.

35. This photograph is used as the cover picture in Edgar Wolfrum, *Geschichtspolitik in der Bundesrepublik Deutschland, Der Weg zur bundesrepublikanischen Erinnerung 1948–1990,* Darmstadt: Wissenschaftliche Buchgesellschaft, 1999.

36. Seibt, "Das Brandenburger Tor," 83.

37. Helmut Börsch-Supan, "Zum Geleit," in *Das Brandenburger Tor: Ein deut-sches Symbol,* ed. Michael S. Cullen and Uwe Kieling (Berlin, 1999), 10. Translation by the authors of this chapter.

38. König, "Symbolische Bedeutung," 135.

39. Friedrich Karl Fromme, "Kein Übergang unter vielen," *Frankfurter Allgemeine Zeitung,* December 23, 1989. Translation by the authors of this chapter.

40. Most relevant: Celina Kress, Marc Schalenberg, and Sandra Schürmann, eds., special issue, *Urban Icons: Informationen zur modernen Stadtgeschichte* 2 (Berlin, 2011).

41. Georg Franck, "Medienästhetik und Unterhaltungsarchitektur," *Merkur* 54, no. 615 (2000): 590–604. Translation by the authors of this chapter.

42. Having said that, a dramatic architectural structure does not guarantee visibility, as Christa Kamleithner and Roland Meyer point out. They explain that urban icons develop from a complex process of promoting architectural works as canonic and embedding them into the collective memory at the same time. This assertion has been most significantly proved with implementing the Berlin Memorial for the Murdered Jews of Europe as an iconic site. Christa Kamleithner and Roland Meyer, "Urban Icons: Architektur und globale Bildzirkulation," special issue, *Urban Icons: Informationen zur modernen Stadtgeschichte* 2 (2011): 17–31.

43. Lydia Haustein, *Global Icons: Globale Bildinszenierungen und kulturelle Identität* (Göttingen, 2008), 25. Explicitly following Aby Warburg, Lydia Haustein focuses on the global exchange of images, particularly how African, Asian, and South American artists transfer Western images into their own artworks.

44. Vicki Goldberg, *The Power of Photography: How Photographs Changed Our Lives* (New York, 1991), 135.

45. Haustein, *Global Icons,* 25.

46. Claire Colomb analyzes the plural strategies and projects that Berlin city marketing deployed to make beneficial usage of the multiple selling points that exist in the city, such as "metropolis," "global service metropolis," or *"Schaustelle."* The latter branding played with the German *Baustelle* for "construction site" and the verb *schauen* for "having a look." *Schaustelle* pointed to the staging of Berlin as a living exhibition of its history and its continuous and rapid transformation. This marketing strategy aimed to promote Berlin to the creative industry; the famous slogan "Poor, but sexy" still circulates today. Clair Colomb, *Staging the New Berlin: Place Marketing and the Politics of Urban Reinvention Post-1989* (New York, 2012).

47. Simon Frost, "Berlin lieben und investieren," *Der Tagesspiegel,* December 16, 2013, http://www.tagesspiegel.de/wirtschaft/stadtmarketing-berlin-lieb en-und-investieren/9226934.html. Translation by the authors of this chapter.

48. Ibid.

49. Nina Apin, "Berlin ist ein dickbäuchiger Typ in meinem Alter: Montagsinterview mit Typograf Erik Spiekermann," *Tageszeitung,* July 10, 2011, http://www.taz.de/!5116706/2011.

50. The self-appointed "makers" of this campaign justify it as follows: "[W]hen the Berlin Senate commissioned Berlin Partner GmbH in the summer of 2007 to develop and implement a strategy for an image campaign under the auspices of the Senate Chancellery, an opinion poll conducted by market researchers TNS Infratest found that although Berlin was viewed nationally as full of joie de vivre and internationally as having great potential, the German capital did not have a clear profile." Berlin Partner für Wirtschaft und Technologie GmbH, "Berlin—eine Stadt mit Profil," *sei.berlin.de,* accessed February 21, 2015, http://www.sei.berlin.de/kampagne.

51. Cityguide AG Stadtmarketing, "Berlin—die Hauptstadt App," accessed October 26, 2015, https://itunes.apple.com/de/app/berlin-die-hauptstadt-app/id545721936?mt=8.

52. Fromme, "Kein Übergang unter vielen."

53. Most relevant, see James E. Young, "Horst Hoheisel's Counter-Memory of the Holocaust: The End of the Monument," *Center for Holocaust and Genocide Studies,* accessed October 26, 2015, http://chgs.umn.edu/museum/memorials/hoheisel/.

54. dpa, "Neuer Anlauf für Einheitsdenkmal—Aber nicht in Berlin," in *Berliner Morgenpost,* July, 30, 2016, accessed January, 16, 2017, http://www.morgenpost.de/bezirke/mitte/article207968213/Neuer-Anlauf-fuer-Einheitsdenkmal-aber-nicht-in-Berlin.html. Translation by the authors of this chapter.

55. Florian Mausbach, "Über Sinn und Ort eines nationalen Freiheits- und Einheitsdenkmals," in *Der Weg zum Denkmal für Freiheit und Einheit,* ed. Andreas H. Apelt (Schwalbach, 2009), 12.

56. Evelyn Finger, "Mehr Revolution wagen!," *Die Zeit,* July 9, 2009.

57. Florian Mausbach et al., "Initiative Denkmal Deutsche Einheit, Brief der Initiatoren, Mai 1998," in *Der Weg zum Denkmal für Freiheit und Einheit,* ed. Andreas H. Apelt (Schwalbach, 2009), 33. Translation by the authors of this chapter.

58. Deutscher Bundestag, "Errichtung eines Einheits- und Freiheitsdenkmals auf der Berliner Schlossfreiheit," *Drucksache* 14/3126 (2000), 53. Translation by the authors of this chapter

59. Mausbach et al., "Initiative Denkmal," 34.

60. See Schlögel, "Wir brauchen die Wippe nicht": "Aber nirgendwo fallen Ort und historisches Ereignis so sehr zusammen wie am Brandenburger Tor." (Nowhere else but here, at the Brandenburg Gate, history and place coincide.)

61. Ibid., 14. Translation by the authors of this chapter.

62. Deutscher Bundestag, "Errichtung eines Einheits- und Freiheitsdenkmals," 53.

63. Lea Rosh, "Kriegsdenkmäler—ja, Holocaust-Denkmal—nein?," in *Vorwärts* 45, November 5, 1988, cited in *Der Denkmalstreit—das Denkmal? Die Debatte um das "Denkmal für die ermordeten Juden Europas," Eine Dokumentation,* ed. Ute Heimrod, Günter Schlusche, and Horst Seferens (Berlin, 1999), 52. Translation by the authors of this chapter.

64. Dorothee Wilms, "Was sollte ein Freiheits- und Einheitsdenkmal versinnbildlichen?," *Deutschland Archiv* 40, no. 5 (2007): 870.
65. Marko Demantowsky, "Das geplante neue Berliner Nationaldenkmal für 'Freiheit und Einheit': Ansprüche, Geschichte und ein gut gemeinter Vorschlag," *Deutschland Archiv* 5 (2009): 884. Translation by the authors of this chapter. Demantowsky is here adapting a tripartite typologization of signs first proposed by Winfried Speitkamp, Winfried Speitkamp, "Denkmalsturz und Symbolkonflikt in der modernen Geschichte: Eine Einleitung," in *Denkmalsturz, Zur Konfliktgeschichte politischer Symbolik,* ed. Winfried Speitkamp (Göttingen, 1997), 5–21, esp. 6. Demantowsky's term "repository of symbolic meaning" ("Symbolträger") is Speitkamp's "memory sign". According to Speitkamp's system, 'first-degree memory signs' are signs that "have only been produced for purposes of symbolization, such as flags and anthems, but also 'classic' monuments"; 'second-degree memory signs' "serve a practical purpose", like coins or postage stamps; and 'third-degree memory signs' are those which "were not originally conceived as such" but "were accorded symbolic content by a group using them in reaction to conditions it had experienced". The third group is the understanding of symbol used in the present chapter.
66. Demantowsky, "Das geplante neue Berliner Nationaldenkmal," 884.
67. Ibid., 885.
68. Ibid., 886.
69. Schlögel, "Wir brauchen die Wippe nicht."
70. Ibid.
71. Ibid.
72. Mausbach, "Sinn und Ort," 12. Translation by the authors of this chapter.

Bibliography

Apin, Nina. "Berlin ist ein dickbäuchiger Typ in meinem Alter: Montagsinterview mit Typograf Erik Spiekermann." *Tageszeitung,* July 10, 2011. Accessed March 13, 2017. http://www.taz.de/!5116706/2011.

Berlin Partner für Wirtschaft und Technologie GmbH. "Berlin—eine Stadt mit Profil." *sei.berlin.de.* Accessed February 21, 2015. http://www.sei.berlin.de/kampagne.

Börsch-Supan, Helmut. "Zum Geleit." In *Das Brandenburger Tor: Ein deutsches Symbol,* edited by Michael S. Cullen and Uwe Kieling, 7–10. Berlin: Berlin Edition, 1999.

Bothe, Rolf. "Edle Einfalt, falscher Friede." *Frankfurter Allgemeine Zeitung,* August 30, 1991.

Cityguide AG Stadtmarketing. "Berlin—die Hauptstadt App." Accessed October 26, 2015. https://itunes.apple.com/de/app/berlin-die-hauptstadt-app/id545721936?mt=8.

Colomb, Claire. *Staging the New Berlin: Place Marketing and the Politics of Urban Reinvention Post-1989.* London: Routledge, 2012.

Cullen, Michael S., and Uwe Kieling. *Das Brandenburger Tor: Ein deutsches Symbol.* Berlin: Berlin Edition, 1999.

Demantowsky, Marko. "Das geplante neue Berliner Nationaldenkmal für 'Freiheit und Einheit': Ansprüche, Geschichte und ein gut gemeinter Vorschlag." *Deutschland Archiv* 5 (2009): 879–87.

Demps, Laurenz. *Das Brandenburger Tor: Ein Symbol im Wandel.* Berlin: Verlagshaus Braun, 2003.

———. *Geschichte Berlins: Von den Anfängen bis 1945.* Berlin: Dietz Verlag, 1987.

Deutscher Bundestag. "Errichtung eines Einheits- und Freiheitsdenkmals auf der Berliner Schlossfreiheit." *Drucksache* 14/3126 (2000).

dpa. "Neuer Anlauf für Enheitsdenkmal—Aber nicht in Berlin." *Berliner Morgenpost,* July 30, 2016. Accessed March 13, 2017. http://www.morgenpost.de/bezirke/mitte/article207968213/Neuer-Anlauf-fuer-Einheitsdenkmal-aber-nicht-in-Berlin.html.

Dreyer, Claus. "Politische Architektur als Bedeutungsträger: Ästhetik und Repräsentation." *Wolkenkuckucksheim* 6, no. 1 (2001). Accessed May 9, 2015. http://www.cloud-cuckoo.net/openarchive/wolke/deu/Themen/011/Dreyer/dreyer.htm.

Eco, Umberto. *Einführung in die Semiotik.* Munich: Wilhelm Fink, 2002.

———. *Zeichen: Einführung in einen Begriff und seine Geschichte.* Frankfurt: Suhrkamp, 1977.

Finger, Evelyn. "Mehr Revolution wagen!" *Die Zeit,* July 9, 2009.

Franck, Georg. "Medienästhetik und Unterhaltungsarchitektur." *Merkur* 54, no. 615 (2000): 590–604.

Fromme, Friedrich Karl. "Kein Übergang unter vielen." *Frankfurter Allgemeine Zeitung,* December 23, 1989.

Frost, Simon. "Berlin lieben und investieren." *Der Tagesspiegel,* December 16, 2013. Accessed March 12, 2017. http://www.tagesspiegel.de/wirtschaft/stadtmarketing-berlin-lieben-und-investieren/9226934.html.

Göhler, Gerhard. "Der Zusammenhang von Institution, Macht und Repräsentation." In *Institution—Macht—Repräsentation: Wofür politische Institutionen stehen und wie sie wirken,* edited by Gerhard Göhler et al., 11–62. Baden-Baden: Nomos, 1997.

———. "Symbolische Politik—Symbolische Praxis, Zum Symbolverständnis in der deutschen Politikwissenschaft." In *Was heißt Kulturgeschichte des Politischen? Zeitschrift für historische Forschung. Beiheft 35,* edited by Barbara Stollberg-Rilinger, 57–69. Berlin: Duncker & Humblot, 2005.

Goldberg, Vicki. *The Power of Photography: How Photographs Changed Our Lives.* New York: Abbeville, 1991.

Haustein, Lydia. *Global Images: Globale Bildinszenierungen und kulturelle Identität.* Göttingen: Wallstein, 2008.

Jencks, Charles. *The Iconic Building: The Power of Enigma.* London: Frances Lincoln, 2005.

Kamleithner, Christa, and Roland Meyer. "Urban Icons: Architektur und globale Bildzirkulation." Special issue, *Urban Icons: Informationen zur modernen Stadtgeschichte* 2 (2011): 17–31.

König, Norbert. "Die symbolische Bedeutung des Brandenburger Tores." In *Das Brandenburger Tor: Wege in die Geschichte; Tor in die Zukunft,* edited by Stiftung Denkmalschutz Berlin, 113–35. Berlin: Jovis Verlag, 2003.

Kress, Celina, Marc Schalenberg, and Sandra Schürmann, eds. Special issue, *Urban Icons: Informationen zur modernen Stadtgeschichte* 2 (2011).

Kurz, Gerhard. *Metapher, Allegorie, Symbol.* Göttingen: Vandenhoeck Ruprecht, 2004.

Mausbach, Florian. "Über Sinn und Ort eines nationalen Freiheits- und Einheitsdenkmals." In *Der Weg zum Denkmal für Freiheit und Einheit,* edited by Andreas H. Apelt, 12–30. Schwalbach: Wochenschau Verlag, 2009.

Mausbach, Florian, et al. "Initiative Denkmal Deutsche Einheit: Brief der Initiatoren, Mai 1998." In *Der Weg zum Denkmal für Freiheit und Einheit,* edited by Andreas H. Apelt, 33–35. Schwalbach: Wochenschau Verlag, 2009.

Meyer, Robert and Lutz Haarmann. "Das Freiheits- und Einheitsdenkmal, Die geschichtspolitische Verortung in der Ideengeschichte der Bundesrepublik." *Bpb: Bundeszentrale für politische Bildung.* Accessed January 10, 2017. http://www.bpb.de/geschichte/zeitgeschichte/deutschlandarchiv/53296/freiheits-und-einheitsdenkmal.

Norberg-Schulz, Christian. *Logik der Baukunst.* Frankfurt: Ullstein, 1965.

Reiche, Jürgen. "Symbolgehalt und Bedeutungswandel eines politischen Monuments." In *Das Brandenburger Tor: Eine Monographie,* edited by Willmuth Arenhövel and Rolf Bothe, 270–316. Berlin: Verlag Willmuth Arenhövel, 1991.

Rosh, Lea. "Kriegsdenkmäler—ja, Holocaust-Denkmal—nein?" *Vorwärts* 45 (November 1988). Cited in *Der Denkmalstreit—das Denkmal? Die Debatte um das "Denkmal für die ermordeten Juden Europas": Eine Dokumentation,* edited by Ute Heimrod, Günter Schlusche, and Horst Seferens, 52. Berlin: Philo, 1999.

Schirmer, Dietmar. "Politik und Architektur: Ein Beitrag zur politischen Symbolanalyse am Beispiel Washingtons." In *Sprache des Parlaments und Semiotik der Demokratie: Studien zur politischen Kommunikation in der Moderne,* edited by Andreas Dörner and Ludgera Vogt, 309–39. Berlin: Walter de Gruyter, 1995.

Schlögel, Klaus. "Wir brauchen die Wippe nicht." *Die Welt,* May 28, 2011. Accessed March 12, 2017. http://www.welt.de/print/die_welt/vermischtes/article13399337/Wir-brauchen-die-Wippe-nicht.html.

Schröder, Richard, et al. "Brauchen wir ein Nationales Freiheits- und Einheits-Denkmal? Erstes Hearing der Deutschen Gesellschaft e.V. am 9.11.2006 im

Berliner Rathaus." In *Der Weg zum Denkmal für Freiheit und Einheit,* edited by Andreas H. Apelt, 58–82. Schwalbach: Wochenschau Verlag, 2009.

Schwerk, Ekkehard. "Die verwickelte Wahrheit des gewandelten Wahrzeichens." *Der Tagesspiegel,* August 3, 1991.

Seibt, Gustav. "Das Brandenburger Tor." In *Deutsche Erinnerungsorte II,* edited by Etienne François, and Hagen Schulze, 67–85. Munich: Verlag C. H. Beck, 2009.

Senatsverwaltung fur Wirtschaft, Technologie und Frauen. "Tourismuskonzept Berlin: Handlungsrahmen 2011+." Accessed October 26, 2016. http://www .dehoga-berlin.de/images/dehoga/005_daten_fakten/daten_fakten_pdf/ tourismuskonzept_2011.pdf

Smend, Rudolf. "Verfassung und Verfassungsrecht." In *Staatsrechtliche Abhandlungen und andere Aufsätze,* edited by Rudolf Smend, 119–276. Berlin: Duncker and Humboldt, 1994.

Wilms, Dorothee. "Was sollte ein Freiheits- und Einheitsdenkmal versinnbildlichen?" *Deutschland Archiv* 40, no. 5 (2007) 868–72.

Wolfrum, Edgar. *Geschichtspolitik in der Bundesrepublik Deutschland, Der Weg zur bundesrepublikanischen Erinnerung 1948–1990.* Darmstadt: Wissenschaftliche Buchgesellschaft, 1999.

Young, James E. "Horst Hoheisel's Counter-Memory of the Holocaust: The End of the Monument." *Center for Holocaust and Genocide Studies.* Accessed October 26, 2015. http://chgs.umn.edu/museum/memorials/hoheisel/.

CHAPTER 7

Disappearing History
Challenges of Imagining Berlin after 1989

Ayse N. Erek and Eszter Gantner

Berlin faced two major challenges at the beginning of the 1990s: ful-filling the role of a new national capital and, at the same time, meeting the requirements of globalization (especially the global competition of cities). With the relocation of the government and ministries from Bonn, the formal capital of the Federal Republic, it became clear that the re-unified Germany's old-and-new capital Berlin had inherited a heavy and difficult historical burden. The unified city needed redefining. Its Senate drew heavily upon a variety of images from Berlin's intense past, includ-ing the golden Weimar years, the bifurcation into East and West, and even its Nazi period, to achieve such recasting. The image campaigns produced by the marketing company *Partner für Berlin*[1] employed var-ious topoi throughout the 1990s, such as Berlin "as a bridge between Eastern and Western Europe," Berlin as "a leading digital economy cen-tre," and Berlin "as an art metropolis."[2] On the other hand, increasingly, a variety of new practices are also coming to reimagine it, such as arts, civic activities, and global interventions like establishing urban gardens in Mauerpark and in Moritzplatz (called *Prinzessinnengarten*). Each of these influences currently plays enormous roles in the production of Berlin's unique metropolitan identity.

Globalization has shifted cities and metropolises all over the world into the foreground and elevated a subset of them to the category of "world cities."[3] European cities, like their Asian and North and South American counterparts, compete with one another to become preem-inent centers of economic and cultural exchange and, by extension, of tourism as well. The ethnic and cultural diversity, history, and heritage of these cities, and their effective representation, play important roles in this competition. Such cultural heritage constitutes a form of capital that is part of a symbolic economy broadcasting a city's image and accruing concrete economic advantages to it by, for example, increasing tourism and attracting creative industries.[4] To succeed in this symbolic economy, cities undertake "self-culturalization" and "self-historization" by shaping and disposing their distinctive features to appear in the most favorable light.[5]

The renovation and reinterpretation of particular quarters, the staging and promotion of events, the fashioning of an image unique to a given city, and the marketing of its history—mostly through architectural heritage—manifests such processes of self-culturalization and self-historization. Cities consciously cultivate a brand and communicate it to the world by adopting an approach similar to that used in the marketing of consumer products. City branding efforts profit from the unique history attached to place, for instance through the creation of museum districts and the reconstruction of ethnic quarters such as the *Marais* in Paris and the *Kazimiercz* in Krakow as Jewish quarters. In their article in this volume, Stefanie Eisenhuth and Scott H. Krause also consider such processes, using the well-known Cold War sites Checkpoint Charlie, the Normannenstraße Stasi compound, and *Tempelhof* Airport field to examine struggles around the multiple interpretations of history involved in designing Berlin today. They seek to "illustrate how Berlin is not a coherent, unequivocal *lieu de mémoire,* but rather an arena of battlefields for interpretational sovereignty." Our examination also shows that the intensive use of new discourses on history in "imagineering" processes were characteristics of the fabricating of Berlin at the beginning of the 1990s, while going on to argue for a more recent, slow phenomenon of *disappearing history.*[6]

In the 1990s, in the context of economic challenges such as the loss of most of Berlin's industrial base[7] and political debates about German unification and the new role of Berlin, the main issues present in the local media and public debates centered on concrete urban development.[8] These discourses raised questions about the city's identity in relation to its Nazi and Communist past.[9] Because of this difficult history and heritage, there were loud pleas to select an epoch upon which positive identity-building and image construction could take place.[10] Weimar Berlin and the "Golden Twenties," or "Roaring Twenties," became that reference point in the June 20, 1991, parliamentary debate on Berlin as capital. In this historic deliberation of the German *Bundestag,* the main question was symbolic: Why relocate from Bonn when Berlin was "so freighted with heavy historical baggage"?[11] In that spectacular session, only a slim majority of eighteen votes approved Berlin's capital status. MPs of the Free Democrats (FDP) and of Social Democrats (SPD) argued in a very emotional debate *for* Berlin, due to its democratic heritage rooted in the Weimar period. In their argumentations *for* or *against* Berlin, they cited both "dark" periods, such as the Nazi past, and bright ones, such as the Weimar Republic.[12]

Yet, finally, "choosing" the Weimar period as the primary historical reference point solved the dilemma of Berlin's "heavy historical baggage," and, therefore, during the 1990s the city seemed to be inseparable from the myth of the "Golden Twenties." As sociologist Sybille Frank emphasizes in her research on the revitalization of the emblematic Potsdamer Platz, "the memory images in the myth remain conspicuously limited to the 1920s."[13] The concepts from which this myth has been constituted include Weimar as experimental and as laboratory, Americanization, mass culture, crisis, and modernity.[14]

While the republic persisted as locus for the urban imaginary during the 1990s, by the 2000s, parallel with the strengthening political situation of Berlin, new historical themes moved into focus, among them the difficult heritage of the city, the NS-Past (Nazi past). But by the year 2000 Berlin's political position was strong enough to openly face this historical burden. Through the newly emerged memory district,[15] which includes the Jewish Museum (2001), the Memorial of the Murdered Jews of Europe (2005), and the Topography of Terror, not only the *moral duty* of facing with the past had been fulfilled, but at the same time by this act a new iconic architecture had been established in the urban space. This architecture, connected with the city's difficult history, had become one of *the unique selling points* of Berlin.[16]

Parallel to these developments, from the middle of the 1990s onward, the growing art scene has played an increasingly important role in the process of reimagining the city. The establishment of Berlin's art fair, the Art Forum 1995, and, three years later, the Berlin Biennale, point not only to the significant number of galleries and artists but also to the growing support of major agents in Berlin's marketing, such as the Berlin Senate.[17] In 2000 a real gallery boom started, and, with each opening, more international and German collectors frequent the capital. The official tourism website "Visit Berlin" illustrates the extent to which the Berlin Senate is aware of this development: "From artists, gallery owners and curators, to critics and collectors—Berlin is an artistic hub and the place to be for all art professionals. Berlin is long been said to be one of the most vital and exciting centers of art. This is why many artists come to the German capital, whether for a few weeks or months, a couple of years, or forever."[18] Indeed, much research shows that the city government actively supports the arts as part of imagineering efforts.[19]

In this context, our chapter analyzes the paradoxes of image production—or *urban imagineering*—of Berlin over the last two and a half decades with a focus on the phenomenon of disappearing history. The term *urban imagineering* was coined by Charles Rutheiser to describe successive waves of organized and systematic promotion in linked but not always well-coordinated acts. The German anthropologists Rolf Lindner and Alexa Färber develop the concept further and have applied it to the study of Berlin. Each understands urban imagineering as a differentiated discursive field of practices, especially by professionalized groups of stakeholders. One such stakeholder is the marketing agency of Berlin's municipality,[20] which actively generates the unique images, narratives, and symbols of the city. In this selection and production of publicly communicated images,[21] we argue, both ethnic and cultural diversity and history play significant roles.[22]

This chapter proceeds in two steps to illuminate how particular narratives of history, diversity, the "new" are deployed in fabricating the German capital. The first aim of our analysis is to illustrate the selection of historical themes as inherent to the urban imagineering of Berlin through two case studies, the former Jewish Girls' School in Berlin's Mitte district and the "Be Berlin" campaign. The two very different cases exemplify the various mechanisms of disappearing history: while the Jewish Girls' School demonstrates how architectural heritage forfeits its history, "Be Berlin" shows the use of historical motifs in a campaign aimed at reimagineering Berlin. The second aim is to examine what replaces history in imagining the New Berlin. In this case, the "new" is attached to art and creativity to reimagine the city. The analysis moves on to conceptualizing disappearing history as a consequence of such urban imagineering. Disappearing history describes a process whereby agents of urban imagineering, such as the Berlin Senate, select and use those values and images that are in synchrony with globalization and emphasize the "new"—instead of using and referring to other specific urban knowledges and histories—in order to reimagine Berlin. Our investigation demonstrates how urban imagineering has refashioned Berlin through such selective articulation with a focus on the global and the new, and we analyze at the same time how history is disappearing in this process.

Disappearing History

The redevelopment of the former Jewish Girls' School in the August-straße exemplifies disappearing history. Through a careful selection of certain historical and thematic elements, its admittedly beautiful renovation refashions the building in a completely new image. This image not only has the additional effect of recasting the area around it but also rewriting the history of it. In the new context, the difficult history of the structure provides the building and its new functions nothing more than an exotic touch. As a result of its transition, the former Jewish school—for years unrenovated and empty—is now one of the fashionable hubs in Mitte.

Although the building has had several uses over the years, its significance in the new Berlin primarily involves Jewish culture. The school in the Auguststraße was built between 1927 and 1928, based on the plans of architect Alexander Beer with a usable area of about three thousand square meters. It was one of the last prewar buildings of the Jewish municipality of Berlin upon which construction was completed. Consisting of fourteen classrooms, a gymnasium, and a roof garden, the school was one of the most modern ones in the city. By the time it was closed in June 1942, most of the pupils and teachers had been deported and killed in various concentration camps. The building then served as a military hospital until 1945. Between 1950 and 1989, it was used as a school in the German Democratic Republic. Between 1996 and 2009, the abandoned building hosted temporary exhibitions such as "Davka—Jüdisches Leben in Berlin" of the Jewish artists group Me-shullash 1998[23] and the fourth Berlin Arts Biennale in 2006. It was only in 2009 that the structure was officially handed over to the Jewish community. The community's lack of funds to renovate the building, which is on a historic register, compelled them to lease it to the Michael Fuchs gallery for twenty years. The gallery owner had redeveloped the structure and tried to establish a new concept of revitalization in the building by developing it as a space of art, commemoration, and gastronomy. The history of the building served as a basis for a production of a new "stylish" and exotic image of "Jewishness" that played an enormous role in recentering the building on the map of Berlin's fashionable, cosmopolitan areas.[24]

The former Jewish Girls' School and its history were "recycled" by mixing components of luxury and exotic (Jewish) for the reopening of the building to the public in 2012. Due to this mixing, the building and its past legitimized particular forms of "Jewishness" and the same legitimacy provided the restaurant Mogg & Meltzer a touch of "exotic" as well. The strategy for the reuse of the building underlay an imagineering process in which selected motifs and images of Jewish-German history and culture were decontextualized and marketed. As a result, the local Jewish culture and the history of the building and of the area were reduced to certain motifs, such as food like matzo ball soup or music like klezmer or certain traditional practices like kashrut in one of the restaurants of the building "Kosher Classroom." These motifs generated a new narrative of "Jewishness" marketed as "history." The home page of the building management firm supported this reading, stating, "After effectively demonstrating how the building would both honor the past and become part of Berlin's creative future, this newly refurbished space aims to combine the experience of history, art and gastronomy."[25]

This imagineering of a stylish and "exotic," in terms of "ethnically different,"[26] urban Berlin that accepts and embraces cultural difference, having overcome its difficult past, succeeded here symbolically. *Merian,* one of the best-known magazines for travel and tourism in Germany, celebrated the newly imaged Jewish Berlin in 2013 the following way:

> Das Jüdische in der Hauptstadt ist in den letzten Jahren vor allem dank des Zustroms aus Russland, Israel und den USA viel sichtbarer geworden. Und hinter diesem neuen jüdischen Berlin steckt die Sehnsucht nach Normalität—ohne die Geschichte dabei zu vergessen. …. Immer öfter gelingt dieser Spagat. Zum Beispiel in der Ehemaligen Jüdischen Mädchenschule.[27]

In this quote, the history of the building was utilized as a reservoir of motifs fed by an exotified Jewishness. Interestingly, the generations-old stereotypical "Image of the Jew" of Holocaust, World War II, and perhaps Israel fame[28] is slowly being replaced with new motifs based on the aforementioned cultural clichés, like music, clothes, or eating habits. This process suggested some of the implications of creating a new Jewishness despite a "difficult history."[29]

More recently, the ongoing process of the disappearance of the history has resulted in the full disappearance of these historical motifs of the German–Jewish past. With the exception of one tableau in the small exhibition at the entrance, nothing else reflects the history of the building. The restaurants have changed their menus, becoming global, and in the spaces of the building, new galleries have opened new art exhibitions. History has been replaced by art. Even the so-called Kennedy Museum in the building does not contradict this process: it is a collection of the Camera Work gallery showing hundreds of pictures connected to the Kennedy Family. But according to the Camera Work gallery's website,[30] its main focus is the exhibition of contemporary artists.

The refurbishment of the Jewish Girls' School testifies to the ongoing process of disappearing history, in this case of German-Jewish history. The building's past served as a resource for its reimagineering and relocation into a new and creative cosmopolitan area with a developed art scene.[31] There has been little discussion of new and creative up to this point. The difficult German-Jewish history, overshadowed by the Holocaust and connected with issues such as historical responsibility and the duty of commemoration,[32] does not fit in all its complexity into the newly imagined, creative, and hip Berlin. Instead, the building and its multifaceted history has been reduced to internationally decodable images of Jewish culture (or what is thought to be Jewish culture), and for now even these images have slowly disappeared. An architectural manifestation of the German-Jewish past has been transformed into an artistic and gastronomic hub, into a place of globalizing urban culture replacing complex history.

The "Be Berlin" Campaign

In 2004, the German urban planner Dieter Hassenpflug famously declared, "The resources for the production of future urban habitats lie in the past."[33] He points to one of the most discussed correlations between heritage, identity, and history within urban studies research. Against this widely shared conviction,[34] we employ disappearing history to argue that history and images with historical content now play less of a role in the projected urban future than even five years ago. By understanding urban imagineering as a differentiated discourse and field of practice, it is possible to capture and analyze the practices and the most influential agents involved in selecting the tools used to create the future-oriented image of Berlin.

The image campaign "Be Berlin," organized and released by the marketing agency Berlin Partner GmbH under the supervision of the Berlin Senate in 2008, offers one case by means of which to examine the change in the imagining of the city from a focus on the past to a focus on the future. This imagining influences the selection of images of Berlin in the campaign, whose mandate is to give the capital a *clear profile*. The imagineering of a "New Berlin" is based on the following two principles:

1. Avoid large spectacular actions or brisk slogans, rather thematize the diversity and creativity of the 3.4 million Berliners "who make our city so unique and who contribute every day to its transformation."[35]
2. Systematically expose the different facets of Berlin, such as business, science, culture, industry, modern sports, and community.

The first principle expresses the clear message that Berlin is the place where every city dweller, newcomer, and even tourist can experience being part of a community in their own individual ways. "Be Berlin" perceives this diversity of individuals and the coexistence of these various people as driving forces for creativity, change, and innovation. These attributes—and here we follow the logic of the campaign—are the basis for developing the city as an attractive economic location. The second principle, based on the first one, connects the diversity of city dwellers with the six main areas of urban production. In the first year of the campaign, and in the campaign opening speech of the mayor Klaus Wowereit, city dwellers were invited to participate actively in it. This *participatory* element was not meant only rhetorically. From 2008, thousands of people took part in the campaign through testimonials or in the form of the various competitions, both of which became integral parts of the promotion. The campaign produced several thematic images every year around an established topic, and various images were created and set in place. The following chart provides an overview of the chosen topics (and their slogans) over the last six years. The summary of the campaign activities between 2008 and 2014 serves as a basis for the chart.

As the chart shows, comparatively few historical topics were selected; 2013 saw the fiftieth anniversary of John F. Kennedy's visit to Berlin, and the Fall of the Wall is recurrent. Much more than historical images and topics, future visions are projected onto the city: digital worlds, clean technology, the future itself. The present is "socially" related and is reflected in basic principles: diversity, society, and creativity. This focus means that Berliners themselves are thematized, as the slogan "We in Berlin" suggests. In contrast, the "New Berlin" of the future focuses more on images of "digital" and "scientific" visions for a city of new technologies and sciences as well as design and art. This *less historical,* present and future-oriented "New Berlin" points to another phenomenon requiring consideration as well; namely, that this image of a smart and green Berlin is a vision that, demographically speaking, is *shared* by a high percentage of the populace. The "Be Berlin" campaign

Table 7.1. Five-Year Summary of "Be Berlin" Campaign: 2008 to 2014

"Be Berlin" campaign	2008	2009	2010	2011	2012	2013	2014
Historical topics	Unification of Germany (Day of German Unification)	—	—	—	—	Be John F. Kennedy	—
Future-related topics (STS)	—	—	Future made in Berlin; Clean-Tech World	—	City of Chances; Science in Berlin; Startups in Berlin	—	Digital Capital; E-Mobility; Technology and Innovation; "Typical Berlin: Everywhere Space to Think"
Present-time topics	The longest love letter to our city on eight Berlin S-Bahn stations	Berliners with Heart & Gob; Berlin the place to be	Berlin your face; Social city; Industry: Showcase	"We in Berlin" "be Berliner"	"Ideas in Berlin"; "Culture in Berlin"; "Work in Berlin"; "Nature in Berlin"	"Your idea for Berlin"	Families and Talents "Bring your children to Berlin! They will be here later anyway!"
Events turned into images	Festival of Light Fashion Week	Festival of Light Fashion Week	Festival of Light Fashion Week	Berlin Music Week (BMW); Fashion week; Festival of Light	Fashion Week; Festival of Light; BMW	Fashion Week; Festival of Light; BMW	Fashion Week; Festival of Light; BMW

was built on the diversity of the city dwellers—the new vision of Berlin therefore must be sharable by those already in the city and also by those intending to move or transition there. Its future vision must *include* and *not exclude,* as many narratives of history do.

The historical images of Berlin are mostly based on the commonly experienced past of the nation. Although it was perhaps always a "European" metropolis, as the capital of imperial Germany, the Weimar Republic, and Nazi Germany, it simultaneously played a national-political and cultural role. After 1945 again, the historical experiences of the *Berliner Bürger* could not have been separated from the fate of the two Germanys. However this national historical narrative, and even the fall of the Wall, *excluded* those who were not part of this *national* historical experience. Due to globalization and with it the migration to Berlin, this national historical narrative of *exclusion* is disappearing from the imagineering of the city. It is replaced by a new, *shareable* future vision of the city offered by the "Be Berlin" campaign. Based on values and issues, such as science, ecology, technology, design, culture, and creativity, this vision must necessarily imply the future in its endeavor to be shared by everyone.

The Rise of the New Berlin as an Art City

Within the variety of practices coming to reimagine Berlin as of the present and future rather than the past, arts has a specific role in introducing the "new," while the emphasis on history diminishes. Nevertheless, the intersection of art and urban centers in global cities are unique in the twenty-first century. Global cities become laboratories that generate a particular type of creative process and various discussions addressing the global city as a particular kind of social field, with specific cultural dynamics.[36] They serve as marketplaces for the quest for cosmopolitanism by offering a multiplicity of cultural influences.[37] The arts play an important role in this setting, since the close connection between cultural industries and the cultural dynamism of global urban contexts provide the inhabitants with diverse cultural resources.[38] The global age marks the cultural turn where both arts and its world are progressively taking a role in imagining a city. As the global city had to find a way to brand itself to find a place in the new conditions of globalization, it had to create an image to appeal to the competitive global economy.[39] Branding the city through arts connects its financial activity, tourism, and expectations to economic growth, where arts become components in reproducing the political, economic and symbolic economy of cities.[40]

The city of Berlin has been characterized by culture and arts periods throughout the twentieth century, but after 2000, intensified cultural contact in Berlin created a unique opportunity for it to cater to cosmopolitan interests. The 1990s defined Berlin as a city of contemporary arts and alternative culture; youth cultures, activist movements, and street art—all young and global—took on a new role in the public spaces. Officially promoted by the Senate as having "long been said to be one of the most vital and exciting centers of art" and "an artistic hub and the place to be,"[41] the capital saw an increase in investment in the arts. Funds raised from the early 2000s led to a new and dynamic art world, reimagining Berlin as a new center for alternative global lifestyles.

At this time, the increase in art fairs, the relocation of art galleries to Berlin, and the arrival of artists from all around the world helped the process of imagining the "new" Berlin and defining it as a global capital of the arts. The material consequences of this are observable in the redefinition of its neighborhoods and its architectural heritage. The first three Berlin Biennales directly thematized Berlin as "a city of art." The first, in 1998, titled "Berlin," focused on artists who had moved there permanently and even temporarily as they "found a departure (for their work) by taking a look at this exciting city."[42] The 1990s were defined as a lively time for the arts in Berlin, and the event was defined as an inspiration for the arts. The curator of the major sponsor *Hauptstadt-kulturfonds Berlin,* Adrienne Goehler, had defined the biennale as being highly relevant to the capital city, and the minister also emphasized the "great future potential" of the exhibition.[43] The destruction of the Wall was chosen as "the historical and the conceptual starting point" for the contemporary art exhibition, while the choice of *Kunstwerke* or *Martin-Gropius-Bau* as venues to exhibit international art simultaneously linked Berlin to the "international developments" within art, an endeavor that could be interpreted as the desire to be part of the global and to connect the city and its spaces with the rest of the world through arts.[44] In 2004, Christina Weiss, the state minister at the Federal Chancellery and the Federal Government Commissioner for Cultural and Media Affairs, defined it as a "hub for the contemporary art world" and a "charismatic city with an historical touch, political connotations and newly defined urban spaces,"[45] pointing out that history is not the main force for imagining the city but that in addition arts and its urban spaces define it anew.

Apart from exploring the aesthetic terrain of Berlin, the emphasis was on "giving each new generation of new arrivals to Berlin the opportunity to improvise their very own new Berlin."[46] Its depiction of being in a state of "relative poverty and relaxed laissez faire" attitude due to the surfeit of accommodation and business space[47] furthered this notion that there was room for everyone. Berlin's characterization as the art capital of Europe is associated with "artistic authenticity" as well as "transgressive and Bohemian lifestyles."[48] Isabelle Graw argues that "the alternative," "minoritarian," and "bohemian" connotations of today's Berlin "conform to a professional profile that is in high demand in what is described as 'network capitalism.'"[49] Relatedly, Ingo Niermann observes a new direction in the market that involves social networking in biennales, festivals, art fairs, and openings, declaring that "the times are over when the lives and the looks of bohemians were exotic enough to sell [their works]."[50]

The Senate's official choice of Berlin as art city had material consequences, such as an increase of art spaces spread throughout, spaces that transformed the architectural heritage and the neighborhoods to suit their new uses and were also embraced by the real-estate market. The city now hosts approximately four hundred galleries, most of which opened in the last ten years and some of which relocated from other cities like Cologne; several galleries from around the world opened branches in Berlin, which needed to compete with New York as a major global center for arts in the twenty-first century.[51] Gallery Weekend founded in 2005 and followed by the inauguration of Berlin Art Week in 2012 "sought to underscore the importance of the city as a center for contemporary art, placing a focus on the city as a place that attracts visitors from all around the world."[52] In 2008, Gallery Weekend evolved into an international art fair ABC (Art Berlin Contemporary), "with a common interest in promoting Berlin as an art market and bringing its protagonists together."[53] Other successors of the Art Forum (created in 1996) include Preview Berlin Art Fair, founded in 2005, and the *Berliner Liste,* initiated in 2008. The recently founded Positions announced itself with the promise of "depicting the quality and currentness of the international art scene comprehensively and independently from established categories, inviting the visitor to discover new positions."[54]

While urban space and art spaces are brought together as never before, the old neighborhoods are undergoing renovation for the new Berlin: renewed and refunctioned. This reconstruction includes the choice of iconic spaces in the city for use as galleries, as well as the transformation of previously existing buildings into such spaces. Designing Berlin occurs in parallel with designing its galleries in accordance with the new architectural face of the city. Artnet recently chose Berlin's ten best art spaces, selecting several galleries that work with iconic and disused city structures in accordance with its new guides for contemporary art.[55] For example, the influential contemporary art gallery Blain I Southern, which moved into the old cavernous hall that previously held the printing press of the Berlin newspaper *Tagesspiegel*, exemplifies this endeavor in the newly emerging gallery quartier around Potsdamer Straße. The former Catholic church of St. Agnes is being renovated as the new venue for young artists associated with König Gallery, which in 2006 moved to a former industrial space near Potsdamer Platz, famously known as the center of the Weimar Republic and now a symbol of the postmodern city. The "monumentality" of the new space, St. Agnes Church, is emphasized on the gallery website as part of the description for a sound-art installation.[56] *Galerie Kewenig*, which moved to Berlin in 2013 from Cologne, purchased and revamped a 1688 baroque townhouse, one of the city's oldest, near the museum island. Artnet also lists the "ostalgic" spaces that link the new art world to the former east of Berlin; notably, the *Galerie Neu* now occupies three spaces in Mitte, including a GDR *Plattenbau* (prefabricated) apartment block previously used as an electric plant, and both *Capitain Petzel* and *Peres Projects* now inhabit the former commercial spaces of Karl-Marx Allee near Alexanderplatz.[57]

The renewal of cities involves removing old buildings to build new ones, yet the urge to transform historical spaces and provide them new functions is also a part of the global world: new, dynamic, and forward-looking. As most cities have had to reinvent themselves to accord with global conditions, so urban spaces and iconic buildings have gained new functions through art. In Berlin, many new projects that involve architectural design have become a part of the landscape of public art institutions opened after 2000. For example, the Contemporary Fine Arts exhibition space, a museum of nineteenth-century art, design, and technology on Mitte's Museum Island, was designed and built by David Chipperfield Architects (2003–7), and the same studio restored the *Neues Museum*, which reopened in 2009.[58]

Berlin's policymakers are proud of the existence of contemporary art in the city. In spring 2007, local newspapers reported that the new branding strategy promoted by then-mayor Klaus Wowereit was "Berlin: City of Change." He declared that the aim was "to promote Berlin as a casual and relaxed, international and open metropolis, radiating joy and creativity, and where it is a pleasure to live."[59]

Conclusion

The process of image production by professionals and stakeholders has generated a variety of images, narratives, and symbols for Berlin since the 1990s. Within this urban imagineering, some interest has been focused on memory and historical narratives. On the other hand, the rise of art and its institutions—entangled with the urban fabric, real-estate investments and their marketing, new strategies of imagining Berlin through publicity campaigns, and new discourses on history—imply a change in how Berlin is imagined. Today's Berlin is depicted primarily as a metropolis of present and future that charts a process of disappearing history: history is disappearing from the present self-image and future vision of the city.

Our case studies reflect on somewhat different aspects of the history and historical heritage of the city in illustrating the process of this disappearing history. The case of the former Jewish Girls' School connects image creation with tangible heritage, while the campaign "Be Berlin" uses select historical events as tools in its urban imagineering. If the practice of disappearing history produces a new instrumentalization of history that looks forward to the future, then the official decision undertaken to introduce a "new" Berlin produces cultural and material consequences in the city: arts and creativity become motives for the production of Berlin's contemporary image, which in return takes a crucial role in redefining the neighborhoods, places, and buildings of the city. Within this process, particular histories of spaces play a rather marginal role. The case studies examined in this paper clearly demonstrate this. They show how the past has been treated—reduced to certain selected images—and how these images are no more than added "details" in a new vision of Berlin defined through the notions of change, dynamism, cosmopolitism, and, especially, the "new." Globally understandable and sharable values and slogans—such as technology, smart, digital, green, as well as artistic and creative—belong to the repertoire of this future image of Berlin. In addition, this vision is globally attractive and promises openness and internationalism for everyone. In the call for the new and the city to be shared globally, the past is imaged by spectacularizing history, which is a way of opening up the city to the laws of global processes, as is required of a global city. In this regard, in the discourse of imagining Berlin, art plays an especially definitive role: it replaces history as the city's master discourse, evolves within the spirit of the contemporary, and defines itself in accordance with the dynamic and the new. Many urban researchers record the phenomenon of Berlin's self-historicization[60]; our work here counters that this focus on the past marks a previous phase of the imagineering of Berlin, one characteristic of the late 1990s and early 2000s. The metropolis imagined a decade earlier is already fading away.

Ayse N. Erek is associate professor of art history at Kadir Has University, Istanbul. Her research focuses on urban imaginaries in the context of political and cultural discourse in Istanbul and Berlin and issues of modern and contemporary art and exhibiting practices. She coedited a special issue of *Visual Resources Journal* in 2014.

Eszter Gantner is Post-Doc researcher and project coordinator (LOEWE) at the Herder Institute for Historical Research on East Central Europe, Marburg. Her research concentrates on 19th and 20th century urban history in East Central Europe and heritage studies with focus on former socialist countries.

Notes

1. The company, *Partner für Berlin Holding Gesellschaft für Hauptstadt-Marketing mbH,* was established by the Berlin Senate in 1994.
2. Claire Colomb, *Staging the New Berlin: Place Marketing and the Politics of Urban Reinvention Post-1989* (London, 2012), 137.
3. Ulf Hannerz, "The Cultural Role of World Cities," in *Humanising the City? Social Contexts of Urban Life at the Turn of the Millennium,* ed. Anthony P. Cohen and Fuki Katsuyoshi (Edinburgh, 1993), 67–84.
4. Sharon Zukin, *The Culture of the Cities* (New York, 1996).
5. Andreas Reckwitz, "Die Selbstkulturalisierung der Stadt: Zur Transformation moderner Urbanität in der 'Creative City,'" *Mittelweg 36* 18, no. 2 (2009): 2–34.
6. Beate Binder, *Streitfall Stadtmitte: Der Berliner Schlossplatz* (Vienna, 2007), 37–43.
7. Colomb, *Staging the New Berlin,* 83.
8. Ibid., 106–7.
9. Sharon Macdonald, *Difficult Heritage: Negotiating the Nazi Past in Nuremberg and Beyond* (New York, 2009).
10. Binder, *Streitfall Stadtmitte,* 37–43.
11. David Clay Large, *Berlin* (New York, 2000), 547.
12. See, for example, the speech of the social democrat MP Hans-Jochen Vogel, "Berlin-Debatte / Wortlaut der Reden: Vogel," *Deutscher Bundestag,* accessed February 12, 2016, http://www.bundestag.de/kulturundgeschichte/geschichte/debatte/bdr_017/246560.

13. Sybille Frank, "Mythenmaschine Potsdamer Platz," in *Selling Berlin*, ed. Thomas Bischkup and Marc Schalenberg (Stuttgart, 2008), 295.

14. Eszter Gantner, *Budapest-Berlin: Die Koordinaten einer Emigration* (Stuttgart, 2011), 187.

15. Tobias Brinkmann, "Neighborhood Memorials: 'Jewish' Space in New York and Berlin," in *Taking Up Space: New Approaches to American History*, ed. Christoph Ribbat and Anke Ortlepp (Trier, 2004), 123–38.

16. Eszter Gantner, "Jewish Quarters as Urban Tableaux," in *Jewish and Non-Jewish Spaces in Urban Context*, ed. Alina Gromova, Felix Heinert, and Sebastian Voigt (Berlin, 2014), 10–20.

17. Many different and often interconnected reasons account for the current success of contemporary art in Berlin. The existence of well-established institutions was not the only crucial reason for Berlin's development into a metropolis of fine arts. Its history and culture, different communities, and the living conditions in Berlin also played a critical role. For more on the city's art development, see Carsten Zorn, "Art System and Society of Control: Exhibition vs. Autonomy; On Recent Changes in Form and Function of Structural Coupling," *Österreichische Zeitschrift für Geschichtswissenschaften* 17, no. 2–3 (2006): 98–126.

18. "Berlin's Gallery Scene," *Berlin Tourismus & Kongress GmbH*, accessed April 20, 2016, http://press.visitberlin.de/en/news-release/berlin-epicentre-of-contemporary-art.

19. Ibid.

20. The main task of Berlin's first public-private partnership, formed in 1994, was to develop and implement new strategies and messages for a concentrated urban and site marketing. The brand perception of Berlin had to be revitalized, and a new and positive image of the German capital had to be created. The "New Berlin" campaign was thus addressed to newly defined target groups: the city's population and economy, the German population as a whole, potential investors, and visitors to the capital ("5 Years").

21. Sandra Schürmann and Jochen Guckes, "Stadtbilder und Stadtrepräsentationen im 20. Jahrhundert," *Informationen zur modernen Stadtgeschichte* 1 (2005): 5–11.

22. Gisela Welz, *Inszenierungen kultureller Vielfalt* (Berlin, 1996).

23. "Davka–Jüdisches Leben in Berlin: Traditionen und Visionen von der Gruppe Meshulash," *haGalil.com*, accessed February 23, 2016. http://www.hagalil.com/archiv/98/11/davka.htm.

24. Dirk Ludigs, "Juden in Berlin: Sie Kommen, Um Zu Bleiben," in *MERIAN Berlin: Die Lust am Reisen* (Hamburg, 2013), 115–17.

25. Ibid., 117.

26. For further discussion, see Dagmar Horn, *Das selkupische Ethnizitätsgebäude: Zur gegenwärtigen ethnischen Identität der südlichen Selkupen (Westsibirien)* (Trier, 2002).

27. Ludigs, "Juden in Berlin," 115. "Jews in the capital have become more visible during the last years above all thanks to migration from Russia, Israel, and the United States. And behind this New Jewish Berlin lies a longing for normality—but without forgetting history.... More and more often this balancing act succeeds. For example, in the former Jewish Girls' School."
28. Gantner, "Jewish Quarters as Urban Tableaux," 10–20.
29. For further discussion, see Sharon Macdonald, *Difficult Heritage*.
30. Camera Work, accessed February 2, 2017, http://camerawork.de/en/cam era-work/.
31. "Tour 10—Fahrradtour durch Mitte: Jüdisches Leben in der Mitte Berlins," *Berlin Tourismus & KongressGmbH,* accessed Feburary 24, 2016, http://www.visitberlin.de/de/artikel/tour-10-fahrradtour-durch-mitte.
32. Eszter Gantner and Jay (Koby) Oppenheim, "Jewish Space Reloaded: An Introduction," *Anthropological Journal of European Cultures* 23, no. 2 (2014): 1–10.
33. Friedrich Eckardt and Dieter Hassenpflug, eds., *Urbanism and Globalization* (Frankfurt, 2004), 82.
34. Markus Tauschek, *Kulturerbe: Eine Einführung* (Berlin, 2014).
35. Berlin Partner für Wirtschaft und Technologie, "5 Years of be Berlin—A Review," *beBerlin.de,* accessed April 12, 2016, http://www.be.berlin.de/campaign/campaignyears.
36. For further discussion, see Stuart Hall, "Creative Cities and Economic Development," *Urban Studies* 37, no. 4 (2000): 639–49; Zukin, *Culture of the Cities.*
37. Zukin, *Culture of the Cities.*
38. Pilar Rojas Gaviria and Julie Emontspool, "Global Cities and Cultural Experimentation: Cosmopolitan-Local Connections," *International Marketing Review* 32, no. 2 (2015): 181–99.
39. For the discussion of imaginary city through various cases around the world, see Ayse N. Erek and Ayse H. Köksal, "The Imaginary City in the Twenty-First Century," *Visual Resources: An International Journal of Documentation* 30, no. 4 (2014).
40. Setha Low, "The Anthropology of Cities: Imagining and Theorizing the City," *Annual Review of Anthropology* 25 (1996): 383–409.
41. "Berlin's Gallery Scene," accessed February 20, 2015.
42. Tanja Lelgemann, Thomas Wulffen, and Hans Ulrich Obrist, eds., *Berlin Biennale for Contemporary Art Exhibition Catalogue* (Berlin, 1998), 7.
43. Ibid.
44. Klaus Biesenbach, "Berlin Biennial," in *Third Berlin Biennial for Contemporary Art Exhibition Catalogue,* ed. Uta Meta Bauer, Sonke Gau, and Vanessa Adler (Cologne, 2004), 8–9.
45. Christina Weiss, foreword to *Third Berlin Biennial for Contemporary Art Exhibition Catalogue,* ed. Uta Meta Bauer, Sonke Gau, and Vanessa Adler (Cologne, 2004), 6.

46. Biesenbach, "Berlin Biennial," 10.
47. Ibid.
48. Isabelle Graw, "The Myth of Remoteness from the Market: Notes on Berlin's Rise as an Art Metropolis," *Texte Zur Kunst* 24 (2014): 34.
49. Graw employs the term "network capitalism" in reference to sociologists Luc Boltanski and Eva Chiapello's *The New Spirit of Capitalism*. See Graw, "Myth of Remoteness," 36.
50. Ingo Niermann, "Expanded Prostitution," *Spike* 37 (2013): 90.
51. Graw, "Myth of Remoteness," 34.
52. "Berlin Art Week," *e-flux.com,* accessed June 3, 2016, http://www.e-flux .com/announcements/berlin-art-week-2012/.
53. "ABC: About," *Art Berlin Contemporary,* accessed November 10, 2014, http:// www.artberlincontemporary.com/about/.
54. Ibid.
55. Alexander Forbes, "Berlin's 10 Best Gallery Spaces," *Artnet,* October 13, 2014, https://news.artnet.com/art-world/berlins-10-best-gallery-spaces-127917.
56. Enrico, "Alicja Kwade: Nach Osten / Johann König at St. Agnes, Berlin," *VERNISSAGE TV: The Window to the Art World,* May 2, 2013, http://vernissage .tv/2013/05/02/alicja-kwade-nach-osten-johann-konig-at-st-agnes-berlin/.
57. Ibid.
58. Ibid.
59. Colomb, *Staging the New Berlin,* 259.
60. For further discussion, see Zukin, *Culture of the Cities*; Richard Florida, *Cities and the Creative Class* (New York, 2005); Reckwitz, "Die Selbstkulturalisierung der Stadt," 2–34.

Bibliography

"ABC: About." *Art Berlin Contemporary.* Accessed November 10, 2014. http:// www.artberlincontemporary.com/about/.
"Berlin Art Week." *e-flux.* Accessed June 3, 2016. http://www.e-flux.com/ announcements/berlin-art-week-2012/.
Berlin Partner für Wirtschaft und Technologie. "5 Years of *be Berlin*—A Review." *beBerlin.de.* Accessed April 12, 2016. http://www.be.berlin.de/campaign/ campaignyears.
Berlin Tourismus & Kongress GmbH. "Berlin's Gallery Scene." Accessed April 20, 2016. http://press.visitberlin.de/en/news-release/berlin-epicentre-of-contemporary-art.
Biesenbach, Klaus. "Berlin Biennial." In *Third Berlin Biennial for Contemporary Art Exhibition Catalogue,* edited by Uta Meta Bauer, Sonke Gau, and Vanessa Adler, 8–10. Cologne: Walter König, 2004.
Binder, Beate. *Streitfall Stadtmitte: Der Berliner Schlossplatz.* Vienna: Böhlau, 2007.

Brinkmann, Tobias. "Neighborhood Memorials: 'Jewish' Space in New York and Berlin." In *Taking Up Space: New Approaches to American History,* edited by Christoph Ribbat and Anke Ortlepp, 123–38. Trier: WVT Wissenschaftlicher Verlag Trier, 2004.

Camera Work. Accessed February 2, 2017. http://camerawork.de/en/camera-work/.

Colomb, Claire. *Staging the New Berlin: Place Marketing and the Politics of Urban Reinvention Post-1989.* London: Routledge, 2012.

Eckardt, Friedrich, and Dieter Hassenpflug, eds. *Urbanism and Globalization. The European City in Transition 2.* Frankfurt: Peter Lang, 2004.

Enrico. "Alicja Kwade: Nach Osten / Johann König at St. Agnes, Berlin." *VERNISSAGE TV: The Window to the Art World,* May 2, 2013. Accessed March 12, 2017. http://vernissage.tv/2013/05/02/alicja-kwade-nach-osten-johann-konig-at-st-agnes-berlin/.

Erek, Ayse N., and Ayse H. Köksal, eds. "The Imaginary City in the Twenty-First Century." Special issue, *Visual Resources: An International Journal of Documentation* 30, no. 4 (2014).

Florida, Richard. *Cities and the Creative Class.* New York: Routledge, 2005.

———. *The Rise of the Creative Class: And How It's Transforming Work, Leisure, Community, and Everyday Life.* New York: Basic Books, 2002.

Forbes, Alexander. "Berlin's 10 Best Gallery Spaces." *Artnet,* October 13, 2014. Accessed March 12, 2017. https://news.artnet.com/art-world/berlins-10-best-gallery-spaces-127917.

Frank, Sybille. "Mythenmaschine Potsdamer Platz." In *Selling Berlin,* edited by Thomas Bischkup and Marc Schalenberg, 291–327. Stuttgart: Franz Steiner, 2008.

Gantner, Eszter. *Budapest-Berlin: Die Koordinaten einer Emigration.* Stuttgart: Franz Steiner, 2011.

———. "Jewish Quarters as Urban Tableaux." In *Jewish and Non-Jewish Spaces in Urban Context,* edited by Alina Gromova, Felix Heinert, and Sebastian Voigt, 10–20. Berlin: Neofelis, 2014.

Gantner, Eszter, and Jay (Koby) Oppenheim. "Jewish Space Reloaded: An Introduction." *Anthropological Journal of European Cultures* 23, no. 2 (2014): 1–10.

Gaviria, Pilar Rojas, and Julie Emontspool. "Global Cities and Cultural Experimentation: Cosmopolitan-Local Connections." *International Marketing Review* 32, no. 2 (2015): 181–99.

Graw, Isabelle. "The Myth of Remoteness from the Market: Notes on Berlin's Rise as an Art Metropolis." *Texte zur Kunst* 24 (July 2014): 34–59.

Hannerz, Ulf. "The Cultural Role of World Cities." In *Humanising the City? Social Contexts of Urban Life at the Turn of the Millennium,* edited by Anthony P. Cohen and Fuki Katsuyoshi, 67–84. Edinburgh: Edinburgh University Press, 1993.

Horn, Dagmar. *Das selkupische Ethnizitätsgebäude: Zur gegenwärtigen ethnischen Identität der südlichen Selkupen (Westsibirien)*. Trier: Universität Trier, 2002.

Large, David Clay. *Berlin*. New York: Basic, 2000.

Lelgemann, Tanja, Thomas Wulffen, and Hans Ulrich Obrist, eds. *Berlin Biennale for Contemporary Art Exhibition Catalogue*. Berlin: H & P Druck, 1998.

Low, Setha. "The Anthropology of Cities: Imagining and Theorizing the City." *Annual Review of Anthropology* 25 (1996): 383–409.

Ludigs, Dirk. "Juden in Berlin: Sie kommen, um zu bleiben." In *MERIAN Berlin: Die Lust am Reisen*, 110–17. Hamburg: Jahreszeitenverlag, 2013.

Macdonald, Sharon. *Difficult Heritage: Negotiating the Nazi Past in Nuremberg and Beyond*. New York: Routledge, 2009.

Niermann, Ingo. "Expanded Prostitution." *Spike* 37 (Autumn 2013): 90–93.

Nishen, Dirk. *Info Box: Der Katalog*. Berlin: Nishen, 1998.

Reckwitz, Andreas. "Die Selbstkulturalisierung der Stadt: Zur Transformation moderner Urbanität in der 'Creative City.'" *Mittelweg 36* 18, no. 2 (2009): 2–34.

Schürmann, Sandra, and Jochen Guckes, eds. "Stadtbilder und Stadtrepräsentationen im 20. Jahrhundert." *Informationen zur modernen Stadtgeschichte* 1 (2005): 5–11.

Tauschek, Markus. *Kulturerbe: Eine Einführung*. Berlin: Dietrich Reimer, 2014.

"Tour 10—Fahrradtour durch Mitte: Jüdisches Leben in der Mitte Berlins." *Berlin Tourismus & KongressGmbH*. Accessed February 24, 2016, http://www.visit berlin.de/de/artikel/tour-10-fahrradtour-durch-mitte.

Vogel, Hans-Jochen. "Berlin-Debatte / Wortlaut der Reden: Vogel." *Deutscher Bundestag*. Accessed February 12, 2016. http://www.bundestag.de/kultur undgeschichte/geschichte/debatte/bdr_017/246560.

Weiss, Christina. Foreword to *Third Berlin Biennial for Contemporary Art Exhibition Catalogue*, edited by Uta Meta Bauer, Sonke Gau, and Vanessa Adler. Cologne: Walter König, 2004. Accessed February 17, 2016 at: http://blog .berlinbiennale.de/en/publications/ute-meta-bauer-in-the-catalogue-of-the-3rd-berlin-biennale-12519.

Welz, Gisela. *Inszenierungen kultureller Vielfalt*. Berlin: Akademie, 1996.

Zorn, Carsten. "Art System and Society of Control: Exhibition vs. Autonomy; On Recent Changes in Form and Function of Structural Coupling." *Österreichische Zeitschrift für Geschichtswissenschaften* 17, no. 2–3 (2006): 98–126.

Zukin, Sharon. *The Culture of Cities*. New York: Blackwell, 1995.

PART III

Reimagining Integration

CHAPTER 8

Governing through "Ethnic Entrepreneurship"

Barış Ülker

"Neukölln rocks," declared the front page of *Zitty*, a magazine that publicizes local events and editorializes Berlin politics and lifestyle. In the March 2008 lead article, Daniel Boese reflected on transformation in this district associated with low migrant "integration" levels, unemployment, and youth violence.[1] Neukölln was transforming into a trendy neighborhood (as opposed to "ghetto") with new bars, cafes, and restaurants. This echoed features of urban development in districts such as Prenzlauer Berg, which had experienced its own changes from the 1990s onward.[2]

This narrative seemed to contradict another image associated with Neukölln, the image of violence and "integration" problems among migrants in the *Rütli Hauptschule* (secondary school).[3] However, Boese pointed out that the school's development through the *Campus Rütli* project—initiated by Heinz Buschkowsky (former mayor of the Neukölln municipality) and the Foundation for the Future of Berlin (supported by leading local enterprises)—provided groundwork for the transformation of northern Neukölln.[4] *Campus Rütli* was presented in the mass media as a project that could be implemented in other cities[5] and utilized as a marketing instrument to increase Neukölln's attractiveness to the "creative classes."[6] Referring to this model of urban development, Boese concluded his article by promoting the district's entrepreneurial spirit, which could produce a "multicultural economic" miracle.[7] Although scholars have criticized this thinking in terms of the negative social consequences of gentrification in Berlin,[8] the "multicultural entrepreneurial" spirit—historically associated with the concept of "ethnic (or migrant) entrepreneurship" in Germany, Europe, and the United States—has only been discussed to a limited extent.[9]

The aim of this chapter is to explore the transformation of human beings into subjects ("ethnic entrepreneurs") within the struggles of power between policymakers (experts, scholars, and institutions) and migrants. To examine these power relations as productive entities, unlike the interpretations of liberal and Marxist schools,[10] it is crucial to look at the intersection of two technologies: technologies of domination (the ways that individuals are governed by others) and technologies of the self (the ways that individuals govern themselves). These technologies constitute what Foucault calls governmentality.[11] Technologies of domination determine the management of individuals, directing them to certain goals. Technologies of the self allow individuals to transform their ways of being to reach a form of perfection, alone or with the help of others. To illustrate the contact points of technologies of the self and technologies of domination, this chapter focuses on the story of Rojda Jiwan (a migrant from Turkey) and her daycare services in Berlin, further considering her connections to the Neighborhood Management (*Quartiersmanagement*) program in Neukölln.

Methodologically, the chapter derives from my ethnographic research.[12] By looking at the experiences of Rojda Jiwan as a case study[13] based on concrete context-dependent knowledge, this chapter does not intend to make any generalization about "ethnic entrepreneurship" in Berlin, nor does it intend to fit this singular narrative into a "natural flow of history" by creating falsifications and verifications about this body of knowledge. It also does not aim to present the success story of an entrepreneur with "migration background" who is "thriving" due to "successful" local and national government policies. Rather, by examining Jiwan's practices, the chapter indicates the ways in which she presents herself as an "ethnic entrepreneur," while also examining the rules for this way of operating and the truth claims made in this context. At stake are the power struggles or strategies between policymakers (experts, scholars, and institutions) as they embody technologies of domination and an "ethnic entrepreneur" as she embodies technologies of the self.

However, this chapter does not interpret the transformation of Rojda Jiwan into an "ethnic entrepreneur" as part of the ideological state apparatus (à la Althusser).[14] It does not consider this transformation as a result of top-down state policies or hegemonic discourses (e.g., parallel societies). See Johanna Schuster-Craig's contribution to this volume for a discussion on integration policies and responses of artists to these discourses in Neukölln. Instead, this chapter goes beyond the analysis of "integration" policies in Germany. Rojda Jiwan is not the docile recipient of any policy or knowledge. She is an active participant in the economic, political, and social domains of life in Berlin, and she has the capacity to redefine her "ethnic entrepreneurship" through daily practices and reflections. This chapter investigates a mode of reasoning ("ethnic entrepreneurship") that derives from the self-responsibility of an individual or group of people with "migration background," interacting with technologies of domination and technologies of the self through freedom and consent. Consequently, the chapter points out the practices of power concealed and revealed in "ethnic entrepreneurship."

The chapter is organized into four parts. The first introduces the concept of "ethnic entrepreneurship" in the form mostly used by policymakers, experts, scholars, and institutions. The second illustrates Rojda Jiwan's motivations in developing her own company, while the third part reflects on "culture-specific" elements of Jiwan's daycare service. The fourth section briefly portrays Rojda Jiwan's contribution to Neighborhood Management through her "ethnic entrepreneurship" in Neukölln. The conclusion returns to the question of why this particular model of entrepreneurship has made a place for itself in Berlin especially since the late 1980s.

Background on "Ethnic Entrepreneurship"

In the intellectual history of Europe, the concept of entrepreneurship associated with personal initiative, management, risk-taking, competitiveness, and opportunism emerged in the mid-eighteenth century.[15] The concept of "ethnic entrepreneurship," however, arrived a century later. Appearing in Germany with various formulations in the late nineteenth and early twentieth centuries,[16] it has been reproduced by scholars in the United States and Europe since the mid-1970s. The concept derives from theories of ethnic economy in which any immigrant or ethnic group maintains a private economic sector and controlling ownership stake.[17]

Five scholarly approaches—middleman minorities,[18] disadvantage,[19] ethnic enclave,[20] interaction,[21] and mixed embeddedness[22]—have been used to analyze "ethnic entrepreneurs" in terms of successes and failures, a form of political economic calculation. Although there are divergences and convergences in historical contexts and methodologies, two interrelated explanations seem to dominate within these approaches, used by policymakers, experts, and institutions as a technology of domination in Berlin. First, there are explanations privileging the structural conditions of a country. These explanations try to find reasons in the most unitary structure available (e.g., general employment trends in labor markets, and liberalization of legal principles such as the German Foreigners' Law). There is also an array of explanations running from essentialist to constructionist models of culture that refer to the productive interpretation of power (à la Foucault) and its subjects (migrants/others). These explanations differ from the accounts presented in populist/pejorative discourses that refer to "parallel societies" or top-down/repressive politics of "integration."[23] Essentialist models, associating a specific space with a pre-given identity and considering it natural, underline the ways that "ethnic entrepreneurs" do business. Constructionist models, acknowledging the social embeddedness of these economic agents in laws, institutions, and social networks, emphasize cultural coexistence,[24] as well as the potential of "ethnic entrepreneurs" (again, this assessment of potential is a form of political economic calculation); associated concepts include "transculturalism," "multiculturalism," "interculturalism," and "cosmopolitanism."

The body of knowledge on "ethnic entrepreneurship" in Germany, particularly in Berlin,[25] has been developing since the late 1980s. This development represents adaptation to the crises of Fordism and post-Fordist relations of production, and legacies of Ordoliberalism (German neoliberalism) in the Kohl and Schröder administrations.[26] Emphasis on entrepreneurial form and reformulation of juridical institutions marked Ordoliberal practice in the constitution of contemporary German policy.[27] These analyses assert competition and market mechanisms as the driving forces of society, in combination with legal and institutional interventions by public authorities. Ordoliberal thinking on entrepreneurship (focused on efficient utilization of resources and coping with crises/difficulties) is thus a response to the question of "governing too much or too little."[28] Classical and neoclassical economic theorists, as well as social economists like Georg Simmel, Werner Sombart, and Max Weber, dealt with this question by examining the dynamics of freedom and control in modern capitalism.[29] In the context of such neoliberal thought, economic agents pursuing their own and other interests are free to act within the logic of competition, forming an enterprise society. By doing so, these individuals do not disassociate themselves from society. On the contrary, they are socially embedded through institutions and a framework of law guaranteed by the state.

Consequently, "ethnic entrepreneurship" (functioning with self-restricting economic freedom) emerges as an expression of the Ordoliberal understanding of social market economy; it belongs to the realm of social policy according to which relations between political rationale and people with "migration background" can be defined and regulated. Policymakers, experts, scholars, institutions, and migrants themselves use the term interchangeably with "migrant entrepreneurship," "entrepreneurs with migration background," and "Turkish-German or Kurdish-German entrepreneurs." Even if the population is qualified to belong to the category of "German" through citizenship, focus remains on the "migration background" or *Herkunft* (origin), which

> often involves a consideration of race or social type. But the traits it attempts to identify are not the exclusive generic characteristics of an individual, a sentiment, or an idea, which permit us quantify them [for example] as "Greek" or "English"; rather it seeks the subtle, singular, and individual marks that might possibly intersect in them to form a network that is difficult to unravel. Far from being a category of resemblance, this origin allows the setting apart, the sorting out of different traits. ... The body—and everything that touches it: diet, climate and soil—is the domain of *Herkunft*. The body manifests the stigmata of past experience and also gives rise to desires, failings, and origins.[30]

It is crucial to examine how these discourses on "ethnic entrepreneurship" have been applied to migrants by migrants themselves (as technologies of the self), as well as experts and policymakers (as technologies of domination). The following sections offer an examination of the daycare services of Rojda Jiwan as entrepreneurial practices, exemplifying the instantiation of this body of knowledge in Berlin.

Daycare Service as "Ethnic Entrepreneurship"

Rojda Jiwan was born in 1960 and lived in Sivas, Turkey, until 1970. Her father came to Berlin in 1969, bringing his wife and children a year later. After *Hauptschule* Rojda Jiwan attended a *Realschule* and got a degree to continue her internship as a nurse. She did her internship in a clinic and became responsible for elderly people.

Jiwan subsequently worked at a hospital for three years. In 1990 she moved to the psychiatry department, where she took advantage of a special university entrance program for people with four years of working experience and a *Realschule* degree; she was admitted to the university in 1994. After getting married in 1995, Rojda gave birth to two daughters in 1996 and 1997. Her experience enabled her to finish her degree at the Technical University of Berlin's Department of Education in

1997, within seven semesters. Her hospital patients constituted the subject of her thesis on the relationship between drug addiction and laws
regarding foreigners. Until 1999, Rojda Jiwan worked at the hospital as
a nurse for patients with substance abuse problems. On the weekends,
she provided a daycare service for elderly people at their homes as an
additional income opportunity.

Between 1997 and 1999, she started a part-time job at a doctor's
clinic in Neukölln, where she kept records of patients who were predominantly migrants from Turkey. The job became a networking chan-
nel through which she could find new patients for her daycare service,
a practice that was unofficially approved by the doctor. In 1999, Rojda
Jiwan and the doctor—also with a "migration background" from Turkey—set up a daycare service through bank credit.

At the end of three months, however, the doctor resigned from the
partnership because of the economic crisis and his miscalculation of
startup capital requirements. Under these circumstances, Rojda Jiwan
asked for financial support from her family. With this financial support
and her own savings, she was able to register in a certificate program
to run the company herself, and in 2001 she received the diploma required in Germany's healthcare system. As a technology of the self,
Jiwan's "ethnic entrepreneurship" can be seen to operate through social relations to produce resources via solidarity, primarily ethnic and
family solidarity. On the one hand, the notion of ethnicity, based on
the belief in ontological difference between cultures associated with
particular spaces, provides for a distinctive business mentality. On the
other hand, the family, understood as the core of this ontologically different culture, serves to cultivate the physical and mental welfare of its
members (where the assessment of welfare is a form of calculation).
Familiarization, as Jacques Donzelot argues, is a catalyst that shapes
the personal capacities of its members in a way that is consistent with
ethics of autonomy and responsibility,[31] with results that can be more
effective than top-down/repressive "integration" policies because familiarization transforms individuals into freely acting subjects.

Since 2001, the employees and patients of Jiwan's company are predominantly people with "migration background" from Turkey, with various ethnic (e.g., Turkish and Kurdish), religious (e.g., Alawi and Sunni),
and political (e.g., liberal, conservative, and leftist) identities. While her
employees are second- and third-generation migrants, patients come
from a range of generations. According to Rojda Jiwan, her company
can bring these groups of people from Turkey together because of the
main objective of the company: "taking care of migrants" in terms of

their health, "integration," and "empowerment." This speaks to Foucault's analysis of pastoral power (a power of care).

Investigating the development of power techniques oriented toward ruling individuals in a continuous way (technologies of domination), Foucault concentrates on the pastoral modality of power.[32] The metaphor of a shepherd's care for his flock rests on the relation between God, king, and man. God, as the shepherd of men, entrusts his flock to the king (subaltern shepherd), who should restore them to God at the end of the day.[33] This power of the shepherd has three features.[34]

First, the shepherd's power is not exercised over a territory but rather over a flock that travels from place to place. The shepherd leads and people have to follow, hence exercising power over a "multiplicity in movement." Second, the aim of this pastoral power is the salvation of the flock, i.e., its subsistence. The shepherd feeds the flock, treats the injured, and keeps an eye out for dangers that may threaten the members. The shepherd's role is to direct care toward others, never toward himself. Third, the shepherd directs the whole flock, but also looks after each member of the flock individually. Thus, pastoral power is an individualizing power. An example of this pastoral modality of power, Rojda Jiwan's daycare service differs from top-down/repressive "integration" policies, which do not involve the individual in the same way.

Broadly speaking, her company provides individual and collective forms of care by keeping an eye on all and on each. Daycare service in patients' homes, provided by nurses or family-workers, is one of the most popular services. For instance, a mother who is pregnant with her second child and categorized as high-risk by her doctors has the option of being supported by this daycare service. In this situation, a family-worker takes care not only of the mother's health but also of the daily needs of the first child. Additionally, this family-worker helps with housecleaning, cooking, monitoring diets, exercise, and attention to medication and appointment schedules—subsistence of the patient is the aim of this pastoral power. For the healthcare system, aiming to minimize socioeconomic costs, this program significantly cuts the cost of the mother's care, from six hundred euros per day in the hospital to fifty euros per day for five hours of care in the patient's own home. The service, separated into shifts, operates seven days a week.

In this type of daycare service, the employees (predominantly women) do not have to accommodate the needs of more than one patient at the same time. With the individualized form of care, she may be engaged with her patient in different places (home, school, café) and at different times (during shopping trips or while the patient sleeps)—

exercising power over a "multiplicity in movement." Hence, daycare service takes into account the details of each patient's life, as in the pastoral modality of power. Providers collect information on patients' physical conditions and psychological well-being. Detailed records enable the daycare service to learn about patients' memories of childhood, migration stories, and working experience. Additionally, through daily engagement, daycare providers get in touch with patients' families (in some cases friends) and connect to their lives and problems.

However, Rojda Jiwan's company provides more than these individual forms of care. In 2003, Rojda Jiwan established a daycare center with the motto of "culture-specific" service, focusing on collective forms of care as well. This daycare center is in the Moabit district, historically regarded as a working-class neighborhood, which has many migrants.[35] The center is part of an old hospital building, located close to the criminal court, prison, and interior ministry. Within this symbolically charged setting, Rojda Jiwan's center functions with a collective understanding of care, keeping an eye on all patients as in the pastoral model. Each patient is picked up from her/his house in the morning and brought to the center by nurse assistants (7:00–9:00). After breakfast together in the center under the supervision of nurses (9:15–10:00), they are taken into the garden or a large room for morning gymnastics. During these sessions (10:30–12:30), some patients participate in mental training exercises, and some participate in ergotherapy. Lunch is communal (a daily menu of Turkish cuisine, 12:30–1:15). The afternoon program generally starts with a rest period (1:15–2:30), followed by physiotherapy. Afterward (2:30–3:30), patients can participate in a variety of activities, (e.g., listening to music and group discussion). Before they are brought home (from 4:15 onward), patients are served tea and coffee (3:30–4:15), and they are encouraged to talk about their daily lives and problems.

Within the structure of this daycare center there is consideration not only of the individual but also of the group as a whole (pastoral power constantly keeps an eye on all and on each). Nurses and their assistants treat each patient individually, and each individual takes care of her/himself to a certain extent. Yet the foremost intention is to direct everyone toward more social interaction and interactive care during dining, therapy, and activities. Group coherence is prioritized at each step with a precise daily schedule. A group identity emerges, demonstrating the benefits of—or need for—collective care, in the process of which each individual can assist in helping themselves and each other. A shared "migration background" facilitates this form of care, in part because it also generates knowledge of shared background, as individuals compare different aspects of experience. Nurses and their assistants provide constant, caring attention. From the perspective of the healthcare system, minimizing socioeconomic costs constitutes the main objective of this collective care, similar to individual care. Doctors appointed by the system make a cost-benefit analysis depending on each patient's health conditions to determine whether the cost of this collective form of day-care service would be less than the sum of patients' individual costs. As a result, collective care becomes a disciplinary form of power (a technology of domination), since it fabricates an individuality that is cellular (by the play of spatial distribution in the center), organic (by the coding of activities), generic (by the articulation of time), and combinatory (by the composition of forces involved in decisions).[36]

In conjunction with the conduct of these individual and collective forms of patient care by her employees, Rojda Jiwan also takes care of herself through recollections and reflections (as a technology of the self). Prior to the establishment of her company and in its early years, her work experiences were similar to those of her employees, who are predominantly migrant women from Turkey. Recalling this parallel with a sense of empathy allows her to define herself and describe the way she experienced entrepreneurship as a woman with "migration background." It enables her to grasp her changing position from Sivas to Berlin, from daycare nurse to entrepreneur. This self-examination, through which she questions her progress in relation to what she has become, generates a feeling of pride and hence becomes a source of pleasure to be practiced constantly. Positioning herself in relation to her employees (with a sense of empathy), she develops a narrative of spiritual direction that orients her everyday life.[37]

Relevant for my examination of "ethnic entrepreneurship" is the way in which this individual turns the gaze inward and takes care of the self (in Greek *epimeleia heautou*).[38] This form of care consists of knowing oneself and hence contributes to the formation of subjectivity, not only in order to discover the truth about oneself but also to take care of others.[39] Through self-care and self-knowledge (as technologies of the self), Jiwan claims an authority of entrepreneurial competence (wisdom in medical care and business planning, as well as understanding derived from being a migrant woman); she recognizes herself as an expert who can act as a role model and give recommendations to other migrant women. She absorbs what she has learned and develops her own interpretation, combining different assets. She is accustomed to the "German way of doing things" to such an extent that she can be considered an "integrated" migrant, or "intercultural" entrepreneur. As a technology of the self, she has the capacity to practice a certain way of life with/in another context. The next section will illustrate this by examining Rojda Jiwan's "culture-specific" services and her self-refection on those services as related to "ethnic entrepreneurship."

"Culture-Specific" Daycare Service

Developing her company's market share by mostly serving migrants from Turkey, Rojda Jiwan has expanded her individual and collective forms of care to various parts of Berlin. She opened offices for home-care services in Wedding (2007), Kreuzberg (2008), Steglitz (2009), and Spandau (2010). Moreover, Jiwan inaugurated her twenty-four-hour intensive care unit (2007), "culture-specific" senior shared flats (2009), intensive care shared flats (2010), and life-care shared flats (2013) in Kreuzberg, Neukölln, and Steglitz. Through these individual and collective forms of daycare (keeping an eye on all and on each—pastoral modality), Jiwan gathers a detailed set of knowledge that makes her care service "culture-specific." This knowledge-gathering is not the priority of "integration" policies; this is one aspect of Jiwan's way of doing business that marks it as "ethnic entrepreneurship." Further, this is what allows Jiwan to take care of herself with the help of self-reflection (as a technology of the self).

The notion of *abdest* offers an example of the complexity of Rojda Jiwan's "culture-specific" service, her way of doing business as "ethnic entrepreneurship" (as a regime of truth),[40] and her own reflections as a form of self-care. An Islamic hygienic custom that a Muslim is obliged to observe, *abdest* is the practice of washing parts of the body with water. This ritual of partial ablution is required for a physical and spiritual sense of cleanliness, or purification in preparation for prayer five times a day. *Abdest* is called for at different moments of daily life, since the emission of semen or blood, vomiting, defecation, urination, passing gas, falling asleep, fainting, and sexual contact are regarded as physical and spiritual impurities. During daycare, *abdest* is practiced as a "culture-specific" service at the request of patients. Rojda Jiwan's company, which has competence in this "culture-specific" service, uses *abdest* as a method of spiritual direction in relation to patients;[41] this way of doing business demonstrates "ethnic entrepreneurship." Three examples illustrate the spiritual direction of *abdest,* in turn exemplifying Jiwan's self-reflections (as technologies of the self).

First, in keeping with the target group for her services—migrants from Turkey—Rojda Jiwan attends to a performance of *abdest* as a traditional, cultural form of care for elderly people; most of the "German" daycare companies cannot provide such service. Familiarity with this "culture-specific" service helps her company to develop a kind of friendship with patients, instead of a hierarchical master-disciple relationship. Patients entrust themselves to Jiwan's care, taking part in a social exchange.[42] The guidance of family workers and nurse assistants comes to be considered a natural, personal experience. Although they may not be physically capable of daily prayer, patients still carry out *abdest* in their homes and the daycare center in Moabit. The ritual does not take place five times a day; it is integrated into the once-daily bathing service. Haircutting or shaving can also become part of this ritual. According to Jiwan, such changes to the prescribed definition of *abdest* (redefinition of truth) do not irritate the cultural sensibilities of her patients. Hence, the company as a reflection of Jiwan's "ethnic entrepreneurship" claims the knowledge to redefine the practice of a cultural form of care. Furthermore, it solidifies her intention of developing "ethnic entrepreneurship" as a practice that shapes her own thoughts (technology of the self) and the thoughts of others (related to technologies of domination).

Second, through this "culture-specific" service, Rojda Jiwan's "ethnic entrepreneurship" also emphasizes its authority in conflicts between "German ways of doing things" and migrants' needs. For example, although a patient can be cleaned in bed or in a bathtub filled with water, Jiwan's patients prefer to stand under running water throughout this process. For Jiwan, this preference has to do with the understanding of hygiene in Islam, no matter if the patient is an Alawi or a Sunni. Since the healthcare system's time regulation of seven minutes for the cleaning process is not sufficient, she claims that her employees work more than a German daycare service would require. This example shows that Rojda Jiwan's "ethnic entrepreneurship" displays the capacity to integrate values from a certain way of life (i.e., the understanding of hygiene in Islam) into another cultural system (i.e., time regulations of the German healthcare system). Such negotiation involves not only making use of cultural distinctions but also suggesting solutions. This intercultural competence turns her company, and primarily Jiwan herself, into a mediator[43] between patients and the healthcare system. As an "ethnic entrepreneur," she has to judge each action in terms of its consequences, possible meanings, and merit. Through this responsibility she takes care of herself and operates according to her reflections (technology of the self).

Third, because of this conflict—"working in a German system according to the culture of migrants,"[44] as she puts it—Rojda Jiwan pays extra attention to training her employees in the understanding of hygiene in Islam and cultural values in Turkey. She thus addresses any ignorance on the part of her employees regarding "culture-specific" service.[45] This has to be taught in order to generate self-reliant employees who can contribute to Rojda Jiwan's "ethnic entrepreneurship." The perception of any kind of ignorance in her employees makes her worried about the future of her company and herself as a role model, and she tries to anticipate issues in advance. Jiwan's reflection functions as a test in which a disturbing prospect is mentally simulated to reduce its possible negative impacts. She frequently sends her employees to medical care programs or seminars led by experts of the healthcare system in Berlin. Additionally, she carries out unofficial extra training that is necessary to better understand the problems and needs of particular patients. As first-generation migrants, these patients have experienced the results of limited German language skills in their daily lives, which may have engendered fear of various local authorities. Addressing patients' consequent reluctance to engage in social contact outside their neighborhoods, Jiwan seeks to optimize communication. Her policies of employing people with "migration background" and providing them with extra training aim to allow patients to express themselves in their mother tongues, with reference to their cultural values, while counting on the fact that they will be readily understood by her employees.

This "culture-specific" service creates a special value for Jiwan's "ethnic entrepreneurship," which she describes as threefold. First, a service designed in this way makes a patient believe that the company takes good care of his/her health. This feeling creates a trust mechanism; emerging from the relationship between patient and employee, this trust is eventually associated with Rojda Jiwan. This association spreads via patients and their families, and in turn functions to promote her company. Second, her employment policies aim to improve the qualifications of women with "migration background," contributing to their "integration" in Berlin. According to Jiwan, her employees prove that they can be self-sufficient. Third, this small business owner underscores the role of "culture-specific" knowledge. As a technology of the self, this investment in knowledge enables her to contribute to the urban space in which she lives, participating in the production of power (à la Foucault). The next section will explore her involvement in the city through the Neighborhood Management program.

Neighborhood Management and "Ethnic Entrepreneurship"

Rojda Jiwan's "ethnic entrepreneurship" clearly corresponds with the objectives and methods of Neighborhood Management in Berlin. Broadly speaking, Neighborhood Management is one of the tools of the program "Districts with Special Development Needs—The Socially Integrative City," created by an initiative of federal and state governments in 1999 to combat sociospatial polarization in urban areas throughout Germany. This program can be considered a technology of domination in the urban context, as it entails managing individuals and directing them to certain goals.[46] With its motto of "helping others to help themselves," Neighborhood Management relates to the governmental question of "how not to govern too much" that emerged in the transformation from *raison d'État* (mercantilism and diplomatic-military systems between the sixteenth and mid-eighteenth century) to modern governmental reason.[47] As part of modern governmental reason, political economy as an intellectual instrument (a form of calculation and rationality) prioritizes the question of success or failure (in keeping with utilitarian philosophy).[48] In this broader framework, Neighborhood Management Berlin has a more subtle strategy than top-down/repressive "integration" policies. It is coordinated by the Senate Department for Urban Development and local municipalities of Berlin. Between 1999 and 2015, various projects have been funded with contributions from the Federal State of Berlin, the European Union, and the federal government.

Although the goals of Neighborhood Management depend on the starting conditions, problems, and resources of each area, its mandate can be listed as follows:

> [S]ocial and ethnic integration; improving neighborly community life; employment and education for local residents; placement on the primary labor market; economic revitalization; support for the local economy; redevelopment and modernization measures; improving the residential environment; linking investment measures in urban renewal with non-investment social and employment measures; improving transport infrastructure and accessibility; improving social and cultural infrastructure; integrating infrastructural facilities such as schools, youth and senior citizen facilities into district work; the promotion of children, young people, and families; improving (residential) security in the neighborhood; public relations, image development.[49]

Pursuing these goals, Neighborhood Management teams in "problem" areas work to activate the commitment and responsibility of inhabitants, as well as local entrepreneurs, pressure groups, and institutions. Neighborhood Management teams encourage the development of projects and networking possibilities of various actors. Each team has a local office, working with a coordinator from the Senate Department for Urban Development and a coordinator from the particular borough. Team members have different skills, e.g., job training, entrepreneurship, urban design, and pedagogy. The Neighborhood Management teams bring representatives of interest groups and inhabitants of the area together to form Neighborhood Councils. A maximum 49 percent of members are representatives of interest groups and a minimum 51 percent of council members are inhabitants. The Neighborhood Councils have fifteen to thirty members. Neighborhood size is the decisive factor; there is at least one member per one thousand inhabitants.[50] Designed with a bottom-up approach (attempting "not to govern too much"), the councils are platforms that give voice to inhabitants and interest groups, and they play a special role in decisions regarding the allocation of funds. As a rule, the councils define the requirements of the area, collect project ideas, select the most promising projects together with the Steering Committee (composed of the Neighborhood Management team, borough coordinator, and in some cases members of the Neighborhood Council), and decide on implementing partners.

Acknowledging differences in the conditions, problems, and resources of each area, project teams seek out the most feasible and appropriate solutions. The aim is not to construct homogenous areas; rather, it is to discover particular resources through the responsibilization of inhabitants (economic government à la Foucault). In order to achieve this,[51] various sets of knowledge about the problem area and its inhabitants are prioritized in the scope of different projects. Furthermore, the existing potential of the inhabitants becomes the main focus of the Neighborhood Management program.

The potential of Rojda Jiwan's "ethnic entrepreneurship" was discovered by Fuat Yakın's consultancy service in one of the Neighborhood Management offices in Neukölln. With degrees in economics from Ankara and Berlin, Fuat Yakın worked with the first Senate Commissioner of Berlin for Integration and Migration. Later, he operated his own consultancy service in the framework of the Turkish-German Entrepreneurs' Association Berlin-Brandenburg. Since the late 1990s, he has been working with different research institutions on entrepreneurship and qualification seminars for migrants. These experiences laid the groundwork for Yakın's Neighborhood Management project: making close contact with "ethnic entrepreneurs" is regarded as a crucial factor in mobilizing the capabilities of a neighborhood. Three examples illustrate the contribution of Rojda Jiwan's "ethnic entrepreneurship" to Neighborhood Management in Neukölln. These contributions were possible in part thanks to Fuat Yakın's political economic guidance, processed through Jiwan's self-reflection.

First, Rojda Jiwan's activities were recognized and leveraged by policy organizations to exemplify "ethnic entrepreneurship," used as an instrument of "helping others to help themselves" (technology of domination in urban space). For instance, Fuat Yakın organized small panels in several Neighborhood Management offices in Neukölln, where Rojda Jiwan explained her migration story and business philosophy. Later she participated in activities organized by the Association of Economy and Labor Neukölln, which cooperates with Neukölln's employment office, Neighborhood Management, and over sixty Neukölln enterprises to mobilize underused potential, develop dialogue among entrepreneurs, work against unemployment, and bring together financial resources. Since 2007, Rojda Jiwan has also participated in local activities like *Karşılaşma—ein deutsch-türkischer Abendsalon* (a German-Turkish meeting), to discuss ethnic economy and healthcare in Neukölln. These activities and meetings function as rituals of imagining herself (technology of the self). Through these social interactions related to "ethnic entrepreneurship" she finds convergences and divergences between herself and those entrepreneurs whom she admires or hates. She seeks truth on "ethnic entrepreneurship" by paying attention to the life stories of her role models in Neukölln. At stake in these life stories are not only the prescriptions (e.g., having culturally informed employees) but also the ways of practicing them (e.g., being honest) that she finds substantial and applies in her daily life. By articulating her own structures of truth regarding "ethnic entrepreneurship" or collecting those of others, she examines herself continuously and develops this particular form of subjectivity.

Second, going beyond these official organizations, Rojda Jiwan accepted two interns recommended through the initiatives of Fuat Yakın and a Neighborhood Management office. These two interns (categorized as young people with learning problems) had already been through a drug-addiction program before they started working with her. She knows her employees very well. Recalling the pastoral modality of power, her knowledge and concern are focused on young migrants in the neighborhood of Neukölln; she seeks to "integrate" each one into society, developing their qualifications, taking care of their physical and mental health, encouraging their self-sufficiency, and even keeping them from crime and violence. Such concern for others enables her to have a kind of cognitive map of migrant inhabitants. This knowledge, one of the main instruments of Neighborhood Management teams, is also crucial in dealing with the problems of particular districts in Neukölln. At the same time, Jiwan claims to be a role model for her two interns. In their training, she asserts her belief that there is a correct way to practice entrepreneurship. This training in turn operates as an opportunity for self-examination, in which Jiwan considers her past and cultivates her "ethnic entrepreneurship" for the future (technology of the self).

Third, inspired by the achievements of Neighborhood Management in Neukölln (judged in utilitarian terms of success and failure), Rojda Jiwan developed her own future business project, the construction of two connected buildings. Jiwan will manage its realization while profiting from having sold her idea to a construction firm that undertakes projects for the Senate Department for Urban Development. According to architectural plans, the buildings look like two staircases. Each floor is divided into flats and has a huge terrace. There is a view to each terrace from the top of each building. Designed to have plenty of daylight, flats of different sizes are meant to accommodate people with differing incomes and life circumstances: single mothers, elderly people who live alone, small families, single people, and people with disabilities. According to the plans, the project will also provide other facilities. A daycare center is already integrated so that elderly inhabitants do not have to be transported elsewhere, and regular health checks can be conducted easily. This daycare center will share the ground floor with a supermarket, pharmacy, and several health clinics. A playground for children and a café where "people can chat even if it rains"[52] are also included in the plans. All of these facilities will also be available to people who do not live in the two buildings, which will make the project a center for inhabitants of the neighborhood, creating the possibility of lasting relationships among neighbors. The main model behind the particular design of these buildings is the model of communication in small towns. In a way, Rojda Jiwan wants to bring village life into a part of the city populated mainly by people with "migration background." This structure aims to prevent isolation.

Through this continuous dialogue, migrants can grow accustomed to their milieu and get involved with the problems of those around them, which fits into the motto of Neighborhood Management: "helping others to help themselves." Consequently, this interaction functions to reinforce strategies or tactics of power. On the one hand, it paves the way to materialize an idea, i.e., creating an urban environment in which people with "migration background" will take care of themselves and others (another contact point of technologies of the self and technologies of domination). On the other hand, it serves to solidify Jiwan's way of practicing "ethnic entrepreneurship" and generates the objectification of knowledge associated with this practice, a circle of truths that can be broadened with new reflections (technology of the self). Although Rojda Jiwan has not yet completed this project, her business initiatives in "culture-specific" forms of care were already awarded with Berlin's integration prize in 2008, and she was Berlin's entrepreneur of the year in 2010. Both of these recognitions serve to validate the calculation of success according to the reasoning of political economy.

Conclusion

From a broader historical perspective, three periods have to be kept in mind to contextualize relations between Berlin and migrants from Turkey and to explain why this particular model of entrepreneurship has made a place for itself especially since the late 1980s.[53] During the first period, from the construction of the Wall (1961) until the ban on recruiting foreign labor forces (1973), West Berlin benefitted from state subsidies and tried to improve its economic and political position as an island in the German Democratic Republic with the help of guest-workers whose presence was considered a "state of exception."[54] During the second period, from 1973 until the fall of the Wall (1989), migrants became a permanent part of West Berlin, which was meanwhile trying to cope with economic crises and restructuring in Germany and across the world. The population of migrants was diversifying and increasing through family reunification and asylum seeking, and hence migrants became associated with social concern, fear, and risk in the city. At the end of this period, Berlin was focused on the "integration" of migrants, while businesses formed by migrants were beginning to emerge. In the post-Wall period that continues today, Berlin is facing the social, economic, and political impacts of reunification and restructuring. The city deals with migrants as a source of social concern while simultaneously attempting to promote "ethnic entrepreneurship."

In this context, against a backdrop of the declining profitability of mass-production industries and the crisis of welfare policies since the second half of the 1980s, the "ethnic entrepreneurship" of Rojda Jiwan is about creating jobs, offering training, paying taxes, providing services, generating economic profit, and maintaining existence without the need for direct political intervention. She is an enterprising individual who has autonomy over her own everyday practices and existence.[55] She is not simply an owner of remittances from Germany to Turkey.[56] Nor can her practices be explained entirely with the classical conceptualization of *homo oeconomicus*; she is not only an individual acting rationally for her own well-being, defined through optimization of needs with the least possible costs. Going beyond these formulations, Rojda Jiwan is an entrepreneur who constitutes her own capital, as the producer of her own earnings.[57]

Rojda Jiwan's entrepreneurship is care-oriented in a manner that recalls Foucault's analysis of taking care of the self and others. On the one hand, she takes care of others in different ways: attending to patients' health (physical and psychological); responding to their cultural needs and values; trying to improve the education and job qualifications of her employees; keeping records of their problems; and giving advice. Her engagement takes place in the office, at the daycare center, in patients' homes, and on the streets. She not only contributes to the rational calculation of capabilities and costs but also keeps an eye on the well-being of people with "migration background." In a way, her "ethnic entrepreneurship" is connected to the idea of an enabling state,[58] as the state encourages this mode of confronting the challenges of economic restructuring and the political and social impacts of reunification in Berlin. "Ethnic entrepreneurship" thus fits into the objectives and methodologies of Neighborhood Management (technologies of domination), which are more subtle than top-down/repressive "integration" politics. On the other hand, Rojda Jiwan's "ethnic entrepreneurship" is a way of taking care of the self (technologies of the self). It works through self-reflections and reflections regarding her relationship to employees and patients, the functioning of her company, development of her new project, and involvement in social activities at the district level. These practices cannot be reduced to an internalization of "ethnic entrepreneurship" or top-down/repressive "integration" discourses. Rather, her thoughts, conduct, and way of being function as mechanisms to constitute herself as an "ethnic entrepreneur." It is at the intersection of these two technologies (governmentality) that one can examine her transformation into a subject who governs herself and others.

Barış Ülker is research fellow in the Center for Metropolitan Studies at the Technical University, Berlin. He authored *Enterprising Migrants in Berlin* and coauthored *Challenges and Inspirations: Ernst Reuter as* *an Urban Reformer in Turkey.* His research interests focus on governmental subjectivities, colonial and postcolonial relations, and urban restructuring.

Notes

Parts of this chapter have been published in my book, *Enterprising Migrants in Berlin* (Bielefeld: transcript Verlag, 2016), based on research funded by the German Academic Exchange Program, the Transatlantic Graduate Exchange Program: Race, Ethnicity and Migrations Studies, the German Research Foundation, and the Center for Metropolitan Studies. All of the names of people in this the chapter are pseudonyms. I am particularly indebted to Jennifer Hosek and Karin Bauer as editors of this volume for their invaluable comments to improve the chapter, and Sage Anderson for her critical reading. All remaining errors and inadequacies are mine alone.

1. Daniel Boese, "Neukölln Rockt," *Zitty,* March 2008, 15.
2. Andrej Holm, "Berlin's Gentrification Mainstream," in *The Berlin Reader: A Compendium on Urban Change and Activism,* ed. Andrej Holm, Britta Grell, and Matthias Bernt (Bielefeld, 2013), 171–87.
3. See Klaus Brinkbäumer et al., "Die verlorene Welt," *Spiegel* 14 (2006): 22–36; Caroline Schmidt und Holger Stark, "Das System ist krank," *Spiegel* 49 (2006): 54–58.
4. Boese, "Neukölln Rockt," 15.
5. Florentine Anders, "Auf dem Rütli-Campus lernen jetzt auch Kitakinder," *Berliner Morgenpost,* April 12, 2014, http://www.morgenpost.de/berlin-ak tuell/article126874333/Auf-dem-Ruetli-Campus-lernenjetzt-auch-Kitakinder .html.
6. Richard Florida, *Cities and the Creative Class* (New York, 2005); Stefan Krätke, "'Creative Cities' and the Rise of the Dealer Class: A Critique of R. Florida's Approach to Urban Theory," *International Journal of Urban and Regional Research* 34, no.4 (2010): 835–53; Claire Colomb, *Staging the New Berlin: Place Marketing and the Politics of Urban Reinvention Post-1989* (London, 2011). See Ward's contribution in this volume for a discussion on the notion of creative class.
7. Boese, "Neukölln Rockt," 16.
8. Andrej Holm, *Wir Bleiben Alle: Gentrifizierung–Städtische Konflikte um Aufwertung und Verdrängung* (Münster, 2010).
9. Felicitas Hillmann, *Marginale Urbanität: Migrantisches Unternehmertum und Stadtentwicklung* (Bielefeld, 2011).
10. Michel Foucault, "The Subject and Power," in *Michel Foucault, Beyond Structuralism and Hermeneutics,* ed. Hubert L. Dreyfus and Paul Rabinow (New York, 1982), 208–26.
11. Michel Foucault, "Technologies of the Self," in *Technologies of the Self: A*

Seminar with Michel Foucault, ed. Luther H. Martin, Huck Gutman, and Patrick H. Hutton (Amherst, 1988), 18.

12. The chapter comes out of four years of fieldwork, during which I relied on different research techniques, e.g., interviews (with "ethnic entrepreneurs," experts, and policymakers), participant observations, and analysis of textual and visual materials. I was able to conduct in-depth interviews with eighty-nine "ethnic entrepreneurs." To put together these case studies as concrete context-based knowledge, I used the networks of business associations in Berlin established by migrants from Turkey, snowball technique in different districts, information from the Yellow Pages published since 1996 related to migrants from Turkey, textual and visual materials concerning these businesses, and contacts of local and federal policymakers, experts, and institutions. The "ethnic entrepreneurs" in these case studies are the owners of small-size enterprises who have migration background from Turkey, active in different branches of the "formal economy" in Berlin. Their customers can be individuals, companies, and public/private institutions in Berlin, Germany, Europe, and Turkey. In order not to fall into a methodological trap in defining "ethnic entrepreneurship," I used the wording of various experts, policymakers, institutions, and "ethnic entrepreneurs" themselves, since they are the actors who define the features of this subjectivity. For a detailed explanation of the methodology behind this study, see Barış Ülker, *Enterprising Migrants in Berlin* (Bielefeld, 2016), 17–31.

13. For a general discussion on the values of case-study research, see Bent Flyvbjerg, "Five Misunderstandings about Case-Study Research," *Qualitative Inquiry* 12, no. 2 (2006): 219–45.

14. Louis Althusser, *Lenin and Philosophy and Other Essay,* trans. Ben Brewster (New York, 1991), 127–86.

15. Donald F. Kuratko and Richard M. Hodgetts, *Entrepreneurship: A Contemporary Approach* (Orlando, 1988).

16. Georg Simmel, *The Philosophy of Money,* ed. David Frisby (London, 1990); Werner Sombart, *Economic Life in the Modern Age,* ed. Nico Stehr and Reiner Grundmann (Piscataway, NY, 2001); Max Weber, *Economy and Society* (Berkeley, 1978).

17. Ivan Light and Steven Gold, *Ethnic Economies* (San Diego, 2000), 9.

18. Edna Bonacich, "A Theory of Middleman Minorities," *American Sociological Review* 38 (1973): 583–94.

19. Ivan Light and Carolyn Rosenstein, *Race, Ethnicity, and Entrepreneurship in Urban America* (New York, 1995).

20. Kenneth L. Wilson and Alejandro Portes, "Immigrant Enclaves: An Analysis of the Labor Market Experiences of Cubans in Miami," *American Journal of Sociology* 86, no. 2 (1980): 295–319.

21. Roger Waldinger, Howard Aldrich, and Robin Ward, "Opportunities, Group Characteristics, and Strategies," in *Ethnic Entrepreneurs: Immigrant Busi-*

ness in Industrial Societies, ed. Roger Waldinger, Howard Aldrich, and Robin Ward (Newbury Park, CA, 1990), 13–49.

22. Jan Rath, ed., *Immigrant Business: The Economic, Political and Social Environment* (Houndmills, 2000).
23. See Schuster-Craig in this volume for the connotations of culture as presented in populist/pejorative discourses that refer to "parallel societies" (criticized by Bukow et al.) or top-down/repressive politics of "integration" (criticized by Nghi Ha).
24. Slavoj Žižek, "Tolerance as an Ideological Category," *Critical Inquiry* 34 (2008): 660–82.
25. Hillmann, *Marginale Urbanität*; Robert Pütz, *Transkulturalität als Praxis: Unternehmer Türkischer Herkunft in Berlin* (Bielefeld, 2004); Antoine Pécoud, "Weltoffenheit Schafft Jobs: Turkish Entrepreneurship and Multiculturalism in Berlin," *International Journal of Urban and Regional Research* 26, no. 3 (2002): 494–507; Czarina Wilpert, "Germany: From Workers to Entrepreneurs," in *Immigrant Entrepreneurs: Venturing Abroad in the Age of Globalization,* ed. Robert Kloosterman and Jan Rath (Oxford, 2003), 233–60; Hillmann, *Marginale Urbanität*.
26. Jeremy Leaman, *The Political Economy of Germany under Chancellors Kohl and Schröder: Decline of the German Model?* (New York, 2009).
27. Anthony James Nicholls, *Freedom with Responsibility: The Social Market Economy in Germany, 1918–1963* (San Diego, 1994).
28. Michel Foucault, *The Birth of Biopolitics: Lectures at the Collège de France, 1978–1979,* ed. François Ewald and Alessandro Fontona (New York, 2008), 9–13
29. Ibid., 75–157.
30. Michel Foucault, "Nietzsche, Genealogy, History," in *Aesthetics, Method and Epistemology: Essential Works of Foucault 1954–1984,* ed. James Faubion and Paul Rabinow (London, 1994), 373–75, emphasis in the original.
31. Jacques Donzelot, *The Policing of Families* (Baltimore, 1997).
32. Michel Foucault, *Security, Territory, Population: Lectures at the Collège de France, 1977–1978* (New York, 2007), 123.
33. Ibid., 124.
34. Ibid., 125–29.
35. Senatsverwaltung für Gesundheit, Umwelt und Verbraucherschutz, *Sozialstrukturatlas Berlin 2008, Gesundheitsberichterstattung Berlin Spezialbericht* (Berlin, 2009), 60.
36. Michel Foucault, *Discipline and Punish: The Birth of the Prison* (London, 1995), 141–67.
37. Foucault, "Technologies of the Self," 18.
38. Michel Foucault, *The Hermeneutics of the Subject: Lectures at the Collège de France 1981–1982* (New York, 2005), 10–15, 217–23, 229–41.
39. Foucault, *Hermeneutics of the Subject,* 174–79.

40. Michel Foucault, "Truth and Power," in *Power: Essential Works of Foucault,* ed. James Faubion (New York, 2000), 111–33.
41. For a detailed analysis of the use of spiritual direction, see Foucault, *Hermeneutics of the Subject,* 136–44.
42. For a broader explanation of friendship as a form of care, see ibid., 192–95.
43. See ibid., 129–30, for the role of the philosopher as mediator in the spiritual guidance of individuals.
44. Rojda Jiwan, interview with author, May 18, 2008.
45. See Foucault, *Hermeneutics of the Subject,* 128–29, for the interplay between ignorance and memory in governing the self and others.
46. DIfU, Deutsches Institut für Urbanistik im Auftrag des Bundesministeriums für Verkehr, Bau- und Wohnungswesen, *Strategien für die Soziale Stadt, Erfahrungen und Perspektiven—Umsetzung des Bund-Länder-Programms "Stadtteile mit besonderem Entwicklungsbedarf—die soziale Stadt"* (Berlin, 2003).
47. Foucault, *Security, Territory, Population,* 285–306, 311–41; Foucault, *Birth of Biopolitics,* 9–13.
48. Ibid., 13–19.
49. Thomas Franke and Rolf-Peter Löhr, "Neighborhood Management:—A Key Instrument in Integrative Urban District Development," *Deutsches Institut für Urbanistik Occasional Papers* (2001): 11.
50. SenStadt, *The Neighborhood Councils within the Neighborhood Management Process* (Berlin, 2010), 11.
51. Jacques Donzelot, "The Mobilization of Society," in *The Foucault Effect: Studies in Governmentality,* ed. Graham Burchell, Colin Gordon, and Peter Miller (Chicago, 1991), 173.
52. Rojda Jiwan, interview with author, April 22, 2009.
53. Ülker, *Enterprising Migrants in Berlin,* 75–101.
54. Giorgio Agamben, *Home Sacer: Sovereign Power and Bare Life* (Stanford, 1998), 15–29.
55. Nikolas Rose, *Inventing Our Selves: Psychology, Power, and Personhood* (Cambridge, 1998).
56. Serdar Sayan and Ayca Tekin-Koru, "Remittances, Business Cycles and Poverty: The Recent Turkish Experience," *International Migration* 50 (2012): 151–76.
57. Foucault, *Birth of Biopolitics,* 219–26.
58. Bundesministerium des Innern, *Moderner Staat—Moderne Verwaltung: Das Programm der Bundesregierung* (Berlin, 1999), 7–9.

Bibliography

Agamben, Giorgio. *Home Sacer: Sovereign Power and Bare Life.* Palo Alto: Stanford University Press, 1998.
Althusser, Louis. *Lenin and Philosophy and Other Essay.* Translated by Ben Brewster, 127–86. New York: Monthly Review Press, 1991.

Anders, Florentine. "Auf dem Rütli-Campus lernen jetzt auch Kitakinder." *Berliner Morgenpost,* April 12, 2014. Accessed March 13, 2017. http://www.morgen post.de/berlin-aktuell/article126874333/Auf-dem-Ruetli-Campus-lernen jetzt-auch-Kitakinder.html.

Boese, Daniel. "Neukölln rockt." *Zitty,* March 8, 2008.

Bonacich, Edna. "A Theory of Middleman Minorities." *American Sociological Review* 38 (1973): 583–94.

Brinkbäumer, Klaus, et al. "Die verlorene Welt." *Der Spiegel* 14 (2006): 22–36.

Bundesministerium des Innern. *Moderner Staat—Moderne Verwaltung: Das Programm der Bundesregierung.* Berlin: Druck Center Meckenheim GmbH, 1999.

Colomb, Claire. *Staging the New Berlin: Place Marketing and the Politics of Urban Reinvention Post-1989.* London: Routledge, 2012.

Deutsches Institut für Urbanistik im Auftrag des Bundesministeriums für Verkehr, Bau- und Wohnungswesen. *Strategien für die Soziale Stadt, Erfahrungen und Perspektiven—Umsetzung des Bund-Länder-Programms "Stadtteile mit besonderem Entwicklungsbedarf—die soziale Stadt."* Berlin: Mercedes-Druck, 2003.

Donzelot, Jacques. "The Mobilization of Society." In *The Foucault Effect: Studies in Governmentality,* edited by Graham Burchell, Colin Gordon, and Peter Miller, 169–79. Chicago: University of Chicago Press, 1991.

———. *The Policing of Families.* Baltimore: Johns Hopkins University Press, 1997.

Florida, Richard. *Cities and the Creative Class.* New York: Routledge, 2005.

———. *The Rise of the Creative Class: And How It's Transforming Work, Leisure, Community, and Everyday Life.* New York: Basic Books, 2002.

Flyvbjerg, Bent. "Five Misunderstandings about Case-Study Research." *Qualitative Inquiry* 12, no. 2 (2006): 219–45.

Foucault, Michel. *The Birth of Biopolitics: Lectures at the Collège de France, 1978–1979.* Edited by François Ewald and Alessandro Fontana. New York: Palgrave MacMillan, 2008.

———. *Discipline and Punish: The Birth of the Prison.* London: Vintage Books, 1995.

———. *The Hermeneutics of the Subject: Lectures at the Collège de France 1981–1982.* New York: Picador, 2005.

———. "Nietzsche, Genealogy, History." In *Aesthetics, Method and Epistemology: Essential Works of Foucault 1954–1984,* edited by James Faubion and Paul Rabinow, 269–78. London: Penguin Books, 1994.

———. *Security, Territory, Population: Lectures at the Collège de France, 1977–1978.* New York: Palgrave MacMillan, 2007.

———. "The Subject and Power." In *Michel Foucault: Beyond Structuralism and Hermeneutics,* edited by Hubert L. Dreyfus and Paul Rabinow, 208–26. Chicago: Chicago University Press, 1982.

———. "Technologies of the Self." In *Technologies of the Self: A Seminar with Michel Foucault,* edited by Luther H. Martin, Huck Gutman, and Patrick H. Hutton, 16–48. Amherst: University of Massachusetts Press, 1988.

———. "Truth and Power." In *Power: Essential Works of Foucault 1954–1984*, edited by James Faubion, 111–33. New York: New York Press, 2000.

Franke, Thomas, and Rolf-Peter Löhr. "Neighborhood Management: A Key Instrument in Integrative Urban District Development." *Deutsches Institut für Urbanistik. Occasional Papers* (2001). Accessed March 14, 2017. https://difu.de/publikationen/occasional-papers.html?page=1.

Hillmann, Felicitas. "A Look at the Hidden Side: Turkish Women in Berlin's Labor Market." *International Journal of Urban and Regional Research* 23, no. 2 (1999): 268–83.

———. *Marginale Urbanität: Migrantisches Unternehmertum und Stadtentwicklung*. Bielefeld: transcript Verlag, 2011.

Holm, Andrej. "Berlin's Gentrification Mainstream." In *The Berlin Reader: A Compendium on Urban Change and Activism*, edited by Andrej Holm, Britta Grell, and Matthias Bernt, 171–87. Bielefeld: transcript Verlag, 2013.

———. *Wir Bleiben Alle: Gentrifizierung—Städtische Konflikte um Aufwertung und Verdrängung*. Münster: Unrast-Verlag, 2010.

Krätke, Stefan. "Creative Cities and the Rise of the Dealer Class: A Critique of Richard Florida's Approach to Urban Theory." *International Journal of Urban and Regional Research* 34, no. 4 (2010): 835–53.

Kuratko, Donald F., and Richard M. Hodgetts. *Entrepreneurship: A Contemporary Approach*. Orlando: Dryden Press, 1998.

Leaman, Jeremy. *The Political Economy of Germany under Chancellors Kohl and Schröder: Decline of the German Model?* New York: Berghahn Books, 2009.

Light, Ivan, and Carolyn Rosenstein. *Race, Ethnicity, and Entrepreneurship in Urban America*. New York: Walter de Gruyter, 1995.

Light, Ivan, and Steven Gold. *Ethnic Economies*. San Diego: Academic Press, 2000.

Nicholls, Anthony James. *Freedom with Responsibility: The Social Market Economy in Germany, 1918–1963*. Oxford: Clarendon Press, 1994.

Pécoud, Antoine. "Weltoffenheit schafft Jobs: Turkish Entrepreneurship and Multiculturalism in Berlin." *International Journal of Urban and Regional Research* 26, no. 3 (2002): 494–507.

Pütz, Robert. *Transkulturalität als Praxis: Unternehmer türkischer Herkunft in Berlin*. Bielefeld: transcript Verlag, 2004.

Rath, Jan, ed. *Immigrant Business: The Economic, Political and Social Environment*. Basingstoke: MacMillan Press, 2000.

Rose, Nikolas. *Inventing Our Selves: Psychology, Power, and Personhood*. Cambridge: Cambridge University Press, 1998.

Sayan, Serdar, and Ayca Tekin-Koru. "Remittances, Business Cycles and Poverty: The Recent Turkish Experience." *International Migration* 50 (2012): 151–76.

Schmidt, Caroline, and Holger Stark. "Das System ist krank." *Der Spiegel* 49 (2006): 54–58.

Senatsverwaltung für Gesundheit, Umwelt und Verbraucherschutz. *Sozialstruk-turatlas Berlin 2008, Gesundheitsberichterstattung Berlin Spezialbericht.* Berlin: Senatsverwaltung für Gesundheit, Umwelt und Verbraucherschutz, 2009.

SenStadt. *The Neighborhood Councils within the Neighborhood Management Process.* Berlin: Senatverwaltung für Stadtentwicklung, 2010.

Simmel, Georg. *The Philosophy of Money.* Edited by David Frisby. London: Routledge, 1990.

Sombart, Werner. *Economic Life in the Modern Age.* Edited by Nico Stehr and Reiner Grundmann. Piscataway, NY: Transaction Publishers, 2001.

Ülker, Barış. *Enterprising Migrants in Berlin.* Bielefeld: transcript Verlag, 2016.

Waldinger, Roger, Howard Aldrich, and Robin Ward. "Opportunities, Group Characteristics, and Strategies." In *Ethnic Entrepreneurs: Immigrant Business in Industrial Societies,* edited by Roger Waldinger, Howard Aldrich, and Robin Ward, 13–49. California: Sage Publications, 1990.

Weber, Max. *Economy and Society.* Berkeley: University of California Press, 1978.

Wilpert, Czarina. "Germany: From Workers to Entrepreneurs." In *Immigrant Entrepreneurs: Venturing Abroad in the Age of Globalization,* edited by Robert Kloosterman and Jan Rath, 233–60. Oxford: Berg Publishers, 2003.

Wilson, Kenneth L., and Alejandro Portes. "Immigrant Enclaves: An Analysis of the Labor Market Experiences of Cubans in Miami." *American Journal of Sociology* 86, no. 2 (1980): 295–319.

Žižek, Slavoj. "Tolerance as an Ideological Category." *Critical Inquiry* 34 (2008): 660–82.

CHAPTER 9

Resisting Integration
Neukölln Artist Responses to Integration Politics

Johanna Schuster-Craig

Before the district of Berlin-Neukölln began to gentrify, it held symbolic status as the site of national concerns about the "integration" of immigrants. In the early 2000s, there was a series of events that brought attention to the district, such as the 2004 utterance by mayor Heinz Buschkowsky that multiculturalism had failed[1]; the 2005 "honor" murder of Hatun Sürücü on the border of Neukölln and Tempelhof, as well as outrageous comments made by students which were picked up by the media after her death[2]; and the Rütli-Schule scandal of 2006, where teachers demanded intervention in their failing school.[3] These scandals contributed to the rising pitch of integration debates, which reached new fervor in 2010 when Thilo Sarrazin published his racist polemic, *Deutschland schafft sich ab* (Germany does away with itself).[4] Echoes of Sarrazin's work continue to reverberate among citizens and politicians of the Right in 2016 as more than a million refugees have entered Germany.[5] Finally, Sarrazin himself continues to demand attention. In 2016 the cable network RTL brought back a talk show called *Der heiße Stuhl* (*Hot Seat*). Their first guest was Thilo Sarrazin, who argued that Muslim immigrants and refugees cause problems that other groups do not.[6]

Neukölln occupied a central role in integration debates because the district was instrumentalized by journalists and politicians as the national figurehead for the trope of a "parallel society" (*Parallelgesellschaft*), according to which immigrants are portrayed as refusing to assimilate to German norms und follow German law. This trope builds upon long-standing stereotypes of cultural "deficits" associated with immigrant groups, such as resistance to education, criminality, and traditional familial roles, especially gender roles. The purported resistance to abandoning "tradition" prompts—in this trope—a failure to integrate. In response to such "failures," integration politics (*Integrationspolitik*), which had existed in multiple incarnations since the late 1960s, shifted again in the early 2000s. This shift did not target new immigrants but rather was aimed at long-term (primarily Muslim) residents, who were depicted as both isolated and dangerously separate from a mythical German mainstream. Assimilative integration policies, such as integration and orientation courses, targeted this purported isolation as a social threat that would lead to the disintegration of the nation. The metaphor of a parallel society thus became one of the primary tropes to describe the de facto segregation of immigrant populations in German cities—and integration was widely held up as the antidote to segregation.

The discourse of a parallel society that describes minority groups as willfully separate illustrates a conflict between majority and minority groups. Parallel lines never meet; similarly parallel societies are portrayed as societies forever separated by incommensurable distance.[7] This metaphor typically implicates immigrant populations as responsible for keeping their distance. In contrast (and rarely defined in this way), a parallel society can also depict German society as a space that immigrants are unable to access and will never be able to shape. Artists of immigrant backgrounds and community organizations working in Neukölln do not accept either narrative of minority isolation. This chapter will explore first how the spatial metaphors of parallel societies and integration have shaped the imagined spaces of Neukölln. Then, by analyzing two cultural products—a comic book and a series of panel discussions—I will show how local narratives endeavor to recast the neighborhood (and by extension, the nation) as a place created through contact rather than isolation.

Despite such attention to parallel societies, a truly "parallel" location—a space that is separate and closed off from the world around it—is neither plausible nor probable in contemporary urban spaces. For instance, Barış Ülker's ethnographic attention to a network of geriatric care facilities for immigrants in this volume shows how these societies interact while at the same time illustrating how nuanced our understanding of neighborhood contact must be to comprehend the complexities of integration and integration politics. While Ülker's chapter—in stark contrast to the rhetorical analysis I undertake here—does not question integration as an operative term, his portrait of Rojda Jiwan's "ethnic entrepreneurship" hints at Jiwan's deep understanding of how everyday neighborhood life can be structured through contact. Jiwan not only understands how to navigate the German system of health-care in order to create culturally specific elder care for immigrants of the first generation who often have had negative interactions with state authorities, but she also won an integration prize in 2008, which shows how German policy and immigrant cultural practice come into contact with each other as a matter of course. Furthermore, Jiwan's cited vision of a socially connected neighborhood in which multiple generations of residents are interdependent is defined spatially rather than in terms of ethnic identity. Residence is the prerequisite for contact, and culturally specific business models are not necessarily dis-integrative.

As Wolf-Dietrich Bukow, Claudia Nikodem, Erika Schulze, and Erol Yildiz persuasively argue in their edited volume *Was heißt hier Paral-lelgesellschaft? Zum Umgang mit Differenzen* (*What Do You Mean, Par-allel Society? On Engaging with Differences*):

> The term [parallel society] implies the existence of institutionally sepa-rate and well-defined societies that exist side by side. And this associa-tion does not fit forms of urban coexistence common today, much less the rising and already sizeable mobility or the increasingly all-encom-passing infrastructural, economic, educational, administrative and com-municative systems in a long-since globalized culture and economy.[8]

These authors characterize the pervasiveness of the parallel metaphor as the product of two historical conditions. Due to West Germany's broad recruitment of immigrants from multiple countries in the 1960s, decades passed before immigrants with similar backgrounds were pub-lically recognized as groups.[9] The parallel society metaphor depends on a critical mass of immigrants with common backgrounds sharing residential space. This critical mass must also be large enough to cre-ate complex codes of social organization that can attend to the mate-rial, social, and cultural needs of a group—i.e., a society. When looking at the specific case of Neukölln, the preconditions for establishing this critical mass can be partly traced to the *Zuzugsperre* (Immigrant Resi-dency Ban) of 1975 that prohibited certain ethnic groups (such as Turks) from settling in the districts of Tiergarten, Wedding, and Kreuzberg.[10] This ban was created explicitly to stop the segregation of immigrants in districts described as "overwhelmed" (überlastet).[11] By trying to hinder individual immigrant groups from becoming segregated in one district, authorities hoped to develop neighborhoods that were ethnically di-verse rather than ethnically homogenous. As a 2013 study for the Berlin Senate Administration for Urban Planning and the Environment (*Sen-*

atsverwaltung für Stadtentwicklung und Umwelt) points out, this ban was discontinued not because it was discriminatory but rather because it was inefficient.[12]

Neukölln shares a border with the neighboring district of Kreuzberg. Although Turks were not permitted to settle in Kreuzberg for several years after 1975, there were no prohibitions on settling in Neukölln. North-Neukölln was thus strategically positioned to become what Bukow et al. call an "ethnic colony" and grew into a desired location for new immigrants who might have otherwise settled in Kreuzberg. Ethnic colonies develop when new immigrants settle or are settled in one neighborhood, and are also generally occupied only in the short term. Immediately after arrival, ethnic colonies can provide new immigrants with support through language, trusted friends or family members, shared experiences, and adaptation to a new environment. Once immigrants find their footing, they will move up the social and economic ladder and into a variety of other neighborhoods as their preferences develop. If immigrants are unable to find stability in the new country, however, they may remain in an ethnic colony due to linguistic or economic disadvantage or to other conditions that reflect the precarity of their social status.[13] Surprisingly, considering this history, in 2016 the German government passed a new "integration law" for refugees—the first of its kind. This law reintroduced residency requirements—in this instance for refugees who wish to seek asylum in Germany—with the stated aim of prohibiting the construction of "ghettos."[14]

The discourse of parallel societies took root because of a renewal of nationalist thought (*nationalstaatlichen Denkens*) that Bukow, Nikodem, Schulze and Yildiz posit was only possible after reunification.[15] The two Germanies had vastly different economies, institutions, and cultures. Reunification was a demanding project that required West German policymakers to absorb these differences and create a sense of national homogeneity. In the economic shifts that took place in West Berlin after reunification, many unskilled workers lost their jobs. Consequently, many immigrants found that they fell down the economic ladder instead of climbing it. An economic underclass of low-skilled workers of immigrant background began to emerge, and conditions thus became ripe for discourses that vilified the "ethnic colony."[16] Importantly, the parallel metaphor is not used to describe elite gated communities or migration to the suburbs: Bukow et al. point out that in contemporary discourse, a foreign-language sign or the construction of a mosque is enough to declare a neighborhood a "parallel society."[17] The term in its current usage thus carries xenophobic and Islamophobic connotations that target people such as the large Turkish-German and Arab-German populations that reside in North-Neukölln.

The discourse of insularity within a "parallel" metaphor would not be possible without the concept of integration. Integration is the dominant linguistic metaphor for the incorporation of immigrants, especially immigrants of color. In context, it hints strongly at assimilation and has been rejected as an offensive term by many, who argue that democratization and participation are the desired goals for immigrants.[18] In contrast to integration, democracy and participation are not linked to compulsory assimilation and loss of culture and/or identity. Integration and assimilation are demands directed only at immigrants and alienate some members of those groups from participating in civic life.[19] In this context, immigrants are thus more likely to remain in ethnically homogenous neighborhoods because their mobility is variously restricted:

> Alongside economic crises which inhibit mobility, in many countries there is another reason why immigrants stay in such neighborhoods long-term: structural conditions [Bedingungen] which restrict mobility.... In this way an "ethnic proletariat" develops which must remain in precarious neighborhoods and thus is marginalized over the long-term.... This happens time and again in Europe where political, economic or racist barriers block migrants' path into society.[20]

Thus, the trope of a parallel society does not accurately reflect immigrant desire but rather reflects the exclusionary mechanisms and attitudes held toward immigrants by those in power. Invoking this trope is thus an act of exclusion, not of description. The call to integrate reflects directly how difficult it can be to access German civic and social life.

Just as Bukow et al. disrupt the trope of a parallel society by showing how mobility can be restricted at the level of neighborhood, postcolonial theorist Kien Nghi Ha problematizes "integration" by showing its theoretical relationship to colonial practices designed to infantilize and assimilate ethnic others seen as culturally backward (kulturell rückständig) and threatening (bedrohlich).[21] In Nghi Ha's essay "Deutsche Integrationspolitik als koloniale Praxis" ("German Integration Policy as a Colonial Practice"), he argues both that integration policy has been accepted across the political spectrum, and that this broad acceptance obscures social realities like structural racism while reinforcing Germany's self-perception as an open and morally superior democracy.[22]

Rather than allowing vulnerable populations to access knowledge and participate in shaping society, integration courses—the case study of Nghi Ha's essay—are unsuccessful in promoting upward social mobility because integration policy is based on an "exclusionary German immigration policy" (*Ausländerpolitik*).[23] State attempts to integrate new immigrants—sometimes forcibly, by legally designating them "in need of integration"—also stoke prejudice: "This rhetoric [of integration and defensive democracy] appeals to a German sense of unity [*Wir-Gefühl*] and constructs [*inszeniert*] the German society as a victim of religious fundamentalism as well as threatening, expanding 'parallel societies.'"[24] The desire for border controls and limiting immigration requires integration as its opposite, according to Nghi Ha: "[E]xternal seclusion requires inward integration."[25] Limiting entry and demanding assimilation complement each other to create coherent policy. The negotiations of the German federal government with Turkey, Afghanistan, and other countries to limit refugee migration after 2015 suggests that Nghi Ha's analysis is especially prescient.

Thilo Sarrazin's polemic *Deutschland schafft sich ab* (*Germany Does Away with Itself*) targets Neukölln directly as a parallel society: "[Parallel societies] easily take on the character of a ghetto where the population with under-employment survives mostly from welfare subsidies. That applies to North-Neukölln with its Turkish and Arab population just as it used to apply to black Harlem in New York [*das schwarze Harlem*]."[26] In the following chapter in Sarrazin's book, he argues that the failure of integration policy is that it is not enforced. He then lists suggestions for policing integration, many of which sound a lot like forced assimilation.[27] In journalistic debates, Sarrazin has been praised publicly for breaking "the silence" about resentment directed toward (Muslim) immigrants. He has since been criticized for his "genetic" theories—what Sander Gilman called "a popular misuse of very, very bad science"—which are simultaneously philo-Semitic and Islamophobic.[28] Gilman traces the origins of Sarrazin's racialized arguments. They stem from both nineteenth-century European debates about the Jewish "race" and twentieth-century US research about "race" and evolutionary biology. Gilman's analysis of the theoretical foundations of *Deutschland schafft sich ab* shows how racial theory flows through Sarrazin's book and illuminates how "race" masquerades as both religious identity and phenotype.

Amid the Sarrazin controversy, then–federal president Christian Wulff gave an important speech commemorating twenty years of unified Germany. In this speech, President Wulff does not directly confront the racist scaffolding of Sarrazin's arguments; however, the most famous line of this speech—"Islam also belongs to Germany"—is constructed in direct opposition to the Sarrazinian debates circulating at that historical moment:

> Even though we've come farther than the current debate suggests, it's clear that we have not come far enough. ... But what we need first and foremost is a clear position. An understanding of Germany that does not restrict belonging to a passport, a family history or a belief, but which is fashioned more broadly. Christianity, without a doubt, belongs to Germany. Judaism, without a doubt, belongs to Germany. That is our Christian-Judaic history. But by now Islam also belongs to Germany.[29]

As a speech given to commemorate the *reunification* of Germany, Wulff's rhetoric aims to strengthen national identity by developing a clear stance on Germany's relationship to minorities. His chosen language here is quite interesting: first, he asserts that Germans as a whole are "further"—i.e., more progressive—than the Sarrazin scandal would imply. Second, he emphasizes religion by grouping Christianity and Judaism as religions that "without a doubt" (*zweifellos*) hold a place in German culture—and then adds Islam to the list as a religion that, "by now," is part of Germany. With this move, President Wulff hesitates. The hesitation that creeps into his rhetoric in the phrase "by now" (*inzwischen*) can be read as evidence of the obstacles faced by immigrants as they try to claim a position in national narratives. Wulff's speech is an extension of Nghi Ha's theory that political utterances and policies work hard to protect national identity and German "ethnic and cultural homogeneity"—even as they purportedly try to include othered groups.[30]

In what follows, I explore two very different cultural objects that emerged in 2010 in the context of debates about integration and parallel societies. The first, *Weltreiche erblühten und fielen* (*Empires Rose and Fell*), is a graphic novel written by Anna Faroqhi, edited by Dorothea Kolland, commissioned by the *Kulturamt Neukölln,* and published in 2010, the same year Sarrazin's book was released. The second, the "Playing in the Dark" series, consisted of three community conversations about racism curated by Philippa Ebéné and the *Werkstatt der Kulturen* in Neukölln in response to the lack of press attention in 2010 to hold Thilo Sarrazin accountable for his racist theories. Although different in form and content, both objects have a similar goal: they disrupt the myth of German ethnic homogeneity and resist the idea that immigration populations are "in need of integration" (*integrationsbedürftig*).[31] Read alongside each other, they point to the cultural labor already undertaken by many to reimagine narratives of the German nation as heterogeneous. Finally, these two projects resist integration discourses and policies in different ways. Grouping these two products together does not mean that these two organizations work together or view each other's work necessarily in favorable terms. The political interactions between organizations would be the subject of a different kind of analysis.

Since they are both attempting to reach a general audience, these kinds of cultural artifacts are quite useful for adding nuance to journalistic discourses that are necessarily (due to word limits) or intentionally (due to bias or accepted tropes) reductive. Two unique objects hardly constitute a fully formed topographical landscape; however, they can offer insight into local nodes of cultural production worthy of exploration in multiple directions. Similarly, many contributions to this volume explore both immigration policies and their critique. For instance, Simon Ward treats the effects of gentrification through and on the "creative class." Given that Neukölln is rapidly gentrifying, it would be interesting to consider whether and how the *Kulturamt Neukölln* and the *Werkstatt der Kulturen* may be forced to adapt their programming in the New Berlin.

Weltreiche erblühten und fielen was published by Dağyeli Verlag, a local publisher on the Karl-Marx-Straße in Neukölln.[32] Former director of the *Kulturamt,* Dr. Dorothea Kolland, was charged with developing a *Festschrift* for the 650th anniversary of the founding of the district celebrated in 2010. The commemorative texts generally commissioned for anniversaries have been dry, lofty tomes with tables about population growth and harvestable acreage.[33] Kolland wanted to do something different, primarily to fulfill the mission of the *Kulturamt,* which requires serving the district's diverse constituents. There are 160 nationalities said to be represented in Neukölln, and the rapidly gentrifying district is home to upwardly mobile young people, a traditionally blue-collar German population, and many groups of immigrants with various educational and economic backgrounds.[34] According to Kolland:

> DK: [T]he contemporary Neuköllners, especially those in North-Neukölln, no longer predominantly consist of people of a German background. They have come to Neukölln from many, many countries, but also from other German regions. And they are not the kind of people who—in terms of education—all have a college degree or are the kind who read academic works. And I thought it important to try [at least] ... to communicate history—I mean, to communicate knowledge about history—not just to put out a glossy thing [*Hochglanzding*] ... ; and secondly, to set a special focus on those who live in Neukölln today.[35]

Kolland's task, as she articulates here, is to transmit knowledge about history to current residents of Neukölln who are either unlikely or unable to profit from a traditional academic text. Reaching her constituents requires Kolland to make this historical information accessible rather than elite—since Neukölln, in Kolland's words, "was and is a poor district."[36] A text can incorporate implicit gatekeeping into its production. Formats, genres, and styles seen as elite, or even something as simple as a moderately high price, can make a text unappealing. An episodic graphic novel paperback that sells for less than ten euros, *Weltreiche erblühten und fielen* is designed to attract a broad readership. Both Kolland and Faroqhi even reject academic language when discussing the text, choosing to call the book a "comic" rather than a "graphic novel."[37]

> DK: And that's why [we] chose the comic form consciously, as an attempt—in this case—to tell the history of the district in all of its complexity.... [In order] to build a bridge, so that the people who live here and are poor notice that they are in the right place, and that they are supported here, because poverty ... and migration, that was always an issue here, in this district. And ... [the district] always somehow accepted it and coped with it, whether that was with the Bohemians [Moravians]; with the, the many [people] who flocked here after 1900; with the atheists, who were accepted by the Christians; and the devil knows what else.[38]

By insisting that immigration was not new for Neukölln but was a historical constant of the district *and* always moved along a long arc in which immigrants are eventually incorporated into the nation, Kolland refuses to portray immigration as a national threat. She is well aware of how revising the narrative of immigration-as-threat positions her against more conservative political narratives. During our interview, Kolland described a local celebration curated by the *Kulturamt,* criticizing politicians for seeing deficits where they could see potential:

> DK: We have people, who had come to Neukölln—there were descendants of the Bohemians [Moravians] there, there was one person from the GDR, but predominantly it was the whole world, with the thought, the potential that these people, who have come to Neukölln from all over the world, contain; [we wanted to] make this potential fruitful—visible—and fruitful [*fruchtbar*]. Really as potential and not a problem. Politics always links that to a problem. And a deficit.[39]

Kolland's commission of the comic book was thus informed by an explicit resistance to contemporary political and media discourses about immigrants in Neukölln. As the leader of a cultural institution, Kolland consciously chooses formats (the comic) and topics (immigration) that are designed to reach a broad swath of residents, especially new *Neuköllner.*

Kolland commissioned writer and visual artist Anna Faroqhi to develop the comic, who worked in concert with Kolland's educational and promotional mission. Faroqhi's ethnic identity complicates the stereotypical association of Neukölln with the two largest immigrant communities in the district: those with Arab or Turkish backgrounds.[40] In the text, Anna describes herself as having "Muslim-Indian forefathers." She then remarks critically upon being able to "pass" for white while looking into a mirror that reflects a different version of identity than the one offered by outside appearance. With this image, Faroqhi effectively disrupts a common misconception that racial and ethnic identity can be discerned by outsiders, and she also hints at the privileges she may carry by effectively passing. As this image of the protagonist communicating with herself in the mirror suggests, Faroqhi's characters are simply drawn: her faces often no more than dots and lines; her frames and gutters drawn by hand with gray shadings that sometimes move beyond the

Figure 9.1. "I myself have Muslim-Indian forefathers, but you can't see any of that anymore."[41]

boundaries of the frame. The cartoon style of her figures, however, reflects the power of comics to prompt identification.

Scott McCloud, the astute graphic novelist and comics theorist, sees great potential in the reduced, simple facial sketches common to cartoons. This simplicity, according to McCloud, both mirrors the general awareness we have of our own features and prompts identification on behalf of the reader: "Thus, when you look at a photo or realistic drawing of a face—you see it as the face of *another*. But when you enter the world of the *cartoon*—you see yourself."[42] On a landscape where media tropes like parallel societies and "fake" asylum seekers (*Scheinasylanten*) dominate and demand that we see Muslims, immigrants, and refugees as different from ourselves, these facial forms and their ability to prompt identification actively resist this othering.

Faroqhi uses her family (herself, her husband Haim, and their children: Prosper, Emily, and Sita) to frame historical episodes that move from the middle ages to the present day. Their story is only one of the many contemporary narratives that inform the text. Moreover, the historical episodes of the comic book are linked to Anna's self-reflective process of writing and drawing. As a narrator, Anna moves into and out of her historical framework, and frequently moves between time frames and through locations by portraying family walks. She and her family wander through Neukölln much like Baudelairean *voyeurs*.[43] Through the walks of the characters in the district, readers are introduced to its architecture, memorials of specific historical events placed in space, and the different "faces" of Neukölln embodied by various *Zuwanderer* (immigrants), who literally wander through the panels. Prosper, for example, asks his father fairly early on why he—a Moroccan-Israeli Jew—decided to come to Germany. His father explains he no longer wanted to live in Israel after his military service and the death of his brother. As Haim and Prosper discuss the place of Jews in post-Holocaust Germany, Christiana W., a refugee from Sierra Leone, wanders past the outside café where they are sitting.

It may be problematic that Haim supposes a woman of color must be a refugee or an immigrant; but Haim's reference to Christiana also smooths the transition to this sidebar for readers. Such narrative devices facilitate the incorporation of more stories in the comic than Haim's autobiographical framework alone would allow. The three characters

Figure 9.2. Prosper: "I think I will go to Israel after I finish high school."
Haim: "I think the same thing every winter! But this country is a refuge for many. Maybe also for this woman …"
Caption: Christiana W., born 1963 in Portloko in Sierra Leone. The place was destroyed by rebels who murdered or drove people out. Christiana fled in 1982 from the atrocities of the political conflicts. She had to leave her daughter behind. Not until nine years later, as the civil war broke out in 1991, was she able to bring the child and her [Christiana's] four siblings to Berlin. Christiana runs a restaurant on Boddin Street.[44]

in this one panel—Prosper, Haim, and Christiana—all have different relationships to Germany, and according to Faroqhi, these differences are to be treasured. In the joint interview with Kolland that I conducted, Faroqhi stated that one of her aims in this comic is to value the multiple, individual stories deemed unimportant by the broader public:

> AF: For me this comic was [a way of] finding many small stories, because that's the whole point, to tell these stories or to find them from people who don't leave a story [Geschichte] behind.... I think it's incredibly important to take that seriously, these ... really small, hard to discern [stories], and the little treasures [Kostbarkeiten] of all these many lives and all these many unseen lives. I don't know where I'm going with that, but in the moment my motivation to do something myself is minimized because I find it so incredible, the great wealth [Größe] of stories, which are all around me.[45]

For Faroqhi, the narrative elements that surround her as a resident of Neukölln are both great and small. The greatness emerges from the sheer quantity of stories; the small treasures emerge in simple stories that require her to exercise discernment as she develops her narrative arc. The reductive grand narrative of defensive isolation inherent to the parallel-society metaphor is inadequate in the face of individual stories that coalesce to form a grand collection. By including as many individual stories as possible, Faroqhi works hard to create a differentiated portrayal of individuals in Neukölln.

In 2010 the *Werkstatt der Kulturen* curated three panel discussions about racism in response to the debates about Thilo Sarrazin and his book, *Deutschland schafft sich ab.* The WdK is an arts organization near Hermannplatz, merely two subway stops away from the *Kulturamt Neukölln.* Sarrazin's controversial book essentializes ethnic groups through pseudoscientific genetic theories, which are based on assumed inheritable intelligence and supposedly predict the group's ability to add value to the national economy. The "Playing in the Dark" series at the WdK was developed to resist racializing arguments and educate the public about how racist ideologies function. Beginning a mere six weeks after the publication of *Deutschland schafft sich ab,* the panels in October, November, and December 2010 drew large audiences.[46] The three events highlighted different mechanisms of racist ideology: the politics and policy of integration; the racist socialization of children; and discriminatory language in politics, the media, and everyday life. Each panel had four or five participants and was moderated by the polemic TV journalist Michel Friedman, host of the N24 talk show *Studio Friedman.*

If journalists have deemed parallel societies to be an immigrant problem, politicians have deemed immigrant integration to be their social solution. The first panel discussion at the WdK thus focused on integration politics. This focus was especially topical given Sarrazin's emphasis on "failed" integration in his book. Five guests took the stage: Prof. Dr. Naika Foroutan, then a researcher of migration at the Humboldt University of Berlin; Dr. Kien Nghi Ha, political scientist and cultural studies scholar; Anetta Kahane, the chairperson of the Amadeu Antonio Foundation; Mekonnen Mesghena, the head of the Migration and Diversity Department at the Heinrich Böll Foundation; and Maryam Stibenz, the commissioner of integration for the District of Berlin-Mitte.

Just as *Weltreiche erblühten und fielen* assembled a large cast of characters and collected a variety of stories from residents to create a differentiated portrait of the district of Neukölln, the *Werkstatt der Kulturen* brought together a variety of public intellectuals, artists, public servants, and scholars to offer a variety of viewpoints about the controversies at hand. Similar to the way that the *Kulturamt* rejected the idea of producing a traditional academic text to celebrate the anniversary of the district, deciding instead for an engaging and accessible comics format, the "Playing in the Dark" series refused to allow the mainstream media to dictate the terms of a discussion about race. The result in both cases was a product or performance that was highly accessible to a general audience. In this short space, I will not be able to do justice to every participant, but I will analyze a few moments as illustrative of the kinds of responses present throughout the three-event series.

Michel Friedman, the moderator for the panel discussion at the WdK, states quite clearly in his introduction that this panel discussion stands in stark relief to the Sarrazinian arguments and media debate. What Friedman finds problematic in the "phenomenon" of Sarrazin is what he calls the "emotionalization" (*Emotionalisierung*) of these debates. First, Friedman asserts that uncontrollable affect is dangerous, and states that he will try to bring reason and argument back to the debate. Friedman even shows that he is aware of his polemic reputation, stating that he has nothing against emotion, but "emotions without content" are dangerous and problematic. Everyone in a romantic relationship, he jokes, already knows this. Second, Friedman asserts that the role of this panel is to let minorities speak for themselves—but with a desire to prevent the common dynamic in so many conversations where minorities assert that critical statements about their groups do not apply to them as individuals.[47]

Friedman found immediate opportunity to pursue his stated goals. Naika Foroutan, a migration researcher from the Humboldt University in Berlin, was the first guest to speak. Friedman posed several questions to Foroutan about Muslim identity in the context of former federal president Wulff's statement earlier that month that "Islam belongs to Germany." Foroutan answers most of these initial questions like an academic, citing definitions, statistics, and methods. Friedman then asked Foroutan personally what kinds of effects these conversations have on her. Foroutan initially resisted giving personal responses, replying in exactly the way Friedman wanted to avoid: she insists that such statements are not directed at her.

> MF: What has changed in your everyday life [due to the current controversies]? ...
>
> NF: Well, I have to admit that I've been asking myself exactly this question thematically as part of my research ... um, and they don't really mean me; that's what I've been investigating all this time, who do they mean, how are they marked –
>
> MF: They mean you.
>
> NF: Yeah, ok, the question is, um, actually through these TV appearances ..., what's become more or less clear to me is that by speaking about phenotype and self-identification as Muslims is that a whole lot of people have been excluded from the indigenous German society; many people also from the center—...
>
> MF: What effect does that have on you?
>
> NF: Since—Since I research this academically, ... at least I was prepared in a certain way [*in gewissem Maße*].
>
> MF: And in uncertain ways? [*Reden wir vom nicht gewissen Maße.*]
>
> NF: *Ja* [*laughter in the audience*]. Well, it's not comfortable, of course.[48]

Through this insistence on speaking about the personal, Friedman artfully reproduces the emotional response in Foroutan that he criticized in his introduction—the protective tendency of minorities to insist that hurtful statements do not apply to them as individuals. As Friedman's questioning continues, Foroutan explains why she deflects questions by analyzing her emotional response.

> MF: Yeah, that [*more laughter*] took a while.... What effect does that have on you?
>
> NF: Yes, now I know where you're heading. ... Actually, I've developed an obstinate feeling inside, this feeling, *uff*, what? I belong here and

no one can tell me that I don't belong here. And that … produces in me actually, as far as I can tell, for the first time, moments come up where I use words like "my country," "my Germany," but still not in a constructed way, but rather stubbornly.

MF: Did you emphasize that before, when you spoke? My country?

NF: *Nee* –

MF: My Germany?

NF: *Nee*—I never said it.

MF: But now you do.

NF: Now I do.[49]

Foroutan asserts that Sarrazin's theses and the media attention they garnered served to exclude many members of German society, but especially those from the "center." Foroutan and Friedman narrate this exclusion: Friedman resists Foroutan's quantitative responses about Muslim populations as incomplete by insisting that the Sarrazin debates most certainly have hailed her as a subject and have excluded her as well. Foroutan first resists this exclusion, and then recounts her recent, sudden insistence that Germany is her country; that she belongs no matter what exclusionary tactics are chosen. She glosses her claim as obstinacy: "my Germany" is not a patriotic construct, but rather a stubborn one—and a position that has developed against the backdrop of current events.

Yet, by insisting that Foroutan speak about her personal feelings rather than facts, Friedman risks a different kind of exclusion—he insists that her position as a minority is more telling than her expertise as a researcher. Insisting on felt emotions as proof of the destructive effects of the debate excludes this professional from the "center" of a profession. The first responses during the question-and-answer session produced precisely this critique from an audience member who—if memory serves—was frustrated that minority scholars were being forced to speak personally and who argued that this style of questioning was itself racist.[50]

Other panelists, however, approached the resistance to seeing oneself as part of the group named by Sarrazinian arguments as arising from a colonial past. Mekonnen Mesghena, head of the Migration and Diversity Department of the Heinrich Böll Foundation, spoke about the theoretical consequences of excluding those who do not hold dominant power and how this exclusion was part and parcel of colonial rule. Asked by Friedman if racism would disappear if all immigrants became "productive forces," Mesghena described this formulation as a strategy of "divide and rule" (English in the original). Mesghena states, "When racists draw a blank, then they show up with this strategy of 'divide and rule'—this means, one creates hierarchies."[51] Dividing up immigrant groups into those who are productive and those who are ostensibly unproductive, those who are integrated and those who are not, is a foundation of racist ideology. The "group dynamic"—the refusal to see themselves named by Sarrazinian arguments—that Friedman finds so frustrating in his introduction could also be interpreted as a direct consequence of policies of "divide and rule." By insisting that—in the words of Friedman—"they don't mean me," individuals could be inhibiting the development of coalitions that could resist racism. Mesghena pointed out that focusing on analyzing Sarrazin and integration is only the beginning of the kind of engagement that is necessary to dismantle structural racism:

> MM: And that's where we would have had to go further and talk less, it's less about integration, and constructive criticism was hardly present, but we could have used this opportunity [the Sarrazin debates] to talk about racism. Which we still remain silent about in spite of all the people who got involved: it's precisely about those—what you said—sociopolitical questions. We live primarily in a no-win society [*chancenlos*], where for part of society, when we're talking about immigrants [*Migranten*], [they] are caught on a dead-end street, and can hardly ... reach a certain kind of social advancement, much less upward mobility, because the systems, the institutions, see to it that people are limited in their achievements and are not encouraged, and are selected much too early and too frequently—we know this debate from the educational sector and the lack of integration in the workforce, etc., etc. These are, first of all, the most urgent questions that we have to engage with, and precisely these questions are always concealed and avoided through a debate, which just distracts us [from seeing] what we're actually lacking.[52]

The issue, according to Mesghena, is not cultural difference or intentional separation from the mainstream. Racism and the sociopolitical access it limits need to be discussed, rather than productivity or "integration." Mesghena's answer strongly echoes the critiques of the parallel society metaphor offered by Bukow et al. and critiques of integration policies offered by Nghi Ha. The metaphor of a parallel society bases itself upon some notion of agency by those minorities who "choose" to live apart; however, what Mesghena is asserting is that because "we" do not speak about racism, "we" cannot notice the real, material sociopolitical exclusions that prevent minorities from accessing the most important homogenizing institutions: higher education and the workforce.

Over the course of the discussion, similar points were emphasized and the nuances of racialized dynamics were discussed. Most often, these utterances emphasized the persistence of structural racism within integration politics. In his closing remarks, Friedman pointedly declared that this conversation will never end. The dynamics of exclusion are mutable, and the protean nature of racism can easily transfer resentments from one group to another. Rather than see this statement as an excuse for racism, however, I suggest below that understanding how racism mutates helps shape our analysis in ways that allow us to track racism even when racist language appears in new formulations.

The two projects analyzed here both resist passive acceptance of the tropes of a parallel society and of the need to integrate foreigners through state-sponsored assimilation. They do so in a variety of ways—collecting and facilitating expression of stories and voices, resisting fitting into certain media-proscribed boxes, and redefining concepts like integration and neighborhood. The difficulty in reaching large audiences with these kinds of resistance is evident in the types of reviews both works have received. *Weltreiche erblühten und fielen* received primarily local newspaper reviews.[53] Despite Kolland's attempts to make history accessible, she was surprised by the resistance of educators to the comics format:

> DK: And I actually hadn't suspected that in Germany—even at the level of research … that the resistance and skepticism—among teachers as well—would be so great. I really hadn't planned for that.
>
> …
>
> JSC: What are a couple of examples where you both recognized that this opening isn't there, or that the resonance [for this project] wasn't there?
>
> DK: Well … in the sales figures, which aren't so common, but what I found particularly regrettable was: … We offered reduced prices for classroom sets, and that was only taken advantage of with great hesitation.[54]

Faroqhi and her husband, Haim Peretz, conduct a variety of local comics-drawing workshops in schools and nonprofit organizations in Neukölln based upon their work on *Weltreiche erblühten und fielen*. What Kolland implies is that the comic was less influential than it could have been, due primarily to structural hurdles: the skepticism among teachers and the lukewarm reaction of the market to the comic and its content.

The last in the series of panel discussions about race at the Werkstatt der Kulturen was reviewed by *Der Spiegel*, where it did not enjoy a particularly favorable reception. The review of this last "Playing in the Dark" event, which focused on racist language, included a portrait of Michel Friedman, eyes closed, forefingers pointing directly into the air, unceremoniously framed by the title of the review, "N——-prinzessin."[55] When Philippa Ebéné, the curator of the series and artistic director of the WdK, showed me this layout during a conversation we had after the events had concluded, my shock was audible. On the interview recording, I can be heard gasping with an distinct "Hooooh!"[56]

Ebéné then offered me her interpretation of the composite image of the headline and Friedman's portrait. Not only was the language in and of itself racist—this was the source of my audible shock—but it was also featured prominently in a national magazine. Ebéné stated that she sees this kind of offensive language more and more frequently. More importantly, Ebéné argued in our conversation that this title performs the kinds of mutations Michel Friedman hinted at when he declared that racist structures both persist and are highly adaptive. According to Ebéné, this combination of picture and title provided the author of the *Spiegel* review, Christoph Scheuermann, with multiple opportunities to discredit the work of Michel Friedman at the event itself. Second, the language chosen allowed Scheuermann to other Michel Friedman—but he stopped short of publishing an anti-Semitic slur (Friedman, the most well-known of the panelists, is the child of Polish-Jewish Holocaust survivors). Finally, using what Ebéné calls a "colonial racist" term allows Scheuermann to hide the true dynamics of who is offending whom. The mismatch between the term in its historical usage and the photo of Friedman—which is highly unflattering—makes it more difficult to map exactly how this slur applies to Friedman. Yet, the prominence of title and photo make clear that no one else besides Friedman could be meant as the recipient of this attack, and the language is highly offensive in a way that cannot be reclaimed.[57] I would also add that the feminine form of the slur, which ends with "princess," implies a misogynist slant to the choice of title and portrait, and aims to feminize Friedman as an added insult.

Ebéné's astute commentary on the protean nature of racism in journalism illustrates how slurs can be applied in indirect ways that make resistance invisible and perpetuate structural racism. Ebéné's response to national media coverage also suggests that while some artists, activists, and intellectuals living and working in the district of Neukölln resist the stories told about them, the national press has little interest in listening to what these experts have to say. Instead, reporters use racist language to both discredit their subjects' work and silence their critiques. These structural obstacles are deeply embedded within German culture and are the foundation prompting the proliferation of other tropes, such as "parallel societies" and the need for "integration." Racist rhetoric, while prominent, is not all encompassing, precisely because of the fact that in the examples observed here, artists, activists, and intellectuals are offering solutions and redefinitions despite being ignored by the national press and local institutions (such as schools).[58]

One of the clearest examples of this conflict between traditional tropes and redefinition became quite clear in the press coverage that followed the criminal activities in Cologne on New Year's Eve in 2015. While some journalists and especially the right wing were quick to target Muslim men and revive Orientalist tropes of savagery, there were strong countering voices that argued that sexualized violence is a problem for all patriarchal societies, including traditional German society.[59] Change is slow because of competing, conflicting narratives, in spite of the variety of stories all around us, the expertise of researchers, and the work of curators with knowledge of the dynamics of racism. Narratives of integration and parallel societies should be treated skeptically, as they are produced by institutions that actively work to resist other narratives from entering mainstream discourse.

Acknowledgments

Funding for this research was provided by the Alexander von Humboldt Foundation German Chancellor Fellows program for 2010–11. Many thanks to Philippa Ebéné, Anna Faroqhi, and Dorothea Kolland for agreeing to be interviewed for this project, and to the editors for their helpful suggestions in revising this text.

Johanna Schuster-Craig is an assistant professor of German and global studies at Michigan State University. Her previous publications have appeared in *German Life and Letters* and *Tulsa Studies in Women's Literature*. She is at work on a book about integration politics.

Notes

1. Werner van Bebber, "Neuköllns Bürgermeister: Multi-Kulti ist gescheitert," *Der Tagesspiegel,* November 13, 2004, http://www.tagesspiegel.de/berlin/neukoellns-buergermeister-multi-kulti-ist-gescheitert/562396.html.
2. Newspaper coverage of the Sürücü murder has been extensive and ongo-

ing. Turkey recently charged two of her brothers who fled Germany with murder, ten years after her death. See "Türkei erhebt Mordanklage gegen Brüder von Hatun Sürücü," *rbb-online.de,* July 27, 2015, http://www.rbb-on line.de/politik/beitrag/2015/07/tuerkei-erhebt-mordanklage-gegen-brued er-von-hatun-sueruecue.html. For thematic coverage, see "Mord an Hatun Sürücü," *Spiegel Online Panorama,* accessed October 2, 2015, http://www .spiegel.de/thema/mord_an_hatun_sueruecue/.

3. The Rütli School scandal was also heavily documented: Bundeszentrale für politische Bildung, "Schule und Integration," *Bundeszentrale für politische Bildung,* April 3, 2006, http://www.bpb.de/politik/hintergrund-aktuell/70206/schule-und-integration-03-04-2006; Franziska Manske, "Die Gewalt-Kids von der Terror-Schule: Sie nennen deutsche Mädchen Hurentöchter," *Bild.de,* December 10, 2007, http://www.bild.de/news/2006/schule-terror-287834.bild.html; Lorenz Maroldt, "Jugend trainiert für das Ghetto," *Der Tagesspiegel,* March 30, 2006, http://www.bild.de/news/2006/schule-terror-287834.bild.html; Brigitte Pick, *Kopfschüsse: Wer PISA nicht versteht, muss mit RÜTLI rechnen* (Hamburg, 2007). Teachers published a letter asking for help from government officials and described conditions that included violence, disrespect for property, and the lack of teachers of color to serve their population. Finally, they noted that the school had been unsuccessful in placing its graduates in apprenticeships, the necessary next step for upward mobility for *Hauptschule* students.

4. Thilo Sarrazin, *Deutschland schafft sich ab: Wie wir unser Land aufs Spiel setzen* (Munich, 2010).

5. BMI, "2015: Mehr Asylanträge in Deutschland als jemals zuvor," *Bundesministerium des Inneren,* January 1, 2016, http://www.bmi.bund.de/Shared Docs/Pressemitteilungen/DE/2016/01/asylantraege-dezember-2015.html.

6. Arno Frank, "Mangelnder Anstand als Sendungskonzept," *Spiegel Online,* December 13, 2016, http://www.spiegel.de/kultur/tv/der-heisse-stuhl-bei-rtl-mangelnder-anstand-als-sendungskonzept-a-1125612.html.

7. For analysis of the phrase "incommensurable difference," see Rita Chin, *The Guestworker Question in Postwar Germany* (Cambridge, 2009), 141–90.

8. Wolf-Dietrich Bukow et al., *Was heißt hier Parallelgesellschaft? Zum Umgang mit Differenzen* (Wiesbaden, 2007), 13–14. Unless otherwise noted, translations are my own.

9. Ibid., 13.

10. Udo Gößwald and Kerstin Schmiedeknecht, *Wie zusammen leben: Perspektiven aus Nord Neukölln* (Berlin, 2009), 16; "Türken in Berlin—'die Heimat hast du hier,'" *Der Spiegel* 5 (1980): 39.

11. Nikolai Roskamm, "Studie: Das Leitbild von der 'Urbanen Mischung,'" (Berlin, 2013), 22, http://www.stadtentwicklung.berlin.de/staedtebau/baukultur/iba/download/studien/IBA-Studie_Urbane_Mischung.pdf.

12. Ibid., 23.

13. Bukow, et al., 11–12.

14. Lisa Caspari, "Besser Arbeiten, Schneller Scheitern," *Zeit Online*, May 24, 2016, http://www.zeit.de/politik/deutschland/2016-05/integrationsgesetz-fluechtlinge-wohnsitz-parlament-meseberg/seite-2.
15. Bukow, et al., 13.
16. Ibid.
17. Ibid., 15.
18. Philippa Ebéné, in discussion with the author, February 10, 2011.
19. Anna Böcker, "Integration," in *Wie Rassismus aus Wörtern spricht: (K)Erben des Kolonialismus im Wissensarchiv deutsche Sprache. Ein kritisches Nachschlagewerk*, ed. Susan Arndt and Nadja Ofuatey-Alazard (Münster, 2011), 347–64.
20. Bukow, *Parallelgesellschaft*, 12.
21. Kien Nghi Ha, "Deutsche Integrationspolitik als koloniale Praxis," in *Re/visionen: Postkoloniale Perspektiven von People of Color auf Rassismus, Kulturpolitik und Widerstand in Deutschland*, ed. Kien Nghi Ha, Nicola Lauré al-Samari, and Sheila Mysorekar (Münster, 2007), 123.
22. Ibid., 117.
23. Ibid., 121.
24. Ibid.
25. Ibid., 122.
26. Thilo Sarrazin, *Deutschland schafft sich ab*, 294.
27. Ibid., 260–330.
28. Sander L. Gilman, "Thilo Sarrazin and the Politics of Race in the Twenty-First Century," *New German Critique* 39, no. 3 (2012): 50–59.
29. Christian Wulff, "Rede zum 20. Jahrestag der Deutschen Einheit," *Der Bundespräsident*, October 3, 2010, http://www.bundespraesident.de/SharedDocs/Reden/DE/Christian-Wulff/Reden/2010/10/20101003_Rede.html.
30. Nghi Ha, 116–17.
31. "Zuwanderungsgesetz," *Auswärtiges Amt*, August 28, 2007, http://www.auswaertiges-amt.de/DE/EinreiseUndAufenthalt/Zuwanderungsrecht_node.html.
32. Anna Faroqhi, *Weltreiche erblühten und fielen*, ed. Dorothea Kolland (Berlin, 2010).
33. Johannes Schultze, *Rixdorf-Neukölln: Die geschichtliche Entwicklung eines Berliner Bezirks* (Berlin, 1960).
34. "Kulturarbeit in Neukölln," *Fachbereich Kultur, Bezirksamt Neukölln von Berlin*, October 6, 2015, http://kultur-neukoelln.de/ueber-uns-konzept.php.
35. Anna Faroqhi and Dorothea Kolland, in discussion with the author, March 23, 2011.
36. Anna Faroqhi and Dorothea Kolland, *Weltreiche erblühten und fielen* (presentation, *Linke Medienakademie*, Berlin, March 11, 2011).
37. Lynn M. Kutch's contribution to this volume explores this split between high and low cultural products in the context of comics. This split may be what Kolland and Faroqhi are reacting to by consistently calling their book a "comic."

38. Faroqhi and Kolland, discussion.
39. Ibid.
40. For an analysis of the creative class in Berlin, which would include most of the writers and artists in this chapter, see Ward in this volume. Barış Ülker's contribution to this volume also includes a framework for understanding ethnic entrepreneurship in Neukölln.
41. Faroqhi, *Weltreiche erblühten und fielen*, 11.
42. Scott McCloud, *Understanding Comics: The Invisible Art* (Northampton, MA, 1993), 36.
43. See Kutch in this volume for an analysis of the term *Flaneursjournalist* in the context of graphic novelist Ulli Lust.
44. Faroqhi, *Weltreiche erblühten und fielen*, 43.
45. Faroqhi and Kolland, discussion.
46. The title, which plays on Toni Morrison's book about whiteness and the literary imagination, was chosen consciously by Ebéné.
47. Werkstatt der Kulturen, "1. Spieglein, Spieglein an der Wand, wer ist der Integrierteste im ganzen Land?," YouTube video, 17:47, posted by "wdkberlin," January 16, 2012, https://www.youtube.com/watch?v=ad04Dnvk2Nk.
48. Ibid.
49. Ibid.
50. Fieldwork notes, October 27, 2010.
51. Werkstatt der Kulturen, "2. Spieglein, Spieglein an der Wand, wer ist der Integrierteste im ganzen Land?," YouTubevideo, 14:47, posted by "wdkberlin," January 25, 2012, https://www.youtube.com/watch?v=pIHTsUFLj1g.
52. Ibid.
53. Jörg Sundermeier, "Politik in der Hasenheide," *Berliner Zeitung*, July 14, 2010, http://www.berliner-zeitung.de/archiv/-weltreiche-erbluehten-und-fie len—-anna-faroqhis-lehrreicher-comic-ueber-650-jahre-neukoelln-poli tik-in-der-hasenheide,10810590,10729852.html.
54. Faroqhi and Kolland, discussion.
55. Christoph Scheuermann, "N****prinzessin," *Der Spiegel* 51 (2010): 71, http://magazin.spiegel.de/EpubDelivery/spiegel/pdf/75803471.
56. Ebéné, discussion.
57. Ibid.
58. This list is not exhaustive. Antiracist interventions can be found in various sectors, including journalism. See the glossary developed by the Neue deutsche Medienmacher for journalists. "Neue deutsche Medienmacher: Glossar," *Neue deutsche Medienmacher*, http://glossar.neuemedienmacher.de/.
59. The coverage of the events in Cologne is extensive. *Die Zeit* published several articles in the month of January: Anonymous, "Angefasst," *Die Zeit* 4 (2016): 55; Miriam Lau and Khuê Pham, "Der Albtraum"; and Elisabeth Raether, "Sex und Macht: Woher kommt die Gewalt gegen Frauen?" *Die Zeit* 2 (2016): 2. The events were so drastic that *Der Spiegel* published an article in English about them, something they often do for events of importance: *Spiegel*

Staff, "How New Year's Eve in Cologne Has Changed Germany," *Spiegel Online*, January 8, 2016, http://www.spiegel.de/international/germany/co logne-attacks-trigger-raw-debate-on-immigration-in-germany-a-1071175 .html. The TV station 3SAT offered on January 12, 2016, a video conversation with literary scholar Barbara Vinke critiquing the trope of violent foreign men: "Kulturzeit-Gespräch mit Barbara Vinken zur Sexismus-Debatte in Deutschland," http://www.3sat.de/mediathek/?mode=play&obj=56368. See also Bassam Tibi, "Junge Männer, die die Kultur der Gewalt mitbringen," *Welt Online*, May 8, 2016, https://www.welt.de/debatte/kommentare/ article155134929/Junge-Maenner-die-die-Kultur-der-Gewalt-mitbringen .html.

Bibliography

Anonymous. "Angefasst." *Zeit Online*. Accessed March 13, 2017. http://www.zeit .de/2016/04/sexuelle-gewalt-opfer-missbrauch-bewaeltigung.

Böcker, Anna. "Integration." In *Wie Rassismus aus Wörtern spricht: (K)Erben des Kolonialismus im Wissensarchiv deutsche Sprache. Ein kritisches Nachschlagewerk*, edited by Susan Arndt and Nadja Ofuatey-Alazard, 347–64. Münster: Unrast Verlag, 2011.

Bukow, Wolf-Dietrich, Claudia Nikodem, Erika Schulze, and Erol Yildiz. *Was heißt hier Parallelgesellschaft? Zum Umgang mit Differenzen*. Wiesbaden: VS Verlag für Sozialwissenschaften, 2007.

Bundesministerium des Inneren. "2015: Mehr Asylanträge in Deutschland als jemals zuvor." Accessed February 9, 2016. http://www.bund.de/SharedDocs/ Pressemitteilungen/DE/2016/01/asylantraege-dezember-2015.html.

Bundeszentrale für politische Bildung. "Schule und Integration." Accessed October 7, 2015. http://www.bpb.de/politik/hintergrund-aktuell/70206/schule-und-integration-03-04-2006.

Caspari, Lisa. "Besser Arbeiten, Schneller Scheitern." *Zeit Online*. Accessed March 13, 2017. http://www.zeit.de/politik/deutschland/2016-05/integratio nsgesetz-fluechtlinge-wohnsitz-parlament-meseberg/seite-2.

Chin, Rita. *The Guestworker Question in Postwar Germany*. Cambridge: Cambridge University Press, 2007.

Ebéné, Philippa. Discussion with Johanna Schuster-Craig. February 10, 2011.

Faroqhi, Anna. *Weltreiche erblühten und fielen*, edited by Dorothea Kolland. Berlin: Dağyeli Verlag, 2010.

Faroqhi, Anna, and Dorothea Kolland. Discussion with Johanna Schuster-Craig. March 23, 2011.

———. "Weltreiche erblühten und fielen." Presentation, *Linke Medienakademie*, Berlin, March 11, 2011.

Frank, Arno. "Mangelnder Anstand als Sendungskonzept." *Spiegel Online*, December 13, 2016. Accessed March 12, 2017. http://www.spiegel.de/

kultur/tv/der-heisse-stuhl-bei-rtl-mangelnder-anstand-als-sendungs konzept-a-1125612.html.

Gilman, Sander L. "Thilo Sarrazin and the Politics of Race in the Twenty-First Century." *New German Critique* 39, no. 3 (2012): 50–59.

Gößwald, Udo, and Kerstin Schmiedeknecht. *Wie zusammen leben: Perspektiven aus Nord-Neukölln.* Berlin: Museum Neukölln, 2009.

Ha, Kien Nghi. "Deutsche Integrationspolitik als koloniale Praxis." In *Re/visionen: Postkoloniale Perspektiven von People of Color auf Rassismus, Kulturpolitik und Widerstand in Deutschland,* edited by Kien Nghi Ha, Nicola Lauré al-Samari, and Sheila Mysorekar, 113–28. Münster: Unrastverlag, 2007.

"Kulturarbeit in Neukölln." *Fachbereich Kultur, Bezirksamt Neukölln von Berlin,* October 6, 2015. Accessed March 12, 2017. http://kultur-neukoelln.de/ue ber-uns-konzept.php.

Kulturzeit. "Kulturzeit-Gespräch mit Barbara Vinken zur Sexismus-Debatte in Deutschland." 3sat Mediathek video, 5:53. January 12, 2016. Accessed March 12, 2017. http://www.3sat.de/mediathek/?mode=play&obj=56368.

Lau, Miriam, and Khuê Pham. "Der Albtraum." *Zeit Online,* January 21, 2016. Accessed March 12, 2017. http://www.zeit.de/2016/02/koeln-sexu elle-uebergriffe-arabische-maenner-vorurteile.

Manske, Franziska. "Die Gewalt-Kids von der Terror-Schule: Sie nennen deutsche Mädchen Hurentöchter." *Bild.de,* December 10, 2007. Accessed March 12, 2017. http://www.bild.de/news/2006/schule-terror-287834.bild.html.

Maroldt, Lorenz. "Jugend trainiert für das Ghetto." *Der Tagesspiegel,* March 30, 2006. Accessed March 12, 2017. http://www.bild.de/news/2006/schule-terror-287834.bild.html.

McCloud, Scott. *Understanding Comics: The Invisible Art.* Northampton, MA: Kitchen Sink Press, 1993.

"Mord an Hatun Sürücü." *Spiegel Online Panorama,* October 2, 2015. http://www.spiegel.de/thema/mord_an_hatun_sueruecue/.

"Neue deutsche Medienmacher: Glossar." *Neue deutsche Medienmacher.* Accessed March 13, 2017. http://glossar.neuemedienmacher.de/.

Pick, Brigitte. *Kopfschüsse: Wer PISA nicht versteht, muss mit RÜTLI rechnen.* Hamburg: VSA-Verlag, 2007.

Raether, Elisabeth. "Sex und Macht: Woher kommt die Gewalt gegen Frauen?" *Die Zeit* 2 (2016): 2.

Roskamm, Nikolai. "Studie: Das Leitbild von der 'Urbanen Mischung.'" Berlin: Senatsverwaltung für Stadtentwicklung und Umwelt, 2013. Accessed March 12, 2017. http://www.stadtentwicklung.berlin.de/staedtebau/baukultur/iba/download/studien/IBA-Studie_Urbane_Mischung.pdf.

Sarrazin, Thilo. *Deutschland schafft sich ab: Wie wir unser Land aufs Spiel setzen.* Munich: Deutsche Verlags-Anstalt, 2010.

Scheuermann, Christoph. "N****prinzessin." *Der Spiegel* 51 (2010): 71. Accessed October 7, 2015. http://magazin.spiegel.de/EpubDelivery/spiegel/pdf/75803471.

Schultze, Johannes. *Rixdorf-Neukölln: Die geschichtliche Entwicklung eines Berliner Bezirks.* Berlin: Bezirksamt Neukölln, 1960.

Spiegel Staff. "How New Year's Eve in Cologne Has Changed Germany." *Spiegel Online,* January 8, 2016. Accessed March 12, 2017. http://www.spiegel.de/international/germany/cologne-attacks-trigger-raw-debate-on-immigration-in-germany-a-1071175.html.

Sundermeier, Jörg. "Politik in der Hasenheide." *Berliner Zeitung,* July 14, 2010. Accessed March 12, 2017. http://www.berliner-zeitung.de/archiv/-welt reiche-erbluehten-und-fielen—-anna-faroqhis-lehrreicher-comic-ueber-650-jahre-neukoelln-politik-in-der-hasenheide,10810590,10729852.html.

Tibi, Bassam. "Junge Männer, die die Kultur der Gewalt mitbringen." *Welt Online,* May 8, 2016. Accessed March 12, 2017. https://www.welt.de/debatte/kommentare/article155134929/Junge-Maenner-die-die-Kultur-der-Gewalt-mitbringen.html.

"Türkei erhebt Mordanklage gegen Brüder von Hatun Sürücü." *rbb-online.de,* July 27, 2015. Accessed March 12, 2017. http://www.rbb-online.de/politik/beitrag/2015/07/tuerkei-erhebt-mordanklage-gegen-brueder-von-hatun-sueruecue.html.

"Türken in Berlin—'die Heimat hast du hier.'" *Der Spiegel* 5 (1980): 38–44.

van Bebber, Werner. "Neuköllns Bürgermeister: Multi-Kulti ist gescheitert." *Der Tagesspiegel,* November 13, 2004. Accessed March 12, 2017. http://www.tagesspiegel.de/berlin/neukoellns-buergermeister-multi-kulti-ist-gescheitert/562396.html.

Werkstatt der Kulturen. "1. Spieglein, Spieglein an der Wand, wer ist der Integrierteste im ganzen Land?" YouTube video, 17:47. January 16, 2012. Accessed March 12, 2017. https://www.youtube.com/watch?v=ad04Dnvk2Nk.

———. "2. Spieglein, Spieglein an der Wand, wer ist der Integrierteste im ganzen Land?" Accessed March 12, 2017. YouTube video, 14:47. January 25, 2012. https://www.youtube.com/watch?v=pIHTsUFLj1g.

Wulff, Christian. "Rede zum 20. Jahrestag der Deutschen Einheit." *Der Bundespräsident,* October 3, 2010. Accessed March 12, 2017. http://www.bundespraesident.de/SharedDocs/Reden/DE/Christian-Wulff/Reden/2010/10/20101003_Rede.html.

"Zuwanderungsgesetz." *Auswärtiges Amt,* August 28, 2007. Accessed March 12, 2017. http://www.auswaertiges-amt.de/DE/EinreiseUndAufenthalt/Zuwanderungsrecht_node.html.

CHAPTER 10

The Revival of Diasporic Hebrew in Contemporary Berlin

Hila Amit

The emergence of political Zionism was accompanied by what is considered the "revival" of Hebrew. However, there have in fact been several revivals at different periods in different places (Babylonia, Spain, Russia). In this respect, the title of this chapter should also be put in quotation marks, as the ways in which contemporary Berlin manifests a "revival" of Hebrew, if at all, remains in question. I will explore here the ways in which contemporary Israeli activists living in Berlin undermine the inseparable connection between the Hebrew language and the territory of Israel by pointing to the consequences of this historical event: the Zionist attempt to interfere with the flow of Hebrew over time and space and to suture it to one specific territory, breaching the possibilities it embodied by virtue of it being surrounded and affected by various languages.

The implications of this Zionist attempt stood at the center of a discussion between Gershom Scholem and Franz Rosenzweig during the 1920s. For both, political Zionism and the secularization of Hebrew meant distortion and destruction of the character of the Hebrew language.[1] They believed that Hebrew was always in a process of renewal and is characterized by forms of dialogue with foreign cultures. Zionism was to prevent this dialogue from taking place by transforming it into a territorial language, a language of "Boden und Blut" (soil and blood).[2] Scholem saw in the Hebrew of Zionism the crime of forgetfulness of tradition. The results, he claims, are to be seen in Zionist militarism and national heroism.[3]

Rosenzweig argued that the nature of Hebrew lies beyond its national or individual implications in the present and that Hebrew is bound up with the past and committed to the universe. It is exactly its "diasporic" or "peripheral" character that represents the essence of Hebrew. Hebrew, he claimed, enhances all languages with an ethical horizon that is based on a time structure of the "noch nichts" (not yet). This is a structure of the past in Hebrew that is open endlessly toward the future, thus manifesting a time structure of hope.[4]

This chapter will show how the principle of hope plays a significant role in this new "revival" of Hebrew in Berlin. The activists I will describe here see in the diasporic use of Hebrew a horizon full of possibilities. The radical potential they speak of lies in the political significance of Hebrew's deterritorialization and the reclamation of its diasporic and "open" character. By reviving Hebrew outside of the territory of Israel they seek to bring Hebrew back to where it once belonged; the diaspora, and especially Berlin, which was the center of cultural Hebrew in the first half of the twentieth century.[5] Furthermore, it can be said they are de facto "reviving" it, as they engage in political activities and personal relationships with non-Israelis who take up learning Hebrew as part of their lives. This chapter, thus, explores the ways in which Israeli emigration contradicts the ideology and political project of Zionism and the Israeli state. It highlights the emigrants as "traitors" of the nation-state while simultaneously questioning the effectiveness of the political project of establishing a Hebrew culture in Berlin.

Zionism and Zion

Zionist ideology and movement aspired to the establishment of Jewish political autonomy in the biblical land of Israel. Statehood Zionism was accompanied by the transformation of the image of the feminized disaporic Jew into a powerful, dominant, masculine Jew.[6] As Daniel Boyarin has aptly put it, Zionism can be constructed as a male "return to Phallustine, not Palestine."[7] The Zionists were aiming to normalize not just the image of the Jew but also the image of the nation and the Jewish people. The goal of Zionism was to become normal, "a nation like all other nations."[8]

As Dani Kranz and Hadas Cohen show in their chapter of this volume, the gathering of the exiles became the institutionalized raison d'être of the country. This was addressed both in the declaration of independence and by various Israeli officials. Mainly, the new state established the Law of Return, a legislation securing the right of each Jew to immigrate to Israel and receive full citizenship. The emigration of Jews out of Palestine, and later on out of the state of Israel, was always seen

under a negative perspective. As I show elsewhere, since the establishment of Israel Zionist ideology has invested in discouragement of emigration and has portrayed the image of the emigrant as a traitor, just like
soldiers fleeting the battle field.[9]

Since Israel proclaimed independence in May 1948, dominant national discourses have deployed the Holocaust (*Shoah*) as the definitive
mark of the national identity.[10] Kranz and Cohen in this volume write in
detail on the meaning of the Holocaust in the Israeli narrative, as well
as the place of the Holocaust in the narrative of contemporary Israeli
emigrants in Berlin. The *Shoah* has been and remains a launchpad for
nationalism, a foundation upon which to construct a collective memory
of the public.[11] The *Shoah* was manipulated to serve nationalist objectives, as well as invoked to justify the occupation of Palestine.[12] In addition, Israel can be identified as a militaristic society, and this militarism is
based on the construction of the Israel-Palestinian conflict as a routine
reality. A state of emergency, which was declared in 1948, was never
canceled and still allows the government and army to act for "security
reasons," privileging national needs over human rights.[13] The army's role
in the formation of the Israeli society in general and its place as one of
the most central institutions in Israel cannot be questioned.[14]

The centrality of army service, the Holocaust, and a high birth rate[15]
still characterize contemporary Israel quite accurately. However, other
aspects of Israeli collectivism have been fractured, and questions regarding central Israeli ethos and institutions are starting to appear. Religious,
nationalist, and socialist Zionism is now infected with rifts between religious and secular communities, *Mizrahim* and *Ashkenazim,* rich and
poor, men and women, Jews and Arabs.[16] Aliza Solomon argued that
"Jewish Israelis are increasingly regarding themselves not primarily as
actors in the Zionist drama of Return but as distinct citizens deserving
of privacy and liberal rights."[17]

Uri Ram suggests the 1970s to be the decisive years where social
and political undercurrents have transformed Israeli society. Ram refers
to the dissolving of the Labor's hegemony and the rise of widespread
skepticism toward conventions and "sacred cows."[18] In *The Globalization
of Israel: McWorld in Tel Aviv, Jihad in Jerusalem,* he describes the impact
of globalization on the development of two opposite camps in contemporary Israel, symbolized by Tel-Aviv and Jerusalem.[19] Ram argues that
globalization bifurcates the "Jewish and democratic" unison of the state
of Israel and splits the "Jewish" and the "democratic" dimensions into a
Jewish-Jihad trend, which Ram terms "Neo-Zionism," and an Israeli-
McWorld trend, which he terms "Post-Zionism."[20] The transformation

of the Israeli society follows these two extremes. Neo-Zionism is to be found in the continuing settler colonialism of the West Bank, apartheid mechanisms, Jewish terrorism, and the movement of radical right-wing elements from the margins to the center of the political spectrum. The McWorld model signifies the transformation from nation-building and collective responsibility (Zionism) to a theology of consumerist individualism and a general decline from a collective ethos of solidarity to an "every man for himself" notion of society (Post-Zionism). This terminology can explain a wider acceptance of civil society by young Israelis who end up not serving in the army, thus undermining the "sacred cow" of "The People's Army." These changes are also manifested in the shifting attitudes toward emigration, which used to be considered a national problem.

Israeli Emigration

Most ethnographic projects tend to imply that Israeli emigrants feel a strong connection to Israel, that they left for mainly economic reasons, are sad to have left, and wish to return.[21] This literature lacks any description of Israeli emigrants who mention they have no wish to ever return to their homeland. In addition, Israeli emigrants who articulate emigration as motivated by a criticism of the Israeli regime or of Zionist ideology are almost completely missing in this literature.[22] Most of this literature is quantitative and based on questionnaires filled out by Israeli emigrants contacted through embassies and consulates, which suggests an already-existing positive connection between the emigrants and the homeland. Kranz and Cohen's chapter in this volume reflects a different story, according to which Israelis do leave as a result of the situation in Israel/Palestine. My previous research also follows Israeli emigrants who portray a negative sentiment to their homeland.[23]

Yinon Cohen indicates that ideology was always (and still is) part of the data presented to the public regarding the numbers of Israeli emigrants.[24] Organizations advocating for the Zionist demographic mission and Israeli government officials tend to offer, Cohen shows, higher numbers of emigrants than other research sources.[25] Presenting a higher migration rate can legitimize state policy for bringing emigrants back, and it can also create a discourse mobilizing Israeli citizens – convincing individuals not to emigrate and convincing individuals who have emigrated to return. This was the case in 2003 when the Israeli Ministry of Absorption claimed that 750,000 Israelis are living outside of the homeland. The specific Zionist anxiety regarding the numbers of emigrants is not a recent phenomenon, and Cohen shows similar examples of exaggeration in numbers as early as the 1970s.[26] Debates about the size of the Israeli emigrant population tend to be more pervasive and heated than those concerning outbound emigration rates from other countries, due to the involvement of Zionist ideology.[27] Just as there is no precise number of the Israeli emigrants, no institute can sufficiently indicate the current number of Israelis in Berlin. Estimations run between ten and forty thousand.

Jewish *Haskalah*, Hebrew Literature and Zionism: The Berlin Connection

Berlin stood as the origin of the Jewish *Haskalah* (enlightenment) movement taking place in Europe between 1780 and 1880. This movement pressed for exiting the Jewish ghetto and integrating into European society, not just physically but also mentally and spiritually. The movement called for increasing education in secular studies and advocated developing literature and poetry in Hebrew.[28] Berlin was known as a secular, multicultural, and multiethnic center. This made Berlin a fertile environment for the *Maskilim,* who were paving a way from religious study into much more critical and worldly studies. The movement is often referred to as the *Berlin Haskalah,* though it later spread across Eastern Europe.

Hebrew was a significant element in the eyes of the *Maskilim,* who asked to "re-invent" Hebrew literature and poetry, which were almost extinct in the Jewish world of Eastern and Central Europe.[29] The *Maskilim* revived Hebrew as a literary language, and they did so by establishing Hebrew journals and publishing houses. The first Hebrew literary journal, *Kohelet Musar*, was established in Berlin in 1755 by Moses Mendelson.[30] In 1783 another journal was established, called *Hameasef.* From 1784 onward, journals and publishing houses started to appear, promoting Hebrew authors and translators. In the first decades of the twentieth century, Berlin became a flourishing center for Hebrew creation. In 1912 the author and Nobel Prize winner Shmuel Yosef Agnon even left Palestine to join the Hebrew cultural scene in Berlin, where he stayed until 1924.[31]

Berlin was also a significant center for the Zionist movement during the first half of the twentieth century, and it was the center for innovative ideas and critical engagement with Zionism. Among the scholars situated in Berlin in the years before the Holocaust we can find Hannah Arendt, Martin Buber, Gershom Scholem, Hans Koch, Mordechai Kaplan, and others. The struggle for a Jewish sovereign state, "statehood-Zionism," was only one fragment of the Zionist movement in its early stages. It wasn't until the 1940s that statehood became the official policy of the Zionist movement.[32] Among these scholars and Zionists situated in Berlin was Simon Rawidowicz, who spent his formative years in Berlin, where he joined a circle of leading Hebrew authors, created the first international association of Hebrew speakers, and later opened a Hebrew publishing house. Rawidowicz is important to mention here in detail because of his emphasis on the Hebrew language as the basis for national solidarity. His proposition for the future of the Jewish people in the first two decades of the twentieth century was "global Hebraism."[33] This notion reflects a model introduced by Rawidowicz which promotes a deterritorialized and decentralized Jewish nationalism.[34] Global Hebraism rejected the primacy of Palestine and envisioned, instead, national life flourishing regardless of location or political context. According to his model, the Hebrew language and the culture of textual interpretation "would generate fluid boundaries, creating a dynamic equilibrium between integration and autonomy far more consistent with centuries of Jewish life than state-framed definitions of Jewish nationality."[35] In his view, the Jewish nation was united by a language and not by territory and citizenship.

In order to challenge the centrality that Israel was gaining within the Zionist movement, he developed an understanding of Jewish nationalism by proposing the concept of *Babylon* and *Jerusalem* as symbolic alternatives to constructing national myths around a territorial nation-state.[36] By introducing *Babylon* and *Jerusalem,* Rawidowicz attempted to undermine the significance of Zion (Israel/Palestine) to Jewish thought, offering Babylon as another Jewish center, which could symbolize, like Jerusalem, the importance of different diasporic Jewish centers.

The Revival of the Hebrew Language in Berlin

Similar to Rawidowicz's engagement with the Hebrew language as a political framework, contemporary Israeli emigrants in Berlin also attribute political importance to the place of Hebrew language and culture. In what follows, two figures of Israeli emigrants and their activities in contemporary Berlin will be presented. Analyzing their activities will demonstrate the ways in which the call for the revival of the Hebrew language in Berlin position the city as a new destination for a Jewish political movement. While I will not be able to provide a detailed account here, it must be mentioned that Israeli emigrants are also calling for Israelis to join the diaspora and move to Berlin, thus contributing to the mystification of Berlin as the new Zion.[37]

Tal Hever-Chybowski

On August 1, 2014, the Israeli emigrant Tal Hever-Chybowski organized an evening in Berlin focusing on texts written in Hebrew during World War I. The event was called "Tribute Night for the Slackers of the First World War in Hebrew Literature," and it was held in Hebrew in a small Berlin Café. Hever-Chybowski, a PhD student in history, had collected texts written in Hebrew in the early twentieth century, which deal with European Jews (real individuals as well as literary characters) who wanted to avoid military service during World War I. The topic of the texts and the date of the event must be read for their political implications.

The event took place in the midst of the 2014 war between Israel and Gaza (Operation Offensive Shield).[38] Though he said he had planned this event before the war began, Hever-Chybowski created a Facebook invitation on July 18[t] which was the tenth day of war and the day the government of Israel decided to physically enter the Gaza Strip, a military act that meant the war would not end soon and was about to become even more offensive.[39] One of the texts read during the evening is from Gershom Scholem's autobiography:

> My time as a young soldier – in Anelshtein in East Prussia—was short and stormy and I don't wish to discuss it in length. I was against everything that was happening there and I behaved in a way that basically left them only two options: either to put me on trial, or to release me as a madman. They chose the second option and I was released two months later, as, they told me, a "psychopath" … The truth is that I don't remember any other period in my whole life during which I had such a "clear understanding" as in those weeks.[40]

Hever-Chybowski himself insisted that this evening should be read not as a contrast to what was happening in Israel at the same time but as a mere reflection of the opportunities diasporic Hebrew enables. In his concluding remarks, Hever-Chybowski addressed the contemporary political context precipitating the selection of the texts:

> The texts read in this evening were mostly written in diasporic Hebrew, in a language that was not the language of the state or the army, but of a minority scattered in different countries and nations. It wasn't the language of one country, but of many countries and many nations. …

> This evening was dedicated to an attempt to try and expose, here – in Berlin, and in Hebrew, that there were, and there are still, political options in Hebrew which challenge the nationalist equation of "one people – one language – one land," an equation that stands again and again at the heart of wars. This evening tried to point out, even if very generally, the existence of an non-heroic and non-militaristic Hebrew, which stems from different places and responds to organized violence and erupting militarism in a way that avoids taking part, joining armies and militancy.[41]

Hever-Chybowski's closing remarks, as well as the texts he selected, did criticize the Israeli regime directly. The challenge of the model of "one people – one language – one land," for him, is not just a challenge to Zionism but to nationalism in general. Diasporic Hebrew, he argues, used to unite Jews from various states in Europe, who objected to the war that was devastating the continent. It was not a language of a state, and it was not connected to a territory or a nation but to a people living in many nations. Thus, in the days of World War I, Hebrew had a radical potential, as it did not align itself with nations and armies, and as such enabled a possibility for radical political and cultural activities. However, as Hever-Chybowski keeps his suggestion open and somewhat vague an evening like this leaves the audience to imagine what can constitute "political options in Hebrew," and his offer could not be separated from criticism of the events in Israel/Palestine.

Hever-Chybowski also established the first literary journal to be published in Hebrew in Europe since 1944. In 2012, he opened a Facebook page for the journal *Mikan Ve'eilakh* (*From Here and Onward*). Hever-Chybowski described the journal in the following words:

> *Mikan ve'eilakh* is a Hebrew diasporic journal established in Berlin. The goal of the journal is to become a literary cultural platform for non-hegemonic and non-sovereign Hebrew, a Hebrew that is free from the shackles of nationality and territory. The return of Hebrew to Berlin is accompanied with recognition of the historical position of the city as the center for diasporic Hebrew in the previous century.[42]

In a lecture Hever-Chybowski gave in Berlin in February 2015, he expressed the political motivations he sees in the emergence of Hebrew in the diaspora. According to Hever-Chybowski, the establishment of Israel has transformed the fluid nature of diasporic Hebrew, which was used by different people in different locations, into a national language, which now expresses only one collective in one location, the point of view of the Jews of the State of Israel. As an opposition to the "Israeli"

Hebrew, Hever-Chybowski calls to rethink of a Hebrew that is not connected to Israel: a Hebrew that does not constitute itself as the peripheral Hebrew, which is always used against and in light of the cultural center, the State of Israel, but a separate Hebrew, an independent fluid language, as it used to be before the establishment of Israel.

One of the interesting examples he offers is in regard to the use of the word *ha'aretz* (the country). In the past, he argues, if a story was written in Hebrew in 1755 in Russia and the word *ha'aretz* appeared in it, it was obvious that the writer was referring to the country in which the story was written. The meaning of the word *ha'aretz* would function in a similar way to refer to Berlin, Warsaw, or London. However, since the establishment of Israel, when the word *ha'aretz* appears in Hebrew (either in a literary text, but also as part of a conversation), it no longer matters *where* the text was written or where the conversation was happening, since *ha'aretz* can only mean one country, Israel. Hever-Chybowski is not criticizing the fact that the word *ha'aretz* refers nowadays to "the land of Israel." His critique centers on the loss of all the other possibilities the word *ha'aretz* used to have.

Similarly, Hever-Chybowski shows how the name "Israel" used to mean "Jew," while today its only meaning is the "State of Israel." Hever-Chybowski also refers to the long history of literary journals published in diasporic Hebrew, including the first modern Hebrew literary journal, *Kohelet Musar,* which was published in Berlin in 1755. He ponders whether Israelis can write in Hebrew without a nation-state in which Hebrew is the hegemonic language: "I want to create a Hebrew which eradicates its nationality and returns to a position it once had, before a state was attached to it."[43]

Hever-Chybowski's project and the political meaning he attributes to the journal are fascinating. It is also fascinating that for four years, the journal had a web page and a Facebook page, and Hever-Chybowski regarded the journal as if it was already published, even though it was not officially out until the summer of 2016. This notion of discussing in public things that are not yet there, as if they *are* there, is the focus of the following discussion of the revival of Hebrew in Berlin.

Mati Shemoelof

Mati Shemoelof, a well-respected poet and author, has been living in Berlin since 2013. Kranz and Cohen in this volume also mention speaking with Shemoelof. Reflecting on his Jewish–Middle Eastern–Israeli–*Mizrahi* identity, he is associated with representing yet another political aspect of living in Berlin. I interviewed him after he published an article titled "A Glimpse of the Day in Which Zionism Will No Longer Control Hebrew Culture" in *Ha'aretz,* an Israeli newspaper.[44] The provocative title seemed at first unrelated to the topic of the article. Shemoelof wrote about the activities of a Hebrew library established in Berlin, which was described as having more than "3000 books for children and adults" and "more than 800 members." The manager of the library, an Israeli emigrant, had also organized a public reading of Hebrew poetry at the Jewish Museum and hosted prominent Israeli authors for book launches and talks. Shemoelof considers the Hebrew Library as part of several cultural activities in Hebrew taking place in Berlin, including a Hebrew newspaper called *Spitz,* Hebrew lectures and discussions in a gallery in Mitte, and Hever-Chybowski's [not yet published] journal *Mikan Ve'eilakh.* However, the last section of the article posed an interesting and quite provocative statement regarding Zionism and Hebrew literature. Shemoelof talks about the day in which there will be an "independent diasporic Hebrew center, one that is not submissive to the territorial borders the state has structured within the culture." Not only does Shemoelof use the same language as Hever-Chybowski and talks about the deterritorialization of the Hebrew language, he also refers to a specific event in earlier Hebrew literature and which sheds an interesting light on the contemporary Hebrew world.

Shemoelof describes the "Brenner events" that changed the face of the Hebrew literary community in pre-state Palestine. In short, in 1910, when Hebrew literature started to appear in Palestine, it was fully funded by diasporic Jewish centers. A committee sitting in Odessa, Ukraine, one of the largest Jewish centers in the nineteenth century, decided to stop funding a journal after Joseph Hayyim Brenner, one of the authors in Palestine, wrote a provocative article calling for the disconnection between nationality and religion. This exercise of diasporic hegemony over the minority Jewish community in Palestine seemed like censorship. It mobilized the literary community in Palestine and transformed it to an independent community, which started funding its literary journals without the economic support from the diaspora. Shemoelof's article envisions a future in which a similar event will happen, "the day that a large enough Hebrew community will settle outside the boundaries of Zionist nationality and will start thinking independently." He concludes his article with this provocative description:

> At these very moments the variety of Hebrew creation, including the *Hebrew Library in Berlin,* contains subversive elements, since the con-

temporary Zionist trend in Israel does not see in a positive light the possibility for sovereign, Jewish, Hebrew independent life outside of Israel. And one day things will change, and maybe the *Hebrew Library in Berlin* will send Hebrew authors to Israel.

Shemoelof wants to dismantle Israeli hegemony on Hebrew literary creation and sees this as a challenge to Zionism itself. His vision is directly connected to Hever-Chybowski's goal upon establishing the journal. Shemoelof's and Hever-Chybowski's activities can be linked to Rawidowicz's proposal for a collective united by language and culture and not by territory and nationality. While Hever-Chybowski is calling for creating a model of diasporic Hebrew that is separated from the Israeli state and language, Shemoelof calls for destabilizing the contemporary Zionist regime. A regime, he claims, not only has devastating consequences on the Hebrew language itself, but on Hebrew culture in general. Just like Rawidowicz, Shemoelof objects to a perspective that views Israel as the only center for the Jewish people and for Hebrew creation.

Apart for his political call, the most interesting aspect of Shemoelof's article is not his description of the developments in Hebrew culture in contemporary Berlin but the fact that what he was describing does not necessarily reflect the reality of contemporary Hebrew culture in Berlin. Many criticized Shemoelof's article, and this criticism appeared in Facebook groups of Israelis in Berlin as well as in comments to the article on the *Ha'aretz* website. His political perspective was not the focus of the public disagreement; rather, it was the facts that were contradicting what he articulated in the article. The "library" was actually someone's living room bookcases. Though this living room was filled with books, and though these books were available for free for public use, it could hardly be described as a "library" per se. Michal Zamir, who initiated the idea and hosts "the library" in her own private family home, opens her house to the "members of the library" approximately once a month, for two hours only. Her house is located in a neighborhood in West Berlin, far from the center of the city or the neighborhoods most Israelis inhabit. And though people can check out or donate books, the inventory is unknown to the public, and maybe even to Zamir herself. The library's' register book, which keeps track of the books checked out and returned, is a simple notebook. Furthermore, Shemoelof exaggerated the number of members, as the eight hundred "members" he mentions are simply eight hundred "likes" on the Facebook page of the Hebrew Library in Berlin. At most, and I have attended three of these open-house library events, a group of ten to twenty people – usually the same ten to twenty people – arrive, check books in and out, and stay for a short coffee and chat with the others. Though poetry and culture events take place there from time to time, they attract a small number of participants – again, usually from the same social circles. These events definitely do not engage a substantial number of the Israelis in Berlin. Shemoelof was happy to elaborate and explain the gap between reality and what he describes in his article:

> It is imaginary, this is what I wish would be here, the wish of my heart. And yes, it is possible that nothing of what I've described actually exists in reality, it is possible that it is completely ungrounded in facts, absurd, but let's changed that, let's make it real. I believe we need to create these imaginary thoughts. This is what I dream of. I'll go to the extent and say that I want an exilic government to be established. We need to re-think the structure of Israel. It is rotten from its very basic elements.[45]

Thus, Shemoelof is aware of the big difference between how he described things and how they really are, and he is aware of the limits of what he can personally do to change reality. Yet, he believes that in writing about an imagined reality on a public platform, he is promoting change. Shemoelof thinks that if he manages to create the appearance of a Hebrew cultural revival, people might actually believe it to be true and initiate real events and activities, which eventually, if added to those that already exist in Berlin, can lead to what he imagines. For him, the "white lies" in his article are purely politically motivated. Shemoelof's political activism is the creation of a fake reality using nothing but his words.

Berlin: The New Zion?

Zionism was imagined not only to solve "the Jewish question" but also to serve as a light to the nations, "an outpost of civilization against barbarism."[46] Some even thought that the revival of the Jewish people in the holy land would establish an example for the entire human race.[47] Zionism offered a utopia, a social paradise in the world.[48] The political and ideological leaders of the movement took the place of prophets in a religious mythology, and the nation was perceived as an "exemplary, chosen society that is fulfilling an ancient prophecy under divine supervision."[49] Zionism was the cure for the experience of the *Galut* (the exile), "living a perverted existence by means of surrogates for reality."[50]

The creating of the imagined utopian society, as structured by early Zionists, resembles in many aspects the way Shemoelof and Hever-

Chybowski portray the utopian possibilities of the Israeli emigrants in the diaspora, and in Berlin specifically. In this respect, I want to return to the author Joseph Hayyim Brenner, mentioned above as responsible for the "Brenner Events." In 1914, in an article titled "Self-Criticism," Brenner outlined his critique of Zionism, articulating it as nothing but another form of storytelling, an imaginary dream: "We have no colonists, no workers, no laborers; all we have are pipe dreams of speculation worthy of the heirs of Reb Leib the Melamed."[51] Reb Melamed is not a real Rabbi but a fictional character, a hero of a well-known short story written in 1892 by the famous Jewish author Mendele Mokher Sefarim (Shalom Jacov Avramovitz). The story was written as a satirical reaction to the early Zionist movement. While Zionist leadership was rosily describing the joys awaiting those who moved to Palestine, many European Jews rushed to offer themselves as would-be settlers. In his story, Mendele Mokher Sefarim described Reb Leib the Melamed as one of these Jews who failed to succeed in the Jewish ghettos of Eastern Europe, thus dreaming of the glory awaiting him in Palestine. I turn to Brenner's criticism as he points out, through this reference to Mendele Mokher Sefarim's story, the status of the Zionist movement in his time. In his view, though Zionism attempts to articulate the Zionist movement as a great colonial undertaking, there were only a "handful of young men [that] can be found among 12 million to give their sweat" to the building of the Jewish state in Palestine.[52] In this article Brenner attempts to motivate the establishment of the true Zionist dream – a solution to "the Jewish question" in the form of a Jewish state in Palestine:

> We live now without an environment, utterly outside any environment. We have to start all over again, to lay down a new cornerstone.... In order to create such an environment ourselves – our character must be radically changed.
>
> We are at an impasse, but the pen is still at hand. Our literature lives with Mendele Mokher Sefarim and with all of who have succeeded him, and it continues to seek the way, with a true self-criticism for a guide. Our literature cries out.[53]

It is impossible to overlook the similarities between Brenner's call for action and the declarations made by Shemoelof and Hever-Chybowski. Brenner identifies the ways in which the Zionist movement is basically selling out those who adhere to the lies about the glory awaiting those who arrive in Palestine. While the protagonist of Mendele Mokher Sefarim's story follows the glorifying descriptions of the Zionist leadership in Eastern Europe, Brenner seeks to abandon the imaginary tales and start up a true "realistic" movement aimed at achieving the dream of the Jewish state. He asks his readers to start something new, to create new frameworks for a different vision, and to do this through the force of writing: "the pen is still at hand."

Similar to Brenner, Hever-Chybowski and Shemoelof turn to literature and the written text in order to promote their aspirations. Shemoelof even recognizes the need, just as the Zionist movement had recognized, to use "his pen" as praxis to promote his political aspiration: to describe things that are not yet there, and to glorify things out of their proportion.

Whether the attempt is to draw other Israelis to emigrate, to create a threat for the Israeli regime, or to bring back to the Hebrew language the open and fluid character it once had, Hever-Chybowski and Shemoelof carry out the same practices as the early Zionist movement. One may even say that Brenner in 1914 and Shemoelof in 2014 are pursuing the same goals: they are part of a political movement in its early stages, and they are prescribing the actions that need to be taken in order to promote their agendas. While Brenner turns to literature in order to reflect on the imaginary stage the Zionist movement is caught up in (and by doing so creating an additional "imaginary project"), Shemoelof turns to literature as the symbol of the imaginary project of the Israeli emigrants in Berlin. And as a prophet of this movement, just like Brenner, with the "pen in hand," he writes a fictive "story," aimed at motivating others to real actions.

Conclusion

In this chapter I have attempted to draw a connection between Jewish-Israeli activists working in contemporary Berlin and between Jewish activists who were active in Berlin at the beginning of the twentieth century. As diasporic Hebrew was a significant element in the writing and thought of many Jewish scholars and activists who were objecting the "Jewish state" paradigm, the activists I described here promote a diasporic Hebrew that works and develops separately from Israel. This disconnection undermines the inherent relationship between Israel and Hebrew, a relationship that has not been questioned since the establishment of the state. And, in a way, it undermines the existence of the state of Israel altogether.

I have articulated the ways in which the Zionist endeavor sought to "create a new land and a new culture ... something out of nothing ...

to criticize the past and to replace it with an alternative reality."[54] The endeavor of Israeli emigrants in Berlin, I argue here, shares similarities with the utopian aspiration of Zionism. Though not aspiring to create "a new culture in a new land" per se, they are aspiring to create a new function of the Hebrew culture in a different "new-old" land, that of the diaspora. If Zionism wished to create this new culture and new land "out of nothing," then Shemoelof's writing is the example of harnessing the "nothing" itself in the attempt to reach the goal.

Contemporary Israeli emigrants in Berlin, thus, are mirroring the same practices of the Zionist movement in its early days. As Brenner may have seemed ridiculous in his time, we can say the same of the contemporary project of the "revival" of the diasporic Hebrew in Berlin. However, as Brenner's vision eventually became a reality, only time will tell if this contemporary "revival" of diasporic Hebrew will have significant implication on the "Israeli" Hebrew, or even on the Israeli regime.

Hila Amit submitted her dissertation at the Center for Gender Studies in the School of Oriental and African studies (SOAS), University of London, in 2016. She is working at the intersection of queer and postcolonial theory, migration and diaspora studies, and the Israeli-Palestinian conflict.

Notes

1. Galili Shahar, "The Sacred and the Unfamiliar: Gershom Scholem and the Anxieties of the New Hebrew," *Germanic Review: Literature, Culture, Theory* 83, no. 4 (2008): 304.
2. Ibid.
3. Gershom Scholem, Od Davar (Tel Aviv, 1997), 61–62.
4. Shahar, "Sacred and the Unfamiliar," 306.
5. Uzi Shavit, *Ba'alot Hashachar* (Tel Aviv, 1996).
6. See, for example, Daniel Boyarin, "Colonial Drug: Zionism, Gender, and Mimicry," *Theory and Criticism* 11 (Winter 1997): 124–44; Michael Glozman, *The Zionist Body: Nationalism, Gender and Sexuality in the New Hebrew Literature* (Tel Aviv, 2007).
7. Boyarin, "Colonial Drug," 22.
8. Amnon Raz-Krakotzkin, "Exile within Sovereignty: Toward a Critique of the Negation of Exile in Israeli Culture," *Theory and Criticism* 4 (Fall 1993): 23.
9. Hila Amit, "A Queer Way Out: Israeli Emigration and Unheroic Resistance to Zionism" (PhD diss., SOAS, University of London, 2015).
10. Don Handelman, Nationalism and the Israeli State: Bureaucratic Logic in Public Events (New York, 2004), 171–99.

11. Danny Jacoby, ed., *Nation Building* (Jerusalem, 2000).

12. Tom Segev, *The Seventh Million: The Israelis and the Holocaust* (New York, 1993).

13. Baruch Kimmerling, "Militarism in the Israeli Society," *Theory and Criticism* 4 (1993), 123–40.

14. See, for example, Ronit Chacham, *Breaking Ranks: Refusing to Serve in the West Bank and Gaza Strip* (New York, 2003), 2–14; Uri Ben-Eliezer, "From Military Role-Expansion to Difficulties in Peacemaking: The Israeli Defense Forces 50 Years On," in *Military, State, and Society in Israel: Theoretical and Comparative Perspectives,* ed. Daniel Maman, Eyal Ben-Ari, and Zeev Rosenhek (Piscataway, NJ, 2001), 137–72.

15. See, for example, Orna Donat, *From Me and Beyond* (Tel Aviv, 2011); Sigal Goldin, "Technologies of Happines: Managing Fertility in a Pronatalist Welfare State," in *Citizenship Gaps: Migration, Fertility and Identity in Israel,* ed. Yossi Yona and Adriana Camp (Jerusalem, 2008), 167–206.

16. Yaron Ezrahi, *Rubber Bullets: Power and Conscience in Modern Israel* (New York, 1997), 83.

17. Alisa Solomon, "Viva La Diva Citizenship: Post-Zionism and Gay Rights," in *Queer Theory and the Jewish Question,* ed. Daniel Boyarin, Daniel Itzkovitz, and Ann Pellegrini (New York, 2003), 155.

18. Uri Ram, *The Changing Agenda of Israeli Sociology* (New York, 1995), 9.

19. Uri Ram, *The Globalization of Israel: McWorld in Tel Aviv, Jihad in Jerusalem* (New York, 2008).

20. Ibid., 7.

21. See, for example, Moshe Shokeid, *Children of Circumstances* (Ithaca, NY: Cornell University Press 1988); Zvi Sobel, *Migrants from the Promised Land* (New Brunswick, NJ & Oxford: Transection Books, 1986); Lilach Lev Ari, *Returning Home: Research on Former Israeli Migrants Returned to Israel* (Jerusalem: Ministry of Absorption, 2006); Lilach Lev Ari, *The American Dream – For Men Only? Gender, Immigration, and the Assimilation of Israelis in the United States* (El Paso: LFB Scholarly Publishing LLc,2008); Steven J. Gold, *The Israeli Diaspora* (Seattle: University of Washington Press. 2002); Naama Sabar, *Kibbutzniks in the Diaspora* (Albany: State Universty of New York Press, 2000).

22. Amit, "Queer Way Out."

23. Ibid.

24. Yinon Cohen, "Migration Patterns to and from Israel," *Contemporary Jewry* 29, no. 2 (2009): 115–25.

25. Ibid., 120.

26. Ibid.

27. Gold, *Israeli Diaspora,* 23.

28. Shavit, *Ba'alot Hashachar,* 12.

29. Ibid., 13.

30. Ibid., 10.
31. Dan Laor, *The Life of Agnon* (Tel Aviv, 1998), 68.
32. Noam Pianko, *Zionism and the Roads Not Taken* (Bloomington, 2010), 10.
33. Ibid., 4.
34. Ibid., 9.
35. Ibid., 10.
36. Simon Rawidowicz, *Bavel Veyerushalayim [Babylon and Jerusalem]* (Waltham, MA, 1957), 198.
37. Amit, "Queer Way Out."
38. This is not, by any means, to regard the Gaza Strip as a separate entity, but as a part of the occupied Palestinian Territories. The mentioned attacks, or war, was mainly directed at the Gaza Strip but was felt in the West Bank as well.
39. "Israeli Military Begins Ground Offensive in Gaza," *The Guardian*, July 18, 2014, http://www.theguardian.com/world/2014/jul/17/gaza-crisis-humanitarian-truce-due-to-start-live-updates.
40. Gershom Scholem was a German Jew, a historian, and a philosopher. This quote is taken from his autobiographical book *From Berlin to Jerusalem: Memories from My Youth* (Tel Aviv, 1982), 46. Unless otherwise noted, translations are my own.
41. Hever-Chybowski's text can be found on the "Tribute Night for the Slackers of the First World War in Hebrew Literature" Facebook page, posted August 1, 2014, accessed June 1, 2016, https://www.facebook.com/events/340886716062543/permalink/348482401969641/.
42. *Mikan Va'eilach* Facebook page, accessed January 7, 2016, https://www.facebook.com/mikanve/. Translations of quotes to English are my own.
43. Eirad Ben Itzhak, "Diasporic Hebrew: A Conversation with Tal Hever-Chybowski," *Hashuel Ha'haviv* (blog), October 21, 2012, accessed June 1, 2016, https://derchawiw.wordpress.com.
44. Mati Shemoelof, "A Glimpse of the Day in Which Zionism Will No Longer Control Hebrew Culture," *Ha'aretz*, January 11, 2015, http://www.haaretz.co.il/literature/study/.premium-1.2533139.
45. Mati Shemoelof, in discussion with the author, September 20, 2014.
46. Teodor Herzl, "The Jewish State," in *The Zionist Idea: A Historical Analysis and Reader*, ed. Arthur Hertzberg (New York, 1997), 204–26.
47. Oz Almog, *The Sabra: The Creation of the New Jew* (Berkeley, 2000), 74.
48. Ibid., 18.
49. Ibid.
50. Jacob Klatzkin, "Boundaries (1914–1921)," in *The Zionist Idea: A Historical Analysis and Reader*, ed. Arthur Hertzberg (New York, 1997), 323.
51. Joseph H. Brenner, "Self-Criticism (1914)," in *The Zionist Idea: A Historical Analysis and Reader*, ed. Arthur Hertzberg (New York, 1997), 307–12.
52. Ibid.

53. Ibid., 311–12.
54. David Ohana, *The Origin of Israeli Mythology: Neither Canaanites nor Crusaders* (Cambridge, 2012), 15.

Bibliography

Almog, Oz. *The Sabra: The Creation of the New Jew.* Berkeley: University of California Press, 2000.

Amit, Hila. "A Queer Way Out: Israeli Emigration and Unheroic Resistance to Zionism." PhD diss., SOAS, University of London, 2015.

Ben-Eliezer, Uri. "From Military Role-Expansion to Difficulties in Peacemaking: The Israeli Defense Forces 50 Years On." In *Military, State, and Society in Israel: Theoretical and Comparative Perspectives,* edited by Daniel Maman, Eyal Ben-Ari, and Zeev Rosenhek, 137–72. Piscataway, NJ: Transaction Publishers, 2001.

Brenner, Joseph H. "Self-Criticism." In *The Zionist Idea: A Historical Analysis and Reader,* edited by Arthur Herzberg, 307–12. New York: Hertzel Press, 1914.

Boyarin, Daniel. "Colonial Drug: Zionism, Gender, and Mimicry." In *Theory and Criticism* 11 (1997): 124–44.

Chacham, Ronit. *Breaking Ranks: Refusing to Serve in the West Bank and Gaza Strip.* New York: Other Press, 2003.

Cohen, Yinon. "Migration Patterns to and from Israel." *Contemporary Jewry* 29 (2009): 115–25.

Donat, Orna. *From Me and Beyond.* Tel Aviv: Hakibbutz Hameuchad, 2011.

Ezrahi, Yaron. *Rubber Bullets: Power and Conscience in Modern Israel.* New York: Farrar, Straus, and Giroux, 1997.

Glozman, Michael. *The Zionist Body: Nationalism, Gender and Sexuality in the New Hebrew Literature.* Tel Aviv: Hakibbutz Hameuchad, 2007.

Gold, Steven J. *The Israeli Diaspora.* London: Routledge, 2002.

Goldin, Sigal. "Technologies of Happiness: Managing Fertility in a Pronatalist Welfare State." In *Citizenship Gaps: Migration, Fertility and Identity in Israel,* edited by Yossi Yona and Adriana Camp. 167–206. Jerusalem: Van Leer, 2008.

Handelman, Don. *Nationalism and the Israeli State: Bureaucratic Logic in Public Events.* New York: Berg, 2004.

Harpaz, Yossi. "Israelis and the European Passport: Dual Citizenship in an Apocalyptic Immigrant Society." Master's thesis, Tel Aviv University, 2009.

Herzl, Teodor. "The Jewish State." In *The Zionist Idea: A Historical Analysis and Reader,* edited by Hertzberg Arthur, 204–26. New York: Herzl Press, 1997.

Jacoby, Danny, ed. *Nation Building.* Jerusalem: Magnes Press, 2000.

Klatzkin, Jacob. "Boundaries (1914–1921)." In *The Zionist Idea: A Historical Analysis and Reader,* edited by Arthur Hertzberg, 316–27. New York: Herzl Press, 1997.

Kimmerling, Baruch. *Immigrants, Settlers, Natives: Israel between Plurality of Cultures and Cultural Wars.* Tel Aviv: Am Oved, 2004. (Hebrew)

Kimmerling, Baruch. "Militarism in the Israeli Society," *Theory and Criticism* 4 (1993), 123–40. (Hebrew)

Laor, Dan. *The Life of Agnon.* Tel Aviv: Schoken, 1998.

Ohana, David. *The Origin of Israeli Mythology: Neither Canaanites nor Crusaders.* Cambridge: Cambridge University Press, 2012.

Peled, Yoav. "Citizenship Betrayed: Israel's Emerging Immigration and Citizenship Regime." *Theoretical Inquiries in Law* 8, no. 2 (2007): 603–28.

Pianko, Noam. *Zionism and the Roads Not Taken.* Bloomington: Indiana University Press, 2010.

Ram, Uri. *The Changing Agenda of Israeli Sociology.* Albany: State University of New York Press, 1995.

———. *The Globalization of Israel: McWorld in Tel Aviv, Jihad in Jerusalem.* New York: Routledge, 2008.

Rawidowicz, Simon. *Bavel Veyerushalayim [Babylon and Jerusalem].* Waltham, MA: Ararat Publishing Society, 1957.

Rapaport, Lynn. *Jews in Germany after the Holocaust.* Cambridge: Cambridge University Press, 1997.

Raz-Krakotzkin, Amnon. "Exile within Sovereignty: Toward a Critique of the Negation of Exile in Israeli Culture." *Theory and Criticism* 4 (1993): 23–55.

Scholem, Gersum. Od Davar. Tel Aviv: Am Oved, 1997. (Hebrew)

———. *From Berlin to Jerusalem: Memories from My Youth* (Tel Aviv, 1982). (Hebrew)

Segev, Tom. *The Seventh Million: The Israelis and the Holocaust.* New York: Hill and Wang, 1993.

Shahar, Galili. "The Sacred and the Unfamiliar: Gershom Scholem and the Anxieties of the New Hebrew." *Germanic Review: Literature, Culture, Theory* 83, no. 4 (2008): 299–320.

Shavit, Uzi. *Ba'alot Hashachar.* Tel Aviv: Hakibbutz Hameuchad, 1996.

Shemoelof, Mati. "A Glimpse of the Day in Which Zionism Will No Longer Control Hebrew Culture." *Ha'aretz,* January 11, 2015.

Shokeid, Moshe. *Children of Circumstances: Israeli Emigrants in New York.* Ithaca, NY: Cornell University Press, 1988.

Solomon, Aliza. "Viva La Diva Citizenship: Post-Zionism and Gay Rights." In *Queer Theory and the Jewish Question,* edited by Daniel Boyarin, Daniel Itzkovitz, and Ann Pellegrini, 149–65. New York: Columbia University Press, 2003.

Yiftachel, Oren. *Ethnocracy: Land and Identity Politics in Israel/Palestine.* Philadelphia: University of Pennsylvania Press, 2006.

Yona, Yossi. "The State of All Its Citizens, a Nation-State or a Multicultural Democracy: Israel and the Boundaries of Liberal Democracy." *Alpayim* 16 (1998): 238–63.

CHAPTER 11

Berlin's International Literature Festival

Globalizing the Bildungsbürger

Marike Janzen

In the late summer and autumn of 2015, Germany was on the forefront of the largest influx of refugees to Europe since the end of World War II.[1] Syrians, Iraqis, and Afghans, among people of other nationalities, fled war and its aftermath in their own countries and made their way across Eastern Europe to Germany. In August 2015 Germany expected to "register 800,000 asylum applications... quadruple the number of applications processed [in 2014]."[2] Of those asylees, nineteen thousand had registered in Berlin, more than in the years 2013 and 2014 combined.[3]

In the midst of this sudden arrival of a large number of non-Europeans to Germany, the nation's capital was host to the fifteenth annual *internationales literaturfestival berlin* (international literature festival berlin), or *ilb*, one of Germany's biggest and most prestigious literary events.[4] The festival, which director Ulrich Schreiber describes as "the most international of all international literature festivals,"[5] spans twelve days and draws over a hundred authors from around the world and thirty thousand visitors to Berlin.[6] Supported primarily through city and federal grants, the *ilb* takes place in venues across the city and comprises standard public literary activities, for example, readings by world-renowned writers such as Wole Soyinka and Salman Rushdie and panel discussions on contemporary global issues that feature well-known intellectuals, including Gayatri Spivak. Beyond these large-scale public events, the *ilb* aims to bring world literature and non-German writers into the smaller spaces of Berliners' everyday lives. The festival organizes readings in prisons, invites residents to serve as hosts to individual visiting writers, and calls on Berliners to read books out loud in the city. In its own words, the *ilb* aims to create a "lively, polyglot forum by and for literature enthusiasts"[7] where one can "[experience] literary diversity in times of globalization."[8] Through the breadth of literary engagement it offers, the *ilb* implicitly claims for Germany's capital the status of a city responding to the cultural exigencies and opportunities of globalization—including immigration—that shape it. Festival programming makes explicit the *ilb*'s mission as a literary project that can effect cultural exchange and cross-cultural understanding.[9] In 2015, for example, the *ilb* declared the refugee crisis of that fall—and, more generally, the refugee condition—a key festival theme. It did so by featuring new novels about refugees in Germany, staging public readings of texts on the topic of asylum seekers and refugees (*Asylsuchende* and *Flüchtlinge*),[10] and publishing a collection of poems and short prose pieces that "[contemplate] the fates of refugees and asylum seekers in literary form."[11]

The *ilb*'s conjunction with and interpretation of the refugee crisis that took place in fall 2015 offers a productive site for examining how national institutions and events articulate conceptions of global identity. The *ilb* justifies its work through the view that in globalization, "literature enthusiasts" should experience as much literature from as many places as possible. In its assertion of books as a self-evident good, the festival reflects a specifically German tradition of noninstrumental intellectual self-formation, or *Bildung,* through reading.[12] Historically, this conception of *Bildung* for its own sake correlated with the sensibility of an educated social class, the *Bildungsbürgertum.*[13] This sensibility, in turn, informed, in Dominic Boyer's words, "a collective social being" that extended to conceptions of German-ness.[14] Seen in this way, the *ilb* supports citizens' intellectual self-formation that will potentially shape a national feeling of global awareness and global citizenship. In fall 2015, the *ilb,* a national site for global *Bildung,* spoke on behalf of the world that was coming to Germany, and Berlin.

As a large number of non-German citizens arriving in Berlin sought to gain a foothold in the city, participants in the German literary sphere—the majority of whom were likely German speakers and German citizens—attended the *ilb* to access the world. In this chapter I consider the relationship between the refugee and the *ilb* in the festival's claims to globality. Specifically, I show how, in the way that the *ilb* takes for granted the fusion of education and citizenship on a national and world scale, the perspective of the not-yet-citizen may be present in the "global" character of the festival, but it does not represent itself. I argue that rather than one creating a transnational dialogue, *ilb*'s efforts to transform Berlin into a comprehensive space of reading texts from around the world can be seen as an enterprise that draws on and reinforces a German national project. I maintain that the *ilb* constitutes a performance of privileged "globalness" that sharply circumscribes the refugee experience it seeks to highlight.

In the following, I examine the national-ness of the *ilb* by looking at distinct sites where the "international" is approached in a specific German way. Here, Berlin's role as national capital and home to prominent national institutions of *Bildung*—for example, the Humboldt University, the city's network of art and ethnography museums such as the *Humboldtforum,* and the *Haus der Kulturen der Welt* (House of World Cultures)—inform ways that the "non-German" is integrated into Germanness through *Bildung.* I begin my discussion by highlighting how the *ilb*'s founding and continued growth relates to German state initiatives to support the development of a "normal" German national identity during the early 2000s that occurred in conjunction with Berlin's reinstatement as the nation's capital. The *ilb*'s self-definition as a world space aligns with larger efforts to highlight Germany's rejection of xenophobic nationalism and embrace of tolerant democracy. I then turn to two festival venues of the 2015 *ilb* that addressed the problematic of "the refugee." Specifically, I examine how the novelist Jenny Erpenbeck's 2015 novel *Gehen, ging, gegangen* (*Going, Went, Gone*), publicly presented for the first time at the *ilb,* theorizes the *Bildungsbürger*-refugee relationship through the story of a retired Berlin professor who volunteers to help African asylum seekers in the city.[15] Next, I investigate citizen-organized public readings of texts about refugees and an *ilb* publication on the same theme. In the case of Erpenbeck's novel and the public readings and publication, the refugee story enters public space primarily through others' descriptions of it. In this way, the refugee story serves the purpose of fostering readers' and listeners' self-cultivation and world awareness, but within the context of the *ilb*—a state-sanctioned space largely for an international literary elite—the refugee voice becomes subsumed within an individualistic national project rather than part of a transnational communicative space.

The *ilb* and Global *Bildung* for the Capital of a "Normal," Tolerant Germany

In a 2014 interview, Thomas Böhm, the *ilb*'s program manager from 2012 until 2014, explained the impetus behind the festival's founding.[16]

In 1998 Ulrich Schreiber, founder and director of multiple cultural initiatives and festivals across Germany and around the world, including Mumbai, Kiev, and New York, attended the *Poetenfest* in Erlangen. At this major literature festival founded in 1985, Schreiber wondered why there was no similar event in Berlin "that corresponds to the metropolis Berlin in terms of its international scope, its diversity, and its size. In response to his own question, he started it."[17] The first *ilb* took place in 2001.

Böhm does not explain Schreiber's successful creation of a major showcase for international literature in Berlin in terms of the city's reestablishment as Germany's capital in 2000. Nevertheless, the *ilb's* founding, and Böhm's claim that the festival allows visitors to experience "literature as a bridge between cultures"[18] (*Literatur als eine Brücke zwischen den Kulturen*) must be understood in the context of a specific transition in practices and discourses about Berlin's role as the capital of a new "normal" nation that had shed intolerant nationalism.[19] To emphasize the nation's renewed identity, multiple cultural and commercial initiatives characterized Berlin as open to the world, or "weltoffen." Katrina Sark notes that marketing campaigns promoting Berlin in the mid-2000s described the city as "free" and emphasized its identity as a "creative" and "liberal" space.[20] As host of the 2006 World Cup, Germans welcomed the world to their capital while simultaneously expressing nationalist sentiment and prominently displaying the German flag—a practice that had been taboo only a few years before.[21] All of these examples reflect an emphatic coupling of German identity with "Weltoffenheit."

Institutions such as the *Humboldtforum,* a new museum located at the site of the old Berlin palace's reconstruction in the middle of the city, explicitly link a German tradition of *Bildung* with both past and future *Weltoffenheit* in Germany. The *Humboldtforum* aims to become a space "dedicated to the dialogue between the cultures of the world and will act as a forum for debate and analysis of historical and current issues of global significance."[22] As Sean Franzel notes, the initiative "[projects] ... a confident self-image as the [enabler] of global *Bildung.*"[23] Specifically, it does so by drawing on the national heritage of learning embodied in the historical figure of Wilhelm von Humboldt, founder of Berlin's Humboldt University and philosopher of *Bildung* as the process of self-formation through exposure to the world. The University, founded in 1810 as the University of Berlin, signifies Humboldt's instantiation of a new educational norm, or *Bildungsideal,* that defined learning as a holistic practice of subject formation fostered through the mutually reinforcing habits of research and practice.²⁴ This vision of education marked a shift from paradigms that prioritized knowledge accumulation in isolation from a world context. Rather than acquiring a catalog of facts, a person educated according to the Humboldtian *Bildungsideal* would learn to make connections between what she observed and her own experience. Though self-formation lay at the core of Humboldt's understanding of *Bildung*, it was not a self-serving practice since the worldly relevance of education' depends on and extends from the educated self, a perspective that Humboldt articulated in his famous exhortation "form your self and then act on others through that which you are" (*Bilde dich selbst und dann wirke auf andere durch das, was du bist*.)²⁵ Ultimately, *Bildung* produces someone who lives in and shapes the world, a citizen of the world, a "Weltbürger."²⁶ Organizers of the Humboldt Forum, as Franzel puts it, draw on the Humboldt name to connote an "unsullied, cosmopolitan pre-Nazi Germanness that is spiritually noble" and cite his philosophy of education—to "connect with as much of the world as possible" (*Soviel Welt mit sich verbinden als möglich*)—to showcase a German national tradition as the path to global awareness within the heart of Germany's capital.²⁷

The *ilb*, which receives funds from the *Hauptstadtkulturfonds* (Capital City Culture Funds), Germany's Ministry of Foreign Affairs, and the Federal Ministry for Education and Research, aligns with state-supported initiatives, such as the *Humboldtforum*, that link "Weltoffenheit" with the project of *Bildung*.²⁸ Though the *ilb* does not feature the term "Bildung" in its self-presentation, on its extensive website, or in auxiliary materials such as *ilb* publications, its linkage of "international-ness" and Berlin with books—the primary tool for subjects' self-formation—suggests global *Bildung* as its goal. The *ilb* manager Böhm's description of the festival as a cultural bridge suggests the *ilb*'s potential to bring people into a world beyond Germany. Further, the Berlin entertainment guide *Zitty* noted that the *ilb* enjoys the moniker of the "Berlinale of books" (*Berlinale der Bücher*). This comparison of the *ilb* with Berlin's famous film festival underscores both the festival's capacity to bring significant books and authors to Berlin as well as its power to attract attention from around the world.²⁹

While the *Humboldtforum* distinctly defines the museum venue as a space of learning, the festival nature of the *ilb* offers a different framework, the public reading, to support intellectual self-formation, or *Bildung*. Even though, according to Thomas Wegmann, there is an overall increase in the number of literature festivals and books published in Germany, individuals' solitary engagement with books through reading alone is on the decline.[30] Nevertheless, by offering people the opportunity to listen to books being read within a group context, what Wegmann describes as a "socially relevant event," the *ilb* links books to *Bildung* through the access to sensibilities and experiences beyond one's immediate context.[31]

Yet, the *Weltoffenheit* that initiatives such as the *ilb* proclaim potentially foreclose from its space the "world" that is in Berlin. A year before Schreiber imagined the *ilb* and the literature festival that would become a major international event in Germany's to-be new capital, Andreas Huyssen published the essay "The Voids of Berlin," in which he highlighted how the design of a "new" Berlin was intended to "enhance the desired image of Berlin as capital and global metropolis of the twenty-first century."[32] Huyssen's concern is the top-down creation of an "international" Berlin that seeks to "decorate the corporate and governmental sheds to better attract international attention," a process that forecloses the potential for the city's heterogeneous dwellers to form the city-in-transition into a "multiply coded text."[33] This is a process that reflects an all-too-eager desire to fill the "voids" of Berlin, the spaces left empty as a consequence of the city's historical upheavals, with structures and spaces that support Berlin's position within global capitalism.[34]

There is little possibility for those without access to this process—to put it bluntly, people like the non-German *Gastarbeiter* (guest workers) brought to West and East Berlin during the Cold War, or people like the refugees now in Berlin—to have a say in the way that these official international and global spaces are created. And yet, what the *ilb* did not specifically highlight in its publicity for the festival, and—as Jennifer Hosek and Karin Bauer argue in the introduction to this volume—what Huyssen's focus on Berlin's voids obscures, is the fact of the city's long-term creation and interpretation by immigrants. Christiane Steckenbiller offers an example of such practice in her chapter in this volume, "Transnational Cityscapes," a study of Turkish-German writer Emine Sevgi Özdamar's 2003 novel *Seltsame Sterne starren zur Erde*. Steckenbiller argues for reading Özdamar's portrayal of a Turkish-German woman inhabiting and navigating a divided Berlin in the 1970s as an "[inscription of] a transnational narrative into the master narrative of postwar Germany." Such texts, Steckenbiller notes, require us to understand the "New Berlin as a product of over fifty years of migration history."

Significantly, the transnational ties that have long characterized migrant life in Berlin do not find representation in an official discourse about the city's global openness. But if migrants have little say in Berlin's self-articulation as a global city, they engage in a different kind of "globalization" of Berlin, one in which the city serves as a platform for maintaining and forging transnational connections that bypass national public spheres. Anthropologist Regina Römhild identifies maintenance and creation of such ties, for example, in the way that Tolga, a Frankfurt native and "son of Turkish *Gastarbeiter* [guest workers]" engaged in hip-hop and reggae music and thus linked his identity with US and Jamaican traditions, as "transnationalism from below."[35] Römhild argues that "transnationalism from below" more accurately explains the way that immigrants to Germany negotiate relationships across borders than an assimilationist model, which assumes that the natural course for immigrants is to "adjust to an apparently given social and cultural setting."[36] The *ilb*'s form as a state-supported project for global *Bildung* did not create space for the refugee voice to "challenge and transform" the "container" of Germany.[37]

Theorizing Refugees' Voices in Berlin, from the Perspective of the *Bildungsbürger*

The *ilb* reinforces the creation of global awareness as a national project but offers little space for the non-German citizen living in Germany to shape the discussion about what a global Germany can or should be. It was within this cultural form, however, that the German author Jenny Erpenbeck presented her 2015 novel *Gehen, ging, gegangen,* which explores the relationship between the *Bildungsbürger*'s understanding of the globe and the presence of refugees in Berlin. *Gehen, ging, gegangen* tells the story of a retired Humboldt University literature professor whose volunteer work with African refugees to Berlin in the years spanning 2012 to 2014 transforms his worldview.[38] On the one hand, the work critiques the limited global vision held by representatives of Germany's intellectual class by showing how Richard's encounter with non-citizens leads to a radical reorientation of the paradigms by which he makes sense of the world. On the other hand, by featuring Richard the professor as narrator and protagonist whose perspective is broadened after he gets to know asylum seekers, the novel largely limits the entrance of the non-citizen voice into a German sphere to the apprehension of this voice by the *Bildungsbürger*. Erpenbeck posits Richard's "globalization" as a positive counterpoint to institutional and intellectual barriers that prevent the non-citizen from being known and heard. Nevertheless, his self-motivated project of self-formation, an enactment of the Humboldtian *Bildungsideal,* neither depends on nor occasions structural change.

Erpenbeck draws a connection between the reformation of Richard's geographical and intellectual reference points and his encounter with refugees in sites of *Bildung,* specifically classrooms that have either been repurposed by them or created for them. In *Gehen, ging, gegangen,* these spaces demonstrate the constraints for refugees to engage productively with Berlin and Germany. In this way they represent the failure of state structures to facilitate exchange between non-citizens and citizens and thus to help refugee voices enter a public sphere.

Richard first encounters asylum seekers at a meeting in the abandoned Kreuzberg secondary school, or *Gymnasium,* that they have occupied in protest of restrictive German asylum laws. Refuges have repurposed the school as a place to live and organize politically against regulations stating that those seeking asylum must remain in the place where they first requested it; they want to achieve more freedom of movement within Germany. This occupation, and the stand-offs between refugees and city officials it occasions, posits the school as a space of confrontation and division between non-citizens and the state.

A second "school scene" links spaces of learning with asylum seekers' marginal status in Germany. A group of refugees who occupied Berlin's *Oranienplatz*—also in protest of asylum laws—are resettled by the city to a retirement home on Berlin's eastern outskirts. Here, an Eritrean woman sets up an improvised classroom to offer the refugees German lessons, and asks Richard to help teach the more advanced students. The purpose of German instruction is to aid refugees' integration. Yet the classroom, decorated with posters of significant Berlin architectural sites, as well as the lessons that occur within it, do not support the project of refugees' assimilation into their new home. Instead, as Richard observes, the project to teach asylum seekers German underscores their alienation within Germany.

Paradoxically, two instances of successful language lessons highlight this problem. In one case, the young teacher wants to make clear how "auxiliary verbs" function in the present perfect tense in German. She asks students to identify men who are always in pairs. Khalil and Mohamed and Moussa and Yaya come forward. The teacher explains that these pairs of friends represent how this verb tense is always made up of two elements, namely, the helping verb "to be" or "to have" and the past participle. She then asks men to identify someone who is always alone in order to demonstrate the contrast between the present perfect and the simple past tense, which is formed by a single verb. Rufu comes forward. The teacher has managed to illustrate a grammatical concept, but she has also highlighted Rufu's loneliness in this new context.[39] In a second scene, Richard helps a refugee improve German skills while drawing attention to the man's marginality. Richard works with Yussuf by teaching him how to speak about the jobs he has had, finally coaching him to say the word "Tellerwäscher" (dish washer), in perfectly accented German. However, Richard realizes that this kind of learning—being able to accurately pronounce one's low-paying and unrespected work history—does not provide a path to social integration. When the teacher dismantles the classroom and takes down her posters of Berlin, Richard considers that these images likely offer no point of reference to the students who have come to German class in order to negotiate the city depicted in them.

Erpenbeck contrasts these scenes of schools as sites that block, rather than foster, refugees' integration into a German social context with Richard's individual project to expand his own awareness of the refugees' backgrounds and lives. In a countermove to the restrictions placed on refugees to reclaim and redefine the "globalness" of Berlin through their encounter with its spaces of learning, Richard works to "globalize" his own knowledge through deeper engagement with refugees. This is a process that leads him to question the parameters by which he has known the world up until then. Ultimately, this work leads to the "cosmopoliticization" of his own modes of learning and the re-characterization of his home from a haven of *Bildung* and solitude to a space open to the world, specifically, the refugees he invites to live there. Yet Richard's openness to the non-citizen voice is a private task, and its effects are felt primarily in the private sphere.

Richard takes on the task of educating himself about the African refugees in Berlin systematically: he reads African history and compiles a series of questions to ask the African asylum seekers. Richard's questionnaire quickly reveals itself as flawed in its dependence on categories of knowledge that do not correspond with the information he receives. He hopes that questions such as "Where did you grow up?" (*Wo sind Sie aufgewachsen?*) or "How did you imagine Europe?" (*Wie haben Sie sich Europa vorgestellt?*) can elucidate the quality of being a refugee by drawing out the distinction between a life as lived there and then and life here, now, and in the future, or, as Richard puts it, "the one life of a person [and] the other life of that same person."[40] Yet the bland questions elide the trauma of refugee experience. Richard asks "did you learn a profession?" (*Haben Sie einen Beruf gelernt?*) and receives answers that he neither expects nor knows what to do with, for example, refugees' stories about witnessing others drowning on the voyage from Libya to Italy just as the Italian coast guard is on its way: "[E]veryone ran to one side of the boat in order to be saved, that's why the boat cap-sized."[41] Richard does not know how to classify this kind of information about despair and unspeakable tragedy.[42]

Just as Richard's work to learn about the refugees in Berlin upsets his preconceived notions of measurable life categories and experiences, his efforts to understand distinctions between refugees' lives "before" and "after" coming to Germany unsettle his conflation of state borders with identity. Even though Richard has lived in multiple Germanys, each one defined by different boundaries, it seems that he only fully realizes the contingency of states' spatial markers via his discussions with refugees. Richard asks a refugee staying in the retirement home where he comes from. The man answers not with the name of a country but with the answer "from the desert" (*del deserto*).[43] The man, a Tuareg from Niger, proceeds to explain how he orients himself in the desert by the way that the sand moves, not by the way that borders are fixed: "If you know how the dunes can shift, then you can recognize the sand underneath the sand."[44] Richard suddenly understands that the borders drawn by Europeans in Africa have more to do with European colonial claims to African space than with describing African identity: "[O]nly now does he realize what kind of arbitrariness becomes clear in such a line."[45] Further, Richard sees how arbitrary borderlines drawn to express state power continue to shape African lives within Berlin. When his refugee friends refuse to comply with the asylum law that requires them to remain in the place where they first requested asylum, the police barricade and surround the building.[46] Richard realizes that the police have imposed a mobile border on an already existing community: "A border, Richard thinks, can also become suddenly visible, can suddenly appear in a place where there never was one—what was being fought out during the past years at Libya's border, or on Morocco's border or the borders of Niger, is now taking place in the middle of Berlin-Spandau. Where before there was only some house, a sidewalk, just everyday life in Berlin, a border suddenly grows up."[47]

In addition to an expanded view of categories of human experience and a revised understanding of the relationship between space and identity, Richard's project to learn about the Africans he meets in Berlin reveals to him the shortcomings of his historical frameworks that he sees as having grown out of German colonial history. He comes to understand that the corpus of texts that he, as an educated person, has read is one that he has only apprehended from a Eurocentric perspective. Learning about Africans leads him to see Europe from the perspective of Africans, a process that reorients his worldview. When he reads

Herodotus now, "the Greek pantheon, which is his area of expertise, shifts and he suddenly understands in a new way what it means that for the Greeks, the world ended where Morocco is today, at the Atlas Mountains, where Atlas held the heaven and earth apart. ... The regions that we today call Libya, Tunisia, Algeria were, in classical times, the region *before* the end of the world, or, in other words, the world."[48]

In the novel, Richard's *Bildung* culminates in his ability to create a "global space" within his own home; he transforms his apartment in a way that mirrors the opening of his worldview. Richard decides to register his apartment as an official lodging for refugees and open his home to refugees who have been granted permission to stay in Berlin. His apartment metamorphoses from an idyllic space of *Bildung* with rooms devoted to books and music to a dormitory for eleven men from various African countries. He puts up Rufu, Abdusalam, Yaya, and Moussa in his library; Khalil, Mohamed, Ithemba stay in his guest room; Apoll and Karon are in the music room; and Zair and Zani sleep in the living room. In the evenings, all gather in the kitchen to eat the food that Ithemba cooks for them.[49] Richard's work to become educated about Africans in Berlin results in a figurative and literal resituation of his own place in the world: he accepts African history and experience as central, not peripheral, to his own and cements this understanding of his connection to Africa by actually offering Africans a place at his table.

The novel celebrates German domestic life radically transformed through the presence of refugees. Yet the "globalization" of the *Bildungsbürger* that occasions this transformation depends on the German citizen's initiative to understand the contingency of knowledge categories and state boundaries; it does not disrupt state institutions that marginalize the non-citizen. Richard sets out on a journey of *Bildung*—self-formation through education—within Berlin. While his journey that brings him into contact with refugees may destabilize his paradigms of *Bildung,* he returns in the end to his same, albeit now refugee-occupied, home. The novel's final scene, a backyard birthday barbecue party for Richard with both refugee and German guests, gestures toward a future in which refugee voices are normal components of conversation in Germany. Yet the work also suggests that this is a future that must begin with the Germans' self-formation. In the end, the novel opts for the status quo–affirming message of the *Bildungsroman*. It leaves behind the radical possibilities through which non-citizens might claim an audience in Germany that the novel's opening scenes of refugees occupying German public space depict.

Considered in the context of the *ilb* reading, a city- and state-sanctioned space occupied primarily by *Bildungsbürger,* the novel's depiction of the *Bildungsbürger*'s development into a *Weltbürger* through integration of refugee knowledge and refugee bodies into German space implicitly critiques the very assumptions that grounded the public reading at the *ilb* at which Erpenbeck read from her novel. *Gehen, ging, gegangen* debunks individuals' encounters with books—and, one might infer, state-sponsored educational programs—as the sole source of socially relevant *Bildung.* Yet the critique, both at the level of the novel's narrative and its presentation, functions in a closed loop, with no "opening" for a refugee voice to enter into the public conversation. The attendees of the *ilb* event, held at the *Haus der Berliner Festspiele,* listened to Erpenbeck read in German about a German perspective: Richard's transformation.

The (Largely) Absent Refugee Voices in the *ilb*'s "Berlin Liest" and the *Berliner Anthologie*

Gehen, ging, gegangen asserts the refugee's agency to claim space within Berlin as well as the refugee's experience of the world to teach Berliners, but upholds the *Bildungsbürger par excellence,* Richard, as a model of the German national subject for whom self-formation is a way to apprehend the world. Nevertheless, the novel theorizes the relationship of the non-citizen and the citizen's education in a way that was absent from the *ilb*'s organization of extrafestival initiatives to insert the refugee perspective and experience into the cityscape in 2015. These fora included the regular *ilb* initiative "Berlin liest," a program that calls for Berliners to read texts of their choice on a particular topic throughout the city, and the annual festival publication, the *Berliner Anthologie,* both of which are supported by the Heinrich Böll Foundation and were, in 2015, dedicated to the theme of *Asylsuchende* and *Flüchtlinge.* The *ilb* called for anyone to participate in "Berlin liest," anywhere, and in any language. The 2015 *Berliner Anthologie* features authors from around the world whose writing "[contemplates] the fates of refugees and asylum-seekers in literary form," and is available from the festival website as a pdf document.[50] Theoretically, these fora could have provided an avenue for the refugee voice to enter the public sphere in a way not possible in the more conventional festival parameters, which require specific linguistic competencies and a ticket purchase. Yet both "Berlin liest" and the *Berliner Anthologie* events, which prioritized *any* story of the refugee experience, highlighted the refugee as a transhistorical and transcendent phenomenon. Neither venue offered reflection on the relationship between the categories of "German/ Berlin," "global worldview" and "refugee," as Erpenbeck does in her novel. "Berlin liest" and the *Berliner Anthologie* provided many texts *about* refugees and asylum seekers but did not theorize, or emphasize, the connection between the refugee voice and experience and citizens' "global Bildung." As such, they primarily provided more opportunities for hearing more stories about non-German experiences, or more *Weltoffenheit,* but did not challenge or refunction primary forms of *Bildung*—practices of self-formation through reading or the university context.

The parameters of "Berlin liest," as I mentioned above, provided the opportunity for inserting a refugee voice into a Berlin public sphere. During the summer of 2015, the *ilb* issued a call on its website for Berliners to read out loud literary texts related to the "situation of refugees and asylum seekers in Europe and around the world."[51] The readings were to take place on the day of the festival's opening, September 9, from 6:00 AM until 5:30 PM in any kind of public space in the city, for example, street corners, train stations, or public squares. Readers were encouraged to draw on texts that the *ilb* had compiled and made available in pdf format or read works of their own choosing, including ones they had written themselves, in any language. Further, readers were asked to inform the *ilb* of their reading plans. This schedule of readings was then compiled and posted on the *ilb* website.[52]

The innovation of the "Berlin liest" project lay in the fact that many people read texts from different contexts in public spaces around Berlin, yet the traditional form of the reading remained intact such that inner development through books—or listening to books being read out loud—served as the venue for gaining an international awareness. It was the "literariness" of the project that mediated the voices as more or less legitimate. The approximately fifty readings held as part of "Berlin liest" took place across the city. Many were held in prominent public places—for example, the Platz der Republik directly in front of the *Reichstag,* the Potsdamer Platz, and the Alexanderplatz. Some readings were held in bookstores across the city, the shopping center *Ka De We,* or at major subway stations and Berlin's main train station. Readers ranged from high school students presenting texts in the Wilmersdorf *Volkspark* to employees of the Federal Foreign Office reading outside of their office buildings.[53]

Despite the breadth of readings, only one "Berlin liest" event co-organized by the libraries of Berlin's Technical University and Berlin's

University of the Arts featured stories that asylum seekers told about their own experiences of flight. Here, the publicly supported university became the space devoted to offering a platform for asylum seekers to "speak for themselves" for an entire afternoon and evening.[54] According to a *Deutschlandfunk* radio broadcast about the event, the reading featured ten refugees, including a Syrian neurologist, Mohammad al-Hashish, and an unnamed Afghan journalist and poet who described the path they took to get to Germany. The thirty or so audience members who listened to al-Hashish, who spoke in German, heard about his life in Syria, specifically about how he was treating those wounded by the war on a daily basis. Al-Hashish also read out loud from a text that he wrote about his flight from Turkey to Greece: "[T]he boat was about nine square meters and held about 50 people. After a week on the island Kos I went to Athens. I stayed in Athens for one month. That is where I bought a fake German passport. That cost 7000 Euros. Then I flew to Germany."[55] Though the reading was of a small scale, al-Hashish's story garnered affective responses from the listeners. A Greek student whom the *Deutschlandfunk* reporter interviewed explained, "I have never heard a refugee 'live.' [What was described] was worse than what the media portray. I had not imagined that [the situation] is so tragic."[56] It remains to be seen what effect the education that the reading offered this Greek woman studying in Germany will have beyond eliciting pathos.

Many of the texts read at the "Berlin liest" event were included in the *Berliner Anthologie* published by the *ilb* and edited by Ulrich Schreiber, Anna Senft, and member of the Heinrich Böll Foundation, Christine Pütz. Just as the "Berlin liest" event did not trouble conventional practices of *Bildung*, the anthology does not challenge the institutional parameters through which the refugee experience might become part of a conception of German-ness. The foreword, written by Ralf Fücks, leading member of the *Heinrich Böll Stiftung* and influential Green Party member, highlights Europe's origins as a "Kontinent der Flüchtlinge" (continent of refugees) and emphasizes Germans' common denominator as immigrants—*not* a cohesive ethnic identity.[57] Yet Fücks also calls for a regulated European-wide immigration policy that distinguishes between "politically persecuted, war refugees, economic migrants, and qualified immigrants" and offers appropriate options for these different groups.[58] For Fücks, the purpose of the anthology is to provoke readers' affective responses to the situation of the refugee, what he calls the first step to "humane und feasible solutions to the new refugee question."[59]

While the framing of the *Berliner Anthologie* reinforces the status quo in terms of Germany's relationship to the world, the texts included in the work do not represent the backgrounds or experiences of the majority of people entering Berlin as refugees in the fall of 2015. With the exception of E. C. Osundo, a Nigerian writer living in the United States, none of the authors represented in the anthology come from Africa or the Middle East.[60] Furthermore, the text is not accessible to refugees in Germany who cannot read English or German. All of the works are published in both German and English and, if not originally written in those languages, are translated into them. The editors do not justify the inclusion of these writers and their texts, some of which are recent and unpublished, others of which have been published over twenty years ago, into the anthology. In sum, the *Berliner Anthologie,* takes for granted the cumulative value of stories about non-Germans for German readers.

Conclusion

In May 2015, the major German newspaper *Die Zeit* published a story about young adult asylum seekers in Bavaria enrolled in German-language and jobs-training courses to better assimilate into their new homes. The title of the piece was "Die Bildungsbürger." Rather than use the term to reference education for its own sake, the piece emphasized how training served to help these not-yet citizens integrate into German society.[61] This raises the question of whether *Bildung,* noninstrumental self-formation, is a practice for Germans and not immigrants.

Berlin's *ilb,* which presents the world to Berliners via books, suggests as much. In this festival, primarily German participants in a literary public sphere are urged to expose themselves to narratives about the world, with the understanding that this is a process that will necessarily contribute to a more global outlook. Such a project is particularly available in Berlin, being supported by the state and through larger cultural practices that link global education with a specific German identity. And yet the world in Berlin, and coming to Berlin, has little opportunity to represent itself within the city's spaces of "global" literary consumption that affirms a German national tradition, reading, as a process of self-formation.

It may be necessary to look beyond explicitly national projects aimed to foster Berlin and, by extension, Germany's *Weltoffenheit* in order to locate non-citizen voices in the public sphere. One example of such a platform for the refugee perspective is the independent "Refugee Radio Network," a forum with the mission to give voice to "refugees and immigrants in precarious life circumstances … in order that they may be heard."[62] The multilingual program, produced in Germany, aims to present stories created and broadcast by people with experiences of flight and migration.[63] Attention to this kind of transnational practice "from below," in Römhild's terms, rather than state-sanctioned educational projects to promote Germans' openness to the world, could offer an important starting point for reorienting the *Bildungsbürger*'s self-understanding within Germany, and the world.

Marike Janzen is assistant professor of humanities at the University of Kansas. Her first book examines authorship and solidarity in the work of Anna Seghers and her contemporaries. She has published articles on Seghers, Peter Schneider, the intersection of rights and narrative in Lynn Nottage and Bertolt Brecht, and pedagogy.

Notes

1. Steven Erlanger and James Kanter, "Plan on Migrants Strains the Limits of Europe's Unity," *New York Times,* September 22, 2015, http://www.nytimes.com/2015/09/23/world/europe/european-union-ministers-migrants-refugees.html?_r=0.
2. Ibid.
3. Yermi Brenner, "Refugees Struggle to Assimilate in Germany," *Al Jazeera America,* August 28, 2015, http://america.aljazeera.com/articles/2015/8/28/berlin-germany-europe-refugees.html.
4. *internationales literaturfestival berlin,* accessed December 30, 2015, http://www.literaturfestival.com/.
5. Emma Martell, "Berlin, a Literary Capital," *Sofitel Berlin Kurfürstendamm* (blog), September 22, 2012, http://blog.sofitel-berlin-kurfurstendamm.com/berlin-a-literary-capital/.
6. "Get Cultured at Berlin's Literature Festival," *mtrip,* August 11, 2011.
7. "15th ilb—International Literature Festival 2015," *Visit Berlin,* accessed December 31, 2015, http://www.visitberlin.de/en/event/09-19-2015/15th-ilb-international-literature-festival-berlin-2015.
8. "International Festival for Literature Berlin," *Creative City Berlin*. The festival is here described as a space where "Arab poets will meet with American short story-writers [sic], South Korean poets with their Russian colleagues, and South African novelists with young, budding Albanian authors. The most interesting, newly discovered authors will stand equally beside literature's most established and respected talents."
9. Dirk Knipphals, "Eröffnung des Literaturfestival Berlin: Alles wird diskutiert," *taz,* September 5, 2012, http://www.taz.de/!5084751/. In this review of the

festival, Knipphals describes how the festival aspires to connect its presentation of books with the goal of creating cross-cultural exchange and understanding: "In Berlin schwingt vielmehr, wenigstens irgendwo im Hinterkopf, der Anspruch mit, zum kulturellen Austausch und vielleicht sogar zur Völkerverständigung beizutragen. … Die 'Konflikte in dieser Welt' hob Festivalchef Ulrich Schreiber in seiner Eröffnungsansprache dann auch als Festivalthema hervor: die Konflikte 'zwischen Religionen und in den Regionen.'"

10. Thomas Hummitzsch, "Wunderkind trifft Flüchtling," *taz,* September 14, 2015, http://www.taz.de/!5231895/. Hummitzsch writes, "Das 15. Internationale Literaturfestival Berlin zeigt sich politisch und rückt die Situation der Flüchtlinge in den Vordergrund."

11. Christine Pütz, Anna Senft, and Ulrich Schreiber, eds., *Woher ich nicht zurückkehren werde/From Where I Shan't Return* (Berlin, 2015), 124.

12. Dominic Boyer, *Spirit and System: Media, Intellectuals, and the Dialectic in Modern German Culture* (Chicago, 2005), 59.

13. Ibid.

14. Ibid.

15. Unless otherwise noted, all translations in the text are mine.

16. "Thomas Böhm verlässt das internationale literaturfestival berlin," *Buchmarkt: Das Ideenmagazin für den Buchhandel,* October 6, 2014, http://www.buchmarkt.de/content/60103-thomas-boehm-verlaesst-das-internationale-literaturfestival-berlin.htm.

17. "Thomas Böhm über das internationale literaturfestival berlin," *Klappentexterin* (blog), September 10, 2014, https://klappentexterin.wordpress.com/2014/09/10/thomas-bohm-uber-das-internationale-literaturfestival-berlin/. "Ulrich Schreiber … fragte sich: warum gibt es eigentlich kein Literaturfestival, das, von seiner Internationalität, seiner Vielfalt, seiner Größe der Metropole Berlin entspricht. Als Antwort darauf hat er es gegründet."

18. Ibid.

19. Ibid.

20. Katrina Sark, "Fashioning a New Brand of 'Germanness': The 2006 World Cup and Beyond," *Seminar: A Journal of Germanic Studies* 48, no. 2 (2012): 254, accessed December 31, 2015, https://vv6tt6sy5c.search.serialssolutions.com/?V=1.0&L=VV6TT6SY5C&SS_searchTypesUsed=yes&SS_searchTypeJournal=yes&S=AC_T_B&C=Seminar.

21. Maria Stehle and Beverly M. Weber, "German Soccer, the 2010 World Cup, and Multicultural Belonging," *German Studies Review* 36, no. 1 (2013): 108, accessed December 31, 2015, https://muse-jhu-edu.www2.lib.ku.edu/journals/german_studies_review/v036/36.1.stehle.html.

22. "Humboldt-Forum Philosophy," *Humboldt-Forum,* accessed December 31, 2015, http://www.humboldt-forum.de/en/home/.

23. Sean Franzel, "Recycling Bildung: From the Humboldt-Forum to Humboldt and Back," *Seminar: A Journal of Germanic Studies* 50, no. 3 (2014): 389,

accessed December 31, 2015, https://muse-jhu-edu.www2.lib.ku.edu/jour
nals/seminar_a_journal_of_germanic_studies/v050/50.3.franzel.html.

24. Or, the "durchgängige Wechselwirkung des theoretischen Verstandes und
des praktischen Willens." Wilhelm von Humboldt, *Wilhelm von Humboldts
Werke, zweiter Band 1796–1799*, ed. Albert Leitzmann (Berlin, 1904), 326.

25. Nicholas Boyle, *Goethe, der Dichter in seiner Zeit, Band II, 1791–1803*, trans.
Holger Fliessbach (Munich, 1999), 47.

26. "Welche Bedeutung hat das Humboldt'sche Erbe für unsere Zeit?," *Humboldt Gesellschaft*, accessed December 31, 2015, http://www.humboldtge
sellschaft.de/inhalt.php?name=humboldt.

27. Franzel, "Recycling Bildung," 390.

28. *internationales literaturfestival berlin*, accessed December 31, 2015, http://
www.literaturfestival.com/.

29. "Pressestimmen," *internationales literaturfestival berlin*, accessed December
31, 2015, http://www.literaturfestival.com/archiv/pressestimmen.

30. Thomas Wegmann, "Zwischen Gottesdienst und Rummelplatz: Das Literaturfestival als Teil der Eventkultur," in *literatur.com: Tendenzen im Literaturmarketing*, ed. Erhard Schütz and Thomas Wegmann (Berlin, 2002), 126.

31. "[E]ines gesellschaftlich relevanten Ereignisses," ibid.

32. Andreas Huyssen, "The Voids of Berlin," *Critical Inquiry* 24, no. 1 (1997):
66–67.

33. Ibid., 69.

34. Ibid., 67.

35. Regina Römhild, "Global Heimat German: Migration and the Transnationalization of the Nation-State," *Transit* 1, no. 1 (2004): 5, accessed December
31, 2015, http://escholarship.org/uc/item/57z2470p.

36. Ibid., 3.

37. Ibid.

38. The novel references specific events of refugee demonstrations and re-
settlement in Berlin that occurred between 2012 and 2014. These include
the occupation of Oranienplatz by refugees from October 2012 until April
2014 and refugees' occupation of the *Gerhart Hauptmann Gymnasium* in
Kreuzberg in December 2012. See Will Coldwell, "Refugees Tell a Different
Story in Berlin," *The Guardian*, November 28, 2015, accessed February 15,
2016, http://www.theguardian.com/travel/2015/nov/28/refugees-tell-a-diff
erent-berlin-story; and Paul Middelhoff, "Flüchtlingsprotest in Berlin-Kreuzberg: Drama auf dem Dach," *Der Spiegel*, June 27, 2014, accessed February
15, 2016, http://www.spiegel.de/politik/deutschland/fluechtlinge-in-berlin-
kreuzberg-drama-um-besetzte-schule-a-977616.html.

39. Jenny Erpenbeck, *Gehen, ging, gegangen* (Munich, 2015), Kindle edition, 57.
Here, Erpenbeck explains how the teacher chooses refugees to represent
"das Hilfsverb *sein* oder *haben* dar, und der andere das Verb, das gebeugt
wird. Khalil und Mohamed sind Freunde, sagt sie, nicht wahr? Ja, sagen alle.
... da die Lehrerin den Gegensatz von Perfekt und Präsens verdeutlichen

will, fragt sie nach einem von ihnen, der immer ganz allein sei, der keinen Freund habe und mit niemandem spreche."

40. Ibid., 52. "Das eine Leben eines Menschen [und] das andere Leben desselben Menschen."

41. Ibid., 61. "Alle [sind] auf die eine Seite des Boots gelaufen, um gerettet zu werden, darum ist das Boot dann gekentert."

42. Ibid., 69.

43. Ibid., 66.

44. Ibid., 67. "Wenn man weiß, wie die Dünen wandern, kann man den Sand unter dem Sand wiedererkennen."

45. Ibid., 66. "Erst jetzt wird ihm klar welche Willkür da sichtbar wird an so einer Linie."

46. Ibid., 258.

47. Ibid., 258–59. "Eine Grenze, denkt Richard, kann also auch plötzlich sichtbar werden, kann plötzlich an einem Ort erscheinen, wo sonst nie eine war—was in den letzten Jahren an den Grenzen Libyens ausgefochten wurde oder an den Grenzen Marokkos oder Nigers, findet nun mitten in Berlin-Spandau statt. Wo es zuvor nur irgendein Haus, einen Bürgersteig, einen Berliner Alltag gab, wuchert plötzlich so eine Grenze."

48. Ibid., 176. "[D]er griechische Götterhimmel der doch eigentlich sein Spezialgebiet ist [verrückt sich für ihn plötzlich auch], und er versteht plötzlich neu, was es bedeutet, dass sich für die Griechen das Ende der Welt da befand, wo heute Marokko ist, am Atlasgebirge, dort stemmte Atlas Himmel und Erde auseinander.… Die Gegenden, die heute Libyen, Tunesien, Algerien heißen, waren in der Antike das Gebiet *vor* dem Ende der Welt, also die Welt."

49. Ibid., 337.

50. Pütz et al., *Woher ich nicht zurückkehren werde/From Where I Shan't Return,* 124.

51. "Call to Take Part in the 'Berlin Liest' Reading Performance on the Situation of Refugees and Asylum-seekers to Launch the 15th International Literature Festival on 9 September 2015," *internationales literaturfestival berlin,* accessed 26 May, 2016, http://www.literaturfestival.com/aktuelles-en/call-to-take-part-in-the-berlin-liest-reading-performance-on-the-situation-of-refugees-and-asylum-seekers-to-launch-the-15th-international-literature-festival-berlin-on-9-september-2015.

52. "berlin liest," *internationales literaturfestival berlin,* accessed December 31, 2015, http://www.literaturfestival.com/programm/berlin-liest.

53. Ibid.

54. "Leseperformance 'Berlin liest' hier im Haus, 9. September 2015, 12-17 Uhr," *Technische Universität Bibliothek,* September 9, 2015.

55. Kemal Hür, "Flüchtlinge beschreiben ihre Erlebnisse," *Deutschlandfunk,* accessed June 5, 2016, http://www.deutschlandfunk.de/literaturfestival-berlin-fluechtlinge-beschreiben-ihre.1773.de.html?dram:article_id=330646.

56. Ibid.
57. Ralf Fücks, "Europa der Flüchtlinge," in *Woher ich nicht zurückkehren werde/ From Where I Shan't Return,* 4–5.
58. Ibid.
59. Ibid., 6–7.
60. The authors represented in the anthology are from Greece, Australia, Italy, Slovenia, Macedonia, Austria, Czech Republic, Norway, Iceland, Vietnam/ United States, South Africa/Australia, Germany, Belarus, Nigeria/United States, Israel, Sweden, Ireland, and Peru.
61. Laura Cwiertnia, "Die Bildungsbürger," *Zeit,* May 28, 2015, http://www.zeit .de/feature/schulabschluss-fluechtlinge-bildung-bayern.
62. "Projektbeschreibung." *Refugee Radio Network,* accessed February 15, 2016, http://www.refugeeradionetwork.net/projekt.html.
63. Ibid.

Bibliography

"15th ilb—International Literature Festival 2015." *Visit Berlin.* Accessed December 31, 2015. http://www.visitberlin.de/en/event/09-19-2015/15th-ilb-international-literature-festival-berlin-2015.

Boyer, Dominic. *Spirit and System: Media, Intellectuals, and the Dialectic in Modern German Culture.* Chicago: University of Chicago Press, 2005.

Boyle, Nicholas. *Goethe, der Dichter in seiner Zeit, Band II, 1791–1803.* Translated by Holger Fliessbach. Munich: C. H. Beck Verlag, 1999.

Brenner, Yermi. "Refugees Struggle to Assimilate in Germany." *Al Jazeera America,* August 28, 2015. Accessed March 12, 2017. http://america.aljazeera .com/articles/2015/8/28/berlin-germany-europe-refugees.html.

Coldwell, Will. "Refugees Tell a Different Story in Berlin." *The Guardian,* November 28, 2015. Accessed March 12, 2017. http://www.theguardian.com/ travel/2015/nov/28/refugees-tell-a-different-berlin-story.

Cwiertnia, Laura. "Die Bildungsbürger." *Zeit,* May 28, 2015. Accessed March 14, 2017. http://www.zeit.de/feature/schulabschluss-fluechtlinge-bildung-bay ern.

Erlanger, Steven, and James Kanter. "Plan on Migrants Strains the Limits of Europe's Unity." *New York Times,* September 22, 2015. Accessed March 12, 2017. http://www.nytimes.com/2015/09/23/world/europe/european-union-ministers-migrants-refugees.html?_r=0.

Erpenbeck, Jenny. *Gehen, ging, gegangen.* Munich: Albrecht Knaus Verlag, 2015. Kindle edition.

Franzel, Sean. "Recycling Bildung: From the Humboldt-Forum to Humboldt and Back." *Seminar: A Journal of Germanic Studies* 50, no. 3 (2014): 379–97.

Fücks, Ralf. "Europa der Flüchtlinge." In *Woher ich nicht zurückkehren werde/ From Where I Shan't Return,* edited by Christine Pütz, Anna Senft, and Ulrich Schreiber, 4–5. Berlin: Verlag Vorwerk 8, 2015.

"Get Cultured at Berlin's Literature Festival." *mtrip,* August 11, 2011. Retrieved from http://www.mtrip.com/berlin-literature-festival/.

Hür, Kemal. "Flüchtlinge beschreiben ihre Erlebnisse." *Deutschlandfunk,* September 10, 2015. Accessed March 12, 2017. http://www.deutschlandfunk.de/literaturfestival-berlin-fluechtlinge-beschreiben-ihre.1773.de.html?dram:article_id=330646.

"Humboldt-Forum Philosophy." *Humboldt-Forum.* Accessed December 31, 2015. Accessed March 12, 2017. http://www.humboldt-forum.de/en/home/.

Hummitzsch, Thomas. "Wunderkind trifft Flüchtling." *taz,* September 14, 2015. Accessed March 12, 2017. http://www.taz.de/!5231895/.

Huyssen, Andreas. "The Voids of Berlin." *Critical Inquiry* 24, no. 1 (1997): 57–81.

"International Festival for Literature Berlin." *Creative City Berlin.* Accessed December 31, 2015. http://www.creative-city-berlin.de/en/event/international_festival_literature_berlin/.

internationales literaturfestival berlin. "berlin liest." Accessed December 31, 2015. http://www.literaturfestival.com/programm/berlin-liest.

———. "The Comic-Manifest: COMICS ARE ART." Accessed March 1, 2016. www.literaturfestival.com/archiv/sonderprojekte/comic/manifest.

———. "Pressestimmen." Accessed December 31, 2015. http://www.literaturfestival.com/archiv/pressestimmen.

———. "Startseite." Accessed December 30, 2015. http://www.literaturfestival.com/.

Knipphals, Dirk. "Eröffnung des Literaturfestival Berlin: Alles wird diskutiert." *taz,* September 5, 2012, http://www.taz.de/!5084751/.

"Leseperformance 'Berlin liest' hier im Haus, 9. September 2015, 12-17 Uhr." *Technische Universität Bibliothek,* September 9, 2015. Accessed December 31, 2015, http://www.ub.tu-berlin.de/en/news/news/detail/952/.

Martell, Emma. "Berlin, a Literary Capital." *Sofitel Berlin Kurfürstendamm* (blog), September 22, 2012. Accessed March 12, 2017. http://blog.sofitel-berlin-kurfurstendamm.com/berlin-a-literary-capital/.

Middelhoff, Paul. "Flüchtlingsprotest in Berlin-Kreuzberg: Drama auf dem Dach." *Der Spiegel,* June 27, 2014. Accessed March 12, 2017. http://www.spiegel.de/politik/deutschland/fluechtlinge-in-berlin-kreuzberg-drama-um-besetzte-schule-a-977616.html.

Pütz, Christine, Anna Senft, and Ulrich Schreiber, eds. *Woher ich nicht zurückkehren werde/ From Where I Shan't Return.* Berlin: Verlag Vorwerk 8, 2015.

Refugee Radio Network. "Projekte." Accessed February 15, 2016. http://www.refugeeradionetwork.net/projekt.html.

Römhild, Regina. "Global Heimat Germany: Migration and the Transnationalization of the Nation-State." *Transit* 1, no. 1 (2004): 1–8. Accessed December 31, 2015. http://escholarship.org/uc/item/57z2470p.

Sark, Katrina. "Fashioning a New Brand of 'Germanness': The 2006 World Cup and Beyond." *Seminar: A Journal of Germanic Studies* 48, no. 2 (2012): 254–66.

Stehle, Maria, and Beverly M. Weber. "German Soccer, the 2010 World Cup, and Multicultural Belonging." *German Studies Review* 36, no. 1 (2013): 103–24.

"Thomas Böhm über das internationale literaturfestival berlin." *Klappentexterin* (blog), September 10, 2014. Accessed March 12, 2017. https://klappentexterin.wordpress.com/2014/09/10/thomas-bohm-uber-das-int ernationale-literaturfestival-berlin/.

"Thomas Böhm verlässt das internationale literaturfestival berlin." *Buchmarkt: Das Ideenmagazin für den Buchhandel,* October 6, 2014. Accessed March 12, 2017. http://www.buchmarkt.de/content/60103-thomas-boehm-verlae sst-das-internationale-literaturfestival-berlin.htm.

von Humboldt, Wilhelm. *Wilhelm von Humboldts Werke, zweiter Band 1796–1799,* edited by Albert Leitzmann. Berlin: B. Behr's Verlag, 1904.

Wegmann, Thomas. "Zwischen Gottesdienst und Rummelplatz: Das Literaturfestival als Teil der Eventkultur." In *literatur.com: Tendenzen im Literaturmarketing,* edited by Erhard Schütz and Thomas Wegmann, 121–36. Berlin: Weidler Buchverlag, 2002.

"Welche Bedeutung hat das Humboldt'sche Erbe für unsere Zeit?" *Humboldt Gesellschaft.* Accessed December 31, 2015. http://www.humboldtgesellschaft .de/inhalt.php?name=humboldt.

PART IV

Berlin Memoryscapes of the Present

CHAPTER 12

Transnational Cityscapes
Tracking Turkish-German Hi/Stories in Postwar Berlin

Christiane Steckenbiller

Since the 1990s, Berlin has been a popular setting for many Turkish-German writers. Yadé Kara, Zafer Şenocak, and most recently Deniz Utlu have chosen the German capital to explore the fall of the Wall, the aftermath of reunification, and the restlessness of a new generation that coincides with the fiftieth anniversary of the Turkish-German guest worker treaty. Yet nowhere does Berlin feature as prominently as in the works of Emine Sevgi Özdamar. While all four authors offer nuanced accounts of the city's unique and tumultuous history, Özdamar's texts cast a wider trajectory. Her persistent focus on Berlin in her overtly semi-autobiographical oeuvre is informed by and interwoven with her own story of coming to Berlin as a Turkish guest worker. She often represents the city as intertwined with the protagonist's migrant identity—as embodied, lived, and practiced—which she does most skillfully in her 2003 novel *Seltsame Sterne starren zur Erde (Strange Stars Stare at the Earth)*, the final installment of her *Istanbul-Berlin-Trilogie*.[1] While all three novels follow the protagonist and first-person narrator on her journey from Turkey to Berlin, *Seltsame Sterne* takes place almost exclusively in Berlin and does not thematize language, integration, or cultural differences between Turkey and Germany. As the subtitle reveals, the text is set in both East and West—in *Wedding–Pankow 1976/77*—and focuses on the narrator's work at the *Volksbühne,* the People's Theater in East Berlin, her constant border crossings, and the diverse range of people and stories she encounters by walking through and residing in the city.

Writing across and beyond borders—between Turkey and Germany, Istanbul and Berlin, and between East and West, past and present— Özdamar assumes a synchronic and diachronic view of history and establishes herself as a highly innovative chronicler of an already transnational city that anticipates the cosmopolitan attitude of the New Berlin today. Özdamar's creative retelling of the East Berlin theater world and her work at the *Volksbühne* in the 1970s could thus also be read as prefiguring the current transnational theater scene and postmigrant theater movement in Berlin. Cultural institutions like the *Ballhaus Naunynstraße* and *Hebbel am Ufer* (HAU), both in Kreuzberg, and the *Maxim Gorki Theater* off Unter den Linden in Berlin Mitte (since 2013 under the direction of Jens Hillje and Şermin Langhoff, previously artistic director of the *Ballhaus Naunynstraße*) have been prominently involved in the postmigrant theater scene since the very beginnings of "postmigrant culture" in 2006.[2] In conjunction with other projects such as the *akademie der autodidakten* (organized by the *Ballhaus Naunynstraße*) or the Refugee Club Impulse (*Jugendtheaterbüro Moabit*), just to name a few, such initiatives need to be understood in the context of migration, minority, and, more recently, refugee discourses in Berlin. As I will highlight in my conclusion, Özdamar's experiences at the *Volksbühne,* as well as her creative work, might be considered an important precursor for such projects and offer a new impulse to look at such institutions and undertakings from a historical and literary perspective while simultaneously reevaluating Özdamar's novel through a contemporary lens.

To view Özdamar as a chronicler of postwar history is not an entirely new argument. *Seltsame Sterne* is perhaps most commonly read as a novel visibly concerned with history and memory, as longing not for the Berlin Babylon of the 1990s, the time period Katrina Sark focuses on in this volume, but perhaps as nostalgic for the Cold War era, the subject of Stefanie Eisenhuth and Scott H. Krause's chapter. Critics have focused on the novel's preoccupation with the Nazi past, the events surrounding 1968 and leading up to German reunification, as well as GDR history.[3] They have argued that Özdamar "preserv[es] for contemporary German culture the disappeared world of the GDR in the 1970s"[4] or that she creates a "countermemory" to dominant memory discourses.[5] Laura Bradley is spot on in positing that the narrator "recover[s] the past" (the Weimar Republic, Holocaust, 1968) and "capture[s] the present," which would be 1976/77, compelling today's readers to piece together these diverse elements and bring them into dialogue with their own pasts and presents.[6] Venkat Mani, too, concentrates on history and memory, suggesting that the task of minority histories like Özdamar's "is not only

a recollection and narration of the subordinated pasts but also account-
ing for the difference between such pasts."[7] Building on Gayatri Spivak,
Mani describes history as inserted and rehearsed—fragmented and incomplete—placed before the reader and immediately replaced by a protagonist whose "memory work is marked by severance and dislocation
from both nations."[8] Ela Gezen has further called attention to the aural
constitution of Berlin, the sounds and music that structure the narrator's
relationships in and to the city and therefore also to its history, especially as such affiliations coincide with theater. Silke Schade has argued
that the narrator reinvents the city as a space of home by endowing
public and private spaces with personal meanings. Finally, Withold Bonner has read the *Volksbühne* as a potential heterotopia where an ideal
socialism becomes possible, while Ottmar Ette insists that the settings
in all of Özdamar's novels are areas of oscillation between Turkey and
Germany, so that Istanbul and Berlin are written into one another in a
form of "transcultural interlacing and traversal."[9]

Bonner, Ette, and above all Gezen and Schade thus recognize the
importance of geographical detail. Yet while Ette and Schade center their
analyses on Özdamar's complete trilogy and only touch on the complexities of *Seltsame Sterne,* Bonner focuses narrowly on the space of
the theater, and Gezen is primarily concerned with the city's aural composition. She highlights inhabitation and walking but unlike Schade does
not read those themes through a lens of human or cultural geography.
Schade, on the other hand, identifies the narrator as a "keen observer of
German history" but does not interrogate this concept any further.[10] I
therefore position my chapter as a new reading of spatiality that brings
cultural geography to the forefront of an analysis of space and memory.
I believe that the novel envisions radically new possibilities for migrants
to attach meanings and symbolism to their everyday lived space. Specifically, I claim that Özdamar constructs a multistratified and textured
landscape that is constituted through narrative and includes memories,
thoughts, impressions, and personal experiences—the narrator's own
and those of others—and allusions to German history, all of which are
filtered through the narrator's first-person account. Unlike the protagonist in Jenny Erpenbeck's *Gehen, ging, gegangen* (*Going, Went, Gone,*
2015)—Richard, a German national and retired professor of languages
and literatures, as discussed in this volume by Marike Janzen—the
protagonist in *Seltsame Sterne* does not merely retell such narratives.
Rather, the narrator and first-person protagonist actively co-constructs
them and in doing so inscribes a transnational narrative into the master narrative of postwar Germany and offers, in Janzen's words, the

"non-citizen voice and perspective" that Erpenbeck's novel is lacking. Through the interlacing of these stories she is able to claim knowledge and ownership of Berlin and comes to establish herself as a resident of history and participant in the making of the city, a practice we could also ascribe to Berlin's postmigrant theater scene today. In the following I will examine how and why the narrator engages in this massive and complex memory work and investigate the implications of this cultural labor for how we might conceptualize the New Berlin today.

Recent studies in political, critical, human, and cultural geography at large have highlighted the dynamic roles of walkers, residents, and the city itself in forging a landscape imbued with and constructed through human perception, experience, and meaning.[11] As a particular type of landscape, the city is socially constructed, layered, and textured, a view that assumes humans and non-humans, as well as the urban space, as actors that constantly shape and reshape the natural and cultural topography. Together, these actors produce constantly shifting realities, narratives, memories, and historical, cultural, political, and symbolic meanings—staged, real, imagined, and contested.[12] The city may also be considered a text. Following Rachel Bowlby, a city can be read, misread, or remain completely illegible. Analyzing its texts (newspapers, signs, schedules), signifiers (buildings, monument, streets), and figures (commuters, tourists, *flâneurs,* residents, workers) requires certain skills and strategies. M. Christine Boyer speaks of the city and its effects as a radical artifice, as a representation to be looked at, experienced, and interpreted. Andreas Huyssen describes the city as a palimpsest and demands that it be embraced not merely as text but in its totality, its materiality and durability, overlapping and often competing temporalities, continuously changing meanings, and its subjective qualities, traces of memories, stories, and personal attitudes that should be read "historically, intertextually, constructively, and deconstructively at the same time."[13]

As a cultural, historical, and geographical discursive construct, the city is heavily fraught with meaning. Particularly in regard to nation-building, strategically useful master narratives and pasts tend to be emphasized, while less useful ones are erased and suppressed. For the British context, Raymond Williams has highlighted how literature has depicted the city as a center of moral depravity while envisioning the countryside as a place of rural innocence onto which a rooted sense of British identity is projected. Karen Till highlights the role of national symbols and monuments as a means for governments to claim or reclaim political control over space; and in the same vein capitals or other iconic cities—like Berlin in this anthology—are representative of its specific historical and geographical contexts promoting a narrative of the nation or a form of national memory that sustains itself through architecture, monuments, street names, symbols, rituals, beliefs, festivals, art, and literature; elements of what Pierre Nora has termed *lieux de mémoire*.[14] This tendency echoes Homi Bhabha's distinction between the pedagogical and performative aspects of the nation, which historian Eleni Bastéa defines as interdependent with the built environment. In his often-quoted article "Diaspora and Nation," Huyssen synthesizes such prominent trends in scholarship and asks how it might be possible to migrate into national memory or "into other pasts" that, although based on forgetting and distortion, are able to draw clear lines of exclusion and inclusion.[15] Juxtaposing national with diasporic memory, which, as Huyssen explains, is in its traditional sense "by definition cut-off, hybrid, displaced, split," he advises that diasporic and national memory inform each other and insists that memory, though aiming at cohesion and completeness, is always, in both forms, unreliable, fragmented, and cut off from the past.[16] He suggests that migrants connect to national memory by what he calls "*recherche*," a process of imaginatively investigating, researching, and comparing the past—the migrant's own past and the new cultural context—rather than a "recuperation" or reconstruction of precise memories.[17]

In looking at *Seltsame Sterne*, I am interested in similar questions: How can the migrant connect to the environment and get to know, or already know, other pasts and presents? How does literature imagine the histories and other stories—personal or public, central or peripheral, widely accepted or contested—that make up the larger cultural landscape of the city? And how does the novel help us arrive at a conceptualization of the city, its history, and its discourses on memory that is transnational and inclusive of its migrant population?

To answer these questions, it is crucial to recognize that the narrator in *Seltsame Sterne* is already familiar with the city. This is no longer the Turkish young adult or guest worker who has just started to learn German and spends most of her time with fellow Siemens workers in a Berlin *Wonaym* (the narrator's Turkish spelling for the German *Wohnheim*, an accommodation for factory workers) before returning to Istanbul in the midst of the turbulences of the 1960s.[18] This is the protagonist in her late twenties who had been dreaming of returning to Berlin all along; who speaks German fluently; whose sense of identity depends on the city; and whose love of Germany, Berlin, and theater turns Berlin into the place where she wants to be, live, and work. Accordingly, the novel's structure and narrative mode emulate the narrator's attitudes, experiences, and the spatial layout of the city. Like Berlin, the text is divided into two clearly separated yet interrelated parts: the first part comprises nonlinear narrative fragments, sprinkled with literary quotations and newspaper headlines, detailing the narrator's arrival in West Berlin, the events leading up to her departure in Turkey, and her first border crossings; the second part is conceptualized as a collection of diary entries, drawings, personal notes, and other texts chronicling her time at the *Volksbühne* and events taking place in East and West Berlin. The diary style lends the text authenticity and immediacy, relating events as they happen, and catapulting contemporary readers back into the 1970s. The narrative is motivated by the people and places encountered and driven forward by the narrator's walks through the city.

The narrator's migrant identity and "privileged position" as the female border crosser significantly shape the narrative and offer a unique way of accessing her past and present.[19] Holding neither a West nor an East German passport, she is seemingly unrestricted in her walks, free to wander and cross borders and encounter myriad people and places on both sides of the Wall. Her background makes her highly aware of the multiethnic makeup of both parts of the city, and memories of Turkey resurface on a daily basis, often triggered by the most common phenomena. On her walks, "the morning atmosphere and smell in the streets of East Berlin" remind her of her grandmother, and the "smell of coal and exhaust fumes" of Istanbul.[20] The narrator's view, however, is not that of the destitute nostalgic, nor does she reinscribe Istanbul onto Berlin. As Leslie Adelson claims, "the national culture of Turkey is not a necessary or primary frame of reference" for the contemporary literature of migration, and therefore Özdamar does not "represent a miniature of otherwise discrete Turkish worlds in Germany."[21] Istanbul and Berlin are "sutured together by acts of remembrance;"[22] and "Turkish fascists" or "military trucks" may haunt the narrator in her dreams.[23] Yet as Mani points out, she is very selective in what she revokes. She vividly and deliberately recalls personal stories connected to her family, friends, and grandmother, but she distances herself from the authoritarian rule that has taken a hold of Turkey. All of this confirms that the hometown and other cities we once inhabited are memorialized and embodied, traveling with the migrant and pervading the present moment, often serving as "the yardstick with which we measure all other cities."[24] As a carrier of what Astrid Erll has theorized as "travelling memory," the narrator debunks the common notion of diasporic memory as cut off and displaced and also discredits the claim that the migrant is severed from her homeland.[25]

Compared to those personal memories, the narrator's depiction of the majority of fellow Turks and Kurds in 1970s Berlin is factual at best. Most of the Turkish men are described as scheming to pick up German women. In the *Alextreff,* a cheap pub in Alexanderplatz, the narrator eavesdrops on their conversations: "They didn't know that I could understand them, so they spoke openly about women and sex."[26] The Kurd who engages her in a conversation at a party and confronts her about her Kurdish background is equally sleazy as he admits, "I'm glad there are so many homosexuals in Germany. I hope there will be more so that we can screw more German women."[27] Other Turks come across as more positive characters. In Wedding she watches Turks as they repair their cars, a pastime that her friend Peter describes as "Turks ... transforming into Germans"[28]; and there is Murat, the friendly bartender in one of the pubs. Littler explains Özdamar's portrayal of fellow countrymen as a strategy that "avoids presenting Turks or Kurds as victims" of racism.[29] Yet I believe it is more accurate to describe the narrator's attitude as an example of Adelson's notion of "touching tales": migrants and locals, their cultural contexts and stories, touch, overlap, or clash in often unpredictable ways.[30] In line with Mani's idea of "multiple and simultaneous affiliations and disaffiliations," relationships, friendships, and other attachments are not necessarily based on ethnicity or a shared background but are contingent on the proximity and openness of the city.[31] The descriptions of those encounters may often lack the precision of an introspective narrator—Mani describes them as merely placed before the reader and then immediately replaced—but as a strategic narrative device I read them as successfully constructing a sense of ordinariness and normalcy. They anticipate what Langhoff, Tunçay Kulaoğlu, and Wagner Carvalho (the latter two artistic directors of the *Ballhaus Naunynstraße*), in discussing the postmigrant theater scene in Berlin, envision as "überflüssig": a time "when diversity has become natural. In life and on stage" (*Wenn Vielfalt selbstverständlich geworden ist. Im Leben wie auf der Bühne*).[32] Most people encountered in the novel are from a place outside Berlin or outside Germany so that Berlin in the 1970s—East and West alike—materializes as a diverse, transnational, transethnic, and transcultural open space where migrants and other newcomers have become an integral part of the cityscape. The narrator's ability to easily cross back and forth between the two halves of the city contributes to this sense of unboundedness, imaginatively exposes the myth of a completely self-contained and homogeneous nation or national memory, and foreshadows the cosmopolitan openness the New Berlin projects today.

Özdamar's representation of fellow Turks, other minorities, and Germans and her seeming lack of specificity further suggest that the narrator's allegiance is with the city and with specific places within it rather than with its people.[33] Most critics depict her as a detached observer, similar to Baudelaire's *flâneur*, "interested, but not excited; disengaged and studiedly detached, but not aloof," yet they overlook that one of the *flâneur*'s key attributes is that he, more so than others, understands and participates in the making of the city.[34] In Bowlby's sense, the narrator is a prototypical urban figure: street names, neighborhoods, buildings, advertisements, graffiti, prints on cigarette packs and various other consumer goods, films, theater performances, words, images, ideas, stories, memories, and other elements of "the language of the street" constantly demand her attention.[35] Faced with a sensory overload of information, she presents the reader with those random texts as she actively negotiates and co-constructs them.

The first pages of the novel are crucial for this argument. They situate the narrator in a particular historical, cultural, and geographical landscape and introduce Özdamar's technique of uncovering the memories of an active past—the narrator's present and more immediate past—a process that operates vis-à-vis the buildings encountered on her daily walks. The novel starts in medias res. The protagonist wakes up in a cold apartment to the sound of a barking dog, which is the first of many references to German or European literature—here, as Littler convincingly argues, to Austrian writer Ingeborg Bachmann's story "The Barking."[36] To block out the noise, she recites an Else Lasker-Schüler poem she had memorized the night before and the first lines of which lend the novel its title. Mani interprets the reference to Lasker-Schüler as the narrator's search for or rehearsal of a subaltern past—Lasker-Schüler was Jewish and fascinated by Middle Eastern culture—and conceives of this brief recitation as an effort to allude to German history that is incomplete and immediately aborted. What the two female writers whose ghosts are conjured up in the first paragraph have in common, however, is that they are considered canonical figures of German literature, yet they defy a simple classification as German. I therefore read this double nod at these two prominent female writers as a first attempt toward pointing out the constructedness of a national narrative or national memory in *Seltsame Sterne* and as affirmation of the possibility that Özdamar and her narrator can inhabit this space too.

Inserted into this intertextual literary landscape are numerous references to geography, history, politics, and culture coalescing in the *Wohngemeinschaft*—or *WG*—a shared living community in West Berlin.

Located "in an old working class neighborhood of Berlin" on a defunct factory floor on top of a shop for seamstresses and ironers, the flat where she lives is shared with seven roommates.[37] These men and women are representatives of the German student and feminist movements of 1968, and they echo the protagonist's own political background and leftist leanings. During the time of the Weimar Republic, communists used to fight in this neighborhood, as her friend Josef from Zurich tells her, and in the more recent past, the previous residents were members of the AA-commune, followers of Otto Mühl, a controversial activist and fervent critic of bourgeois family values. She refers to the lamp in the living room as "a monument to the time of the AA commune," its crookedness and broken light bulbs forever testifying to the activities of the former inhabitants.[38] Other objects she mentions are a "German sausage with frozen ketchup," a Christmas tree, Karl Marx's *Capital,* and newspaper headlines referring to events in Spain, Angola, Vietnam, Italy, and Germany.[39] There is furthermore the "American military underwear" left behind by the commune that, although it can be bought cheaply in the military shop across the street, alludes to the Allied Forces occupying Berlin after World War II.[40] She mentions in passing that one roommate's father was a Nazi and that another roommate failed to prove that he was a pacifist when trying to avoid German military service. Interspersed with these seemingly random impressions are the number 6 million, Hitler, the Stauffenberg plot, and memories of Istanbul kindled by the clothes she finds in the closets. She then ascends to the rooftop terrace, allegedly a former meeting place for members of the RAF. From there she can see the moon and stars over Berlin, another flicker of Lasker-Schüler's poem, and then in the distance the "television tower of East Berlin" which immediately reminds her of the *Volksbühne* in East Berlin where she is a trainee.[41]

It is worth focusing at length on the first pages of the novel—and on the description of the *WG,* in particular—as they set the tone for all that follows. In an approach reminiscent of Gaston Bachelard's *The Poetics of Space,* the narrator's account of the *WG* is not so much a description as it is an examination and systematic excavation of layers of meaning—akin to the digging metaphor that is frequently used to describe the relationship to the past. As Till points out, "[the] past is never settled, sedimented, neatly arranged in horizontal layers," and, similarly, the physical and imaginary expedition through the house (and later the streets of Berlin) is unstructured.[42] The protagonist's thoughts and memories are not neatly organized but drift off, guided by the objects she encounters and decodes and by the spatial arrangement and texture of the building. She neither catalogues facts nor simply reproduces someone else's stories and memories but communicates those stories as they are manifest in place and as they are personally meaningful for her. This process resonates with Walter Benjamin's writings on memory, summarized by Till as follows:

> For Benjamin memory is not just information that individuals recall or stories being retold in the present. It is not layered time situated in the landscape. Rather, memory is the self-reflexive act of contextualizing and continuously digging for the past through place. It is a process of continually making and re-membering the past in the present rather than a process of discovering objective historical "facts."[43]

Phenomenological approaches to geography and anthropology further describe places as vehicles of knowledge. Edward S. Casey, for instance, understands place as intricately intertwined with the body. "There is no knowing or sensing a place except by being in that place, and to be in a place is to be in a position to perceive it."[44] He claims that places "gather," rather than amass or accumulate, material and imaginary objects, experiences, histories, languages, thoughts, and memories that emerge as "local knowledge,"[45] which resonates with Till's demand that places be viewed not as containers but as "fluid mosaics and moments of memory, matter, metaphor, scene, and experience."[46] In a novel in which dwelling places are constructed as representative of German and European political and cultural history, this process is doubly significant. In his influential essay "Building Dwelling Thinking," Heidegger conceptualizes dwelling as the essential way of being in the world, and similarly Kenneth Olwig, in his phenomenological study of landscape, speaks of dwelling as an embodied experience and of "the merging of body and senses that occurs in dwelling" that creates the "woven material" of landscape through an active "doing" instead of a removed "performing on" the landscape.[47] By inhabiting specific places within the city, the narrator becomes a part of this "woven material" and actively contributes to the production of these places and the city as a whole. She has access to and participates in "local knowledge" and epitomizes the idea of collective memory as social and shared, or of shared cultural memories—artifacts, objects, symbols, houses. Paradigmatic of Erll's idea of traveling memory, the narrator espouses a perspective that goes "*across* and *beyond* cultures (emphasis in original)" and nations as she constantly interweaves memories of Turkey and references to East and West Germany and European history at large.[48] Keith H. Basso further contends that the relationship between places and individuals is reciprocal and dynamic and that "places possess a marked capacity for triggering acts of self-reflection, inspiring thoughts about who one presently is, or memories of who one used to be, or musings on who one might become."[49] In a process that he labels "interanimation," places speak to and are at the same time animated by the thoughts and feelings of people passing through or inhabiting that place, which is an accurate characterization of how the narrator experiences the city.

The effect of interanimation is tangible in the description of the *WG* but becomes more evident after the narrator leaves the apartment. Like a scene out of a fairy tale, every object she passes on her walks is awakened or animated by her gaze and touch. Down the street she first passes by a brothel. Turkish men are waiting outside, and the sign on the door reads "milk store," either a remnant of an old shop that is now gone or the name of the current establishment.[50] On the commuter train that moves "like an animal that keeps showing itself, disappearing, and reappearing in the landscape," she passes several discontinued train stations she lists by name.[51] Recalling a memory of a previous train ride, she bestows the train with a strange familiarity and individuality as she thinks back to an old woman she once saw on a train, a man masturbating, and fallen German soldiers and their widows. She picks up a newspaper only to discard it after she rips out a picture of Pasolini who, according to the headlines, has just been viciously killed. Finally, she crosses over to the East, pays for her visa—five marks—and exchanges money for "Eastern currency."[52] Here the sense of interanimation is heightened. The items in the shop windows, the cars and people remind her of a museum, quiet and sleepy, as if she had slipped into a different world or a different past, a "fairy tale."[53] Again, she comments on people's faces, street names, the *Trabant,* the *Brechttheater,* and the bridge over the Spree, and she obsessively reads from signs and packaging. Eventually, she passes by a man walking his dog, a textual strategy that ties this encounter back in with the beginning of the novel. It connects East and West, which, although the narrator at this point claims that she cannot imagine the two as one, are nevertheless linked through her walks and experiences.

The *WG* in the West is complemented by similarly symbolic places in the East, dwelling places for the most part and personally meaningful places the narrator inhabits for a longer period of time. There are, for instance, Katrin's apartment in a "Plattenbau," a grey high-rise typical of Soviet architecture, Gabi Gysi's place in the Prenzlauer Berg neighborhood and later in Pankow, and Benno Besson's apartment in Köpenick.[54] Other sites, and the theater in particular, share attributes commonly as-

tinctive process of knowledge production that could also be examined in terms of what Janzen, in this volume, describes as "a specifically German tradition of noninstrumental intellectual self-affirmation" or *Bildung*.[59] Applying the notion of *Bildung* to *Seltsame Sterne* could offer yet another model of *Bildung* as achieved by the non-German resident, a bottom-up transnational and local production of knowledge that is interdependent with and always already a part of the city and specific public and private spaces within it. The novel thus differs markedly from Janzen's examples earlier in this volume of the *internationales literaturfestival berlin* (international literature festival berlin), or *ilb,* where *Bildung* materializes as a top-down process imposed by the city as a state-sanctioned actor or Erpenbeck's version of *Bildung* as the integration of refugee knowledge into German space via a German citizen.

Similar to the narrator's walks, the *Volksbühne,* too, emerges as an important contact zone between residents and actors, history, and current events, foreshadowing the work of cultural institutions like the *Ballhaus Naunynstraße,* HAU, and *Maxim Gorki Theater* today. Indicative of the pedagogical and performative double narrative of the nation as described by Bhabha, the plays performed—such as Heiner Müller's *Die Bauern (The Farmers),* Manfred Karge and Matthias Langhoff's *Der Bürgergeneral (The Citizen General,* a play by Goethe), or Benno Besson's *Hamlet*—lend historical depth. *Die Bauern,* which depicts the situation of East German farmers after the socialist land reform in the late 1940s, displays a linear pedagogical narrative and idealized view of GDR history that is in line with the antifascist and anticapitalist agenda of GDR politics. At the same time, the productions call attention to the performative and potentially subversive nature of daily life, and to censorship and criticism. Bradley refers to the theater in the GDR as an "enlightened enclave," a public space where it was possible to stage performances and host political meetings directed at covertly criticizing the regime.[60] One character in *Die Bauern,* for instance, picks up a magazine from the West and "reads out an article about the terror the SED regime exerts on the farmers"[61]; and Heiner Müller's comment that, compared to the West, "language is very powerful in East Berlin," through which he helps the narrator understand the audience's comic reaction to Hamlet's famous phrase "Something is rotten in the state of Denmark," points toward both censorship and revolt.[62] Mani interprets the focus on *Die Bauern* as an example of how the narrator "imagines inserting herself into the history of the GDR" and how the novel records and stages history and thematizes the "experience of staging history, captured in the narrator's notes on rehearsals."[63] But the stress on performances is also the mechanism by which the novel emphasizes the constructedness of history and need for multiple histories. The actors actively contribute to this process by performing narratives that are embedded within a larger German or European tradition—like the plays by Goethe or Shakespeare—and their own, like *Die Bauern*. The protagonist's observations on her first day at the theater, as well as her assertion that the rehearsal is not a "substitute for history lessons" touch on this intersection[64]:

> "So these are the people," I thought, "who were born here, walked across the grand boulevards, and grew up in the old houses damaged by the war, who fell in love here and took their children to the kindergarten in the mornings, and who have now come here to play themselves."[65]

The narrator's work as an actress and her engagement with the *Volksbühne* is another way of connecting to the active past. Through her creative cultural labor she co-constructs the *Volksbühne* as a lived space and participates in the performance of everyday life in the GDR and Berlin.

Along those lines, current cultural projects also need to be viewed as interventions in or contributions to contemporary cultural and political discourses in the New Berlin where, arguably, minority and refugee perspectives and voices have become a part of everyday life. Janzen's example of the *ilb* as "an island that draws on and reinforces a German national project" preempts such possibilities.[66] But local theater stages and state-sponsored projects other than the *ilb,* such as the conference and festival *Interventionen: Refugees in Art and Education* (inaugurated in 2015 at the Podewil in Berlin Mitte, an old baroque palace; organized by *Kulturprojekte Berlin* and funded through the Ministry of Culture and Media and the Berlin Senate), help conceptualize the New Berlin as a creative space where Germans and non-Germans work together toward a participatory and performative project of cultural integration and *Bildung.*

The references to performances, acting, and the stage in *Seltsame Sterne* are not limited to the *Volksbühne.* Mirroring Özdamar's own career as an actress and playwright, the narrator attended acting school in Istanbul prior to returning to Germany. Before she comes back to Germany, her friend Josef, who coordinates her living arrangements in West Berlin, advises her to think of the *WG* as a "theater stage," turning both parts of Berlin into one stage where she is at the same time the subject and object of her own narrative and history.[67] Just as Boyer predicts in *The City of Collective Memory,* in which she relates to the city as "the theater of our memory" where "[as] spectators, we travel through the city observing its architecture and constructed spaces, shifting contemporary scenes and reflections from the past until they thicken into a personalized vision," the protagonist emerges as a spectator, actress, walker, and storyteller, and as a producer of and active participant in spatiality and history.[68] This is supported by Gezen, who adds that for Özdamar the act of writing is itself a process of staging, offering her "an opportunity for reinvention and rediscovery through which she can represent the city as a product of her own experiences."[69]

As the centerpiece of the city, the Wall occupies a special position in the narrator's travels through Berlin. Surprisingly, however, compared to other less historically relevant places, the Wall lacks historical depth. It is empty and functional in the novel, and there is no mention of the violence and the numerous deaths associated with the monument. Instead, the protagonist constructs her own stories of visa applications, train rides, Wall acquaintances, smuggled goods, and flirtatious banter with the guards, thereby subverting the authority of the Wall and its dividing function by turning it into a point of intersections. As long as she resides in the West and works in the East she easily crosses back and forth, and later, after her work visa for the East has expired, she can return without difficulty. She has "normalized" the Wall, according to her roommate.[70] Margaret Littler describes the narrator as "one who has inhabited the border and integrated into her way of being in Berlin," an argument that becomes even more powerful if we consider walking as an embodied act that physically connects the migrant to the city.[71] Critics have likened the crossing of the border to instant amnesia as the narrator repeatedly remarks that she tends to forget the other half of the city and that "[i]magining the two as one was just as difficult as imagining Freddy Quinn and Mozart on the same record."[72] Yet this does not diminish the fact that the divided city is connected through her walks, similar to the Berlin she can see from the rooftops, the Berlin covered under a layer of snow, or the Berlin seen from the stars in the novel's title. In the spirit of Boyer and Benjamin, I further argue that the constant crossings result in productive juxtapositions. According to Boyer,

> Benjamin felt that random historical objects from the past such as the debris to be found in flea markets or discrete historical events ... must be allowed to violently collide with others, so that the present may achieve insight and critical awareness into what once had been.[73]

Like the music of Freddy Quinn and Mozart might be found at the same flea market, the narrator combines seemingly random and yet interrelated spatial and temporal stories of East and West Berlin. A modern extension of the *flâneur,* the *flâneuse* becomes a "detective" and an "observer" of space.[74] In a spiral approach, references to politics, history, and culture, personal stories, and memories are constantly supplemented with new perspectives—espoused by the narrator herself and by the people encountered in East and West. Those observations enable the narrator to gain critical insights into Cold War realities.

Making up the crux of the novel, the Wall joins the plethora of other historically resonant places such as the Karl-Marx-Allee and bookstore, Rosa-Luxemburg Platz, Spandau and Stammheim prison, Weimar, Buchenwald, numerous pubs, and other public sites, most of which could be classified as examples of Nora's *lieux de mémoire,* "sites of memory" and substitutes for the lost "real environments of memory."[75] Özdamar might as well have included the sites Eisenhuth and Krause explore in this volume—Checkpoint Charlie, the former Ministry for State Security, and the *Tempelhofer Feld.* Those sites are certainly implicated in the novel's numerous allusions to postwar history and, if mentioned by name, would have further attested to the cultural and historical richness of Berlin's urban memoryscape (before "touristification") and called attention to Berlin's transnational entanglements that Eisenhuth and Krause highlight in their conclusion. Similarly, the sites discussed in the novel are more than mere physical locations. They are "material, symbolic, and functional" and encompass events, rituals, symbols, legacies, histories, and memories that Nora considers typical for a national context.[76] His four-volume monumental work on French history and culture includes chapters on Charlemagne, the Alsace region, the *code civil,* wine, the café, and the Larousse dictionary. For the German context, Etienne François and Hagen Schulze edited a similarly ambitious volume, *Deutsche Erinnerungsorte* (*German Sites of Memory*), in which they dedicate chapters to Goethe, Schiller, Heine, Rosa Luxemburg, the Grimms' fairy tales, the German mark, the German forest, *Schrebergärten,* the Stasi, 1968, Weimar, and the Berlin Wall, all of which are concepts that also permeate the narrator's lived space. However, François and Schulze do not include the guest-worker treaties, the reformation of German citizenship law, or any other developments related to the social and cultural impacts of postwar migration as they consider what constitutes, who produces, and who is impacted by German places of memory. Contrary to the fact that "[m]ultiple generations of migrants lived through every major event in the history of West Germany," migrants and their contributions to German history and culture are strikingly absent in the master narrative of the postwar period.[77] The novel therefore challenges dominant ways of thinking about memory and the exclusive construction of German national history by embracing a transnational or transcultural view. The narrator brings together minority and majority histories—vis-à-vis her migrant subjectivity and through the diverse characters encountered in the novel—and various aspects of German and non-German high and low culture. These are not limited to East or West and include vastly eclectic references to music, literature, art, theater, film, politics, geography, history, and culture, which, in line with Huyssen's notion of "*recherche,*" are explored creatively, historically, and intertextually.

The narrator is thus not an outsider to German memory discourses but firmly emplaced within them. As I have shown, local contexts, knowledge, and memories can be known, experienced, voiced, lived, and contested by consciously being in and sensing place; and by residing in and passing through specific places in Berlin, the narrator emerges as a resident of history and active participant in such local knowledges. Drawing on references to Turkey, Germany, and European or Western culture at large, Özdamar inscribes a transnational narrative into the master narrative of Germany. She illustrates that already in the 1970s, Berlin—both East and West—was a diverse and cosmopolitan space where locals and non-locals, Germans and non-Germans, had become an integral part of the cityscape, "überflüssig" in the words of Langhoff and Kulaoğlu. It is therefore critical to understand the New Berlin today as a product of over fifty years of migration history. Visitors and locals should not be distracted by the newly restored inner city showcasing proud symbols of German or Prussian history, such as the *Reichstag* building, Brandenburg Gate, Neue Wache Memorial, and soon the completely reconstructed Palace; they should not perceive of German division and reunification as a purely German phenomenon; and they should not just look for traces of immigration history in neighborhoods like Wedding, Kreuzberg, or Neukölln. Rather, visitors should look beyond the façades. As mentioned above, local theater venues and other projects such as the *akademie der autodidakten,* Refugee Club Impulse, or *Interventionen* need to be viewed in the context of migration and minority histories, including recent refugee movements, coalescing in the contemporary urban landscape.

In conclusion, I therefore want to call attention once again to Berlin's vibrant postmigrant theater scene and, above all, the *Maxim Gorki Theater* in Mitte, one of the oldest concert halls in Berlin. It is located across from the Prussian City Palace, which is under construction and will soon house the *Humboldtforum,* a museum and therefore a space of learning and knowledge production, despite the controversy surrounding its uncritical engagement with German colonialism. There, according to Janzen, "the 'non-German' is integrated into Germanness through *Bildung*," and the *Gorki*, as a visible expression of migration and minority discourses, physically challenges the idea of a homogeneous German nation in the public sphere.[78] Overshadowed by symbols of German history and agents of German *Bildung* such as the Humboldt University or the planned *Humboldtforum*, the *Gorki Theater* offers a more inclusive concept of *Bildung* as practiced by a wide range of writers, actors, artists, activists, and other practitioners who foreground a multicultural and heterogeneous German society. Places like the *Gorki Theater* physically epitomize the New Berlin as a space of transnational— or Turkish-German—hi/stories,[79] sustained transcultural exchange, and cultural integration, a historical and cultural product whose origins, as Özdamar's literary example reminds us, need to be traced back to postwar realities.

Christiane Steckenbiller is assistant professor of German at Colorado College. She received her PhD and MA from the University of South Carolina and an MA from the Otto-Friedrich-Universität Bamberg. Her research focuses on contemporary German literature, with an emphasis on migration and minority discourses, cultural geography, and urban studies.

Notes

1. Emine Sevgi Özdamar, *Das Leben ist eine Karawanserei, hat zwei Türen, aus einer kam ich rein, aus der anderen ging ich raus* (Cologne, 1992), *Die Brücke vom goldenen Horn* (Cologne, 1998), and *Seltsame Sterne starren zur Erde: Wedding–Pankow 1976/77* (Cologne, 2003), also published as *Sonne auf halbem Weg: Die Istanbul-Berlin-Trilogie* (Cologne, 2006).

2. Following Langhoff's move to the *Maxim Gorki Theater*, Tunçay Kulaoğlu and Wagner Carvalho took over as artistic directors of the *Ballhaus Naunyn-straße*. The beginnings of postmigrant theater are generally attributed to the 2006 "Beyond Belonging" festival taking place under the motto "post-migrant culture" at the Berliner HAU. The festival was organized by Langhoff and co-organized by Kulaoğlu. See Onur Suzan Kömürcü Nobrega "'We Bark from the Third Row': The Position of the Ballhaus Naunynstraße in Berlin's Cultural Landscape and the Funding of Cultural Diversity Work," in *50 Jahre türkische Arbeitsmigration in Deutschland*, ed. Şeyda Ozil, Michael Hofmann, and Yasemin Dayıoğlu-Yücel (V&R unipress, 2011), 91–112, and Ceyda Nurtsch, "Zehn Jahre postmigrantisches Theater in Deutschland: 'Bis wir überflüssig sind,'" *Qantara.de*, November 9, 2016, accessed January 9, 2017, http://de.qantara.de/inhalt/zehn-jahre-postmigrantisches-theater-in-deutschland-bis-wir-ueberfluessig-sind.

3. See Kader Konuk, "Taking on German and Turkish History: Emine Sevgi Özdamar's *Seltsame Sterne*," *Gegenwartsliteratur: A German Studies Yearbook* 6 (2007): 232–56, for the Nazi past; Susanne Rinner, *The German Student Movement and the Literary Imagination: Transnational Memories of Protest and Dissent* (New York, 2013) for references to 1968; and Margaret Littler, "Cultural Memory and Identity Formation in the Berlin Republic," in *Contemporary German Fiction: Writing in the Berlin Republic,* ed. Stuart Taberner (Cambridge, 2007), 177–95, for German reunification. See Laura Bradley, "Recovering the Past and Capturing the Present: Özdamar's *Seltsame Sterne starren zur Erde,*" in *New German Literature: Life-Writing and Dialogue with the Arts,* ed. Julian Preece, Frank Finlay, and Ruth J. Owen (Oxford, 2007), 283–95; Laura Bradley, "From Berlin to Prenzlau: Representations of GDR Theater in Film and Literature," in *The GDR Remembered: Representations of the East German State since 1989,* ed. Nick Hodgin and Caroline Pearce (Rochester, 2011), 19–36; Littler, "Cultural Memory," 177–95; and John Pizer, "The Continuation of Countermemory: Emine Sevgi Özdamar's *Seltsame Sterne starren zur Erde,*" in *German Literature in a New Century: Trends, Traditions, Transitions, Transformations,* ed. Katharina Gerstenberger and Patricia Herminghouse (New York, 2008), 135–52 for GDR history.

4. Littler, "Cultural Memory," 183.

5. Pizer, "Continuation of Countermemory," 135.

6. Bradley, "Recovering the Past," 283.

7. Venkat Mani, *Cosmopolitical Claims: Turkish-German Literatures from Nadolny to Pamuk* (Iowa City, 2007), 91.

8. Ibid., 117. Mani here refers to Spivak's claim in "Acting Bits/Identity Talk" (1992) that experience is always staged.

9. Ottmar Ette, "Urbanity and Literature: Cities as Transareal Spaces of Movement in Assia Djebar, Emine Sevgi Özdamar and Cécile Wajsbrot," *European Review* 19, no. 3 (2011): 376.

10. Silke Schade, "Rewriting Home and Migration: Spatiality in the Narratives of Emine Sevgi Özdamar," in *Spatial Turns: Space, Place, and Mobility in German Literary and Visual Culture,* ed. Jaimey Fisher and Barbara Mennel (Amsterdam, 2010), 334.

11. See Tim Cresswell, *Place: A Short Introduction* (Malden, MA, 2004); Henri Lefebvre, *The Production of Space,* trans. Donald Nicholson-Smith (Oxford, 1991); Doreen Massey, *For Space* (London, 2005) and *Space, Place, and Gender* (Minneapolis, 1994); Edward W. Soja, *Postmodern Geographies: The Reassertion of Space in Critical Social Theory* (London, 1989); Karen E. Till, *The New Berlin: Memory, Politics, Place* (Minneapolis, 2005).

12. See Kenneth R. Olwig, "Performing on the Landscape versus Doing the Landscape: Perambulatory Practices, Sight and the Sense of Belonging," in *Ways of Walking: Ethnography and Practice on Foot,* ed. Tim Ingold and Jo Lee Vergunst (Hampshire, 2008), 81–92.

13. Andreas Huyssen, "Diaspora and Nation: Migration into Other Pasts," *New German Critique* 88 (2003): 7.
14. See Karen E. Till, "Places of Memory," in *A Companion to Political Geography,* ed. John A. Agnew, Katharyne Mitchell, and Gerard Toal (Malden, 2008), 289–301; Pierre Nora, "Between Memory and History: Les Lieux de Mémoire," *Representations* 26 (1989): 7–24.
15. Huyssen, "Diaspora and Nation," 147. Huyssen here rephrases a question that Zafer Şenocak had already posed in 1993 in "Deutschland: Heimat für Türken?," cowritten with Bülent Tulay, published in Zafer Şenocak, *Atlas des tropischen Deutschland: Essays* (Berlin, 1993). Intended as both a call to Turks to critically engage with German history and to Germans to embrace the possibility of shared affiliations between Germans and Turks, Şenocak had asked, "Does immigrating to Germany not also mean immigrating into its most recent past?" All translations here are mine unless otherwise noted.
16. Huyssen, "Diaspora and Nation," 152.
17. Ibid.
18. Özdamar's first two novels focus on the narrator's experiences as a child and young adult in Turkey and her first arrival in Berlin as a Turkish guest worker.
19. Schade, "Rewriting Home and Migration," 333.
20. Özdamar, *Seltsame Sterne,* 81.
21. Leslie Adelson, *The Turkish Turn in Contemporary German Literature: Toward a New Critical Grammar of Migration* (New York, 2005), 13.
22. Ela Gezen, "Staging Berlin: Emine Sevgi Özdamar's *Seltsame Sterne starren zur Erde,*" *German Studies Review* 38, no. 1 (2015): 88.
23. Özdamar, *Seltsame Sterne,* 115, 113.
24. Eleni Bastéa, ed., *Memory and Architecture* (Albuquerque, 2004), 4.
25. Astrid Erll, "Travelling Memory," *Parallax* 17, no. 4 (2011): 4–18.
26. Özdamar, *Seltsame Sterne,* 43.
27. Ibid., 41.
28. Ibid., 76.
29. Littler, "Cultural Memory," 186.
30. Adelson, *Turkish Turn in Contemporary German Literature,* 20.
31. Mani, *Cosmopolitical Claims,* 7.
32. According to Carvalho quoted in Nurtsch, "Zehn Jahre postmigrantisches Theater in Deutschland." For the concept of "Überflüssigkeit" also see the interview with Langhoff and Kulaoğlu in *Das Drama nach dem Drama: Verwandlungen dramatischer Formen in Deutschland seit 1945,* ed. Artur Pełka and Stefan Tigges (transcript, 2011), 408.
33. The narrator is also personally and emotionally attached to Berlin, and proclaims these attachments regularly. Her perceptive descriptions of streets, buildings, and other urban sites suggest an aesthetic and emotional appreciation of the city, as well as a sense of familiarity and comfort.
34. Mani, *Cosmopolitical Claims,* 103.

35. Özdamar, *Seltsame Sterne,* 105.
36. See Littler, "Cultural Memory," 177–95.
37. Özdamar, *Seltsame Sterne,* 48.
38. Ibid., 11.
39. Ibid., 13.
40. Ibid., 12.
41. Ibid., 14.
42. Till, *New Berlin,* 10.
43. Ibid., 8.
44. Edward S. Casey, "How to Get from Space to Place in a Fairly Short Stretch of Time: Phenomenological Prolegomena," in *Senses of Place,* ed. Steven Feld and Keith H. Basso (Santa Fe, 1996), 18.
45. Ibid., 18.
46. Till, *New Berlin,* 8.
47. Olwig, "Performing on the Landscape," 84.
48. Erll, "Travelling Memory," 9.
49. Keith H. Basso, "Wisdom Sits in Places: Notes on a Western Apache Landscape," in *Senses of Place,* ed. Steven Feld and Keith H. Basso (Santa Fe, 1996), 55.
50. Özdamar, *Seltsame Sterne,* 16.
51. Ibid., 16.
52. Ibid., 18.
53. Ibid., 18.
54. Ibid., 79.
55. Ibid., 230.
56. Ibid., 202.
57. Ibid., 51, 52.
58. Ibid., 202.
59. Janzen, "Berlin's International Literature Festival."
60. Bradley, "From Berlin to Prenzlau," 29.
61. Özdamar, *Seltsame Sterne,* 107.
62. Ibid., 215.
63. Mani, *Cosmopolitical Claims,* 114.
64. Özdamar, *Seltsame Sterne,* 88.
65. Ibid., 81.
66. Janzen, "Berlin's International Literature Festival."
67. Ibid., 48.
68. M. Christine Boyer, *The City of Collective Memory: Its Historical Imagery and Architectural Entertainments* (Cambridge, 2001), 31–32.
69. Gezen, "Staging Berlin," 85.
70. Özdamar, *Seltsame Sterne,* 244.
71. Littler, "Cultural Memory," 60.
72. Özdamar, *Seltsame Sterne*, 18.
73. Boyer, *City of Collective Memory,* 5.

74. Walter Benjamin, *The Arcades Project,* ed. Rolf Tiedemann, trans. Howard Eiland and Kevin McLaughlin (Cambridge, 1999), 422.
75. Pierre Nora, "Between Memory and History," 7.
76. Ibid., 18.
77. Rita Chin, *The Guest Worker Question in Postwar Germany* (Cambridge, 2007), 12.
78. Janzen, "Berlin's International Literature Festival."
79. I here take my cues from a 2011 *Colloquia Germanica* special issue, an important contribution to Turkish-German studies, for which the guest editors Ela Gezen and Berna Gueneli compiled a series of essays under the motto "Transnational Hi/Stories: Turkish-German Texts and Contexts." I, too, see my work as fitting into that narrative as an attempt to "offer new insights into the most recent Turkish-German entanglements, encounters, and exchanges." Ela Gezen and Berna Gueneli, "Introduction: Transnational Hi/Stories – Turkish-German Texts and Contexts," in *Colloquia Germanica* 44, no. 4 (2011): 378.

Bibliography

Adelson, Leslie. *The Turkish Turn in Contemporary German Literature: Toward a New Critical Grammar of Migration.* New York: Palgrave Macmillan, 2005.

Bachelard, Gaston. *The Poetics of Space.* Translated by Maria Jolas. Boston: Beacon Press, 2008.

Basso, Keith H. "Wisdom Sits in Places: Notes on a Western Apache Landscape." In *Senses of Place,* edited by Steven Feld and Keith H. Basso, 53–90. Santa Fe: School of American Research Press, 1996.

Bastéa, Eleni, ed. *Memory and Architecture.* Albuquerque: University of New Mexico Press, 2004.

Benjamin, Walter. *The Arcades Project.* Edited by Rolf Tiedemann. Translated by Howard Eiland and Kevin McLaughlin. Cambridge: Harvard University Press, 1999.

Bhabha, Homi. "DissemiNation: Time, Narrative and the Margins of the Modern Nation." In *The Location of Culture,* 139–70. London: Routledge, 1993.

Bonner, Withold. "Vom Cafe Cyprus zu Mitropa und Volksbühne: Räume bei Yadé Kara und Emine Sevgi Özdamar." In *Metropolen als Ort der Begegnung und Isolation: Interkulturelle Perspektiven auf den urbanen Raum als Sujet in Literatur und Film,* edited by Ernest W. B. Hess-Lüttich, Nilüfer Kuruyazici, and Seyda Ozil, 257–72. New York: Peter Lang, 2011.

Bowlby, Rachel. "Readable City." *PMLA* 122, no. 1 (2007): 306–9.

Boyer, M. Christine. *The City of Collective Memory: Its Historical Imagery and Architectural Entertainments.* Cambridge: MIT Press, 2001.

Bradley, Laura. "From Berlin to Prenzlau: Representations of GDR Theater in Film and Literature." In *The GDR Remembered: Representations of the East Ger-*

man State since 1989, edited by Nick Hodgin and Caroline Pearce, 19–36. Rochester: Camden House, 2011.

———. "Recovering the Past and Capturing the Present: Özdamar's *Seltsame Sterne starren zur Erde.*" In *New German Literature: Life-Writing and Dialogue with the Arts,* edited by Julian Preece, Frank Finlay, and Ruth J. Owen, 283–95. Oxford: Peter Lang, 2007.

Casey, Edward S. "How to Get from Space to Place in a Fairly Short Stretch of Time: Phenomenological Prolegomena." In *Senses of Place,* edited by Steven Feld and Keith H. Basso, 13–52. Santa Fe: School of American Research Press, 1996.

Chin, Rita. *The Guestworker Question in Postwar Germany.* Cambridge: Cambridge University Press, 2007.

Cresswell, Tim. *Place: A Short Introduction.* Malden: Wiley-Blackwell, 2004.

Erll, Astrid. "Travelling Memory." *Parallax* 17, no. 4 (2011): 4–18.

Erpenbeck, Jenny. *Gehen, ging, gegangen.* Munich: Albrecht Knaus Verlag, 2015.

Etienne, François, and Hagen Schulze, eds. *Deutsche Erinnerungsorte: in 3 Bänden.* München: Beck, 2017.

Ette, Ottmar. "Urbanity and Literature: Cities as Transareal Spaces of Movement in Assia Djebar, Emine Sevgi Özdamar and Cécile Wajsbrot." *European Review* 19, no. 3 (2011): 367–83.

Gezen, Ela, and Berna Gueneli. "Introduction: Transnational Hi/Stories—Turkish-German Texts and Contexts." *Colloquia Germanica* 44, no. 4 (2011): 377–81.

Gezen, Ela. "Staging Berlin: Emine Sevgi Özdamar's *Seltsame Sterne starren zur Erde.*" *German Studies Review* 38, no. 1 (2015): 83–96.

Heidegger, Martin. "Building Dwelling Thinking." In *Basic Writings,* edited by David Farrell Krell, 343–64. New York: Harper and Row, 1977.

Huyssen, Andreas. "Diaspora and Nation: Migration into Other Pasts." *New German Critique* 88 (2003): 147–64.

Kara, Yadé. *Selam Berlin.* Zurich: Diogenes, 2003.

Kömürcü Nobrega, Onur Suzan. "'We Bark from the Third Row': The Position of the Ballhaus Naunynstraße in Berlin's Cultural Landscape and the Funding of Cultural Diversity Work." In *50 Jahre Türkische Arbeitsmigration in Deutschland,* edited by Şeyda Ozil, Michael Hofmann, and Yasemin Dayıoğlu-Yücel, 91–112. Göttingen: V & R unipress, 2011.

Konuk, Kader. "Taking on German and Turkish History: Emine Sevgi Özdamar's *Seltsame Sterne.*" *Gegenwartsliteratur: A German Studies Yearbook* 6 (2007): 232–56.

Lefebvre, Henri. *The Production of Space.* Translated by Donald Nicholson-Smith. Oxford: Blackwell, 1991.

Littler, Margaret. "Cultural Memory and Identity Formation in the Berlin Republic." In *Contemporary German Fiction: Writing in the Berlin Republic,* edited by Stuart Taberner, 177–95. Cambridge: Cambridge University Press, 2007.

sociated with dwelling spaces. The narrator spends most of her time at the *Volksbühne* where she eats in the cafeteria and sleeps in the theater sauna when she is between apartments. There is a colleague's *Schrebergarten,* a garden plot outside the city, a cameraman's house in the forest, and a restaurant and hotel in Jena where Goethe, too, allegedly used to eat and spend the night. Most of these places are shared apartments where the narrator lives together with other Germans, and they all serve as intimate settings for group gatherings, excursions, and other close encounters.

Replicating the historical and political undergirdings of the West Berlin *WG*, the narratives unearthed in those places are equally representative of the sociocultural and political landscape of the GDR. Discussions of racism, antifascism, communism, and activism in the East substitute for similar conversations about politics in the West. The narrator overhears racist comments in both parts of the city; and references to terrorism in Western Germany are complemented by allusions to state violence and police surveillance in the East. The reader vicariously relives events related to the Red Army Faction, such as Ulrike Meinhof's suicide or the escape of four RAF women from the prison in Moabit, as well as Wolf Biermann's expatriation and the arrest of Rudolf Bahro in the GDR. Gabi, the narrator's roommate, even refers to Bahro as "representing for East Germany what Baader-Meinhof represented for West Germany before they incriminated themselves as the RAF," showing how historical events and cultural products in both parts of Germany are interrelated even before they are filtered through the narrator's subjectivity.[55] Monika Maron's, Heiner Müller's, and Gabi Gysi's conversations about women, Franz Josef Strauß, the "icy relationship between East and West," "the October revolution," and "the history of socialism"[56] correspond to discussions taking place in the West Berlin *WG* where the political magazine *Der Spiegel* is always accessible and where the narrator and her roommates talk about "typically German" thought patterns, "the young generation that ran off to West Berlin," Helmut Kohl's and Strauß's attitude toward the city, and stories about crossing into the East.[57] The narrator may not always be able to fully grasp the content of those discussions—in Gabi Gysi's apartment she feels like attending a "foreign language course"—yet Gabi and others sporadically take the time to explain to her the larger implications of those exchanges. Besides, events and stories are never presented as complete.[58] References to the activities of the RAF, for example, resurface throughout the text. Through walking, the narrator interlinks those elements and begins to construct a bigger and more comprehensive picture of the city, a dis-

———. "The Fall of the Wall as Nonevent in Works by Emine Sevgi Özdamar and Zafer Şenocak." *New German Critique: An Interdisciplinary Journal of German Studies* 116 (2012): 47–62.

Mani, B. Venkat. *Cosmopolitical Claims: Turkish-German Literatures from Nadolny to Pamuk.* Iowa City: University of Iowa Press, 2007.

Massey, Doreen. *For Space.* London: Sage, 2005.

———. *Space, Place, and Gender.* Minneapolis: University of Minnesota Press, 1994.

Nurtsch, Ceyda. "Zehn Jahre Postmigrantisches Theater in Deutschland: 'Bis wir überflüssig sind.'" *Qantara.de.* Accessed January 9, 2017. http://de.qantara .de/inhalt/zehn-jahre-postmigrantisches-theater-in-deutschland-bis-wir-ueberfluessig-sind.

Nora, Pierre. "Between Memory and History: Les Lieux de Mémoire." *Representations* 26 (Spring 1989): 7–24.

Olwig, Kenneth R. "Performing on the Landscape versus Doing the Landscape: Perambulatory Practices, Sight and the Sense of Belonging." In *Ways of Walking: Ethnography and Practice on Foot,* edited by Tim Ingold and Jo Lee Vergunst, 81–92. Hampshire: Ashgate, 2008.

Özdamar, Emine Sevgi. *Das Leben ist eine Karawanserei hat zwei Türen, aus einer kam ich rein, aus der anderen ging ich raus.* Cologne: Kiepenheuer & Witsch, 1992

———. *Die Brücke vom goldenen Horn.* Cologne: Kiepenheuer & Witsch, 1998.

———. *Seltsame Sterne starren zur Erde: Wedding–Pankow 1976/77.* Cologne: Kiepenheuer & Witsch, 2003.

———. *Sonne auf halbem Weg: Die Istanbul-Berlin-Trilogie.* Cologne: Kiepenheuer & Witsch, 2006.

Pełka, Artur, and Stefan Tigges, eds. *Das Drama nach dem Drama: Verwandlungen dramatischer Formen in Deutschland seit 1945.* Bielefeld: transcript, 2011.

Pizer, John. "The Continuation of Countermemory: Emine Sevgi Özdamar's *Seltsame Sterne starren zur Erde.*" In *German Literature in a New Century: Trends, Traditions, Transitions, Transformations,* edited by Katharina Gerstenberger and Patricia Herminghouse, 135–52. New York: Berghahn, 2008.

Rinner, Susanne. *The German Student Movement and the Literary Imagination: Transnational Memories of Protest and Dissent.* New York: Berghahn Books, 2013.

Schade, Silke. "Rewriting Home and Migration: Spatiality in the Narratives of Emine Sevgi Özdamar." In *Spatial Turns: Space, Place, and Mobility in German Literary and Visual Culture,* edited by Jaimey Fisher and Barbara Mennel, 319–41. Amsterdam: Rodopi, 2010.

Şenocak, Zafer. *Atlas des Tropischen Deutschland: Essays.* Berlin: Babel, 1992.

———. *Gefährliche Verwandtschaft.* Munich: Babel, 1998.

Soja, Edward W. *Postmodern Geographies: The Reassertion of Space in Critical Social Theory.* London: Verso, 1989.

Till, Karen E. *The New Berlin: Memory, Politics, Place.* Minneapolis: University of Minnesota Press, 2005.

———. "Places of Memory." In *A Companion to Political Geography,* edited by John A. Agnew, Katharyne Mitchell, and Gerard Toal, 289–301. Malden: Blackwell Publishing, 2008.

Utlu, Deniz. *Die Ungehaltenen.* Munich: Graf, 2014.

Williams, Raymond. *The Country and the City.* Oxford: Oxford University Press, 1975.

CHAPTER 13

Israeli Jews in the New Berlin

From Shoah Memories
to Middle Eastern Encounters

Hadas Cohen and Dani Kranz

Israeli prime minister Yitzhak Rabin's quote "Nefolet shel nemoshot" (the fallen of the weaklings) became an oft-repeated saying to describe—more like bedevil—Israeli Jews who emigrated from Israel. Historically defined as traitors to the Zionist project of the Jewish state, they were reproached for supposedly regarding their own individual desires as more important than their participation in the collective efforts of Israeli Jewry to create a home for the Jewish people. Yet, despite this strong ideological reproach, Israeli Jews have been emigrating from Israel since the state's creation: they returned to Germany,[1] to Poland,[2] and to any previous home country they could return to, or they opted for new shores, mainly the United States, Canada, and Australia.[3] This migration[4] happened against the historical backdrop of the Holocaust and despite the option offered by Israel to live within a Jewish majority state as a self-determined people according to the Declaration of Independence (1948). In this context, leaving Israel for Germany comes to mean a personal moral failure on the side of the migrants and a social act of treason toward Jewish Israeli society.

In the following, we outline the Israeli policies toward Jewish emigrants as a backdrop for the discussion on the significance of Israeli-diaspora relations and Berlin as a special place of Israeli immigration. As we examine the experiences of the migrants in Berlin, we underscore that Israeli migrants might self-classify as emigrants, immigrants, or migrants, while German and Israeli mainstream discourses are conflicted as to what kind of "migrants" these Israelis are. We then argue that while the Zionist discourse, as well as Israeli collective memory of the *Shoah*, shape the initial experiences of present-day Israeli migrants to Berlin, once they arrive in the city, their experiences are much more defined by current Israeli social and geopolitical issues.[5] The ongoing Israeli-Palestinian conflict is particularly influential, as the young migrants experience their ancestral European and Middle Eastern roots to belong to the multitude lifestyle options Berlin offers. Our research is based on a mixed-methods methodology, which included data collected from 100 semistructured in-depth interviews with Israelis living in Berlin and answers to 804 questionnaires of a representative sample across Germany (the total population of Israelis in Germany is estimated at twenty thousand).[6] In addition, we attended as participant observers cultural events, which were initiated by Israelis living in Berlin, and we followed the lives of Israeli individuals and families for a one-year period.[7]

The Idea of a Jewish and Democratic State and the Problem of Being Just That

Upon the founding of the state of Israel, *kibbutz ha'galuyot* (the gathering of the exiles) became the institutionalized raison d'être of the country. It was explicated in multiple documents, including the Declaration of Independence (1948) that called for *aliyah*—which is the immigration of Jews to Israel, and which literally means "to ascend"—the Law of Return (1950), Nationality Law (1952), the Entry into Israel Law (1954), and it even carried into the Anti-Infiltration Law (1954).[8] Furthermore, Israeli citizens had to apply for an exit permit until 1959, and at times they had to litigate to exit Israel.[9] Within the legal sphere, the consolidation process of Israel as a Jewish state was regulated through verdicts, injunctions, and directives.[10] Yet this process is subject to a specific dynamic that changes over time. Presently, *kibbutz ha'galuyot* is less prominent compared to other internal processes within Israel, such as the domestic Judaization, which has been called ethnocratization.[11]

To date, the State of Israel supports *olim* (Jewish immigrants, literally "ascenders") and their families upon undertaking *aliyah*. Israel also engages in programs such as *Taglit* (discovery in Hebrew") or Birth Right. These ten-day trips to Israel are intended to encourage eligible young, diaspora Jews to immigrate to the country.[12] Israel also has a diaspora management policy in some countries that aim to bind diasporic Israelis and their children to their homeland.[13] Other instances include state-assisted return programs for Israeli citizens to entice them to return home.[14] Within the Jewish communities in Germany, as well as in other countries, Zionist organizations ranging from youth movements to women's charters keep Israel in the consciousness of Jewish diaspora. And indeed, in many Jewish diasporas around the world, immigration to Israel is encouraged, while for Jews in Germany it was expected,[15] as no Jew was supposed to remain in the country of the murderers.[16] These different players operate in different areas, ranging from groups within the Jewish community that lobby for *aliyah* and ask for financial support for the Israeli state to those supporting binational joint (business) ventures between Israelis and Germans, which regularly involve Israeli migrants or local Jews on the "German" side. The goal of these programs is to create an ideological affiliation between the different tiers of one main project, namely, maintaining the umbilical cord to Israel.

These developments underpin the fact that leaving Israel contradicts the effort to entice all Jews to join Israel as Jewish citizens and that current efforts have shifted to incorporate "wayward" diasporic Jews and Israeli migrants into their plans of action. Against this backdrop, it is no surprise just how much of a transgression the emigration of Israelis constitutes within Israeli discourse. Until not too long ago, leaving Israel was referred to as *yerida* (descend), and emigrants as *yordim* (descenders), negatively connoted terms that socially stigmatize emigrants. A *yored* (descender) is defined as the opposite of an *oleh* (ascender, Jewish immigrant to Israel); the *yored* enters a lesser form of Jewish existence when leaving Israel and is thought to become part of a vulnerable minority that is at the mercy of the non-Jewish majority.[17] This binary ties in with a number of others that are part of the ideology of Israeli identity construction. They remain highly potent in the Israeli imagination and in practice: Jew vs. non-Jew, diasporic Jew vs. Israeli Jew, and *oleh* vs. *yored*.[18]

The strong currency of these ideological binaries remains palpable in the political sphere as well. Yet, it seems that young Israelis no longer respond to them in the same way. While "emigration" from Israel to Germany historically consisted of German Jews and often German- or Yiddish-speaking Jews, the turn of the millennium, which coincided with the coming of age of the third generation of Israelis, led to a steady increase of Israeli migration to Germany in general and to Berlin in particular. Despite this clear trend, some Israeli politicians do not tire of disparaging emigrants. As late as 2013, the then finance minister of centrist party Yesh Atid (There is a future) Yair Lapid reproached Israeli emigrants, in particular those who migrated to Berlin, averring the old

Israeli hegemonic discourse of *Yerida*. Lapid criticized them for having given up on the Jewish country, which he deemed incomprehensible in the wake of the *Shoah*. Until this strongly worded diatribe, Israeli migrants had either kept quiet, backed down, or pretended they would return to Israel.[19] This time things were different. Young Israeli migrants, who Lapid deemed emigrants par excellence, the majority of whom are third-generation Holocaust survivors,[20] talked back at Lapid, addressing his detachment from their everyday economic hardship and claiming that his comments were "so typical second generation. And it's easy for him to criticize us since he is from Ra'anana [a rich city north of Tel Aviv], so he clearly does not have to worry about the high cost of living in Israel."[21] An Israeli journalist living in Berlin asked angrily, "When did you last have to make ends meet, Mr. Lapid?"[22] Others outlined their dissatisfaction with Israeli society, often spiking their critique with bitter sarcasm. The occupation and the role of Jewish religion in private life were also harshly criticized.[23]

Indeed, data collected in a Germany-wide research project on Israeli Jews who migrated to the country confirmed these sentiments, showing unambiguously that a generational change had occurred. When surveyed anonymously, third-generation Israelis no longer felt the need to apologize for migrating or to defend why they went to Germany of all countries.[24] These findings are all the more striking, as migration to Germany was not only ideologically a taboo but was in the past legally not an option. Until 1956 it was impossible to enter Germany on an Israeli passport, and Israeli passports bore the line "Good for all countries but Germany" until 1956 when *prat le'germania* was abolished.

Yet, Israelis had already migrated to Germany since the founding of Israel, using other passports or finding legal loopholes by way of adopting other citizenships or entering as stateless individuals.[25] Things, however, changed remarkably over the last decade when this trickle became a flow.[26] The Israeli presence in Germany became vocal and visible, and Israelis in Berlin became a mythological feature in German and Israeli popular discourse, media, and politics. Israelis became part of all things Jewish and integral to the New Berlin discourse.[27] Fictional, semifictional, and autobiographically inspired accounts came to the fore, which dwelled on the uniqueness of the German/Israeli/Jewish triangulation and which fed, if not fetishized, the myth of Israelis in Berlin. As interesting as these accounts are, however, more important is the unique perspective they reveal on the phenomenon. Thus, in the following, we endeavor to fill the lacuna in the research on the lives and practices of Israelis in Berlin.[28] We focus on long-term ethnographic fieldwork in Berlin among Israelis while critically reflecting on our own Israeliness, Jewishness, Germanness, and any other attachments that our interlocutors, informants, and friends entrusted to us.[29]

Experiencing Berlin from an Israeli Perspective: Between a Memorial Culture and Self-Definition

Like the rest of Germany, Berlin is afloat with Holocaust memorials, and one enters synagogues typically through a *Gedenkhalle* (memorial hall).[30] Jews, Jewishness, and the Holocaust are inextricably linked in German, German Jewish, and Israeli discourses, but as we will show, the meaning of this discourse has also undergone a generational change. These discourses are reified in Germany even more so than in Israel, since the Holocaust is commemorated in the public space and the memorials are a part of the everyday German experience. One does not have to especially go to a museum to remember. Anybody walking around in Berlin, for instance, will come across one memorial or another,[31] or they will stumble over one of the many *Stolpersteine*. These stones—literally "stumbling stones"—are made of brass and are integrated into the pavement. They are laid upon request of a descendant of a Jew or of a private person and in agreement with the legal descendants in front of a building where a Jew used to live, or in some cases, where he/she used to work.[32] The stone contains the basic details of the individual (name, date of birth, and, if known, date of death, place of death; otherwise last known place before deportation) and is a form of memorial that is both public and personal.

Israelis, on the other hand, are typically not used to an excess of memorials surrounding them in their everyday lives. This sets them apart from the local Jewish population in Germany, the majority of whom had come to Germany as displaced persons from Eastern Europe, emerged from hiding, or were part of the biggest Jewish immigration wave to Germany since the Holocaust from the former Soviet Union. For these Jews, the memorials are part of the physical reality and mental landscape of being Jewish in post-1945 Germany.[33] Yet, the Jewish population in Germany is not monolithic in its attitude to the memory of the Holocaust, and not all Jews are triggered similarly by the commemoration practices. Jewish immigrants from the former Soviet Union, for instance, see themselves as both victors over the Nazis and as victims of the Nazis and the *Shoah*. They differ in this respect from the "local" Jews,[34] who dominate the local discourse.[35] Israelis tend to be ambiguous about where they fit in this binary and vacillate between seeing themselves as descendants of survivors, aligning themselves with the Zionist discourse of the new Israeli-raised Jew, the *Sabra,* or rejecting both positions and narratives as too simplistic (see Amit in this volume).

Israelis among Each Other and Israelis and Other Jews: Not One of a Kind

Considering their highly ideologized Israeli upbringing, it is unsurprising that Jewish Israelis have a complicated relationship with diaspora Jews and among themselves. The idea of a strong independent Israel negates the long history of Jewish life in exile, and the latter has come to define pre-state diasporic "defenseless" life,[36] depicting Jews as a vulnerable minority at the mercy of their host countries,[37] exposed to repetitive violent attacks, with the final catastrophe of the Holocaust.[38] Following the formation of the Israeli state in 1948 and the seemingly miraculous Israeli victory over the Arab countries in the war of independence, the myth at the base of Israeli Zionist nationalism was validated, in which the new "warrior" Jew, the *Sabra,* takes center stage.[39] Furthermore, the continuous wars along with the memory of the Holocaust created a siege mentality in Israel vis-à-vis the surrounding Arab states and the international community, which lead to a specific new, local binary: Israeli (Jews) vs. Palestinians and Arabs, who are often lumped together as "Arabs."[40]

The image of the "New Jew" sharply contrasted with that of the Jewish Holocaust victims who went "like sheep to the slaughter" (an expression fondly used by Gideon Hausner, the state prosecutor at the Eichmann trial),[41] and this attitude was fueled by the fact that most European Jews refused to immigrate to Palestine and join the Zionist project before the Nazis forced them out of Europe.[42] This message has become central to Israeli self-understanding and is being passed on to future generations through youth trips to the extermination camps in Poland during high school years, with the main message being *le'olam lo,* which roughly translates into "never again."[43] In this context, emigrating from Israel stands for the return to a diasporic existence and a betrayal of the Israeli Jewish community as a whole. Migrating to Germany adds another dimension to a downward spiral, given this particular history.

It is not surprising, then, that the Israelis, who are defined as emigrants in Israeli discourse, showed an ambiguous sense of belonging.

Exceptions exist of course, as is the case of German Jews who returned to Germany from British Palestine or Israel after the *Shoah*. The earliest "Israeli immigrants" to Germany consisted of German-speaking Jews who defined Germany as their home. They were joined by mostly German- or Yiddish-speaking Jewish displaced persons from Eastern Europe, who felt more akin to German culture, or were so traumatized that they needed the proximity of the perpetrators to deal with the past.[44] Others of this generation and of following generations became migrants by chance, such as those who came to Germany as exchange students, fell in love with local (non-Jewish) Germans and married them, or were victims of, as one of them reasoned, the idea that "life just happened." The integration of these Israelis did not follow any distinct pattern: some sought out the Jewish communities while others did not; some kept their Israeliness secret while others became active players in the local Jewish communities; yet others completely entered the German mainstream and relinquished their Israeli citizenship in the process.[45] However, as outlined, the number of Israeli migrants of all backgrounds was low until the end of the 1990s, when the third generation came of age. Be that as it may, Israeli emigrants were often not greeted heartily by Jewish diasporic communities either, leading to an ongoing ambiguity.[46]

This ambiguity directly relates to the remnants of the established *yerida* discourse and is regularly expressed by the more conservative factions of the Jewish diaspora as well as the Zionistic factions of Israeli Jewish society. Both provide an unwelcome reminder for the emigrants, reprimanding them for their so-called transgression and insisting that the only place they should live permanently is Israel. While Israeli migrants in other countries and earlier Israeli migrants to Germany commented on and were affected by the reproach, we found that third-generation Israelis in Berlin did not often express these sentiments, nor did they respond to them.

Beyond Jewishness and Israeliness: Encounters with Others

Israelis who migrated to Berlin, where they live as a migrant minority in a cosmopolitan environment, find themselves exposed to the shortcomings of growing up in a predominantly Jewish Israel. "My son can meet all sorts of different kids here, and he can be friends with them. He can get all of these different experiences,"[47] opined a recent arrival, while another reasoned that "I always envied all of those people who can speak different languages, while all I speak properly is Hebrew."[48] At the same time, another one found that "[o]nly here [in Germany did] I [realize] how similar I am to other Moroccans. Actually, more similar than to *Ashkenazim* [European Jews] in Israel. I'd never had that experience back home."[49]

This stands in sharp contrast to the raison d'être of Israel as a Jewish country to which Jews from all around the world can immigrate; Jews are in the majority in Israel, and the presence of the national minorities has been legally and socially problematic since the founding of the state.[50] Any non-Jewish immigration, especially of Palestinians, has been undesirable throughout.[51] As part of the maturation process of Israel as a Jewish majority country, Jewishness, and more so a form of Jewishness in which religion and ethnicity overlap in terms of categorical identity, practice, and political expression, has been gaining in momentum—a fact that a number of Israelis in Berlin criticize.[52] At the same time, despite the terminology used by the different groups in Israel, Israeli society is homogenous, with Jews being the majority and Jewish culture dominant. Native non-Jews are socially and culturally marginal, and encounters between Jewish Israelis and non-Jews (especially Palestinians) are limited by way of stratification and social engineering.[53] When it comes to Israelis in Berlin, however, the story is different. While the Jewish majority in Israel is supportive of the development of a normative Judaization of society, the majority of the Israelis in Berlin are much less *Judeocentric*, and they are open to the new encounters Berlin offers.[54]

Berlin provides in another sense an escape from the limits and boundaries that exist back home. Israeli Jews described the normative and dense structures of Israeli Jewish society as "a pressure cooker."[55] Israelis in Berlin replicated this pattern: "You know how it is! The stress. The pressure. The family,"[56] as well as "I can breathe again"[57] when talking about their feelings in cosmopolitan Berlin. The migrants also stressed how much they enjoyed the intercultural encounters in the city. They contrasted these encounters with their "previous lives" in Israel, which, from their perspective, deprived them of such interactions. However, turning these attitudes into action reflects a specific cosmopolitan approach to life, a hunger for new experiences, which only a minority of all Israeli Jews can and will actualize. The activist who called for "Aliyah to Berlin" failed miserably in the autumn of 2014. While tens of thousands of Israelis had joined the discussion and the social media campaign on Facebook, only a mere 100 attended the campaign's main event on Rabin Square in Tel Aviv, and actual immigration to Berlin did not increase.[58]

Projections as an Expression of Working through the Conflicted Israeliness

The *Shoah* remains central in the popular, media, and political discourse that surrounds the migration of Israelis to Berlin, as the "Milky protest," and the reaction of various outlets, revealed.[59] This very protest used the price of the popular Israeli pudding Milky to underline just how much more expensive it is to live in Israel compared to Germany. Somewhat ironically, the German raison d'être of supporting the existence of Israel and the German endeavors to "make good again" (*Wiedergutmachung*, restitution in a legal and political sense) had such a phenomenal impact on Israeli Jews that they feel very safe in Germany and in Berlin, and the new Germany attracts them. At the same time, they have grown up both within a discourse that depicted emigration from Israel as moral failure and within a Zionistic ethos that penetrates Israeli everyday life, the education institutions, and the legal sphere.[60]

This long-term exposure was reflected in the reactions toward the researchers. During fieldwork in Berlin, where both researchers talked about their work, the reactions they encountered were defined by their positionings. Technically, both are Israeli/foreign dual citizens. Yet, Hadas Cohen is a native *Sabra*-Israeli and Dani Kranz is a native German who visits Israel frequently and speaks German natively.[61] Hadas received mixed reactions concerning her research and—research-related—tenure in Berlin, while Dani was commonly asked specifics about life in Berlin, how to get jobs, or how to solve legal or bureaucratic issues—and met with surprise when she admitted that she does not emotionally relate to the Berlin hype. While the migrants did tell both researchers highly complex narratives and at times conflicting stories about their migration, the narratives that were rendered to each ethnographer showed remarkable differences in their nuances. These differences in and adjustments to the stories they told each researcher are noteworthy. They told Hadas that they felt liberated from the Israeli pressure cooker (which they stressed less to Dani) by escaping from a political climate with which they cannot identify[62] and from economic hardships—the latter point they stressed equally to Dani. Once they arrived in Berlin, all were impressed by the cosmopolitan life they encountered, describing the city as an "adult summer camp" where they can meet other young immigrants like themselves who see immigration to Berlin as an adventure. Interestingly, they did not stress this to Dani at all, most likely because Germany is not that adventurous a place for a German native, and perhaps they felt that she could not share their sentiment as outsiders in Berlin and that the German language was the key parameter of distinction between them and her. Also, Dani was more often asked, "What do Germans mean if they do this?"—an attempt to use her insider's knowledge of German society, culture, and language.

The hardships of immigration was the sentiment expressed especially by immigrants who moved to the city on their own and were not in relationships, especially immigrants in their thirties and early forties who described going through a rough and solitary first winter. Many told Hadas of moments of acute loneliness and hardships, while others uttered in consternation to Dani that "immigration is really a full-time job" or that Germany worked at a much slower pace than they had expected. The weather and the winter was not an issue in encounters with Dani, but instead she was asked about her Jewishness out of curiosity, as post-1945 German Jews are rare, not to say exotic. Complaints about economic hardship in Israel were voiced in concert with appraisals of the relative clarity of German bureaucracy. The latter was interesting but at the same time strange to Dani, who has life-long experience with exactly this bureaucracy and its pursuant legalese and analyzes it as an anthropologist who deals with citizenship and restitution. Yet, no single Israeli migrant defended his/her emigration toward her. Negative reactions toward their emigration were voiced with the assumption that she understands the stigma they had within Israeli society, as she was stigmatized herself in their eyes based on her own—categorical—belongings.

These reactions must be understood in the context of the importance of the *Shoah* to Israeli historiography and the Israeli *Shoah* and *yerida* discourses. Israelis narrate their emigration toward other Israelis differently depending on the status of the Israeli interlocutor. They use specific speech figures, inside humor, and "rational choice" arguments for emigration. In the Israeli context, they feel that they might be put on the spot for their decision to leave Israel, be it temporarily or permanently. They even said so to Dani directly: "It really annoys me when people ask when I plan on coming back to Israel, and if this [emigration to Germany] is good for me," one said, and added why he felt differently with her: "But you are really from here [Germany], so you understand why we love it here."[63] The feeling of having to defend themselves was expressed differently in the relationship to the interlocutors: more were defensive in conversations with Hadas than with Dani.

Navigating the New Berlin: Becoming a Cosmopolitan Minority

The ways Israeli migrants navigate and build their lives in Berlin renders them different from Israelis of other diasporas, but similar to some other migrant populations in Berlin in regard to their economic profiles and the reasons to move there. Similar to American migrants, the majority of Israeli immigrants tend to be highly educated.[64] The same goes for migrants from Southern and Southeastern Europe. Greeks and Spaniards, as well as Romanians and Bulgarians, try to escape their weak economies by moving to Germany. Yet unlike these Europeans, Israelis in Berlin (and Germany) stressed throughout fieldwork interactions their political dissatisfaction in terms of policies and the Israeli/Palestinian conflict and the increasing hold of religion of their private sphere.[65] Yet, this is not to say that the "other" migrants are happy with their governments. Greeks especially stressed their country's strong swing to the right in fieldwork conversations: "I am happy I have a name that can pass as something else [but not Greek]."[66] At the same time, the Israeli migrants who mostly have degrees from the social sciences and the humanities mentioned that their economic hardships in Israel gave them crucial insights into the Israeli economic structures.[67] The Israeli economy is strongly geared around the idea of Israel being the "startup nation" of high-tech companies. However, in order to initiate a startup or work in a startup or a high-tech company, one needs a specific kind of expertise, which is typically not attained by graduates of the social sciences and humanities. Instead, these graduates might enter poorly paid professions for which they are overqualified. Dani encountered two anthropologists during fieldwork in Tel Aviv alone who worked in retail for a mere six thousand shekels (about fifteen hundred USD) a month—before taxes and deductions. Berlin is still a relatively cheap city when compared to London, Paris, or New York. Some migrants said that to them Berlin is the India of Europe, referring to India as the affordable destination for Israeli backpackers but also indicating that they were not averse to living in other locations outside Israel. Unlike India, however, Berlin offers a relaxed and first-world lifestyle at the same time. The combination of relatively cheap rent, a buzzing cultural scene and vivid nightlife, and inexpensive grocery shopping makes the city affordable for students, artists, and young entrepreneurs who want to engage in areas beyond high tech.

These specifics of Berlin result from Berlin's unique history. During the Cold War the city was a heavily subsidized Western enclave that attracted young German men who wished to avoid the military draft and young men and women who formed a specific youth culture: one of the best-known former residents of West Berlin is the late David Bowie. Part of this ethos still lives on. Berlin is politically and socially a very liberal, left-leaning city.[68] That the city kept some of its atmosphere also lies in its infrastructure.[69] After reunification, many apartments vacated in East Berlin entered the local real estate market, which together with a weak city economy kept the city affordable. The whole of Berlin remains heavily subsidized by way of interstate transfers—to the chagrin of many Germans who experience the city as a money pit and not as "poor and sexy" as a previous mayor, the native Berliner Klaus Wowereit, marketed it. One interviewee mused on the fact that he, a philosophy scholar, can still live in Prenzlauer Berg, one of Berlin's hippest neighborhoods: "It is as if a Marxist revolution took place in the city, redistributing the wealth between the rich and the poor. This is how I can afford to live like this with my daughter on a researcher's salary."[70]

Other Israelis felt more inclined to joining a *Wohngemeinschaft*, commonly called by its acronym *WG* in German. This form of alternative living arrangement first gained popularity in the 1960s with students and was part of the rebellion of second-generation Germans against their parents and their parents' lifestyle. At present it remains popular with students, but it has gained a foothold across generations: it is an alternative living arrangement favored by all those who seek a community that is not restricted to a family.[71] For Israelis who come from a close-knit, highly cohesive society and "miss this human closeness," a *WG* offers voluntary proximity. An alternative living arrangement like this is often unavailable in Israel, where marriage and children remain the status quo: "I don't want kids. In Berlin nobody cares while in Israel everybody comments."[72] Thus, while some proximity was appreciated by the Israelis, it was a selective proximity.

The majority of Israelis in Berlin and Germany are politically moderate to left leaning, which means they blend in with the majority of their destination of choice.[73] Their views are pro-peace and in favor of a two-state solution to the Israeli-Palestinian conflict that will allocate each side its own independent state, and some even support the politically radical, far-left one-state solution, which means forgoing defining Israel as a Jewish state. The more extreme support the BDS (boycott, divestment, and sanction) movement, defining themselves as anti-Zionists who "left Israel in disgust."[74] Their everyday encounters with Berlin's cosmopolitan mosaic, and especially with Arab migrants from the Middle East, push back against ethnic stratification in Israel, which often relegates Jews and non-Jews to different geographical terrains and social spheres.

One such local place of encounter is *Café Kotti*—short for Kottbusser Platz in local vernacular—at the heart of Kreuzberg, previously an impoverished, migrant-dominated district now with a cosmopolitan cache. The district was known for its cheap rent and diversity. Post-reunification, this mix attracted both new international and domestic migrants, supporting a lively creative scene. The café serves as a hub for young Arabs from all over the Middle East—activists, scholars, and artists—and is often frequented by Israelis drawn to casually meeting their geographical neighbors from "back home," where meeting them is much more difficult and at times impossible. Mati Shemoelof, a Hebrew-writing Israeli poet and journalist living in Berlin, describes "connecting with my Iranian roots" when starting an ad hoc roundtable discussion at the café with two Iranian immigrants, to whom he introduced himself as an Iranian.[75] Shemoelof described how moving to Berlin and being exposed to the city's artistic worlds and unique culture of protest encouraged him to reflect on his Jewish–Middle Eastern–Israeli–*Mizrahi* identity, and he expressed that he feels his ancestral language should be his present-day language too (also see Amit in this volume). Thus, he adds another layer to the feeling of loss that Israelis realized once they left the country, which goes beyond the common immigration experience of loneliness and missing their home. While Israeli *Ashkenazim* in Israel mourned regularly that they did not speak the European languages of their ancestry, once they were in Berlin they realized just how similar they were to "other" Europeans. *Mizrahi* Israelis, on the other hand, experienced the same sentiment when they encountered other Arabic speakers in Berlin: "Here in Berlin I began to reevaluate my *Mizrahi* roots and interpret them as Arab roots ... which is not bad."[76] Shemoelof articulates the way such encounters and the empowering sentiment they evoke undermine the Israeli national attempt to "erase"[77] the Arab identity and *Mizrahi* Israelis.

Another interviewee, an Israeli woman of European descent who moved to Berlin on her own at the age of thirty-eight, recounted how her initial fascination with the café and the Middle Easterners she met there and "could never imagine meeting in Israel"[78] turned into dread in the face of explicit anti-Israeli sentiment due to the latest Israeli entanglement in Gaza in the summer of 2015. Despite her ambivalence, however, the café made it into a fictional novel she is writing about Israelis in Berlin. Other significant encounters take place in Berlin when Israelis meet Palestinians they would never meet casually back home, such as a Gazan man in his late twenties who frequently attends Israeli cultural events, the Palestinian-Israeli owner of a hummus restaurant called *Kanaan* who comes from what Israeli discourse defines as an "Arab-Jewish" mixed city, or an Israeli Jewish bag designer who teamed with a Palestinian family from East Jerusalem that provides her with Palestinian textiles.[79] These encounters express the political attitudes on both sides, and on a personal level they give rise to rapprochements: "My mum didn't tell me that the black man will come and get me when I was naughty as child. My mum said that the Israelis will come and get me,"[80] mused one Palestinian. Yet, not all Israeli Jews, Palestinian citizens of Israel, or Gaza/West Bank Palestinians were interested in these, at times, very difficult and emotional exchanges. Some were simply happy to "live ... life in peace"[81] in a physical and metaphorical sense.[82]

Israelis in the New Berlin: From the Shoah to the Middle East Encounters

Israeli Jews who migrated to Berlin indeed moved to a "special place," as their ambassador referred to it as late as 2014.[83] Yet the specialty of the place is not limited to the *Shoah,* as a "special place" is a code for a "place of the past." For the Israeli migrants in Berlin, it is only partially a place of the past; more so, it is a place of the present where they can pursue their personal and professional development and encounter others from around the globe, including their closest neighbors geographically in the form of Palestinian migrants. What is striking is that encounters with the latter, the Middle East conflict, and, in particular, the Israeli-Palestinian conflict are of great significance to the majority of the third-generation Israeli Jews living in Berlin. While the *Shoah* was and still is very much present as part of their heritage, the Israeli-Palestinian conflict *is* their present. Thus, German non-Jews, constructed in the old binary as the opposite to Israeli Jews, have been replaced for this generation by a new binary: Palestinians. Both groups, Jewish Israelis, Palestinian citizens of Israel and Gaza/West Bank Palestinians, showed a pronounced interest in engaging with one another, and teamed up as artists, NGO activists, and, along the way, even as friends. This pattern is known for Jews in Germany post-*Shoah* in regard to "other" Germans: while encounters could be tense, shared interest led to interest groups and to friendships.[84]

Besides this very specific feature of the immigrants, what they make of the sea of options on offer in Berlin comes down to personal preferences. One can discover the *Altneuland* (old new land) in an inverse sense of Theodor Herzl's original idea, namely rediscovering Germany as an ancestral home; or, in a twist of the Israeli reality, one can discover one's own Arab roots among migrants from Arab countries. One can also engage with the *Shoah* and its aftermath like some artists and writers do. Others act out a post-Zionist identity, namely remaining Israeli but choosing not to live in Israel temporarily or permanently for whatever reasons. Furthermore, it is of course possible to become a political activist, a mini-ambassador for Israel on the matter of peace and reconciliation, and, of course, to pursue a startup. In other words, Berlin—and Germany—offers a plethora of options that migrants seek out that they feel are not available to them in Israel. All of this is perfectly in line with finds from migration studies: people from countries of the Global North migrate to pursue a specific lifestyle that they feel they could not pursue in their country of origin.[85] At the same time, this pursuit makes immigrants on average happier than those who stayed behind according to global data on German emigrants, and it remains to be seen if and how Israelis fit this pattern.[86] Thus, Israelis in Berlin are perhaps not all that different from other migrants. They have an Israeli twist to things, and the specific baggage from the German/Jewish/Israeli shared history impacts their pursuits. Yet, as ethnographies of this community have shown, the story does not begin and end there but rather lies beyond the past and could perhaps be explicated only in the future from the ways in which this community will develop a home for itself in this charged locality.

Acknowledgments

Hadas Cohen's research for this article was funded in part by a Leibniz-DAAD postdoc fellowship and received institutional and academic support from the Migration, Integration, and Transnationalization Unit at the Berlin Social Science Research Center (WZB). She would like to thank Professor Ruud Koopmans, the head of the Unit, for his assistance and support throughout the research.

Dani Kranz's data was partially generated within the framework of the GIF-supported project "The Immigration of Israeli Jews to Germany since 1990," GIF Grant No. 1186. She would like to thank her colleagues Uzi Rebhun, Nadia Beider, and Maya Shorer-Kaplan (Hebrew University Jerusalem) and Heinz Sünker and Katja Harbi (Bergische University Wuppertal) for their assistance and support.

Hadas Cohen is visiting scholar at the Davis Institute for International Relations at the Hebrew University in Jerusalem. She is a lawyer and holds a PhD in political science from the New School University for Social Research. Her research focuses on national identity formation and the politics of resistance, migration, and integration.

Dani Kranz is a senior researcher and the head of the Israel project at the Bergische University Wuppertal, Germany, and she is the founding director of Two Foxes Consulting. Trained in social anthropology, history, and social psychology, she specializes in the anthropology of migration, legal and political anthropology, interethnic (couple) relationships, and intergenerational transmission processes.

Notes

1. Janni Panagiotidis, "A Policy for the Future: German-Jewish Remigrants, their Children, and the Politics of Israeli Nation-Building," *Leo Baeck Institute Year Book* 60 (2015): 191–206.
2. Marcos Silber, "'Immigrants from Poland Want to Go Back': The Politics of Return Migration and Nation Building in 1950s Israel," *Journal of Israeli History: Politics, Society, Culture* 27, no. 2 (2008): 201–19.
3. Dani Kranz, "Shades of Jewishness: The Creation and Maintenance of a Liberal Jewish Community in Post-Shoah Germany" (PhD diss., University of St. Andrews, 2009).
4. Unless otherwise specified as part of the respective discourses, the term "migrant" denotes Israeli Jews who leave Israel. These individuals might indeed be emigrants, immigrants, returnees, or transnational actors depending on the ideological perspective, which in turn may conflict with self-ascriptions and praxes.
5. The use of the terms "migrant" is deliberate; if we use the term "immigrant" or "emigrant," it refers to the self-positioning of the individual in question or to the discourse of an official body. The background to this paper is the ethnographic research of both authors and furthermore the quantitative and qualitative data sets of the project "The Immigration of Israeli Jews to Germany since 1990," supported by the German Israeli Scientific Foundation for research and development, (GIF) Grant No. 1186. Dani Kranz has been the project head and senior researcher of the German team throughout. The data generated within this project consist of sociodemographic data from German and Israeli (and other relevant) statistical offices, 804 questionnaires of a representative sample across Germany, more than 60 semi-structured interviews with Israelis who had taken part in the questionnaire, as well as participant observation across the country and in Israel conducted between February 2012 and the present. The research languages were Hebrew, German, and English, and the choice of language typically lay with the research partners.

6. Dani Kranz, "Dynamische ethnische Beziehungen mal 2 oder hoch 2? Deutsch/israelisch und inner-israelisch," public lecture given at Johann Guttenberg, Universität Mainz, December 3, 2016.

7. Hadas Cohen followed a select number of individuals during her one-year tenure in Berlin, while Dani Kranz has been following Israelis in Germany ethnographically since 2003. Furthermore, as Kranz outlined in "Where to Stay and Where to Go?" (2015), her embodied experiences that span back her whole life as she is, like Samuel Heilman (1980) put it, a "native anthropologist." Samuel Heilman, "Heilman, Samuel C., Jewish Sociologist: Native as Stranger," *American Sociologist* 15 (1980): 100–108

8. "Declaration of Establishment of State of Israel (May 14, 1948)," accessed June 10, 2016, http://www.mfa.gov.il/mfa/foreignpolicy/peace/guide/pages/declaration%20of%20establishment%20of%20state%20of%20israel.aspx; "Law 5710-1950: Law of Return, 6 June 1950, in Book of Laws 51, p. 151; Law 5730-1970: Law of Return (Amendment No. 2), 10 March 1970, in Book of Laws 586, p. 34," accessed August 24, 2015, http://www.mfa.gov.il/mfa/mfa-archive/1950-1959/pages/law%20of%20 return %205710-1950.aspx; "Law 5712-1952: Nationality Law, 1 April 1952, in Book of Laws 95, p. 146," accessed August 24, 2015, http://www.israellawresourcecenter.org/israel laws/fulltext/nationalitylaw.htm; "Law 5712-1952: Entry to Israel Law, 26 August 1952, in Book of Laws 111, p. 354," accessed August 24, 2015, http://www. israellawresourcecenter.org/israellaws/fulltext/entryintoisraellaw.htm; "Law 5714-1954: Prevention of Infiltration (Offences and Jurisdiction) Law, 16 August 1954, in Book of Laws 161, p. 160," accessed August 24, 2015, http://www.israellawresourcecenter.org/israellaws/fulltext/preventioninfil trationlaw.htm.

9. Silber, "Immigrants from Poland," 201–19.

10. Mazen Masri, "Love Suspended: Demography, Comparative Law and Palestinian Couples in the Israeli Supreme Court," *Social & Legal Studies* 22, no. 3 (2013): 309–34; Ronnie Olesker, "Law-Making and the Securitization of the Jewish Identity in Israel," *Ethnopolitics* 13, no. 2 (2014): 105–21; Yoav Peled, "Citizenship Betrayed: Israel's Emerging Immigration and Citizenship Regime," *Theoretical Inquiries in Law* 8, no. 2 (2007): 603–28; Galia Sabar and Elizabeth Tsurkov, "Israel's Policies toward Asylum-Seekers: 2002–2014," *Instituto Affari Internazionali,* May 20, 2015, http://www.osce.org/networks/165436?download=true.

11. Oren Yiftachel, *Ethnocracy: Land and Identity Politics in Israel/Palestine* (Philadelphia, 2006).

12. Israeli minor citizens are excluded.

13. Nir Cohen, "From Overt Rejection to Enthusiastic Embracement: Changing State Discourses on Israeli Emigration," *GeoJournal* 68, no. 2/3 (2007): 267–78.

14. Nir Cohen and Dani Kranz, "State-Assisted Highly Skilled Return Programs, National Identity and the Risk(s) of Homecoming: Israel and Germany Compared," *Journal of Ethnic and Migration Studies* 41, no. 5 (2014): 795–812.

15. Yvonne Schütze, "'Warum Deutschland und nicht Israel?' Begründungen russischer Juden für die Migration nach Deutschland," *BIOS* 10, no. 2 (1997): 186–208.

16. Martin Löw-Beer, "From Nowhere to Israel and Back: The Changing Self-Definition of German-Jewish Youth since 1960," in *Germans, Jews, Memory: Reconstructions of Jewish Life in Germany,* ed. Y. Michal Bodemann (Ann Arbor, 1996).

17. Dani Kranz, "Quasi-ethnic Capital vs. Quasi-citizenship Capital: Access to Israeli Citizenship," *Migration Letters* 13, no. 1 (2016): 64–83.

18. Guy Katz, *Intercultural Negotiation: The Unique Case of Germany and Israel* (Norderstedt, 2011); Dani Kranz, "Changing Definitions of Germanness across Three Generations of *Yekkes* in Palestine/Israel," *German Studies Review* 39, no. 1 (2016): 99–120.

19. Brent David Harris, "Beyond Guilt and Stigma: Changing Attitudes among Israeli Migrants in Canada," *International Migration* 53, no. 6 (2012): 41–56; Moshe Shokeid, *Children of Circumstances: Israeli Emigrants in New York* (Ithaca, NY, 1988).

20. Kranz, "Israelis in Berlin."

21. Dani Kranz, Uzi Rebhun, and Heinz Sünker, "The Most Comprehensive Survey among Israelis in Germany Confirms the Image: Secular, Educated, and Left," *Spitz,* December 4, 2015, http://spitzmag.de/webonly/7238. Translation of title from Hebrew to English is our own.

22. Hila Weisberg, "One Question before You Speak of Zionism, Mr. Lapid: When Was the Last Time You Thought about Making Ends Meet," *Ha'aretz Online,* October 2, 2013, http://www.themarker.com/career/1.2130595.

23. Kranz et al., "Most Comprehensive Survey."

24. Ibid.

25. Panagiotidis, " Policy for the Future," 191–206.

26. Kranz et al., "Most Comprehensive Survey."

27. See Erek and Gantner in this volume.

28. Dani Kranz, *Israelis in Berlin: Wie viele sind es und was zieht sie nach Berlin?* (Gütersloh, 2015).

29. See endnote 4 for the complete background; https://www.bertelsmann-stiftung.de/de/publikationen/publikation/did/israelis-in-berlin/.

30. Robert Leventhal, "Community, Memory, and Shifting Jewish Identities in Germany since 1989: The Case of Munich," *Journal of Jewish Identities* 4, no. 1 (2011): 13–42.

31. See Erek and Gantner in this volume.

32. They might as well be laid for other victims of Nazi terror; http://www.stolpersteine.de.

33. Yascha Mounk, *Stranger in My Own Country: A Jewish Family in Modern Germany* (New York, 2014); Dani Kranz, "Where to Stay and Where to Go? Third-Generation Jews from in Germany in Germany, Israel, and the UK," in *In the Shadows of the Shadows of the Holocaust: Narratives of the Third*

Generation, ed. Esther Jilovsky, Jordana Silverstein, and David Slucki (London, 2015), 179–208.

34. Dani Kranz, "Forget Israel-the Future is in Berlin! Local Jews, Russian Immigrants and Israeli Jews in Berlin and across Germany," *Shofar*, 34 no. 4 (2016): 5–28

35. Ibid.

36. Shlomo Deshen, "Ethnic Boundaries and Cultural Paradigms: The Case of Southern Tunisian Immigrants in Israel," *Ethos* 4, no. 3 (1976): 271–94; Aziza Khazzoom, "The Great Chain of Orientalism: Jewish Identity, Stigma Management, and Ethnic Exclusion in Israel," *American Sociological Review* 68, no. 4 (2003): 481–510; Kranz, "Changing Definitions of Germanness," 99–120.

37. Cornelia Hecht, *Deutsche Juden und Antisemitismus in der Weimarer Republik* (Bonn, 2003).

38. Joseph Goldstein, *Jewish History in Modern Times* (Brighton, 1995); Tom Segev, *The Seventh Million: Israelis and the Holocaust* (Jerusalem, 1991); Steven J. Gold and Bruce A. Phillips, "Israelis in the United States," *American Jewish Yearbook* (1996): 51–101; Shokeid, *Children of Circumstances,* 1988.

39. Segev, *Seventh Million,* 413.

40. Daniel Bar Tal and Anat Zafran, "The Influence of the Fear and the Self-Perception of Victimhood on the Israeli Understanding of Security Security: The Memory of the Holocaust and Its Implications on the Peace Process," in *In the Name of Security: Sociology of Peace and War in Changing Times,* ed. Maged Al-Haj and Uri Ben-Eliezer (Haifa, 2003). Translation of title from Hebrew to English is our own.

41. Oz Almog, *The Sabra: The Creation of the New Jew,* trans. Haim Watzman (Los Angeles, 2000); Segev, *Seventh Million.*

42. Kranz, "Changing Definitions of Germanness," 99–120.

43. Nadine Blumer, "'Am Yisrael Chai! (The Nation of Israel Lives!)': Stark Reminders of Home in the Reproduction of Ethno-Diasporic Identity," *Journal of Ethnic and Migration Studies* 37, no. 9 (2011): 1331–47; Jackie Feldman, *Above the Death Pits, Beneath the Flag: Youth Voyages to Poland and the Performance of Israeli National Identity* (Oxford, 2010).

44. Kurt Grünberg, "Bedrohung durch 'Normalität'–Juden in der BRD," in *Sozio-Psycho-Somatik: Gesellschaftliche Entwicklungen und psychosomatische Medizin,* ed. Wolfgang Söllner, Wolfgang Wesiack, and Brunhilde Wurm (Hamburg, 1989); Cilly Kugelmann, "Die Identität osteuropäischer Juden in der Bundesrepublik" in *Jüdisches Leben in Deutschland seit 1945,* ed. Micha Brumlik, Doron Kiesel, Cilly Kugelmann, and Julius Schoeps, 177–81 (Frankfurt, 1986); Andreas Kruse and Eric Schmitt, *Wir haben uns als Deutsche gefühlt: Lebensrückblick und Lebenssituation jüdischer Emigranten und Lagerhäftlinge* (Darmstadt, 1999).

45. Kranz, "Shades of Jewishness," 31, 37.

46. Cohen, "From Overt Rejection to Enthusiastic Embracement," 267–78; Kranz et al., "Most Comprehensive Survey."

47. Amirai, interview by Dani Kranz, June 22, 2015.

48. Avraham, interview by Dani Kranz, July 7, 2013.

49. Chaim, interview by Dani Kranz, February 4, 2014.

50. Baruch Kimmerling, *Immigrants, Settlers, Natives: Israel between Plurality of Cultures and Cultural Wars* (Tel Aviv, 2004); Peled, "Citizenship Betrayed," 603–28; Gershon Shafir and Yoav Peled, *Being Israeli: The Dynamics of Multiple Citizenship* (Cambridge, 2002); Yossi Yonah, "The State of All Its Citizens, a Nation-State or a Multicultural Democracy: Israel and the Boundaries of Liberal Democracy" *Alpayim* 16 (1998): 238–63. Translation of title from Hebrew to English is our own.

51. Robin A. Harper and Hani Zubida, "The Israeli Triangle: (De)Constructing the Borders between Israeliness, Jewishness and Migrant Workers," in *Israeli Identity between Orient and Occident*, ed. David Tal (London, 2013), 177–96; Dani Kranz, "Expressing Belonging through Citizenship—Are We Talking Third-Generation Israelis, Third-Generation Yekkes, or Third-Generation Diasporic German Citizens?," in *The Meaning of Citizenship*, ed. Richard Marback and Marc W. Kruman (Detroit, 2015), 95–125; Kranz, "Quasi-ethnic Capital," 64–83; Masri, "Love Suspended," 309–34.

52. See Amit in this volume.

53. Yiftachel, *Ethnocracy.*

54. Darya Maoz, "Young Israeli Backpackers in India," in *Israeli Backpackers: From Tourism to Rite of Passage*, ed. Chaim Noy and Erik Cohen (Albany, 2005), 159–88.

55. Ibid., 150; Kranz et al., "Most Comprehensive Survey."

56. Amitai and Einat, interview by Dani Kranz, June 22, 2015.

57. Gila, interview by Dani Kranz, June 27, 2014.

58. Kranz, *Israelis in Berlin*, 8–10. The campaign and all information ran in Hebrew language only.

59. Ibid., 8.

60. For a more detailed account of a specifically ideologically fraught and complex relationship Israeli emigrants can have with their home country, see Amit's contribution to this volume, where she analyzes the ways in which Israeli activists in Berlin deterritorialize the Hebrew language from its association with Zion, or Israel.

61. Kranz, "Where to Stay," 179.

62. See Amit in this volume.

63. Rani, interview by Dani Kranz, December 16, 2015.

64. Amanda Klekowski von Koppenfels, *Migrants or Expatriates? Americans in Europe* (Basingstoke, 2014).

65. Kranz et al., "Most Comprehensive Survey."

66. Maria, interview by Dani Kranz, April 27, 2015.

67. Ibid.

68. In line with the general right swing of the German population, anti-foreigner and populist sentiments have become more public in Berlin and

moved out of the far-right corner (Nitzan Shoshan, *Managing Hate* [Stanford, 2015])

69. See Erek and Gantner in this volume.

70. Rents in Berlin have increased strongly, and the city is gentrifying. This development has been much debated in particular in the German public, media, and across the local and national political sphere.

71. Family sizes in Germany are smaller compared to those in Israel, families live across the whole country, and weekly visits to parents and grandparents for each Shabbat are uncommon in Germany. Furthermore, the personal space of Germans is generally more pronounced than that of Israelis. One Israeli commented on this—"We pay a very high price for the warmth"—when the matter of proximity came up in conversation (Jana, interview by Dani Kranz, May 14, 2016).

72. Kinneret Lahad, "The Single Woman's Choice as a Zero-Sum Game," *Cultural Studies* 28, no. 2 (2013): 240–66.

73. Kranz et al., "Most Comprehensive Survey."

74. Noam, interview by Dani Kranz, November 7, 2015.

75. Mati Shemoelof, "Here I Sit, with Two Refugees from Mashad," *Haokets,* April 12, 2014, ‏הנה אני יושב עם שני הפליטים ממשהד/‏http://www.haokets.org/2014/ 04/12/.

76. Oren, interview by Dani Kranz, December 20, 2015.

77. Yael, interview by Hadas Cohen, August 5, 2015.

78. Miri, interview by Dani Kranz, October 9, 2015.

79. Kanaan's Facebook page, accessed June 12, 2016, https://www.facebook .com/KanaanRestaurantBerlin/timeline; Noa Provizor, "POD–Design Now," *Headstart,* http://www.headstart.co.il/project.aspx?id=17537&lan=en-US.

80. Ishmail, interview by Dani Kranz, February 2, 2016.

81. Oren, interview by Hadas Cohen, July 22, 2015.

82. Amit's piece in this volume provides another possibility of Israeli existence in Berlin, one that considers the city to be more than simply a carefree home for Israelis migrants. Instead, she argues, based on her ethnographic work with the Israeli activists, in Berlin these migrants are creating a new independent and unique Israeli identity, which, even if diasporic, is parallel rather than a mere satellite to the homeland.

83. Philipp Volkmann-Schluck, "Berlin ist noch immer kein normaler Ort," *Morgenpost,* January 27, 2014, http://www.morgenpost.de/berlin-aktuell/arti cle124251429/Berlin-ist-noch-immer-kein-normaler-Ort.html.

84. Lynn Rapaport, *Jews in Germany after the Holocaust* (Cambridge, 1997); Kranz, "Shades of Jewishness," 23–30.

85. Karen O'Reilly and Michaela Benson, "Lifestyle Migration: Escaping to the Good Life?," in *Lifestyle Migration: Expectations, Aspirations and Experiences,* ed. Karen O'Reilly and Michaela Benson (Farnham, 2009), 1–14.

86. Marcel Erlinghagen, "Nowhere Better than Here? The Subjective Well-Being of German Emigrants and Remigrants," *Comparative Population Studies— Zeitschrift für Bevölkerungswissenschaft* 36, no. 4 (2011): 899–926.

Bibliography

Almog, Oz. *The Sabra: The Creation of the New Jew.* Berkeley: University of California Press, 2000.

Bar Tal, Daniel, and Anat Zafran. "The Influence of the Fear and the Self-Perception of Victimhood on the Israeli Understanding of Security: The Memory of the Holocaust and Its Implications on the Peace Process." In *In the Name of Security: Sociology of Peace and War in Changing Times,* edited by Maged Al-Haj and Uri Ben-Eliezer, 329–68. Haifa: Haifa University Press, 2003. (Hebrew)

Cohen, Erez. "'We Are Staying in Our Country—Here': Israeli Mediascapes in Melbourne." *Journal of Ethnic and Migration Studies* 34, no. 6 (2008): 1003–19.

Cohen, Nir. "From Overt Rejection to Enthusiastic Embracement: Changing State Discourses on Israeli Emigration," *GeoJournal* 68, no. 2/3 (2007): 267–78.

Cohen, Nir, and Dani Kranz. "State-Assisted Highly Skilled Return Programs, National Identity and the Risk(s) of Homecoming: Israel and Germany Compared." *Journal of Ethnic and Migration Studies* 41, no. 5 (2015): 795–812.

Cohen, Yinon. "Migration Patterns to and from Israel." *Contemporary Jewry* 29 (2009): 115–25.

Deshen, Shlomo. "Ethnic Boundaries and Cultural Paradigms: The Case of Southern Tunisian Immigrants in Israel." *Ethos* 4, no. 3 (1976): 271–94.

Diner, Dan. *Rituelle Distanz: Israels deutsche Frage.* Munich: Deutsche Verlags-Anstalt Erlinghausen, 2015.

Ezrahi, Yaron. *Rubber Bullets: Power and Conscience in Modern Israel.* New York: Farrar, Strauss, and Giroux, 1997.

Fabian, Johannes. *Time and the Other: How Anthropology Makes Its Object.* New York: Columbia University Press, 1983.

Feldman, Jackie. *Above the Death Pits, Beneath the Flag: Youth Voyages to Poland and the Performance of Israeli National Identity.* Oxford: Berghahn Books, 2008.

Gold, Steven J. *The Israeli Diaspora.* London: Routledge, 2002.

Gold, Steven J., and Bruce A. Phillips, "Israelis in the United States," *American Jewish Yearbook* (1996): 51–101.

Goldstein, Joseph. *Jewish History.* Brighton: Sussex Academic Press, 1995.

Grünberg, Kurt. "Bedrohung durch 'Normalität'–Juden in der BRD." In *Wurm, Sozio-Psycho-Somatik: Gesellschaftliche Entwicklungen und psychosomatische Medizin,* edited by Wolfgang Soellner and Wolfgang Wesiack, 127–34. Hamburg: Springer Verlag, 1989.

Handelman, Don. *Nationalism and the Israeli State: Bureaucratic Logic in Public Events.* New York: Berg, 2004.

Harpaz, Yossi. "Israelis and the European Passport: Dual Citizenship in an Apocalyptic Immigrant Society." Master's thesis, Tel Aviv University, 2009.

Harper, Robin, and Hani Zubida. "The Israeli Triangle: (De)Constructing the Borders between Israeliness, Jewishness and Migrant Workers." In *Israeli Iden-*

tity between Orient and Occident, edited by David Tal, 177–96. London: Routledge, 2013.

Harris, Brent David. "Beyond Guilt and Stigma: Changing Attitudes among Israeli Migrants in Canada." *International Migration* 53, no. 6 (2012): 41–56.

Hecht, Cornelia. *Deutsche Juden und Antisemitismus.* Bonn: Verlag J. H. W. Dietz, 2003.

Hegner, Victoria. *Gelebte Selbstbilder: Russisch-jüdische Immigranten.* Frankfurt: Campus, 2008.

Heilman, Samuel C. "Jewish Sociologist: Native as Stranger." The American Sociologist 15 (1980): 100–1008.

Katz, Guy. *Intercultural Negotiation.* Norderstedt: Books on Demand, 2011.

Khazzoom, Aziza. "The Great Chain of Orientalism: Jewish Identity, Stigma Management, and Ethnic Exclusion in Israel." *American Sociological Review* 68, no. 4 (2003): 481–510.

Kein Ort der Freiheit: Das Tempelhofer Feld 1933–1945. Berlin: Berliner Geschichtswerkstatt, 2012.

Kimmerling, Baruch. *Immigrants, Settlers, Natives: Israel between Plurality of Cultures and Cultural Wars.* Tel Aviv: Am Oved, 2004. (Hebrew)

———. "Militarism in the Israeli Society." *Theory and Criticism* 4 (1993): 123–35.

Kranz, Dani. "Changing Definitions of Germanness across Three Generations of *Yekkes* in Palestine/Israel." *German Studies Review* 39, no. 1 (2016): 99–120.

———. "Dynamische ethnische Beziehungen mal 2 oder hoch 2? Deutsch/israelisch und inner-israelisch." Public lecture given at Johann Guttenberg, Universität Mainz, December 3, 2016.

———. "Expressing Belonging through Citizenship – Are we talking Third Generation Israelis, Third Generation Yekkes, or Third Generation Diasporic German Citizens?" In *The Meaning of Citizenship,* edited by Richard Marback and Marc W. Kruman, 95–125. Detroit, Wayne State University Press, 2015.

———. "Forget Israel—the Future is in Berlin! Local Jews, Russian Immigrants and Israeli Jews in Berlin and across Germany." *Shofar* 34 no. 4 (2016): 5–28.

———. *Israelis in Berlin: Wie viele sind es und was zieht sie nach Berlin?* [*Israelis in Berlin: How many are there and what drives them to Berlin?*]. Gütersloh: Bertelsmann Stiftung, 2015.

———. "Quasi-ethnic Capital vs. Quasi-citizenship Capital: Access to Israeli Citizenship, Migration Letters." *Migration Letters* 13, no. 1 (2016): 64–83.

———. "Shades of Jewishness: The Creation and Maintenance of a Liberal Jewish Community in Post-Shoah Germany" (PhD diss., University of St. Andrews, 2009).

———. "Where to Stay and Where to Go? Third-Generation Jews from in Germany in Germany, Israel, and the UK," in *In the Shadows of the Shadows of the Holocaust: Narratives of the Third Generation,* edited by Esther Jilovsky, Jordana Silverstein, and David Slucki, 179-208. London, Valentine Mitchell, 2015.

Kranz, Dani, Uzi Rebhun, and Heinz Sünker. "The Most Comprehensive Survey among Israelis in Germany Confirms the Image: Secular, Educated, and Left." *Spitz.* Accessed December 4, 2015 at http://spitzmag.de/webonly/7238.

Kruse, Anderas, and Eric Schmitt. *Wir haben uns als Deutsche gefühlt: Lebensrückblick und Lebenssituation jüdischer Emigranten und Lagerhäftlinge.* Darmstadt: Steinkopff-Verlag, 1999.

Kugelmann, Cilly. "Die Identität osteuropäischer Juden in der Bundesrepublik." In *Jüdisches Leben in Deutschland seit 1945,* edited by Micha Brumlik, Doron Kiesel, Cilly Kugelmann, and Julius Schoeps, 177–81. Frankfurt: Jüdischer Verlag bei Athenäum, 1988.

Lahad, Kinneret. "The Single Woman's Choice as a Zero-Sum Game." *Cultural Studies* 28, no. 2 (2013): 240–66.

Leventhal, Robert. "Community, Memory, and Shifting Jewish Identities in Germany since 1989: The Case of Munich." *Journal of Jewish Identities* 4, no. 1 (2011): 13–42.

Löw-Beer, Martin "From Nowhere to Israel and Back: The Changing Self-Definition of German-Jewish Youth since 1960." In *Germans, Jews and Memory: Reconstructions of Jewish Life in Germany,* edited by Y. Michal Bodemann, 101–30. Ann Arbor: University of Michigan Press, 1996.

Maoz, Darya. "Young Israeli Backpackers in India." In *Israeli Backpackers: From Tourism to Rite of Passage,* edited by Erik Cohen and Chaim Noy, 159–80. Albany: State University of New York Press, 2005.

Masri, Mazen. "Love Suspended: Demography, Comparative Law and Palestinian Couples in the Israeli Supreme Court." *Social & Legal Studies* 22, no. 3 (2013): 309–34.

Mounk, Yascha. *Stranger in My Own Country: A Jewish Family in Modern Germany.* New York: Farrar, Strauss, and Giroux, 1982.

Olesker, Ronnie. "Law-Making and the Securitization of the Jewish Identity in Israel." *Ethnopolitics* 13, no. 2 (2014): 105–21.

O'Reilly, Karen, and Michaela Benson. "Lifestyle Migration: Escaping to the Good Life?" In *Lifestyle Migration: Expectations, Aspirations and Experiences,* edited by Karen O'Reilly and Michaela Benson. Farnham: Ashgate, 2009.

Panagiotidis, Jannis. "A Policy for the Future: German-Jewish Remigrants, Their Children, and the Politics of Israeli Nation-Building." *Leo Baeck Institute Year Book* 60 (2015): 191–206.

Peled, Yoav. "Citizenship Betrayed: Israel's Emerging Immigration and Citizenship Regime." *Theoretical Inquiries in Law* 8, no. 2 (2007): 603–28.

Rapaport, Lynn. *Jews in Germany after the Holocaust.* Cambridge: Cambridge University Press, 1997.

Sabar, Galia, and Elizabeth Tsurkov. "Israel's Policies toward Asylum-Seekers: 2002–2014." *Instituto Affari Internazionali,* May 20, 2015. Accessed March 12, 2017. http://www.osce.org/networks/165436?download=true.

Schütze, Yvonne. "'Warum Deutschland und nicht Israel?' Begründungen russischer Juden für die Migration nach Deutschland." *BIOS* 10, no. 2 (1997): 186–208.

Segev, Tom. *The Seventh Million: The Israelis and the Holocaust.* New York: Hill and Wang, 1991.

Shafir, Gershon, and Yoav Peled. *Being Israeli.* Cambridge: University of Cambridge Press, 2002.

Shemoelof, Mati. "Here I Sit, with Two Refugees from Mashad." *Haokets,* April 12, 2014. Accessed March 12, 2017. http://www.haokets.org/2014/04/12/ ‫.הנה אני יושב עם שני הפליטים ממשהד‬

Shokeid, Moshe. *Children of Circumstances: Israeli Emigrants in New York.* Ithaca, NY: Cornell University Press, 1988.

Shoshan, Nitzan. *Managing Hate.* Palo Alto: Stanford University Press, 2015.

Silber, Marcos. "'Immigrants from Poland Want to Go Back': The Politics of Return Migration and Nation Building in 1950s Israel." *Journal of Israeli History: Politics, Society, Culture* 27, no. 2 (2008): 201–19.

Smooha, Sammy. "Still Playing by the Rules: Index of Arab-Jewish Relations in Israel 2015. Summary of Main Finds." Personal email to Dani Kranz, February 5, 2016.

Volkmann-Schluck, Philipp. "Berlin ist noch immer kein normaler Ort." *Morgenpost,* January 27, 2014. Accessed March 12, 2017. http://www.morgenpost .de/berlin-aktuell/article124251429/Berlin-ist-noch-immer-kein-normaler-Ort.html.

von Koppenfels, Amanda. *Migrants or Expatriates? Americans in Europe.* Basingstoke: Palgrave-Macmillan, 2014.

Weisberg, Hila. "One Question before You Speak of Zionism, Mr. Lapid: When Was the Last Time You Thought about Making Ends Meet." *Ha'aretz Online,* October 2, 2013, http://www.themarker.com/career/1.2130595.

Yiftachel, Oren. *Ethnocracy: Land and Identity Politics in Israel/Palestine.* Philadelphia: University of Pennsylvania Press, 2006.

Yonah, Yossi. "The State of All Its Citizens, a Nation-State or a Multicultural Democracy: Israel and the Boundaries of Liberal Democracy." *Alpayim* 16 (1998): 238–63.

CHAPTER 14

Through the Eyes of Angels and Vampires

Berlin Ruins in Wings of Desire *and* We Are the Night

Peter Gölz

We Are the Night,[1] Dennis Gansel's hip Berlin vampire film, released in 2010, can be read as a response to Wim Wenders's ode to Berlin, *Wings of Desire*,[2] or as a genre-bending contribution to the recent lure of the undead. The love stories of the immortals and the human objects of their desire link the two films on the narrative level, but the more interesting connection is their depiction of Berlin, both as a place of ruinification and reunification. Presenting the divided East and West Berlin of the late 1980s and the metropolis of the new millennium, the two films complement each other's imagery of Berlin and its history. In *Wings of Desire* the past is always present and performs a dialogue with the present, whereas in *We Are the Night* history is compartmentalized both spatially and temporarily and quite literally covered up. However, central locations in the two films, the *Pallasseum* and its bunker and the Devil's Mountain, both exemplify that "no amount of bombing or bull-dozing can fully eradicate the traces of what came before, either in the landscape itself or in the memories and habits of its residents."[3] Or, as Andre Schütze confirms in his "The Uncanny City: Berlin in International Film" in this volume, "the past does not disappear."

Wim Wenders's *Wings of Desire,* released just before the fall of the Wall in 1987, has often been called the prototypical postmodern city movie (German and otherwise), with stunning images by Henri Alekan and highly poetic and stylized dialogues by Peter Handke.[4] Wenders had just returned to Germany after eight years of making movies in the United States[5] where he "came to the conclusion that a new narrative cinema must establish itself against the growing dominance of industry-produced films."[6] Not only did he want to shoot another film in Germany, he wanted to attempt the ultimate Berlin film, a movie that would capture the uniqueness of the city, seen through new eyes and from a totally different perspective—a film that would also pay tribute to the unique history of the city and to the way it memorizes and presents itself.[7] In Wenders's own words,

> When God, endlessly disappointed, finally prepared to turn his back on the world forever, it happened that some of his angels disagreed with him and took the side of humans, saying they deserved to be given a second chance. Angry at being crossed, God banished them to what was then the most terrible place on earth: BERLIN.... All this happened at the time that we today call the end of the Second World War. Since that time these fallen angels ... [have been] condemned to be witnesses, forever nothing but onlookers, unable ... to intervene in the course of history.[8]

This angelic perspective gave Wenders the fresh eyes he needed to look at the city "both as a bridge to the past and as a pivotal city for peaceful coexistence in the world. ... Angels living in Berlin preserve the memory and even presence of Germany's history, while helping the inhabitants bear the burden of the nation's past."[9]

The angels in *Wings of Desire* and the vampires in *We Are the Night* approach the city on airplanes, echoing the Berlin Airlift and the birth of the New Berlin. The fallen angel Peter Falk, playing a fictionalized version of himself (Columbo), flies into Berlin reminiscing about his grandmother, big cities, and his upcoming movie shoot. Damiel, the not-yet-fallen angel accompanies him on the plane, doing what Wenders's and Handke's angels do best—listening to peoples' thoughts and passively recording history. A slow, artistic, black-and-white intro shows an extreme close-up of an all-seeing eye that takes us on the poetic journey of what Wenders called a "vertical road movie."[10] The omniscient view of Berlin continues and moves from the eye to Damiel, perched high on top of the Kaiser Wilhelm Memorial Church looking down at a group of children. They return his gaze and point up to him, stressing the subjective, angelic view of the camera.[11] The site of Damiel's lookout, the bombed-out Memorial Church and its new belfry, is one of the most recognizable Berlin ruins. As a memorial to World War II and the church's destruction in 1943, it is a perfect example of what Jennifer Jordan calls "authentic sites":

The memorial projects constructed in recent years have generally been on "authentic" sites. Many people involved in discussions about memorials and historic preservation distinguish readily between authentic and inauthentic sites, the former being those on which (or in which) recorded and/or remembered events actually occurred.[12]

As an authentic site in Jordan's sense and a popular tourist spot, the Memorial Church used to point to a specific historic period.[13] Its singular reference point is complemented by another central location in *Wings of Desire*, the Victory Column and its multiple layers of authenticity—it refers to the Prussian wars, the Nazis' planned World Capital Germania, and it was used as a symbol for the 1990s Love Parades. More recently, it gained international recognition as the site of Barack Obama's 2008 speech in which he told the world repeatedly to "look at Berlin" and also to look beyond the well-known memory sites and to focus on "the bullet holes in the buildings and the somber stones and pillars near the Brandenburg Gate" instead.[14]

But while the angels often watch the world go by from recognizable sites high above, they also like to mingle with humans and to get as close to them as possible, in the streets or on the subway. Their favorite meeting place, their "primary earthly domicile,"[15] is the public library, the *Staatsbibliothek Potsdamer Platz,* with its futuristic reading room. There they move among the Berliners and listen to their thoughts. "In one of the seemingly arbitrary texts overheard in the library, we find a key to [*Wings'*] historical perspective," Roger Cook explains.[16] The very first thoughts we/the angels hear refer to Walter Benjamin's interpretation of his Paul Klee painting *Angelus Novus,* which perfectly describes the role history plays in *Wings of Desire*:

A Klee painting named *Angelus Novus* shows an angel looking as though he is about to move away from something he is fixedly contemplating. His eyes are staring, his mouth is open, his wings are spread. This is how one pictures the angel of history. His face is turned toward the past. Where we perceive a chain of events, he sees one single catastrophe which keeps piling up wreckage upon wreckage and hurls it in front of his feet. The angel would like to stay, awaken the dead and make whole what has been smashed.[17]

As passive spectators, Wenders's angels have been taking notes and exchanging impressions since the beginning of time, always reminiscent of the past. But when Damiel decides to fall in love with Marion the wing-wearing flying trapeze artist, he is ready to give up his passive, watchful existence so he can finally partake in life's pleasures and the physical aspects of love. As Kolker and Beicken point out, "*Wings of*

Desire proposes that redemption occur with a descent into physicality ... [because] spiritual being is less rewarding than earthly sexual fulfillment."[18] Damiel leaves behind his life as an "Unborn"[19] and his elevated viewpoint by literally falling into the present as a mere mortal. He awakens to his new life next to a colorful section of the Wall.

When Damiel and Marion meet at the end of the film at the bar of the Hotel Esplanade, a former "favorite meeting place for upper-echelon Nazis during the Reich,"[20] their final dialogue culminates in a Nietzschean "postmodern dawning of the gods."[21] Both of them are looking forward to a new life as the Adam and Eve of a new generation of giants, where ancient binaries like male (angel) and female (human), or East and West, are finally united. The Esplanade is another authentic site whose *Kaisersaal* and Breakfast Hall are now memorialized in the Sony Center at Potsdamer Platz.[22] In part through its topography, *Wings of Desire* thus continues its dialogue with the ever-present past even when the topic is the future. With its optimistic outlook, it is also an almost prophetic prediction of the fall of the Wall only two years after its release. The intensity with which *Wings of Desire* portrays the divided city and its memorials, from the Memorial Church to the Victory Column and the Esplanade bar makes it stand out among the Berlin films from the same period, as Schütze explains in his article in this volume.

Twenty-three years after the immortal Damiel had stopped exploring the sky over Berlin to become a mortal, another set of immortals approaches the city through the air, but this time on a private jet. *We Are the Night'*s three female vampires are returning to their city of choice after a shopping spree in Paris with many bags and a dead crew. They jump off the plane and we look down at the dark Berlin through their eyes. Just like at the beginning of *Wings of Desire* and its angelic duo, the striking image of an extreme close-up of an eye points to the vampiric trio watching from high above. The first building we see is the Alexanderplatz TV Tower, easily recognizable as the most popular symbol of the New Berlin, as Ingram states, "[The Brandenburg] Gate has thus far proven unable to compete with the post-socialist TV Tower at Alexanderplatz, which was arguably the city's most popular symbol at the outset of the 2010s."[23] The TV tower in *We Are the Night* has the same leitmotif function as the Memorial Church and the Victory Column in *Wings of Desire,* easily recognizable as the symbol of the New Berlin. A still image of the TV tower also starts the title sequence of *We Are the Night,* which presents Berlin's history as a series of compartmentalized events in a slideshow format. This format is reminiscent of the beginning of *Goodbye Lenin,* which presents a similar historic review with the help of GDR postcards.[24] The slideshow in *We Are the Night* begins in the film's present, twenty years after the fall of the Wall, with the iconic TV tower, previously the icon of the GDR capital and now a symbol for the New Berlin. It continues with another site that also represents the new unity of the formerly divided city, the Berghain Nightclub, whose name is a composite of Kreuzberg in the former West Berlin and Friedrichshain in the former East.

The first member of the vampire trio introduced in the slideshow is Nora, the youngest and the trio's superficial pleasure seeker, born to the vampire's nightlife during a Love Parade. The focus on this event as a central symbol for the three female vampires' histories and their hedonistic lifestyles shows its symbolic significance for the post-Wall Berlin years: "[P]erhaps more than any other cultural movement of the 1990s, [the Love Parade] symbolized utopian dreams in the reunified Berlin Babylon," argues Katrina Sark in this volume. After establishing the vampires' indebtedness to the 1990s hedonistic Berlin, Gansel's retrospective quickly moves on and almost completely skips the divided Germany with only a single slide of the 1960s. He then takes us to the end of the Second World War and bombed-out Berlin. The second member of the vampire trio introduced in the slideshow, Charlotte, became a vampire in a similarly lively and exciting period, the swinging 1920s. She is shown in an edited still from Fritz Lang's *Dr. Mabuse: The Gambler*,[25] coincidentally released the same year as the oldest preserved vampire film, *Nosferatu*, in 1922.[26] Without any references to World War I, the Panoptikum Waxwork Museum at the turn of the century and the 1848 Revolution round up the slideshow, which finally zooms in on the painted face of the head vampire Louise. She gazes out at us from Adolph Menzel's painting *Frederick the Great's Flute Concert in Sanssouci,* in which her face replaces Frederick's sister's in the very center. Three hundred years of history are wrapped up in high speed, giving us a glimpse of the times the three vampires were turned. As befitting a vampire film, in addition to the indirect reference to the birth of the cinematic vampire Nosferatu, the Menzel painting at the end of the slideshow also points to the time when the modern, literary vampire was born in the eighteenth century.[27]

However, the importance of the title sequence lies not only in the choice of historical events but in its kind of *Verangenheitsbewältigung* (coming to terms with the past), or rather its lack thereof: the past, it seems, will be pushed to the side for the rest of the movie to make way for the vampires' hedonistic nightlife in New Berlin. Our first introduction to the vampire trio was on their return from a shopping spree in

Paris. They continue their life of hedonism and consumerism in Berlin during a private nightly no-limits shopping spree at the Alexanderplatz department store, formerly the *HO-Centrum-Warenhaus,* the GDR's largest department store, and now the *Galeria Kaufhof Alexanderplatz.* There Nora succinctly summarizes the trio's credo: "We eat, drink, sniff coke, and fuck as much as we like. But we never get fat, pregnant, or hooked."[28] They live to consume anything and anybody they desire, and their hedonism is only limited by the fear of being discovered. The vampires' credo continuously echoes the anarchic spirit of the early 1990s as well as the present longing for this time, which Katrina Sark in her article in this volume aptly calls the "nostalgia for Babylon."

Representing a city that is more alive during the night than during the day, the vampires personify what producer Christian Becker had in mind: "to show Berlin as a pulsating metropolis."[29] Wenders's pre-unification *Angelus Novus* is replaced, to cite the title of a 1970s classic vampire movie, by a very lively group of *Vampyros Lesbos.*[30] As part of the cinematic history of lesbian vampires, *We Are the Night*'s trio continues the tradition of what Andrea Weiss has called "the most persistent lesbian image in the history of the cinema."[31] They introduce the newcomer Lena to their history, a straightforward feminist revision of common male vampire tales:

> "How many of you are there?"
>
> "Forty women in Europe, one hundred worldwide."
>
> "And the men?"
>
> "Extinct. They were too loud, too greedy, and too stupid."
>
> "Long live emancipation!"
>
> "Yes, for over two hundred years, no man, neither mortal nor immortal, has told me what to do. No king, no boss, no husband. What woman can make that claim?"[32]

The new vampire quartet also shows its indebtedness to classic lesbian vampire tales, particularly when Louise exhibits traces of *Carmilla,* Sheridan Le Fanu's groundbreaking novel from 1872,[33] and, even more so, in relation to Whitley Strieber's novel *The Hunger* as well as Tony Scott's movie of the same name from 1983.[34] In both cases, the female protagonist is a vampire seductress nobody can resist. In the latter, Catherine Deneuve as Miriam Blaylock collects former lovers and endlessly continues her quest to find perfect replacements for them, just like Louise. Blaylock, the *The Hunger*'s metropolitan vampire in New York City, is complemented by Louise in Berlin.

After the quartet's explorations of direct and indirect connections with literary and cinematic lesbian vampires, it comes as a surprise that the conservative and very heterosexual blockbuster *Twilight*[35] has more in common with the conceptualization of *We Are the Night* than the celebration of women's emancipation had suggested. The vampires' nightlives surprisingly end with the death of the original infernal trio and a salute to the heterosexual love story of Lena, the new vampire, and her human lover Tom. Dennis Gansel's three-page exposé "The Dawn," which he had already written in 1996,[36] was actually so close to the record-breaking *Twilight* that he had to rewrite it completely to receive funding. While the plot now has less in common with the blockbuster, the heterosexual desire of vampire and human remains, albeit now with a role reversal of female vampire and male human. While *We Are the Night*'s sexual politics sidestep the film's critical potential, the city as central character succeeds.

The trio's birth to their Berlin nightlife is portrayed in the introductory slideshow by individual stills. Lena's metamorphosis from *Bahnhof Zoo* pickpocket to high-flying vampire, on the other hand, seems much more complicated, and every step of her transformation is described in detail. Her journey begins at her apartment on Pallasstraße, and after a short encounter with her mother and her probation officer, Lena runs away and strolls through the streets of Berlin on a hunt for unlocked cars. She passes a large advertisement that says "Are you ready?"—and she is. Her nightly exploration leads her to the vampire trio's nightclub where Louise keeps a close eye on the club's entrance, always on the lookout for a new companion and lover, somewhat reminiscent of *The Hunger*'s Miriam Blaylock. Lena begins her transformation after she is bitten by Louise, and her physical metamorphosis takes place back in her apartment in the *Pallasseum*.

The *Pallasseum* is the only site that is prominently featured in both *We Are the Night* and *Wings of Desire*. In *We Are the Night*, Lena's apartment is one of more than five hundred apartments for more than two thousand tenants in this immense building complex on the Pallasstraße. In *Wings of Desire*, however, the only part of the *Pallasseum* that is shown is the World War II bunker it was constructed around. Now surrounded by the apartments, the bunker was built by forced laborers from the Soviet Union during World War II. Because it was too dangerous to destroy it without endangering the surrounding buildings, it was repurposed between 1986 and 1989 and turned into the largest civilian bunker in Berlin, with enough space for 4,800 people, and in 2002 it became a "Place of Memory."[37] As Jordan states, it is not unusual at all for Berlin ruins to be integrated in new buildings where they "slip into the fabric of daily life. There are apartments built on the site of Hitler's chancellery, for example, constructed in the 1980s by the East German government, and Sony's European headquarters were built in the 1990s on the site of one of Berlin's most infamous Nazi courts."[38]

Figure 14.1. *Pallasseum Berlin, Blick vom Kleistpark* (View from Kleistpark). Permission Manfred Brückels (Creative Commons Attribution-Share Alike 3.0) https://commons.wikimedia.org/wiki/File:Pallasseum_Berlin_Blick_vom_Kleistpark.jpg.

The *Pallasseum* bunker is a prime example of such an integrated ruin. At the same time, it perfectly symbolizes the two films' dialogue with Berlin history. The *Hochbunker Pallasstraße* remains invisible in *We Are the Night,* just like the apartment building surrounding it can only be seen in the blink of an eye in *Wings of Desire.* But in the end it is the *Pallasseum*'s duality that speaks to the different presentations of history. Or, in Jordan's words, "It is rare that the traces of previous ways of treating the landscape are fully erased. ... The terrain of past political eras combines with new efforts to shape landscapes of memory to create a multiple and even conflicting narrative of different elements of the past."[39]

As the central location in *Wings of Desire* for Peter Falk's movie shoot, the *Pallasseum* bunker is also a "site for confrontation of today's attempts to grasp the past, with all the problems of ... misinterpretations, and it is the place where Peter Falk draws, in an attempt to capture today's thinking of yesterday."[40] As the site of the dialogue between the present and historic past of the film shoot, the bunker also presents the end of Damiel's metamorphosis from angel to human and serves as a site of communication between Damiel and Peter Falk, the two fallen angels.

Wings of Desire focuses on the historic past, and *We Are the Night* seems to hide it. Nevertheless, a closer look at the sites that accompany Lena's transformation shows that it is impossible to ignore the historical layers. While Lena's apartment is located in the former West, the locations that accompany her metamorphosis into a hedonistic vampire are all located in the former East. Lena first encounters the vampire trio at a rave in a derelict former public pool in Lichtenberg that now serves as the vampires' nightclub and hangout. She runs through the abandoned East German *Spreewald* entertainment park and finally learns what it takes to be a vampire in the deserted GDR radio station on Nalepastraße.[41] There she completes her transformation into a vampire predator, who is not running away any more but forcefully fights back and takes a bite out of a Russian pimp who had violently attacked her. And while *Wings of Desire* clearly shows its indebtedness to the West German *Vergangenheitsbewältigung* that was also central for the New German Cinema, Lena the vampire is born from East German ruins, a new life in a unified Berlin that is, like the GDR national anthem stated, "risen from the ruins and facing the future."[42]

But not only Lena rose out of the ruins. The idea of making a vampire movie set in Berlin was reportedly born late one night when director Dennis Gansel walked past ruins along the river Spree:

> After an incredible night at the nightclub Tresor, I walked home through the area around *Schlesisches Tor.* At that time there were factories all along the river. I couldn't believe that in a city of millions and in such a

fancy area there could be derelict, empty buildings in which anything could happen. At home my then-girlfriend had waited up for me. She showed me some photographs of herself. There were all poorly exposed but sexy and sinister. At that point I thought: I have to make a vampire movie. In this city. [43]

These ruins as well as the ones that accompany Lena's transformation serve as reminders that Berlin's reunification also saw a simultaneous ruinification. Unmodified and unmediated, these ruins possess an authenticity that other so-called authentic sites like, for example, the Kaiser Wilhelm Memorial Church have lost. The immediate and unmediated attraction of the three sites of Lena's metamorphosis are perfect examples of what has been poignantly described as "ruin porn." This fascination with images of ruins started in Detroit, and now Berlin has become a poster child for ruinified cities, and the old *Spreepark* is one of the most recognizable ones, as Lyons explains: "The allure of ruin remains prominent in tourism and popular culture, including abandoned amusement parks such as Sydney's Magic Kingdom park, Germany's Cold War-era Spreepark, and Japan's Takakanonuma Greenland in the Fukushima district."[44] As a combination of scopophilic attraction and historic reflection, such ruins "resonate with us today because it is an unmediated experience in a mediated culture. ... The old and decayed buildings are not cleaned up or packaged, frozen as time capsules. They poke through the patina of tourism; there are no postcards here. History is present in our minds, stirring our memories."[45]

While the ruins that had accompanied Lena on her path to become a vampire are all in the former GDR, the final showdown of *We Are the Night* takes place at an abandoned former American spy station, located on top of Berlin's Devil's Mountain. Like the *Pallasseum* and its bunker, it is also built on a monument that was much easier to cover up than to remove. Named for the nearby Devil's Lake just outside Berlin, one wonders if Gansel could have come up with a location more befitting a vampire confrontation. In the original script, the film's showdown was supposed to take place in a run-down hotel close to the airport, but Gansel changed the location to the much more befitting mountain.[46]

Unlike Lena's GDR ruins, Devil's Mountain consists of various authentic layers of Berlin's history, from the Third Reich to the birth of West Berlin, and from the Cold War to the fall of the Wall. It was the place where Hitler had laid the foundation for his *Wehrtechnische Fakultät (military university)*—the fascist university that was intended to complement the *Welthauptstadt* (the "World Capital Germania") designed by his "first architect of the Third Reich," Albert Speer. Hitler had planned

Figure 14.2. One of numerous graffiti in the ruins of the Devil's Mountain spy station (*Teufelsberg*). Permission Peter Gölz.

an East-West axis from the Alexanderplatz to the Victory Column and to the university on Devil's Mountain. But the *Wehrtechnische Fakultät* was never finished, and after the war "the Allies tried using explosives to demolish the school, but it was so sturdy that covering it with debris turned out to be easier. In June 1950, the West Berlin Magistrate decided to open a new rubble disposal on that site."[47] The rubble of the destroyed city finally covered Hitler's megalomaniac plans and made it the highest mountain in Berlin. Six hundred trucks a day deposited debris there because it would have been too expensive to move it further away. As the highest elevation close to the city, it became a ski resort in the 1950s and there were many plans for developing the mountain. However, as an authentic memory site of fascism and postwar renewal in a divided East and West Berlin, it is also a prime monument to the Cold War precisely because it served as a US spy station from 1961 until the fall of the Wall. The spectacular setting and the large towers "have come to assume an aesthetic presence, inviting the viewer to fill out the broken form through the active dynamism of the imagination."[48]

In the ruins of the old spy station, the three-hundred-year old Louise fights with newborn Lena high above the city. Louise promises that she won't harm Lena's boyfriend Tom if she tells her convincingly that she loves her. Lena tries repeatedly but Louise doesn't believe her. She knows that Lena has made her decision and that she will defend her man until the end. Louise shoots Tom but does not kill him in order to force Lena into a decision that will end the film. Louise is defeated and burns up, drifting toward the sun. Lena now has to decide whether or not to save Tom by turning him into a vampire. In the general release version, this question remains unanswered and Lena and Tom just disappear from one cut to the next. A long aerial shot of Berlin ends the film, and just like at the very beginning, we fly past the TV tower one last time. In addition to this ambiguous, open end, there are two alternative endings on the German DVD. The first shows Lena running away and leaving the wounded Tom behind, and the second alternate ending shows Lena biting Tom and turning him into a vampire.

In all cases, and also in *Wings of Desire*'s with its final "To be continued," the couple sets out into their new life, leaving their former partners behind. The thoughtful, passive angels of the past and the hedonistic, action-driven consumer vampires of the present complement each other and describe the New Berlin of the twenty-first century from their viewpoints in the sky over the city. Each in their own way and with differing intensity, the films depict the city's history both as a dialogue with a past that is always present and as an unmediated existence among (and out of) the ruins of the previous century. As such pairs, they show that to come to terms with the old and New Berlin, an outlook that encapsulates both the angels' and the vampires' views is necessary and requires a *Vergangenheitsbewältigung* that continues the dialogue with the Nazi past, is born out of the ruins of the GDR, and is firmly rooted in the present, looking toward the future.

Peter Gölz is associate professor in the University of Victoria's Department of Germanic and Slavic Studies. He served as chair of the department and was president of the Canadian Association of University Teachers of German. Peter has published on SLA, Kafka, Adolf Muschg, William Gibson, Buffy, and humor studies.

Notes

1. *Wir sind die Nacht,* directed by Dennis Gansel (2010; Munich: Constantin Film Verleih, 2011), DVD.
2. *Der Himmel über Berlin / Wings of Desire,* directed by Wim Wenders (1987; Berlin and Paris: Reverse Angle Library and Argos Films, 2009), DVD.

3. Jennifer A. Jordan, *Structures of Memory: Understanding Urban Change in Berlin and Beyond* (Palo Alto, 2006), 23.

4. Berghahn commented on the significance of Handke's script: "In Wenders' early horizontal road movies, stories are encoded visually, whereas in his vertical road movies Wenders relies on voice-over narration to tell a story." Daniela Berghahn, "'Womit sonst kann man heute erzählen als mit Bildern?' Images and Stories in Wim Wenders' *Der Himmel über Berlin* and *In weiter Ferne, so nah!*," in *Text into Image: Image into Text,* ed. Jeff Morrison and Florian Krobb (Amsterdam, 1997), 330.

5. Peter Zander, "Muffensausen beim 'Himmel über Berlin,'" *Welt Online* May 2, 2007, http://www.welt.de/kultur/kino/article846526/Muffensausen-beim-Himmel-ueber-Berlin.html.

6. Roger Cook, "Angels, Fiction, and History in Berlin: *Wings of Desire*," in *The Cinema of Wim Wenders: Image, Narrative, and the Postmodern Condition,* ed. Roger F. Cook and Gerd Gemünden (Detroit, 1997), 175.

7. Wenders quoted in Bordo: "And so I have 'Berlin' representing the world. I know of no place with a stronger claim. Berlin is 'an historical truth.' No other city is such a meaningful image, Such a PLACE OF SURVIVAL, so exemplary of our century. … I say: there is more reality in Berlin than any other city. … Berlin is more a SITE than a CITY. … My story isn't about Berlin because it's set there, but because it couldn't be set anywhere else." Jonathan Bordo, "The Homer of Potsdamerplatz: Walter Benjamin in Wim Wenders' *Sky over Berlin / Wings of Desire,* A Critical Topograhy," *IMAGES* 2, no. 1 (2008): 89.

8. Wim Wenders, "An Attempted Description of an Indescribable Film," Criterion Collection, posted November 2, 2009, accessed March 12, 2017. http://www.criterion.com/current/posts/1289-an-attempted-description-of-an-indescribable-film.

9. Cook, "Angels," 164.

10. Coco Fusco, "Angels, History and Poetic Fantasy: An Interview with Wim Wenders," *Cineaste* 16, no. 4 (1988): 16.

11. Alanis Morissette, celebrating the twenty-fifth anniversary of *Wings of Desire,* pays tribute to this scene in her video "Guardian," where she looks down onto the citizens of Berlin from her angelic perspective. YouTube, accessed January 3, 2017. https://youtu.be/7q0reAgBMYA.

12. Jordan, *Structures of Memory,* 14.

13. Of course the Memorial Church has recently acquired another layer of authenticity as a target of the attack on the 2016 Christmas market. As a memorial site to commemorate the bombing of Berlin, the end of the war, and the beginning of a democratic culture, it has now become the site of one of the worst political attacks in postwar German history.

14. Barack Obama, "Full Script of Obama's Speech," CNN, accessed February 24, 2016, http://edition.cnn.com/2008/POLITICS/07/24/obama.words/.

15. Bordo, "Homer," 90.

16. Cook, "Angels," 184.

17. Russell J. A. Kilbourn, *Cinema, Memory, Modernity: The Representation of Memory from the Art Film to Transnational Cinema* (New York, 2010), 89.

18. Robert Phillip Kolker and Peter Beicken, *The Films of Wim Wenders: Cinema as Vision and Desire* (Cambridge, 1993), 140–41.

19. "Herab von unserem Ausguck der Ungeborenen!," Wim Wenders and Peter Handke, *Der Himmel über Berlin: Ein Filmbuch* (Frankfurt, 1995), 124.

20. Kolker and Beicken, *Films of Wim Wenders*, 156.

21. Ibid.

22. "Hotel Esplanade," Wikipedia, last modified January 11, 2016, https://de.wiki pedia.org/wiki/Hotel_Esplanade_%28Berlin%29.

23. Susan Ingram, ed., *World Film Locations: Berlin* (Chicago, 2012), 7. See also Sarah Pogoda und Rüdiger Traxler, "Branding the New Germany: The Brandenburg Gate and a New Kind of German Historical Amnesia" in this volume.

24. As Nick Hodgin explains: "The opening title sequence of *Good Bye, Lenin!* begins with a montage of picture postcards of East Berlin. These low-resolution images of urban scenes with groups of smiling young East German citizens may imply that the film will offer a nostalgically rendered GDR, but this sequence can also be seen as an attempt to deconstruct that very nostalgia. The postcards are ultimately carefully staged images. The pictorial message they communicate is of an idealised, illusory version of the sunny GDR as a vibrant, modern state populated by bright, young citizens and is in stark contrast to the usual monochromatic representations of the SED state." Nick Hodgin, "Aiming to Please? Consensus and Consciousness-Raising in Wolfgang Becker's *Good Bye, Lenin!*," in *New Directions in German Cinema*, ed. Paul Cooke and Chris Homewood (London, 2011), 109–10.

25. *Dr. Mabuse der Spieler*, directed by Fritz Lang (1922; Munich: Universum Film, 2004), DVD.

26. *Nosferatu*, directed by Friedrich Wilhelm Murnau (1922; New York: Kino International, 2007), DVD. The *Wir sind die Nacht Presseheft* confirms yet another connection with Murnau's *Nosferatu*: all the vampires die the same way Nosferatu had, turning to dust in the sunlight: "Dass die Nachtwandler bei Kontakt mit Sonnenlicht zu Staub verfallen, wurde erstmals in NOSFERATU thematisiert. Fast ein Jahrhundert später hält WIR SIND DIE NACHT dramatisch und bildstark an Murnaus Idee fest."

27. The first vampire poem, "Der Vampir," was published in 1748 by Heinrich August Ossenfelder. See Gordon J. Melton, *The Vampire Book: The Encyclopedia of the Undead* (Canton, MI, 2011), xxiii.

28. *Wir sind die Nacht*, 37:55, Gansel, DVD.

29. Constantin Film, *Wir sind die Nacht: Constantin Film Presseheft* (Munich, 2010), 12.

30. *Vampyros Lesbos*, directed by Jesus Franco (1971; Bloomington, IL: Synapse Films, 2000), DVD.

31. Andrea Weiss, *Vampires and Violets: Lesbians in Film* (London, 1993), 84.
32. *Wir sind die Nacht,* 38:52, Gansel, DVD.
33. Joseph Sheridan Le Fanu, *Carmilla* (London, 1872).
34. *The Hunger,* directed by Tony Scott (1983; Burbank, CA: Warner Bros Home Video, 2004), DVD.
35. *Twilight,* directed by Catherine Hardwicke (2008; Universal City, CA: Summit, 2009), DVD.
36. Constantin Film, *Presseheft,* 7.
37. Bezirksamt Tempelhof-Schöneberg, "Hochbunker Pallasstraße," accessed January 25, 2017, https://www.berlin.de/ba-tempelhof-schoeneberg/ueb er-den-bezirk/gedenken/artikel.358221.php
38. Jordan, *Structures of Memory,* 15.
39. Ibid., 25.
40. Søre Kolstrup, "*Wings of Desire*: Space, Memory and Identity," *p.o.v.: A Danish Journal of Film Studies* 8 (1999): 119.
41. Constantin Film, *Presseheft,* 12–14.
42. "Auferstanden aus Ruinen," Wikipedia, last modified January 7, 2016, https://en.wikipedia.org/wiki/Auferstanden_aus_Ruinen.
43. "Nach einer unglaublichen Nacht im Herbst 1996 im Tresor bin ich nach Hause gelaufen, durch die Gegend am Schlesischen Tor. Damals standen überall am Fluss Fabriken. Ich fand es unfassbar, dass in einer Millionenstadt in bester Lage derart heruntergekommene, verlassene Gebäude stehen, in denen alles passieren kann. Zuhause wartete meine damalige Freundin auf mich. Sie zeigte mir Fotos, die sie von sich hatte machen lassen. Die Bilder waren falsch belichtet, aber sexy und sehr düster. Da dachte ich: Ich muss einen Vampirfilm machen. In dieser Stadt." Jessica Braun, "Ich würde gerne ewig leben: Dennis Gansel Interview," *Zeit Online,* October 25, 2015, http://www.zeit.de/kultur/film/2010-10/dennis-gansel. Translation is my own.
44. Siobhan Lyons, "What 'Ruin Porn' Tells Us about Ruins—and Porn," CNN, accessed January 10, 2016, http://www.cnn.com/2015/10/12/architecture/what-ruin-porn-tells-us-about-ruins-and-porn/.
45. Luisa Zielinski, "Capturing the 'Ruin Porn' of Berlin: Layers of History Beckon with Imperfect Memories," *Nautilus,* November 14, 2013, http://m.nautil.us/issue/7/waste/capturing-the-ruin-porn-of-berlin.2.
46. Constantin Film, *Presseheft,* 15.
47. "Teufelsberg," Wikipedia, accessed January 6, 2017, https://en.m.wikipedia.org/wiki/Teufelsberg#cite_ref-Keiderling_Berlin_1999_42_1-0.
48. Dylan Trigg, "The Place of Trauma: Memory, Hauntings, and the Temporality of Ruins," *Memory Studies* 2, no. 1 (2009): 88.

Bibliography

Berghahn, Daniela. "'Womit sonst kann man heute erzählen als mit Bildern?' Images and Stories in Wim Wenders' *Der Himmel über Berlin* and *In weiter*

Ferne, so nah!" In *Text into Image: Image into Text*, edited by Jeff Morrison and Florian Krobb, 329–38. Amsterdam: Rodopi, 1997.

Bezirksamt Tempelhof-Schöneberg. "Hochbunker Pallasstraße." Accessed March 22, 2017. https://www.berlin.de/ba-tempelhof-schoeneberg/ueber-den-be zirk/gedenken/artikel.358221.php.

Bordo, Jonathan. "The Homer of Potsdamerplatz: Walter Benjamin in Wim Wenders's *Sky over Berlin / Wings of Desire*, A Critical Topography." *IMAGES* 2, no. 1 (2008): 86–109.

Braun, Jessica. "Ich würde gerne ewig leben: Dennis Gansel Interview." *Zeit Online*, October 25, 2010. Accessed March 13, 2017. http://www.zeit.de/kultur/ film/2010-10/dennis-gansel.

Constantin Film. *Wir sind die Nacht: Constantin Film Presseheft*. Munich, 2010.

Cook, Roger. "Angels, Fiction, and History in Berlin: *Wings of Desire*." In *The Cinema of Wim Wenders: Image, Narrative, and the Postmodern Condition*, edited by Roger F. Cook and Gerd Gemünden, 163–90. Detroit: Wayne State University Press, 1997.

Fusco, Coco. "Angels, History and Poetic Fantasy: An Interview with Wim Wenders." *Cineaste* 4 (1988): 14–17.

Hodgin, Nick. "Aiming to Please? Consensus and Consciousness-Raising in Wolfgang Becker's *Good Bye, Lenin!*" In *New Directions in German Cinema*, edited by Paul Cooke and Chris Homewood, 94–112. London: I. B. Tauris, 2011.

Ingram, Susan, ed. *World Film Locations: Berlin*. Chicago: University of Chicago Press, 2012.

Jordan, Jennifer A. *Structures of Memory: Understanding Urban Change in Berlin and Beyond*. Palo Alto: Stanford University Press, 2006.

Keiderling, Gerhard. "Berlin ist endlich trümmerfrei." *Berlinische Monatsschrift* 3 (1999): 39–43.

Kilbourn, Russell J. A. *Cinema, Memory, Modernity: The Representation of Memory from the Art Film to Transnational Cinema*. New York: Routledge, 2010.

Kolker, Robert Phillip, and Peter Beicken. *The Films of Wim Wenders: Cinema as Vision and Desire*. Cambridge: Cambridge University Press, 1993.

Kolstrup, Søre. "*Wings of Desire*: Space, Memory and Identity." *p.o.v.: A Danish Journal of Film Studies* 8 (December 1999): 115–24.

LeFanu, J. Sheridan. *Carmilla*. London: Hesperus Press, 1872.

Lyons, Siobhan. "What 'Ruin Porn' Tells Us about Ruins—and Porn." CNN. Accessed January 10, 2016. http://www.cnn.com/2015/10/12/architecture/ what-ruin-porn-tells-us-about-ruins-and-porn/.

Melton, Gordon J. *The Vampire Book: The Encyclopedia of the Undead*. Canton, MI: Visible Ink Press, 2011.

"Muffensausen beim *Himmel über Berlin*." *Welt Online*, February 5, 2007. Accessed February 24, 2016. http://www.welt.de/kultur/kino/article846526/ Muffensausen-beim-Himmel-ueber-Berlin.html.

Obama, Barack. "Full Script of Obama's Speech." CNN. Accessed February 24, 2016. http://edition.cnn.com/2008/POLITICS/07/24/obama.words/.

Strieber, Whitley. *The Hunger*. New York: Pocket Books, 2001.

Trigg, Dylan. "The Place of Trauma: Memory, Hauntings, and the Temporality of Ruins." *Memory Studies* 2, no. 1 (2009): 87–101.

Weiss, Andrea. *Vampires and Violets: Lesbians in Film*. London: Penguin, 1993.

Wenders, Wim. "An Attempted Description of an Indescribable Film." Criterion Collection, Posted November 2, 2009. Accessed March 12, 2017. http://www.criterion.com/current/posts/1289-an-attempted-description-of-an-indescribable-film.

Wenders, Wim, and Peter Handke. *Der Himmel über Berlin: Ein Filmbuch*. Frankfurt: Suhrkamp, 1995.

Wikipedia. "Teufelsberg," Accessed January 6, 2017. https://en.m.wikipedia.org/wiki/Teufelsberg#cite_ref-Keiderling_Berlin_1999_42_1-0.

Wikiwand. "Der Himmel über Berlin." Accessed March 20, 2017. http://www.wikiwand.com/de/Der_Himmel_%C3%BCber_Berlin.

Zielinski, Luisa. "Capturing the 'Ruin Porn' of Berlin: Layers of History Beckon with Imperfect Memories." *Nautilus,* November 14, 2013. Accessed March 12, 2017. http://m.nautil.us/issue/7/waste/capturing-the-ruin-porn-of-berlin.2.

Filmography

Der Himmel über Berlin / Wings of Desire. Directed by Wim Wenders. 1987. Berlin and Paris: Reverse Angle Library and Argos Films, 2009. DVD.

Dr. Mabuse der Spieler. Directed by Fritz Lang. 1922. Munich: Universum Film, 2004. DVD.

"Guardian." Alanis Morissette. YouTube. Accessed March 20, 2017. https://youtu.be/7q0reAgBMYA.

The Hunger. Directed by Tony Scott. 1983. Burbank, CA: Warner Bros Home Video, 2004. DVD.

In weiter Ferne, so nah! Directed by Wim Wenders. 1993. Berlin: Road Movies, 2000. DVD.

Nosferatu. Directed by Friedrich Wilhelm Murnau. 1922. New York: Kino International, 2007. DVD.

Vampyros Lesbos. Directed by Jesus Franco. 1971. Bloomington, IL: Synapse Films, 2000. DVD.

Wir sind die Nacht. Directed by Dennis Gansel. 2010. Munich: Constantin Film Verleih, 2011. DVD.

CHAPTER 15

The Uncanny City
Berlin in International Film

Andre Schütze

*Even today I have not lost my terror of Berlin. Every stay
evokes for a short moment the same feeling of dread.*
—Hanns-Josef Ortheil[1]

A shot, a scream, a house in Berlin. This city is dangerous, as everyone
knows. However, this gruesome scenario is only a scene from a film.
What the audience supposedly sees is the mysterious, misty city of London, the capital of crime, if we are to believe the many Edgar Wallace
film productions of the 1960s. This series of films is just one example
of the few productions that found success filming in postwar Berlin.[2]
Other cities such as Munich played a more central role in the German
film industry, in terms of production, as well as a place of action. It was
only after the reunification that Berlin was able to initiate a new beginning.[3] But despite the reestablishment of the *Babelsberg* and *Adlershof*
studios in the German film and television market, the significance of
Berlin in the international market remains marginal. The golden age of
the film city Berlin in the twenties and early thirties is long gone and will
likely never be achieved again. Large productions are still exceptions, as
for example, Jackie Chan's *Around the World in 80 Days* (2004), which
was filmed around *Gendarmenmarkt* but whose fictional setting is also
London. Numerous other international film productions have chosen
Berlin, not as a stand-in for another location but as a setting ripe with
historical associations. Berlin is the site for World War II and Nazi movies, for example Kenneth Branagh's recreation of the Wannsee Conference in *Conspiracy* (2001) and Bryan Singer's film version of the events
of the so-called July 20 plot in *Valkyrie* (2008). Steven Spielberg's *Bridge*

of Spies (2015) is set around the events of the prisoner exchange at *Glienicker Brücke* in 1962.

Among these international productions are several similar films that do not portray Berlin in direct connection with its historical past. Instead, these films choose to focus on modern Berlin, but their dark content and imagery suggest that the city is still selected for its unforgettable past as a place of terror. In the following, I discuss four films from different cultural backgrounds in which Berlin functions as the site of violence, split identities, and struggles for domination: Paul Greengrass's Hollywood production *The Bourne Supremacy* from 2004; Jaume Collet-Serra's European coproduction *Unknown* and Farhan Akhtar's Indian blockbuster *Don II,* both from 2011; and finally Ryoo Seung-wan's South Korean *The Berlin File* from 2013. In these films Berlin is portrayed as a modern and globally connected city where one no longer sees concrete evidence of the Wall that once separated the city. The city is now just one of many and is marked by unadulterated communication links and transportation connections to the entire world. The Wall is a distant memory and Berlin's peripheral position at the edge of the free world has seemingly been overcome. Yet the global metropolis is still haunted by its violent history and division. For the films' heroes, the New Berlin is a space filled with violence and full of nerve-shattering experiences. Berlin is not a place where they dwell, it is not their home, their *Heim*. It serves as a transitory space, merely a stage in their life from which they move on. It is also a city marked by danger and uncertainty. This reputation of Berlin has less to do with actual reality than with the images and fantasies connected to its history. These Berlin movies could be transferred to other metropolises only with great difficulty, and it would be a challenge to maintain the same level of visual efficacy.

In these films, Berlin is the city of the "uncanny."[4] As Anthony Vidler noted, the uncanny is not "a property of the space itself nor can it be provoked by any particular spatial conformation: it is, in its aesthetic dimension, a representation of a mental state of projection that precisely elides the boundaries of the real and the unreal in order to provoke a disturbing ambiguity, a slippage between waking and dreaming."[5] Berlin becomes a city of imagination and associations, haunted by its memories. Similar to Freud's description of Italian cities, Berlin becomes a place where the past does not disappear—a place where protagonists get lost circling back to their starting points and places of origin. Like in Freud's characterization of Rome, Berlin becomes a space, "an entity, that is to say, in which nothing that has once come into existence will have passed away and all the earlier phases of development continue to exist alongside the latest one."[6] Layers of uncanny history remain today, and nearly three decades after the reunification, images of discontent linger in a cultural memory very specific to this city. Andreas Huyssen writes, "Berlin-as-text remains first and foremost a historical text, marked as much, if not more, by absences as by the visible presence of its past, from prominent ruins such as the *Kaiser-Wilhelm-Gedächtniskirche* at the end of the famous *Kurfürstendamm* to World War II bullet and shrapnel marks on many of its buildings."[7] But the essence of Berlin is not defined through a rational knowledge of history and an objective understanding of the city, but rather by an emotional discontent. The metropolis in the heart of Europe, a city with stores and street cafes, this city, which would so much like to be the same as other metropolises, conceals behind its facade still the dark memories of something else, specifically the memory of the Nazis, the Holocaust, the destruction during World War II, and the almost impenetrable wall that separated this city and an entire country. The films under discussion here especially draw on the atmosphere of the Cold War, when two highly militarized powers confronted and stalked each other in a doppelgänger city, which mirrors itself through its divide. But the uncanny atmosphere and the sense of darkness and danger lurking behind present events is no longer the result of superpowers' paranoia; rather, they stem from a new development: a battle of the individual against anonymous and rootless organizations of modern capitalism, which operate in a delocalized sphere. Yet the escalation of the conflict between the heroes of the films and their antagonists are fuelled by collective images of the city's past. From the outside, this city may look like other European metropolises, and life may appear more or less like that in other cities. But the memories of Berlin's violent past and the devastation of the war differentiate Berlin from other places in the world. Berlin, as we are well aware, can be terrifying.

Clearly, the New Berlin is still less likely to be the picturesque site for romantic comedies; the mainstream filmic image of the city remains a dark one. For decades, filmmaking and production in Berlin coped with this negative characterization and avoided the problem of its troubling image by simply pretending that Berlin was not Berlin, but another city entirely. Production costs, complications associated with filming offsite, and other considerations make the substitution of one city for another in film a common practice. The ability of a city to adapt and transform itself is essential to its success as a locus of film production. For instance, the characterlessness and mutability of the city of Los Angeles was a great advantage for Hollywood. LA's landscape and cityscape could feign settings for every genre of film, from westerns to classic bible stories to New England romances to Chicago gangster flicks.[8] The ability to simulate these different locales in the same city, and shoot them, one right after the other, allowed LA to become the most filmed city in the Western world, without the audience ever being aware of the deception. Similar to LA, Berlin's long history in connection with movie-making is marked by the substitution of Berlin for other cities, especially after the war.

Movies like Franz Cap's mystery *Die Spur führt nach Berlin* (*Adventure in Berlin*) from 1952 are the exception to the practice of utilizing Berlin to represent another city. This film made use of Berlin as a setting and showcased the various physical conditions of the dilapidated city. Berlin was a city that had a certain international flair, but a flair that was forced upon it by the presence of occupying armies. It was a city full of history, but a history that made every type of crime and violence possible, as evidenced by the Holocaust and Nazi war crimes. It was a city in ruins undergoing massive reconstruction, a configuration that provided the possibility for criminals to flee from one allied sector into another with no chance of pursuit by the authorities.[9] Filming against such a fraught backdrop undoubtedly added to the suspense, but there remained the question of whether or not the German audience was ready to see scenes that so closely reflected their own lives and experiences. The political situation in Berlin is uncannily reproduced in Cap's film, an accuracy that detracts from the pleasure and diversion associated with an entertainment movie.

Something similar occurred with Billy Wilder's 1961 movie *One, Two, Three,* which follows the transformation of a staunch East German communist into a bourgeois representative of the Coca-Cola company, all within the time span of a few hours. This action in the film takes place before the existence of the Wall, but the premiere of *One, Two, Three* was overshadowed by the Wall's sudden construction. The film was initially a critical and popular failure. However, with the distance afforded by the passage of time, the film has finally gained acclaim. But in 1961, film critics often referenced the tumultuous situation in Berlin as a reason for the film's failure. The unrest would not allow for such trenchant satire, which hit too close to home. In an otherwise quite positive review, the *New York Times* maintained, "It is too bad, the present Berlin crisis isn't so funny and harmless as the one Billy Wilder and I. A. L. Diamond have whipped up in their new movie, 'One, Two, Three.' And it is too bad it can't be settled so briskly and pro-Americanly as James Cagney settles the one in this picture."[10]

The Berlin of the sixties is a Cold War "front" city that imparts specific connotations to any film that features it; the city's unique political situation must be front and center. Thus, by cloaking Berlin in the mask of London, the aforementioned Edgar Wallace productions are able to circumvent this politicization and instead deliver pure entertainment and diversion through depictions of crime that were obviously far from real life. In addition to masking postwar Berlin in the trappings of other cities, there were two other strategies film productions used to portray its division. One way was to simply depict the two Berlins as one cohesive city by only concentrating on a single section of Berlin. This was the most obvious choice for the East German film industry. Despite the fact that before 1961 the open border was portrayed time and again as a problem, once the wall was built, it was mentioned only very rarely in DEFA films. East Berlin was always shown as a city by itself, or, according to the official language, as the capital of the first socialist republic in Germany.[11] East Germany never viewed West Berlin as the other half of a city, but rather as a completely different city. This sentiment is conveyed through movies produced in the East, in which West Berlin is never really mentioned. This lack of acknowledgment of the other half of Berlin stands out and only serves to underscore the unnaturalness of the divided city while also subtly moving the existence of the Western portion of the city into the audience's consciousness. More surprisingly, the tendency to depict Berlin as just a normal city is also seen in West Berlin productions, for example in Herbert Vesely's well-made screen adaptation of Heinrich Böll's *Das Brot der frühen Jahre* (*The Bread of Those Early Years*) from 1962. Vesely depicts a kind of estrangement from the *Wunderjahre,* the period of economic revival after the war, by mainly focusing on the areas around the *Gleisdreieck* station, the Moabit district, and the newly built streets around the *Zoo* station, which from the Western perspective became more and more the center of Berlin. Vesely's film does not use the location of Berlin as a means to critique either side of the Wall; the specific political situation of Berlin is not shown, and there is no reference to the city as a political island. Berlin is shown as part of the Western recovery, just one place of many in West Germany. The hugely popular TV show *Ich heirate eine Familie* (*I Married a Family*) from the 1980s can be seen as a charming portrait of a family, but this show is another example in which Berlin is not depicted as Berlin. The city's appearance is just like any other West German city, and Berlin's special status is not portrayed. All of these movies could have been produced in any other German location without detracting from the story. Berlin is not masquerading as a completely different city, and the portrayal does not thematize Berlin's history or status as a divided city. By depicting Berlin as an unhistoric and apolitical city, Berlin is "neutralized."

A few films made in pre-*Wende* Berlin manage to show the city as a divided space, the most famous example of doing so is Wim Wenders's *Der Himmel über Berlin* (aka *Wings of Desire*) from 1987. In his contribution to this volume, Peter Gölz discusses the film and notes that Wenders and scriptwriter Peter Handke manage to maintain a sense of the past and the city's history, even while depicting contemporary Berlin. Numerous other Western film productions represent Berlin by focusing on its unique qualities. Berlin's special status was consciously utilized to emphasize the differences between East and West, and also to exploit and even exaggerate the political danger, which conceivably brought us close to a third world war. There is hardly a spy film in the sixties that did not try to increase its suspense at least partly through references to Berlin. In these films the newly built wall is sometimes only used as interesting set dressing. But many masterpieces of this filmic genre used visual images of violence associated with the wall as a symbol of repression and oppression inherently embedded in the socialist state. A society that could build such a wall, in an attempt to imprison its own people, was clearly capable of anything and was a threat to the free world.

Guy Hamilton's opening scene in *Funeral in Berlin,* a 1966 film from the Harry Palmer series, is unmatched in this juxtaposition and facile identification of good and evil. In the film Michael Caine's performance is an ironic and intelligent play on James Bond. Accompanied by dramatic music, the film opens with a shot of the newly regenerated center of West Berlin. The *Gedächtniskirche* is fully modernized to current tastes, the new Europa Center with its rotating Mercedes Star stands front and center, and the camera gleefully tracks the consumerist pulse of the *Kurfürstendamm*.[12] The film montage in these scenes follows the classic example provided by city films like Ruttmann's *Berlin: Die Sinfonie der Großstadt* (*Berlin: Symphony of a Metropolis,* 1927) with its lively splicing together of big-city traffic scenes with the hustle and bustle of people, intercut with images of coffeehouses, with their relaxed ambiance underscoring the peaceful atmosphere of the new city. Only one short scene showing a war cripple begging on the street gives the beginning sequence dark overtones and provides evidence of the violent history of the city, which actually becomes the central focus of this film. The opening sequence culminates with the recording of traffic crossings and the glittering fountain on the (at one time) highly modern Ernst

Reuter Platz. After being inundated with the previous images, imbued with energy and prosperity, the following scene is a shock. Absolute silence replaces the campy, lively music, and in the dusky gray brown of the no-man's-land at Potsdamer Platz we see the ruins of *Haus Vaterland*, tank barricades, and watchtowers. The area is eerily devoid of human activity, festooned with barbed wire and warning signs, and marked by utter silence until the camera reaches Zimmerstraße near Checkpoint Charlie. Only then do people reenter the scene, walking up wooden platforms and, from this vantage point, taking on the position of tourists as they look down on the newest of Berlin attractions. The music starts again and the opening titles of the film are accompanied with more images of the stretch of the Berlin Wall. The first minutes of the film have already created a clear juxtaposition between West and East Berlin, and no extra commentary is required to explain which side is the good one. But the strength of *Funeral in Berlin* lies in its ability to contradict this clear dividing line. By locating the film in the divided city of Berlin, Hamilton provides a framework that presents a dichotomy that is easy to understand. However, the film undercuts assumptions of what is good and bad and shows that the separation between these two elements is not so simple to discern. In the end, the official propagandas from both sides of the Cold War front are only superficial products. Morals and values are mere commodities that change with fluctuating conditions.

The uncertainty of a precisely defined line between good and evil is also a theme in what is possibly the most famous spy thriller of all time, Martin Ritt's 1965 film version of John le Carré's *The Spy Who Came in from the Cold*. Very few of the scenes are supposed to be in Berlin, and none of them were shot at the actual locations. Yet the most prominent scenes supposedly take place in Berlin and occur at the beginning and end of the movie; the film starts with a failed border crossing at Checkpoint Charlie and ends with a failed flight over the Berlin Wall, an escape stymied by betrayal.

As in *Funeral in Berlin,* despite the clearly defined lines between West and East and good and evil as first presented in the introduction, the position of the individual in the city of Berlin has little to do with his geographical whereabouts in East or West or his political and personal value system, upon which moral decisions are based. This filmic depiction that thrusts Berlin into the center of spy rings and international secret service plots does not provide a clear-cut definition between these physical and metaphorical boundaries but rather reduces people to mere marionettes, who are influenced by unknown sources. This places the hero of the story in a state of constant insecurity. At the end the hero must choose between his own values, independent from the propaganda dictated by those in power, or his ultimate failure.

The four recent films selected for closer analysis are profoundly influenced by these spy movies. They do not portray a historical Berlin but rather a Berlin that conceals layers of division, violence, fear, and feelings of loss under its polished facade. For the heroes of these films, Berlin is a foreign city. Freud noted that the effect of the uncanny is more likely produced and more powerfully experienced in an unfamiliar setting.[13] This feeling is made even stronger through the solitude of the heroes, which renders them without guidance and help. The emphasis on the hero was made famous in classic western films, often featuring the loner in an empty landscape. The four films in my discussion show the same kind of loner among the masses of the metropolis. The uncertainty of their own positions and their feelings of doubt are a part of the arc of suspense inseparably bound to the site of Berlin. The loner of these Berlin films is embedded in the fabric of society, with ties to people and subject to overarching principles and laws already in place. Isolated in the army of millions of other city dwellers, these heroes must find answers in a city that functions like a confusing labyrinth.

The portrait of the loner in the human horde, who surfaces out of anonymity and then disappears again, who must maneuver through the confusion and indefinability of the city space, and who must fight against the incapacitation and homogeneity of the metropolis belongs to the type of big-city dweller that Georg Simmel described. The loner is at the same time both product and opponent of modernity. In his popular lecture *Die Großstädte und das Geistesleben* (The Metropolis and Mental Life, 1903), which focused mainly on Berlin, Simmel already examined the paradox of anonymity in metropolitan everyday life. For Simmel the quality of tolerance that can be found in big cities, in which outsiders and emigrants can carve out their own niches, is the product of a functionalization in human relationships. Individuals are no longer perceived to have enduring personalities amid the daily routine. Rather, humans become the bearers of a specific function, and the knowledge of the many details of their personal lives becomes not only unnecessary but, in the light of the many essential interactions on a daily basis in a metropolis, even impossible. As a defense mechanism against what Simmel calls the "übersteigerte Nervenleben," or the intensification of mental life, city dwellers develop a certain blaséness. This can be defined as a kind of coldness and indifference toward others, which makes meaningful and truly involved interactions in a big city an anomaly, or even worse gives off the appearance of provincial mannerisms. He writes:

> Thus the metropolitan type—which naturally takes on a thousand individual modifications—creates a protective organ for itself against the profound disruption with which the fluctuations and discontinuities of the external milieu threaten it. Instead of reacting emotionally, the metropolitan type reacts primarily in a rational manner, thus creating a mental predominance through the intensification of consciousness, which in turn is caused by it. Thus the reaction of the metropolitan person to those events is moved to a sphere of mental activity which is least sensitive and which is furthest removed from the depths of the personality.[14]

This rationalization and inner division can, on the one hand, lead to a certain tolerance. The city dweller is able to at least theoretically achieve the possibility of self-actualization, which would be impossible within the parameters of the village or a small town. However, at the same time he loses the social solidarity and the stability that comes with the familiarity of a small town. The sociologist Rolf Lindner writes, "[I]n contrast to the pettiness and prejudices that constrain small town inhabitants, the big city dweller is free. But it is this freedom and not just the economic opportunities that accounts for the lure of the anonymous metropolis that we still find today."[15] In this way, the metropolis creates conditions in which the individual is free from the judgment of others, but is subsequently also alone. Each hero of the following movies finds himself in the position of a foreigner, a non-Berliner, who comes to the metropolis and experiences the dissolution of all previous certainties. Among the crowds of people each is left to his own devices, with no one to trust in a city marked by a dark history and violence. But the uncanny city, as James Donald writes, "is not out there in the streets. It defines the architecture of our apparently most secret selves: an already social space, if often a decidedly uncivil form of association."[16]

Simmel explains that the metropolis is characterized by a money economy. This focus on money underlies all four of the films discussed in this chapter. The image of the loner is not just the individual lost in the city; he is actually fighting against the basic principle that defines the city: money. But Berlin is not a financial center. The reason why Berlin is chosen as the setting for this struggle is not because of the clear cut economic conflicts, but because it is a symbol of confrontation between two powers. To choose a city like New York or London would immediately clarify the point of conflict as a fight against economic power. In Berlin it is not so obvious, and the loner must strive to identify the source of conflict. With regards to its economic status, Berlin still lags behind its many global partners. Before the war, Berlin was the economic powerhouse of Germany, a position it still struggles and has failed to regain. This process of trying to reclaim economic dominance does not always coincide with the desires of Berliners, who want to retain the affordable lifestyle unique to Berlin. In his contribution to this volume, Simon Ward describes the process of reconfiguring the economic landscape of Berlin. He focuses on the so-called creative classes that exercise a strong influence on a city's redevelopment. He also cites Berlin's historic authenticity as an asset for this reconfiguration. However, conversely, this development often destroys the very same work and living places for artists, eliminating the diversity from which it had benefitted. In her contribution to this volume, Katrina Sark differentiates between the post-1999 New Berlin, with its focus on development and commercialization, and the pre-1999 Babylon, with its utopian dreams of creativity and alternative models of living. She argues that many newer texts and movies demonstrate a longing for this pre–New Berlin era, which she characterizes as a "nostalgia for Babylon." Post-*Wende* Berlin was a place of open voids and possibilities and provided the opportunity for alternative ways of living. Today, with the influence of global cultures and modernization, Berlin has lost this unique flexibility. The movies in this chapter are produced from an outsider's perspective, but they also replicate this same nostalgia. The fights and struggles in which the heroes must engage in these films are against the exact same forces that are behind the globalization, commercialization, and gentrification of the city, phenomena that many Berliners criticize.

The first and probably most influential of these film productions are the Bourne movies with Matt Damon. They follow Jason Bourne's search for his past. A badly wounded Bourne is rescued from the Mediterranean Sea by fishermen and has no memories of his former life, aside from a few nightmarish flashbacks. Bourne is plagued by hypersensitivity and a heightened sense of alertness. This acute awareness leads him to plumb the depths of his unconscious, revealing memories of his involvement in a highly secret CIA project. As he uncovers more and more of his memories, he soon realizes that the CIA is actively seeking to eliminate him due to the sensitive information he possesses. Berlin is especially prominent in the second film in the series, *The Bourne Supremacy.* Jason Bourne has supposedly achieved peace and respite from persecution at the end of the first film, but in the second he is violently jolted back into his hazy past. The film begins with a vague nightmare scene, which hauntingly conveys Bourne's memories, which he cannot explain.[17] While hiding in India to avoid confronting his previous life, two people in Berlin are killed during a US Secret Service operation, and important documents are stolen. The murderer, who works for a Russian oligarch, leaves behind Bourne's simulated fingerprints, which ostensibly cover the real tracks of the perpetrator. This pushes Bourne into the center of the conflict and makes him the object of pursuit by the US Secret Service.

After an attempt on Bourne's life in Goa, during which his girlfriend perishes, Bourne takes flight back to Europe in order to fill the gaps in his memory of his previous life and to find out about the background of his earlier work for the Secret Service. He realizes that everything that has happened to him is connected to his former life and he must embark upon a new start. Yet without the knowledge of his past, this will not be possible. Berlin, with its own dark, inscrutable past, serves as the ideal location for this search, and Bourne sets out on a trail that leads him to the city in which he supposedly committed murder. For him, the long trip from Italy, where he first arrives on European soil, represents the beginning of a search for himself, in which layer upon layer of his memories are slowly exposed. Berlin is a city that he supposedly does not know but somehow recognizes; it is the city from his nightmares. Bourne has already been to this city, committed a murder there, though a different murder than the one for which he is being sought. It is not surprising that the first images of Berlin we see in Bourne's Proustian *Search of Lost Memory* are of the Walter Benjamin Platz in Berlin's Charlottenburg, not far from the Krumme Straße in Benjamin's *Berliner Kindheit* (*A Berlin Childhood*). However, Berlin is once again impersonating another city.[18] The location is supposedly in Amsterdam, or so the superimposed text would have us believe. In the film Amsterdam serves as an in-between station for the CIA agents flying in to pick up a former coworker of the highly secret Treadstone project. They force her to work with them because she was a psychologist on this project and she knows Bourne, the way he acts, and she will be able to anticipate his next moves. The two parties head to Berlin: a huge team of agents, trying to anticipate the future, and Bourne, alone, trying to remember his past. The dichotomy created by Bourne's and the group of agents' arrival in Berlin underscores the contrast between the CIA and Bourne and also reflects the imagery of the Cold War, visually reproducing the physical separation of the city in the years of the Wall. The film presents the Secret Service entering the city like an invading, superior army. They fly into Berlin, stay in expensive luxury hotels, and begin work immediately in pre-prepared open-plan offices, which are indistinguishable from offices in London or New York. They arrive at the old airport of *Tempelhof,* the classic beginning place for Berlin stories in the West going back to Billy Wilder's 1948 film *A Foreign Affair* or George Seaton's *The Big Lift* from 1950. In their contribution to this volume, Stefanie Eisenhuth and Scott H. Krause discuss the importance of the former *Tempelhof* Airport, known today as *Tempelhofer Freiheit,* as the symbol of the Cold War city.

The Berlin scenes in *The Bourne Supremacy* are set into motion with a panorama shot from *Tempelhof* in the direction of Alexanderplatz, where the offices of the Secret Service are located. With a cavalcade of limousines, the agents move past the *Siegessäule* and the crumbling *Palast der Republik* to their generic offices and later to their hotel in the Friedrichstraße, which the former DDR used as a hotel for high-paying guests from the West and where the arcades for the *Kaisergalerie* were once located. On the one hand these images underscore the position of power and strength; black limousines hurtle though Berlin as if on the former *Protokollstrecke* through *Pankow.* At the same time this display also shows the ignorance of this group and their fundamental lack of connection to Berlin. They blindly careen through a city in which there are unambiguous traces of fallen cultures and warnings against the hubris of power, all of which go unnoticed.

The arrival of Jason Bourne is another matter entirely. He drives alone over the old *Avus,* which is no longer a racetrack, past the *Funkturm,* which lost its status as the highest tower in Berlin a long time ago. He drives until he reaches the *Ostbahnhof,* which was renovated as the main train station in the DDR capital. However, in unified Germany the station was stripped of its importance, and the designation *Hauptbahnhof* was given to the new glass palace, not far from the *Reichstag.* At the *Ostbahnhof* Bourne leaves his car and, unlike his opponents, he immerses himself in the city by actively seeking information, observing everything, and blending in by speaking some German. Without actually knowing the city, he skillfully interacts with his environment and in this way becomes a part of it. This subtle splitting of the city into two different perspectives utilizes the former division of the city to create an obvious demarcation without consciously making reference to the Wall. The film does not provide an easy way for the audience to grasp which side represents good and which evil, a motif that is continually connected to Berlin. Once again the audience must decide for itself. But Bourne's ties to the city give him the upper hand over the Secret Service. He now knows with whom he is dealing, who they are, where they live and work. His biggest advantage is that he allows the city to work for him, and he knows how to manipulate elements of the city to his benefit. He arranges a meeting with the Secret Service in such a way that it coincides with a student demonstration, which he uses as a shield. Bourne does not exploit the students but rather becomes one of them. His struggle is symbolically tied to their cause. Both Bourne and the students are emblems representing the fight against those in power. The continuation of the action carries Bourne out of Berlin, which is typical for all of the movies discussed here. Berlin continues to be depicted as a *"Frontstadt"* (city on the front line) in which important decisions were never made. In the Cold War, these decisions were traditionally made in Russia or America, both countries to which Bourne is compelled to travel. Bourne's trip to Moscow is another opportunity for Berlin to appear as something it is not—this time as the Russian capital. The second part of the series ends in New York, where the big-city motif is picked up again. After Jason Bourne discovers his real name and origins, he disappears and becomes a part of the teeming crowds in the city's urban canyons.

The success of the Bourne films and the charged atmosphere of Berlin clearly played an important role in the decision to shoot other similar productions in this city. The loss of memory and the search for one's true self is at the center of the international coproduction *Unknown,* which, unlike the literary version, plays out in Berlin instead of Paris. The scientist Martin Harris, played by Liam Neeson, is invited to a conference in Berlin. Once there, he is driven by taxi to the middle of the *Oberbaumbrücke,* the former border crossing from Kreuzberg to Friedrichshain, and is involved in a dramatic car crash. The car plummets into the water and Harris survives only through the help of his taxi driver. For many days he lies in a coma, but once he awakens, he exhibits substantial memory loss. He must quickly come to terms with the fact that his old life no longer exists. Once again the hero of the film is a stranger in the metropolis and must rely upon himself. Due to his loss of memory, the film focuses on the question of his true identity. His wife appears to no longer recognize him. Harris is shocked to discover another man at her side, bearing his name and seemingly living his former life for him. Yet in this city of uncertainty, the viewer cannot trust what he/she sees and knows. For soon after, it is revealed that there is no scientist with the name Harris. Who is this eerie replacement and who is the man we know thus far as Harris? Similar to the Bourne films, the individual in *Unknown* must also defend himself against an anonymous, all-powerful organization, which is characterized by its ignorance of and disconnectedness to everyday Berlin. The opposing side celebrates and stays in luxury hotels, in this case the Adlon Hotel, with its proximity to the former Wall delivering fantastic scenery of the *Brandenburger Tor,* the historical symbol of Berlin and its division. In their contribution to this volume, Sarah Pogoda and Rüdiger Traxler discuss the Brandenburg Gate as symbol and icon for Berlin. The Brandenburg Gate possesses a plethora of symbolic meanings. It is seen as a memorial to peace and victory as well as a symbol for both the division and unity engendered by the Berlin Wall. The multifaceted symbolism of the *Brandenburger Tor* contradicts the notion that the gate can be easily appropriated to serve as an icon for the New Berlin.

This film hero now without a name or a past immerses himself once again in the city. His access to information and support do not stem from very glamorous sources but rather from an illegal immigrant from Bosnia named Gina, who earns her money as a taxi driver. He also connects to a former Stasi agent, who refuses to betray him even in the face of great danger. Once again it is clear that in this city, the lines of conflict are not always obvious. Help comes from two economic and political losers, both of whom are not just by chance from the East. The border has disappeared, just as the film shows. The Wall no longer stands, but fresh conflicts are emerging that orient themselves along the lines of old tensions. In the film these conflicts become most obvious when observing the lone hero, who is connected to the city space and anonymous, global, uncontrollable organizations that do not allow themselves to settle in any specific space. The city of Berlin can serve both sides: on the one hand, as the globalized reservoir of real estate that provides the un-transparent elite their office spaces and luxury hotels; on the other, it can also serve as a safe haven. Through its anonymity created by the masses of people, Berlin as a metropolis of layered history and memories offers a hiding place from which one can begin the process of reevaluating personal beliefs and knowledge.

Hardly any other film signifies the image of global Berlin better than the Indian thriller *Don II.* The production of the film in Germany's capital represented a special coup for film marketing in Berlin. The biggest star of Indian film, Shah Rukh Khan, was compelled to come to Berlin and once again take up the role of the gangster boss Don. In *Don II,* Berlin is situated within a global framework, similar to the aforementioned films. The story begins in Thailand and Malaysia, and then leads to Berlin through Zurich. The main character is Don, the king of the Asian underworld, who wants to spread his power to Europe. Out of fear of the new competition, the European united crime cartel plans Don's death. The film deviates from the series of aforementioned films, not only because of the specific film language utilized, which is not solely based on the Western tradition, but also because of the depiction of Berlin and its completely different reception in the film market. More so than in the other films, Berlin's setting comes across strongly as stage scenery. The shots of the city were sought out based on Berlin's photogenic angles and viewpoints. In the film Shah Rukh Khan takes us on a sightseeing tour by bus along *Unter den Linden* and through Friedrichstadt until Alexanderplatz, where he escapes his pursuers by leaping from the roof of the famous Park Inn Hotel. Seeking to capitalize on the film, the Berlin Tourism Board published a brochure for "Don in Berlin." With help from these information leaflets, tourists can follow Don's tracks through Berlin and are led to the city's important sightseeing locations. The advertisement is targeted specifically to those who have seen the movie. The experience allows participants to put themselves in the position of the main character, giving them the chance to leap from the roof of the Park Inn Hotel, supported only by a thin cord. As the brochure points out: "Shah Rukh already did it, now it's your turn to fly."[19] Also in the film, a frenzied car chase leads through all of Berlin, extending the tour of the city, ending directly in front of the *Brandenburger Tor,* where Don escapes his persecutors with his typical smirk.

In contrast to the other film heroes, Don is hardly a vulnerable or contemplative character. He is an absolute hero and is so sure of himself that he appears to not even belong in this city of subtle uncertainty. This film does not focus on a character who sees himself as fighting against a large and hostile organization, devising ways to survive. Don is able to effortlessly evade his opponent, Roma, who works for Interpol and must constantly try to keep up with him, never able to apprehend her nemesis. Don is always one step ahead, and if there is any uncertainty, it is on the part of the audience, who must wait to see if Don's boastful scheming and seemingly unachievable plans are not just exaggerations, as the film often tries to show. In this production it is not the hero who is exposed to uncertainty and feelings of alienation as he traverses the unfamiliar metropolis, but rather the audience itself, plunged into an unknown city being projected throughout cinemas in India. This foreigner is not Don, who feels at home anywhere in the world, but rather the viewer of the filmic introduction to Berlin.

The focus on the many fabulous attractions in Berlin becomes a kind of self-portrait, a first glimpse into a city otherwise known for its gloomy historical events. The dark side of Berlin is only conveyed through a few images of backyard gangsters and car scrapyards, but it nevertheless asserts its presence in the film. This is the city of countless failed military campaigns, the same city wherefrom Don plans to conquer the whole of Europe. Of all places Don chooses the completely empty Olympic Stadium, a space inseparable from Hitler's delusions of grandeur, as the setting to welcome his partner Sameer, who pays homage to Don's criminal mind. It is here he reveals his plans to eliminate the other European gangster groups. Don shows his finesse as a criminal through his plans to execute a complicated bank heist, which is so intricate that the audience only realizes the full scale of his plot at the very end of the movie. Although Don cannot be compared to the outsider figures in the other films, there are some similarities in the ways in which the dynamic between the protagonist and his opponents are represented. Even though Don is rich and powerful, he is mostly portrayed as being alone. Aside from his partner Ayesha, who mostly works in the background, Don's only coworker whom he can trust is the Indian Sameer. Sameer is shown riding through Berlin with his bicycle and lives with his pregnant girlfriend in a small apartment in Kreuzberg, with a view to the noisy *U-Bahn* directly in front of his window. As a young man he hacked into the Tokyo Stock Market and transferred money to an environmental group. The policewoman Roma turns out to be not so much a rival of Don as an admirer, because she is actually quite fascinated by him. The role of Don's opponents is taken over by various managers of a major bank. They are shown in a luxurious auditorium from Gehry's bank building on Pariser Platz, drinking champagne and cocktails on sunny roof terraces or at charity events in the *Schauspielhaus* on *Gendarmenmarkt*. However, in watching these images the audience already knows from former scenes that the gaiety and refinement is only a facade and that these managers do not recoil from violence and murder.

Another film, the *Berlin File* from the South Korean director Ryoo Seung-wan adds another layer to the identity of Berlin, which provides direct political commentary and goes beyond the stunning visuals of the Indian film. The search for one's self is once again at the center of the film. A North Korean agent is the main character in this film. In the very first scene he is shown interrupting the work of the South Korean secret service during the execution of a weapons deal in a hotel familiar to us from the Bourne films. Even before the film title appears there is already a showdown, a climax that many other films would have saved as a finale. In the opening credits we see Berlin in a variety of images, from the *Hackescher Markt* to the Eastside Gallery, from Friedrichstadt and the *Berliner Ensemble* to a demonstration where participants wield the placards with slogans such as "Grass is right." But only the images from the roof of the hotel provide unmistakable evidence as to the location of the action. The camera distances itself from the confrontation of both agents Pyo Jong-seong and Jung Jin-soo with a cut to a panorama of Berlin. It is a scene that opens with the boulevard *Unter den Linden* leading along to the *Tiergarten,* with the *Brandenburger Tor* and the dome of the *Reichstag* in the background. These locations do not just reproduce the path of the former border but also create a direct relation to the divided Korea. Berlin's history represents an example close to Korea's own situation. The choice of a North Korean agent as the hero of the film might at first appear strange. However, the incorporation of the formerly divided city provides a framework that clarifies this. Of course the audience already knows how Berlin's history played out and which side achieved success. If the North Korean is to be the hero of the movie, his loyalty to party directives must be questioned. The Stalinist architecture of the former Soviet embassy's tower, which was the actual center of power of the fallen DDR and which is located almost directly behind the two adversaries in the panorama view, underscores this position and allows the initial defeat of the South Koreans in the fight to seem less humiliating. The setting of Berlin in the film is not simply a facade but rather adds additional meaning to the scenes on screen through images plumbed from its reservoir of history.[20] Without having to give explanation, for example through voiceover, the cultural knowledge about the fall of the Wall, the reunification, and the breakdown of the Eastern Bloc, which is inextricably bound with the *Brandenburger Tor,* puts into perspective and undermines the initially superior position of the North Korean. Even before the beginning of the actual film, it is subtly made clear through the Berlin landscape that the agent is fighting a losing battle. Either he will be defeated or he must reconsider his connection to the Communist Party. The losers of the battle shown at the beginning of the film win at the end. Once again finding one's own position becomes the focus of the movie.

However, the battle lines are not so clearly drawn. In this film the individual is also forced to make decisions for himself. For Pyo Jong-seong this means to question his role of spying on his own wife, who works in the Berlin embassy for North Korea and is suspected of betrayal. Like in the other films discussed here, Pyo Jong-seong needs to extricate himself from the threat of control and the regulation of everything he does. Initially he is just a part of the North Koreans' machinery of control. Symbolically, he learns of the accusations against his wife in front of the last remains of the Berlin Wall. This exchange before the Wall illustrates the necessity of overcoming such divisions. However, he fails to realize this and ransacks their shared apartment for evidence and follows her on her way to the *Brandenburger Tor,* which is once again a symbol of separation, but also of the possibility of escape. The means to flee is no longer over the long-gone wall but rather through help and asylum offered by the newly built American Embassy located right next to the gate. The North Korean ambassador is trying to use this possibility of refuge, because he understands better than anyone that the arrival of the seedy security expert Dong Myung-soo signifies the end of his career.

The conflict does not play out along the same old border, nor does it concentrate on the juxtaposition between East and West and communism and capitalism. Berlin is the historical symbol for these old conflicts; the New Berlin signifies that the battle is over. As in the other movies, we see that a new battle has begun. It is not a clashing of ideologies but rather a fight over economic factors. The South Korean agent Jung Jin-soo is perceived by his superiors as an old-fashioned warrior who is still following the anticommunist lines and cannot adapt to the new times of economic laissez-faire. In this way his superiors are much farther along than he in their understanding, but they forget that these new politics leave the old victims behind. Jung Jin-soo wants to avenge the victims of the fight between the North and South Korean secret service, even if it means going against the will of his bosses. He tries to make sense of the confusing maneuvers of the secret service that are no longer defined by clear political standpoints but rather by business deals. On the other side, Pyo Jong-seong has neither examined nor altered his position regarding communism. When he tells his wife in the depressing darkness of their shared apartment that even though they are poor they can at least hold their heads high, the audience must confront and question this sentiment. It sees a system that forces Pyo Jong-seong's own wife into prostitution, maligns and threatens people, and does not recoil from murder. However, in the film these intrigues are not connected to the ideology of the party but rather to an egotistical abuse of power of a clique of businessmen in Pyongyang. They still quote Stalin, but they are only interested in their own power and personal enrichment. The fight has moved away from political disagreement to economic profiteering, but the battle is no less aggressive. For this film too, the real solution cannot actually be found in Berlin, which only serves as a symbolic battlefield. Those guilty of Pyo Jong-seong's persecution and the final death of his wife are far away in Korea, and the last scene of the film leads back toward the Korean peninsula. Pyo Jong-seong, allowed to escape by his South Korean opponent, buys himself a one-way ticket to Vladivostok to pursue those responsible for his wife's death.

The uncanny is something that is hidden and should remain hidden. But Berlin, more than any other city, shows that the covert past is always around us. Even with the passage of time, the tearing down of the impenetrable Wall, and the reunification of a nation, Berlin's traumatic past lies latent beneath the modern city's polished and globalized atmosphere. The international films presented in this chapter perceive these hidden anxieties and utilize the layers of Berlin's history to explore emerging tensions in the globalized city and to acknowledge its fraught past. The old conflicts are long over, but the portrayal of the New Berlin shows a city that is nonetheless uncanny. This quality of the uncanny, of the city haunted by its past, alters the traditional struggle of the individual in the metropolis. In Berlin, the focus is not just centered on the individual in a vast metropolis and the battle against alienation as described in Simmel's text. As a historical center of conflict, the New Berlin is the locus of new struggles in which the individual is pitted against anonymous organizations that are no longer connected to the city. This fight is intensified by its emplacement in Berlin, the world's historic capital of terror, crime, and struggle for political domination.

In the age of globalism, when boundaries between cultures and societies are quickly dissolving, it seems perhaps unsurprising that these four directors have chosen Berlin as a milieu for their narratives. The decision could come across as merely random or out of practical purposes, given Berlin's reputation as an affordable, world-class metropolis. Yet, I argue that the site of Berlin was chosen deliberately and that these four disparate filmmakers' outsider status provides them with a unique perspective on the city and a different point of access to Berlin's dark past. This can be compared to directors who are already submerged in and connected to Berlin's history and culture and whose proximity might act as a kind of amnesia.

These four international films reveal a profound understanding of what remains unseen beneath Berlin's glossy, modern finish, and they demonstrate a nuanced manipulation of this hidden imagery in order to apply its symbolism to current issues and conflicts. Freud described Rome as a city made up of layers of history that nonetheless persist and are wholly discoverable. Berlin is also a city with a layered past, but one that remains more concealed through the city's rapid generation and modernization. In their contribution to this volume, Ayse N. Erek and Eszter Gantner describe the many challenges the New Berlin faces in its struggle to find its place in a globalized world. The history of Berlin is at the same time both a burden and a selling point. But as the authors show, capitalizing on history has become more and more instrumental to defining a new image for Berlin, and yet doing so actually functions to dehistorize the city.

The exploration of the New Berlin through a foreign perspective helps to preserve this history. The excavation of the past benefits from having filmmakers from the outside who bring with them a certain set of expectations and preconceived notions about the city and whose distance lends them a more penetrating understanding of Berlin's complexities. Many contemporary films focus on the surface of Berlin and simply normalize it through their depiction of a modern, sanitized city. In all four films, the filmmaker as outsider is paralleled through the depiction of the main character as outsider, both of whom seem to possess more insight into the fraught past of the city and its potential as a symbolic backdrop to contextualize contemporary issues. This excavation and mirroring of the old in the new draws a compelling connection between Berlin's past and present. This external viewpoint may not conform to the reality of what the city is today, but this perspective reminds the viewer of a past reality and of Berlin's position as an uncanny city. It brings to the surface from Berlin's many complex layers the terror, destruction and tensions that lie dormant beneath the thriving, modern metropolis. These movies break through the facade and continually make the audience aware of one thing: this city is still dangerous.

Andre Schütze is a visiting assistant professor at Tulane University. His publications include articles on Thomas Mann's *Der Zauberberg,* Walter Benjamin and Bourdieu, Christa Wolf, and Paul Scheerbart, and he has published in journals such as *Weimarer Beiträge* and *Seminar.*

Notes

1. Hanns-Josef Ortheil, *Die Berlinreise* (Köln, 2014), 9. Unless otherwise noted, translations are my own.
2. In addition other places such as Hamburg, Denmark and Schleswig Holstein were used as a substitute setting for London or England.
3. In *One, Two, Three* it was not possible to shoot in front of the *Brandenburger Tor,* so Wilder recreated this structure in a Munich studio. This seems like a fitting symbol for this move away from Berlin.
4. See Freud's "The Uncanny": "It may be true that the uncanny [*unheimlich*] is something which is secretly familiar [*heimlich-heimisch*], which has undergone repression and then returned from it, and that everything that is uncanny fulfills this condition." Sigmund Freud, "The Uncanny," in *Sigmund*

Freud XVII: An Infantile Neurosis and Other Works, ed. James Strachey et al. (London, 1955), 245.

5. Anthony Vidler, *The Architectural Uncanny: Essays in the Modern Unhomely* (Cambridge, MA, 1992), 11.

6. Sigmund Freud, *Civilization and Its Discontents* (New York, 1962), 17.

7. Andreas Huyssen, "The Voids of Berlin," *Critical Inquiry* 24, no. 1 (1997): 60.

8. A few examples of such films are, Fred Zinnemann's *High Noon* (1952); the 1925 production of *Ben Hur,* which moved back to Hollywood after many difficulties in Rome; George Cukor's *Little Women* (1933) or *Philadelphia Story* (1940); and Howard Hawks's *Scarface* (1932) or even the beginning scenes of *Some Like It Hot* (1959).

9. Vienna offered similar scenes in the film *The Third Man,* which was a much more sophisticated and successful film. There are many parallels between these two movies. The most obvious is the position of the Americans in both films. Another parallel is in the beginning scene, which comes across as a reference to the famous Ferris wheel scene in *The Third Man.*

10. Bosley Crowther, "Screen: Berlin Laughter: 'One, Two, Three' Is at Astor and Fine Arts," *New York Times,* December 22, 1961.

11. Gerhard Klein's film *Berlin—Ecke Schönhauser (Berlin Corner Schönhauser)* from 1957 is probably one of the most famous examples of pre-Wall East German movies and its depiction of the Western part of the city. In West Berlin, Kohle watches cheap Hollywood movies in an attempt to forget his troubles. It is also the place where Karl-Heinz turns into a thief and a wannabe gangster. Dieter und Kohle end up fleeing to West Berlin after falsely believing that they had beaten Karl-Heinz to death. They feel that West Berlin, as the center of crime, would not prosecute them for their misdeeds.

12. For the beginning scenes of *One, Two, Three,* Billy Wilder utilizes a similar juxtaposition, but in a much more ironic way. The movie also opens with the hustle and bustle of the big city around the *Gedächtniskirche* and contrasts this image of prosperity with the anti-American demonstrations in the Eastern part of Berlin.

13. Robin Lydenberg describes the setting in a foreign city as one of Freud's techniques of framing his narration but adds, "Freud's Italian anecdote retains a certain disruptive power because it is provoked by and constructed on the uncertain ground of foreign territory, a ground particularly fertile for the production of the uncanny." Robin Lydenberg, "Freud's Uncanny Narratives," *PMLA* 112, no. 5 (1997): 1075.

14. Georg Simmel, "The Metropolis and Mental Life," in *On Individuality and Social Forms,* ed. Donald N. Levine (Chicago, 1971), 326.

15. Rolf Lindner, "Georg Simmel, die Großstadt und das Geistesleben," in *Georg Simmel und die aktuelle Stadtforschung,* ed. Harald A. Mieg, Astrid O. Sundsboe, and Majken Bieniok (Wiesbaden, 2012), 34.

16. James Donald, "The City, the Cinema: Modern Spaces," in *Visual Culture,* ed. Chris Jenks (London, 1995), 81.

17. See Gaines's description of the role of the reprocessing of trauma in the Bourne Trilogy in Vincent M. Gaine, "Remember Everything, Absolve Nothing: Working through Trauma in the Bourne Trilogy," *Cinema Journal* 51, no. 1 (2011): 159–63.
18. When Bourne meets with a former partner from the Treadstone project, we once again see Berlin masked as another city. The superimposed text maintains that it is actually Munich.
19. See the Citymap *Don in Berlin.* "Don: Der Berlin-Stadtplan," *visitberlin.de,* accessed June 3, 2016, http://www.visitberlin.de/de/artikel/don-der-berlin-stadtplan.
20. The film was more or less a failure at the box office. A reason given for this was the younger generation's lack of knowledge regarding the history of Berlin. As written in *Variety,* "By Ryoo's high standards the big budget film was a comparative disappointment and a commercial close shave. It sold 7.17 million tickets in Korea for a gross of KRW52.4 billion (US$43.9 million at current exchange rates), but Ryoo says that the picture failed to fully connect with younger audiences which know little of the Cold War era." See Patrick Frater, "Busan: Ryoo Seung-wan Lines up Sequels to 'Veteran' and 'The Berlin File,'" *Variety,* October 2, 2015, http://variety.com/2015/film/asia/ryoo-seung-wan-sequels-to-veteran-and-the-berlin-file-1201608131/.

Bibliography

Donald, James. "The City, the Cinema: Modern Spaces." In *Visual Culture,* edited by Chris Jenks, 77–95. London: Routledge, 1995.

Freud, Sigmund. *Civilization and Its Discontents.* New York: Norton and Norton, 1962.

———. "The Uncanny." In *Sigmund Freud XVII: An Infantile Neurosis and Other Works,* edited by James Strachey et al., 218–52. London: Hogarth Press, 1955.

Gaine, Vincent M. "Remember Everything, Absolve Nothing: Working through Trauma in the Bourne Trilogy." *Cinema Journal* 51, no. 1 (2011): 159–63.

Huyssen, Andreas. "The Voids of Berlin." *Critical Inquiry* 24, no. 1 (1997): 57–81.

Lindner, Rolf. "Georg Simmel, die Großstadt und das Geistesleben." In *Georg Simmel und die aktuelle Stadtforschung,* edited by Harald A. Mieg, Astrid O. Sundsboe, and Majken Bieniok, 29–37. Wiesbaden: VS Verlag für Sozialwissenschaften, 2012.

Lydenberg, Robin. "Freud's Uncanny Narratives." *PMLA* 112, no. 5 (1997): 1072–86.

Simmel, Georg. "The Metropolis and Mental Life." In *On Individuality and Social Forms,* edited by Donald N. Levine, 324–39. Chicago: University of Chicago Press, 1971.

Vidler, Anthony. *The Architectural Uncanny: Essays in the Modern Unhomely.* Cambridge: MIT Press, 1992.

Filmography

The Berlin File. Directed by Ryoo Seung-wan. 2013. Seoul: CJ Entertainment, 2013. DVD.

The Bourne Supremacy. Directed by Paul Greengrass. 2004. Universal City, CA: Universal, 2004. DVD.

Der Himmel über Berlin / Wings of Desire. Directed by Wim Wenders. 1987. Berlin and Paris: Reverse Angle Library and Argos Films, 2009. DVD.

Don II. Directed by Farhan Akhtar. 2011. Mumbai: Reliance Entertainment, 2011. DVD.

Unknown. Directed by Jaume Collet-Serra. 2011. Burbank, CA: Warner Bros. Pictures, 2011. DVD.

Index

www.ingramcontent.com/pod-product-compliance
Lightning Source LLC
Chambersburg PA
CBHW060346050426
42336CB00051B/2262